HUMAN RIGHTS WITH MODESTY: THE PROBLEM OF UNIVERSALISM

Human Rights with Modesty: The Problem of Universalism

edited by

ANDRÁS SAJÓ

Springer-Science+Business Media, B.V.
2004

A C.I.P. Catalogue record for this book is available from the Library of Congress.

Printed on acid-free paper.

ISBN 978-90-04-13823-0 ISBN 978-94-017-6172-7 (eBook)
DOI 10.1007/978-94-017-6172-7

Originally published by Koninklijke Brill NV, Leiden, The Netherlands in 2004.
Softcover reprint of the hardcover 1st edition 2004

Table of Contents

List of Contributors

Avineri, Shlomo
Hebrew University of Jerusalem

Balaghi, Shiva
New York University

Brems, Eva
University of Gent

Haarscher, Guy
Free University of Brussels

Inoue, Tatsuo
University of Tokyo

Krygier, Martin
University of New South Wales

Mayer, Ann Elizabeth
University of Pennsylvania

Mutua, Makau
Human Rights Center, SUNY—Buffalo Law School

Osiatynski, Wiktor
Central European University

Petrova, Dimitrina
European Roma Rights Center, Budapest

Sadurski, Wojciech
European University Institute, Florence; University of Sydney

Sajó, András
Central European University

Shweder, Richard A.
Committee on Human Development, University of Chicago

Stacy, Helen
Institute of International Studies, Stanford University

Teitel, Ruti
New York Law School

Upham, Frank K.
New York University Law School

Introduction*

András Sajó

Universalism with Humility

We are certainly beginning to feel and perhaps even understand that humankind is indeed interrelated in the global world. Isolation is no longer possible. Consistent protection of human rights seems to be one of only a handful of tools promising sustainable global coexistence. However, the unity of humankind under the current terms, to the extent that unity is at all on offer, is unconvincing to those who feel that this coexistence comes at their expense. During the initial learning period of coexistence, problems that come up time and again include lack of validity, bias, or even complete irrelevance of universal legal solutions to fundamental human problems.

This volume considers the problem of legal universals at the level of the rule of law and human rights. These two concepts have fundamentally different pedigrees. The *rule of law* is an institutional arrangement (based on peculiar principles) of *positive law* in "differentiated," "modern" societies. This foundation is only loosely connected to the sphere of *morals*, which, on the other hand, is itself often perceived to be the basic theoretical source of *human rights*—despite much disagreement over the nature of such foundations, or whether the attempt to locate human rights in morals can be accomplished with any success. Given the juridicization of human rights, rule of

* Earlier versions of the papers collected in this volume were presented in Budapest in 2002 at the 10th "*The Individual v the State*" Conference. The conference was hosted by Central European University, Legal Studies Department. The Open Society Institute, Budapest provided generous funding for the conference.

András Sajó (ed.), Human Rights with Modesty: The Problem of Universalism, *1-29.*

law and human rights expectations have become significantly intertwined. Human rights are served by the rule of law legal system. In terms of politics and policies human rights and the rule of law have developed an intimate relationship. Human rights are enforced with the instruments of the rule of law and are thus limited by the restricted reach thereof.[1] The restrictions on human rights result mostly from inconvenient expediencies of the rule of law. Usually it is not the essence of human rights that is questioned outright, rather at issue is the affordability of rule of law-dictated solutions, in addition to the restrictions of a given legal system. To the extent that the rule of law or specific arrangements under the rule of law are not affordable for (or practically achievable in) a given society, where there is little hope that human rights will be observed, except if there are social alternatives to law, that is to say, complimentary normative systems that are available for human rights protection in the given society.

1. Challenges

The majority of the authors in this volume (and many other theoreticians and activists) realize that there are certain difficulties with human rights in the context of their application, and even in terms of their foundations.

What are these challenges? What purposes do such challenges serve? There is, of course, the challenge of non-observance, but in this scenario the existence of the idea itself is inherently honored in the act of breach. Any reference to an accepted external canonical meaning remains suspicious, at best. Radical critiques of human rights deny its global relevance, arguing that human rights are a limited tribal concept. Other critiques conclude that human rights, as a historical-cultural product, must be subject to the laws of social evolution and that it is up to social actors to shape and renegotiate the meaning of the product. A milder version of cultural relativism argues that human rights in their present form represent a culturally limited experience of dubious political aspirations. Human rights, and the Universal Declaration of Human Rights in particular, are labeled tools of Western imperialism. Shlomo Avineri in his contribution to this volume argues that it is undeniable that respect for universal human rights derives from the biblical tradition "common to the three Abrahamic faiths." "To state this may sound to many as Euro-centric hubris, or another expression of Western

1. "In order to reconcile democracy and human rights, Western policy will have to put more emphasis not on democracy alone but on constitutionalism, the entrenchment of a balance of powers, judicial review..." See Michael Ignatieff, *Human Rights as Politics and Idolatry*, Princeton and Oxford: Princeton University Press (2001) 30.

hegemonism or intellectual imperialism: it is, however, true." Others, like Wiktor Osiatynski in his chapter on the making of the Universal Declaration, indicate that the Declaration itself is not "Western." He points out that the Universal Declaration corresponded to a very special political arrangement where non-individualistic, non-Western considerations played a significant role. "The principal value protected by twentieth-century rights theory is human dignity rather than individual autonomy, as was the case in the eighteenth century. Individual rights were closely linked to economic principles of market economy; human rights are not linked to any economic theory or system." Osiatynski and Ruti Teitel argue that there was universal agreement and acceptance of the concept of human rights among the drafters of the Universal Declaration, who were motivated to consensus by the collective condemnation of gross human rights violations in World War II. "Fifty years later, the very universality of human rights has been fiercely challenged. Human rights were often presented as the ideology of the West, as a secular 'Western religion,' as a tool of Western imperialism, or as a Western neocolonial 'ideology'" (Osiatynski). Makau Mutua formulates a contrasting view. He finds that the original voices "that problematize[d] the idea of human rights and point[ed] to its difficulties from normative, institutional, and multicultural perspectives" have grown silent.

Besides the normative challenge, additional questions are raised on the grounds of practicality or efficiency. These are the arguments relating to the "affordability" of human rights for developing nations. The so-called economic development argument claims that human rights is a concept that becomes relevant only after a certain level of economic development is achieved. Frank Upham presents an interesting combination of the non-affordability and economic development arguments in his chapter, where, using empirical evidence, he shows that the rule of law and human rights dependent on the rule of law are not conducive to development. His stance goes against the mainstream pro-human rights *cum* development position that Amartya Sen relies on, which essentially proclaims that freedom is development.[2]

2. Amartya Sen, *Development as Freedom: Human Capability and Global Need*, New York: Alfred A. Knopf (1999).
Sen's well-known example is India's never having had famine because of her free press, while in Mao's China millions perished in famine because there was no free press to mobilize the public against the suicidal policies of the government. It is interesting how successful this simplistic argument became (Sen's book itself is naturally more sophisticated on the whole). But those who rely on this simple wisdom overlook the one-sidedness of the example. Currently there is no famine, and hunger is diminishing in China, despite the fact that freedom of speech is still lacking. Further, Singapore that had a rule of law system but was deliberately restricting freedom of speech and religion clearly outperformed both China and India. The "feasibility" argument comes up also in John Rawls, "The Law of Peoples" in Stephen Shute and Susan Hurley (eds.), *On Human Rights*, New

The accusations and soul-searching are based on critical theory, as Charles Taylor has put it: "the worrying thought is that the very idea of such a liberalism may be...a particularism masquerading as the universal."[3] Or, as Mutua more constructively words it in his chapter: "This is not to suggest that universality is always wrong-headed, or devious, but it is rather to assume that universality is not a natural phenomenon. In other words, universality is always constructed by an interest for a specific purpose, with a definite intent."

Joseph Raz has contrasted universalism and particularism as two truths: his problem (that may have served as the original question for some authors of the present volume) is "how to combine the truth of universalism with the truth in particularism."[4] To some extent the current panic is more about confronting the *limits* of universality, than it is about questioning the fundamental legitimacy of universality as a valid perspective. By traditional definitions, universality as a concept does not lend itself to limits. However, the truth of the matter is that recent changes in the structure and content of human rights are probably a more significant factor in the current critical disarray. It is perhaps enough to point to the marked increase in the sheer quantity of rights, which has, to some extent, in turn, led to the judicialization of social rights. Another factor is the growing intensity of application, with enforcement increasingly materializing in forms bordering on armed intervention. Arguably such deeper changes make universality less acceptable to many people. Moreover, for many the confrontation with human rights is a much more important *global* experience than it was in 1948 or 1776.

In the past decade, human rights concepts have become simultaneously both somewhat diluted and much overburdened, as they become the source of a "universal language" or default terminology of justice claims across the board, which can be attributed to the disappearance of an alternative Marxist rhetoric of liberation, among other reasons. But human rights, because of a guilt by association with colonialism, encounter difficulties in reestablishing themselves as a language of postcolonial anti-imperialist liberation, at least in their traditional anti-statist individualistic version. A certain confusion over the use of human rights claims emerges. Loosely related claims to entitlements referring to a single undifferentiated notion of human rights

---

York: Basic Books (1993). Rawls finds that decent but hierarchical societies satisfy "law of peoples" principles. Sadurski's chapter discusses the logical inconsistency of the "feasibility" proviso. The Rawlsian shift from the assumptions of *A Theory of Justice* is perhaps one of the most troubling signs of the loss of Western liberal self-confidence which comes from a mistaken self-perception of being intolerant and ethnocentric.

3. Charles Taylor, *Multiculturalism and the "Politics of Recognition"*: an essay, with commentary by Amy Gutmann, Princeton, N.J.: Princeton University Press (1992) 44.

4. Joseph Raz, "Multiculturalism," 11 *Ratio Juris* (1998) 193, 194.

are voiced, and attempts are made to use similar institutional mechanisms to remedy intrinsically different social problems. Given the successful transformation of human rights into an effective international language of victims' claims in general, it has become increasingly difficult to find an intellectually coherent justification for their validity. Critical analysis aims to overcome the "jumping on the bandwagon" effect that has resulted in "semantic pluralization." However, as Dimitrina Petrova points out in her chapter, the enlargement of the concept to provide cover for *social rights* under its growing umbrella had its advantages for it further delayed the legitimacy crisis of human rights. As long as the primary needs of most non-Western groups are discussed in terms of human rights, the irrelevance and Western ethnocentricity arguments cannot be made with full force.

The historically valid, core implication of human rights is that these are actual *rights* (legally enforceable claims, legitimate titles of action) an individual possesses, and thus human rights protection can be called upon by a person to confront governmental oppression. Because human rights are now extended to very different contexts, the core definition has become unsustainable. The model of individual rights with its underlying individualism is counterproductive if used for other goals such as communal or welfare policy. Groups advocating various measures based on this new looser concept of human rights have to rid human rights terminology of its fundamental meaning, insofar as they carry reference to an individual rights structure. The internal conflicts generated in this way result in uncertainties and intellectual criticism. Such criticism comes not only from enemies of human rights who would like to render them irrelevant in order to better sustain their oppressive practices, but also from those who would like to hijack the concepts to be used in backing their humanitarian liberation agenda. Unfortunately, human rights movements not only follow incoherent patterns intellectually, but perhaps even more disappointingly, practical application, too, seems at best rather disjointed. Further, human rights thinking and action often suffer from the predominance of double standards, arrogance, and incompetent absolutism of bystanders. (Regarding this issue, see the criticism in Mutua's chapter; see Upham's and Martin Krygier's chapters for similar conclusions regarding the rule of law).

The authors in this volume identify a number of particularist criticisms that were first voiced in the eighties.[5] Guy Haarscher writes about "frontal attacks" coming from Asian values, Islamism, African values as well as from the European extreme Right. Based on his understanding, Islamism is primarily an anti-secularist attack. Eva Brems identifies similar sources

5. See Raimundo Panikkar, "La notion des droits de l'homme est-elle un concept occidental?", 120 *Diogène* (1982) 87-115.

of attacks (except for the European racist version), but she refers to "critical discourses" instead of "attacks." In her view, anti-universalists have their own normative claims, partly intended to rearrange universal human rights and their worship of individual freedom. Some of these critiques emphasize the importance of cultural diversity which, they argue, would be disregarded by a blanket application of universal human rights principles. A stronger version of this position identifies grounds for particularism in the Universal Declaration and claims that cultural diversity itself is a fundamental human right. Attributing to diversity the status of a value implies a prioritizing of self-determination as a precondition for other human rights.

But where does the concern about particularism come from anyway? There seem to be a variety of competing interests at stake here. What are the implications for those who advocate the particularist position? Particularists tend to repudiate a conception of human rights as universal standards, and at best, advocate the recognition of special group (class of persons) interests or privileges when referring to human rights. Ignatieff has argued elsewhere that this latter attitude is not a problem as long as its adherents rely on "what unites."[6] For example, an ethnic group that demands the right to non-discrimination for its members *vis-à-vis* another ethnicity will rely on universal human rights arguments, that is to say, on rights pertaining to all humans. However, a problem emerges when the "human rights" claim is made in order to *sustain* difference. A generalized instance on difference would have the effect of atomizing society, causing the entire human rights concept to loose its pragmatic charge. A singular claim to difference cannot be deemed sustainable, so long as the principle on which the concept of difference rests applies only to a particular group and cannot be justified in a way that is relevant to human rights. Of course, a particularist claim to difference might still be justified on other grounds (e.g., justice or pragmatic considerations of avoiding conflict).

Notwithstanding the success of the particularists, commonly occurring atrocities committed in the name of cultural identity significantly undermine the credibility of attempts at the deconstruction of human rights. Universalists in the volume are quick to point out that the empirical evidence (so important for diversity/identity) goes against the particularist argument. "The resurgence in the last decade of civil and military aggression justified on grounds of religious, ethnic, and cultural conviction underscores the continuing urgency in articulating a rationale for human rights that can withstand the claim of violence committed in the name of culture" (Helen Stacy). Brems, too, acknowledges that authoritarian governments are eager to abuse the diversity arguments. Haarscher finds the particularist challenge to univer-

6. Ignatieff, *op. cit.*, note 1.

salism a specifically perverse interpretation of tolerance and Enlightenment-based human rights. Human rights violators, with a perverse twist of logic, accuse human rights universalism of intolerance to the extent of not taking "into account the sensitivities of religious majorities (for instance, by outlawing gender discrimination although it may be prescribed by some religions)." Localizing human rights to allow local intolerance in no way fits the human rights agenda and should be considered an irrelevant position. However, at least in my view, the particularist arguments are appealing to large sections of those populations living under dictatorial regimes. This is a particularly troubling development for human rights policies.

Further, it is entirely possible that, contrary to the particularist claim, cultural diversity does not by default represent an unquestionable good in the world[7]—not to mention the suspiciously frequent abuse of the diversity argument in the denial of individual choice and maintenance of tyrannical rule. As Brian Barry, quoted in Wojciech Sadurski's chapter, puts it: "diversity is desirable to the degree, and only to the degree, that each of the diverse groups functions in a way that is well adapted to advance the welfare and secure the rights of its members."[8] Sadurski develops a modified version of this position. He describes the problem by saying, "Let us consider a situation in which our universalistic claims indeed meet genuine resistance by the community upon which we would like to extend our conception of rights, and the ruling elite is at one with a large majority of the community. Under such circumstances, is it really intolerance that is implicated by a universalist discourse of human rights?" Sadurski sees no problem with such an extension, other than that it is sometimes paternalistic. "Paternalism conceived as a response to ignorance and defects in preference formation is not particularly objectionable as long as it is present in proportion to the defect it proposes to remedy; indeed, it may be more objectionable to take at face value the expressed preferences without looking into the preference formation process." Paternalism is objectionable if it inhibits an individual in the determination of her own life. But the "paternalism" objection to a human rights-dictated position is not justified in regard to oppressed women who cannot make their own choices.

Resistance to the particularist challenges is weakened by an intellectual malaise that is related to the universalistic foundations of human rights. Universality is a key concept here as human rights' normativity is assumed to follow from a universalist assumption: human rights are based on moral commands that are general laws, applicable to all. If universal moral precepts are untenable, or if they are incompatible with one another, the validity (gen-

---

7. Brian Barry, *Culture and Equality: An Egalitarian Critique of Multiculturalism*, Cambridge: Polity Press (2001) 134.

8. *Ibid.*

eral applicability) of human rights becomes highly problematic. Note that as early as the eighteenth century the different human rights foundations like enlightened rationalism, religion-inspired dignity, and secular or religious natural law were competing and often mutually exclusive. Moral philosophers find it increasingly difficult to find thick moral grounds for human rights. Rationalism as a basis for human rights looks *passé* in the prevailing postmodernist mood. Rationalism is described as a instrument of false liberation, as a lie, indeed as total failure. Human rights are the victim of a sort of postmodernist inverted *Auschwitzlüge*. The inverted *Auschwitzlüge* goes like this: the rationality of barbarism (the possibility of "Auschwitz") has discredited the dictates of reason. Reason in this postmodernist narrative is never guaranteed to lead to the "best" of all possible solutions because in reality actions and reactions are conjectural and contextual and can easily serve disguised oppression; or simply because reason itself is oppressive.

As a result, rationality as the basis for human rights arguments has become vulnerable and discredited in the postmodern world. Critical analysts are doubtful of human rights as a rational program since reason itself is deemed to be the very source of failure and/or oppression. Human rights are not conducive to moral truth. They are influential only as a predominant language commonly understood within the context of conflict. Stacy's chapter views the human rights/cultural difference dilemma as a discourse—"an international language of claim against an oppressive majority," and against those who benefit from the protection of the majority, as Sadurski would likely add. A discourse presupposes some understanding of the other. Derrida's position, as explicated by Stacy, represents a "maximal" understanding: the proposition is that the "other" be understood as *other*; that is, in her integrity, as she is. The result of this position is the opposite of the present human rights and rule of law system: a new system in which we will have to learn to live "with the instability of plurality." However, as Stacy points out, this does not help us handle issues like a stoning ordered by a *Shari'ah* court, though perhaps it helps us understand the perspectives of those who support the stoning. But comprehension is not necessarily equal to condoning.

The intellectual *malaise* cannot by itself serve to explain the current soul-searching—certainly not in the case of most of the contributions to this volume. The misfortunes of human rights has forced many of its practitioners and theoretical analysts to reexamine their basic thesis irrespective of the *malaise*. In other words, this self-reflection is not just another exercise in some "effeminate," highbrow, Western human rights metareflection. The genuine intellectual challenge is partly related to changes in patterns of contemporary human suffering. Human rights has proved very efficient as a tool of criticism and as a basis for rights protection, but only if understood as a mechanism that actually triggers legal (centrally: judicial) protection against abuses of state power that restrict liberty or human agency. If the Universal Declaration is the answer to Nazism, then it may well also be *the* answer to ultimate sin. But is it an adequate answer to lesser or more differentiated manifestations of evil? The agency-centered model of human rights is challenged because there are problems of a different nature that are in need of a towering intellectual solution. Many contemporary forms of suffering originate at the hands of different actors who are not at all or only indirectly related to the state, its powers, and infrastructure (e.g., oppression by private or multinational entities, perhaps ethnic collectives).

There is also disagreement over the performance of human rights. Haarscher and Sadurski find that human rights is a successful project overall. Their position is corroborated by other studies that contradict the critical position of particularism. There is empirical evidence that the framework of rights successfully mediates between "competing ethnic claims";[9] human rights in its universalism is *the* solution to ethnic (cultural) particularism. Consequently, one may conclude that perhaps, after all, if there is in fact a crisis affecting the human rights movement, then it is not inherent to rights universalism.

Regardless of their positions on the nature and status of human rights, the authors in this volume uniformly grasp that clearly there are challenges to human rights that cannot be left unanswered. Undeniably, human rights have become problematic as they have lost their irresistible evidentiary power exactly at the historical moment after becoming successful within the victorious naturalist paradigm. The more claims were, and are, voiced regarding human rights the less credibility there is for a common core. The likelihood increases that under the guise of additional human rights claims local problem solving is attempted, or global problems are tackled, that have little in common with the "original" problems addressed under the heading of human rights.

The present volume intends to come to terms with the new unease arising from the universal application of human rights. All arguments attempt, in one way or another, to closely examine the contextual implications of the local application of human rights and the rule of law. Some conclude that there is sufficient evidence pointing to a decisive role for context. Others claim that human rights is "preprogrammed" to take contextual differences into account.

---

9. Yash Ghai, "Universalism and Relativism: Human Rights as a Framework for Negotiating Interethnic Claims," 21 *Cardozo Law Review* (2000) 1099.

2. Universality with and without Foundations

Is it possible to have a meaningful discussion on human rights issues within the human rights context? Many among the most influential theoretical formulations of human rights have a rather strong metaphysical foundation. Such a metaphysical foundation is problematic within the "modernist" discourse. Richard Shweder argues in his chapter that the "modernist theoretical framework" is based on very thin metaphysics

> according to which the "real" world (equated with the idea of the "objective world") is understood to be a material world, and hence devoid of all non-material things (such as normative values). The second feature [of the modernist framework] is a (thin) notion of rational justification, which is restricted in modernist thinking to some combination of deductive and/or inductive logic, pure formalism, and direct sense-experience (no divine revelations, revealed truths, or scriptural narratives). That modernist contraction or reduction of what counts as real and as rational has led some scholars to the dismal conclusion that there is no such thing as moral truth.

Tatsuo Inoue's chapter, however, suggests that even a radical contextualism is in need of universalist arguments—in other words, it is not certain that the conclusions of the modernist critique of modernism, which challenge the possibility of universalism, are correct, even if the criticism itself is accepted.

This is not to say that sound metaphysics would necessarily help human rights universalism. As Avineri points out in his chapter discussing the tradition of Judaism, metaphysical-theological concepts of human rights have their own problems with universalism. (Are the theologically valid foundations of various obligations applicable outside the community of believers?) Once the metaphysical foundations are out of the picture, universalism (and foundations in general) become problematic. The moral realist foundation of human rights is seen as inefficient, while religious and natural law foundations are without universally acceptable empirical validity.

When Napoleon discussed with Laplace the new cosmology of the astronomer, the Emperor asked about the place of God in the astronomer's system. Laplace replied: "Sire, I don't need that hypothesis." This applies to all metaphysical foundations of human rights. One might be better off without metaphysics. This is a sign of our coming out of the self-imposed infancy of humankind (*sapere aude*). Because metaphysical traditions differ from one another, a proof offered by one could well be the grounds for rejection when examined by another. This is true about religions too, notwithstanding all the civilized lip service about mutual respect, common core values, and so on.

There are a number of attempts to replace metaphysics with empirical foundations. In the present volume Haarscher is, for example, one of those who find certain basic similarities in all cultures. He thinks that it is not an impossible task to show that the universality of human rights comes from the patrimony of humanity as a whole. There are also normative alternatives. A thin moral justification is not per se precluded after the (alleged) discrediting of metaphysical foundations. This is the strategy of Inoue's chapter; after all, there is no need to expect human rights to lead us to good life. Another option to follow is Michael Walzer's minimalism in morality.[10] Such minimalism is satisfied if "the rule serves no particular interest, expresses no particular culture, regulates everyone's behavior in a universally advantageous or clearly correct way. The rule carries no personal or social signature."[11] Note that Walzer talks about rules, and human rights per se are not necessarily moral precepts, but only standards which may or may not rest on moral foundations, or—to follow Habermas—standards enabling public morality. To this the relativist will object on the grounds that even this universalism is impossible, as human rights are not minimalist since they do indeed have culture-specific traits, and furthermore, in light of the consequences of human rights policies, human behavior is not always regulated favorably or successfully by universal Western human rights.

Even if minimalist and empiricist alternatives were intellectually acceptable, they would still lack the practical power of moral or religious theories in shaping people's behavior. Pragmatism (i.e., arguments based on consequences) is certainly forceful and to some extent can be used as a positive tool in support of human rights claims. Yet pragmatic arguments lack the force of a moral trump and are subject to constant renegotiation and uncertainty, which in turn makes human rights less effective in the local context. Of course, one may conclude that people just have to learn to live with uncertainty, and indeed—as far as I can see—they will be better off if they do. It is perhaps fair to say that the adulthood of humankind began when we first dared to know, while the next phase is characterized by an awareness of the limits of our ability to know. Even if not trumps, human rights might be attractive in view of their consequences. Suffering is reduced if human rights are observed. But what is objectionable here is that, in fact, it is the agent who determines what amounts to suffering, and therefore, even the apparent consensus regarding the need to avoid suffering will inevitably prove to be purely theoretical or fragile at best. Human rights are able to diminish only that suffering which falls within the Western definition.

Female genital mutilation (FGM) (or "modification") is one of the test cases used in a number of chapters to contrast the efficiency of human rights

10. Michael Walzer, *Thick and Thin—Moral Argument at Home and Abroad*, Notre Dame: University of Notre Dame Press (1994) 7.

11. *Ibid.*

with their limits and the process of renegotiation of human rights in the local context. The choice of FGM as a test case is to some extent problematic because as a human rights claim, lack of FGM is probably not near the top of the victims' agenda. The authors here would probably agree that one has to take into consideration victims' perspectives in prioritizing violations. How then could one consider renegotiating a matter when the party to be spoken for does not consider the issue at hand particularly relevant? Well, in truth, the scholar analyzing this problem has little choice. Whatever the objectively calculated rank of FGM among all human rights violations might be, FGM, due to some of its peculiarities, has gathered an extraordinary momentum of its own and is now a *cause celebre* serving as large caliber ammunition in the human rights *Kulturkampf*.

Brems states that notwithstanding her commitment to dialogism and her recognition of a collective right to cultural practices, these cultural considerations apply where, and only if, the individual has the right to "opt out." Shweder has a stronger commitment to moral universalism, although "without the uniformity." On the basis of an impressive collection of anthropological evidence he argues that moral truth claims remain different across cultures. "[F]ully rational, morally decent people from different ethnic groups or cultural communities may have divergent moral responses to particular cases.... Morally decent and fully rational people can disagree about such things, even in the face of a plentitude of shared objective values." Shweder urges a sympathetic understanding of those who differ from us, especially given our own global-media dictated localism. He reviews the latest epidemiology literature on FGM and cites sources reporting that no significant medical complications have been found to result from the practice. When it is possible to point to the presence of what he terms "terminal good," Shweder argues that "outsiders" should accept the practice under a universal moral standard. One ought to understand the moral integrity of local contexts: a "terminal good" can be found within the practice of FGM, namely, in the reaffirmation of identity. FGM is a choice of identity. But this is exactly the point: Is FGM a choice of identity or an imposition of identity by parents, tribe, etc.? What are the actual choices and faculties of the person who understands her identity through FGM? Western human rights reasoning is based on the presumption of rational individuals imagining the acts of other rational individuals. Does a North African mother satisfy such criteria when she turns a blind eye to her daughter's pain and suffering as she undergoes FGM? Is someone who is bound in her most intimate choices by the dictates of her community considered to be acting rationally? Is this question even meaningful where the idea of a "personal" sphere makes little or no sense, in a local context of all-embracing tradition where rites of passage are central to communal identity? If Stacy is right then "it may simply be impossible to coexist peaceably without acknowledging an intractable disagreement with another's cultural commitment." Sadurski finds unacceptable the denial of *genuine* personal choice in the name of diversity—where the insider's culture disallows personal choice.

Shweder refers to interviews by Lane and Rubinstein conducted[12] with circumcised women. As these researchers put it, out of fifty women they "found *only* two" (emphasis added) who reported any complications. From a human rights perspective these two women (four per cent) are a lot. On the other hand, the North African mother and daughter are quite reasonable in submitting themselves to FGM if the alternative of exiting the community is unavailable to them and if accepting the practice is an otherwise unavoidable prerequisite for marriage. The human rights activist should at least understand the reality of this situation before taking any action affecting another person (destructive) or before condemning the practice outright. Whatever the choices and the actual consequences of the practice, the need for critical evaluation of the facts and consequences surrounding FGM is imperative. As Stacy puts it, "the careful receptivity of arguments for the cultural valence...may produce the possibility of contributing to circumstances in which young women can exercise their preference to exit or remain within a community that practices infibulation." Most African countries have outlawed or are in the process of outlawing FGM and other rites of initiation, if applied to minors or without consent. This appears to satisfy the intellectual dictates of agency-based human rights, but unfortunately, even as I write, in Southern Kenya alone there are some three hundred girls in hiding at church shelters, having run away from their parents for the justified fear of being subjected to FGM.

With all the doubts and legitimate criticism, the practical problem of formulating valid culture-independent human rights claims has only become an increasingly bitter battle. For human rights to be acceptable (regardless of their specific foundation) it is assumed that they have to be universal, i.e., that they pertain to all and be applicable to all. But what might be the proper strategy that would allow all humans to be considered a part of the same collectivity? Without some normative force human rights have little practical consequence in action. Is it inevitable that in order for them to be influential the claim to universalism has to be presented as a natural and obvious truth? Brems claims that universalism is a matter of deliberate choice. Where there is a will there will also be a way. Once accepted in principle, human rights gain momentum through further international acceptance. Political theories of the *social compact* or *contract* worked well with a similar assumption of con-

12. Sandra D. Lane and Robert A. Rubinstein, "Judging the Other: Responding to Traditional Female Genital Surgeries," 26 *Hastings Center Report* (1996) 31-40.

sent without necessarily relying on metaphysical foundations—at least for the intermediate term. After all, most people (regardless of their particular cultural association) want—as a minimum—to be respected, and definitely have a strong preference against being tortured. Moreover, once international human rights (through power politics, modernization, or by any other means) gain momentum, the choice of human rights becomes a fact of life, possessing all the normative force of that which is fact. After all, social institutions tend to develop and are accepted by society with little consideration of intellectual foundations, while practical factors like narrow interests, constraints, violence, superstition, and habit assert more influence. This disregard for foundations might be acceptable even from the perspective of normative theory. At least Inoue argues in his chapter that universalism should not be confused with foundationalism. One possible interpretation of this position is that there can be universalism without universal foundations. For Inoue, "[u]niversal validity as the regulative idea is an essential condition for the contextuality and critical open-endedness of our justification....The public justification requirement implied by this conception tells us to transcend our idiosyncratic beliefs and to turn to the dialogical background we share with our dialogical partners for reasons intelligible and acceptable both for them and us."

Is this position gravitating towards relativism by admitting that our human rights belief or that of other people's is idiosyncratic? With the universal validity assumption there remains a possibility for *mutually acceptable* positions that are based on mutually intelligible *reasons*. If religious or idiosyncratic cultural positions do not amount to *reasons*, then there is no place for such relativism even in a dialogical understanding of human rights and justice. One honors another not by accepting that person as *other* but by assuming that the other person can produce reasons or at least has the ability to react reasonably to reasons. To call this "imperialism" is the end of discourse.

In a postmodern world universals have become suspicious per se, exactly because it is accepted that "universal" is a reference for convenient prefab solutions to uncertainties resulting from lack of sufficient information (or too much complexity). By now these references to the universal have proven to be historical illusions. Human rights and rule of law appeal

> to the desire for universal truths in a global world. It simplifies complex realities by transforming social and political behavior into legal categories, and it promises to make mutually comprehensible [transparent in the current jargon] the processes and practices of societies as different as those of Nigeria and Nebraska. Second, the rule of law appeals to our mistrust of politics and political action. It promises order without bureaucracy; governance without government; social choice without politics. Just as the invisible hand

> of the market produces wealth without intentional human agency, the black box of legal reasoning [and neutral courts] resolves social and economic disputes without moral judgment or political bias. In an age when politics and social engineering are reviled as wasteful and corrupt, the rule of law presents itself as the perfect complement for a free-market based view of development, offering to fix whatever problems the market fails to fix on its own. (Upham)

Krygier is more in favor of universal rule of law as a general attempt to reduce uncertainty and arbitrariness, but he, too, finds specific means of the rule of law problematic: "to speak sensibly of the rule of law as a significant element in the life of a society, the law's norms must be socially *normative*."

Of course, the anxiety about the universality of human rights is related to a specific application or caricature of their application. Universal human rights were never as rigid as some people are inclined to represent them. Human rights are neither rules nor rights in the legal sense of the expression, although there is a strong argument (that I would subscribe to) that the primary relevance of human rights is in the context of modern judicially enforced law, i.e., as bona fide legal rights.

The specificity of human rights compared to morals is that they have the potential to become positive law. The great social achievement of human rights is that they are becoming positive, enforceable through a political process. Human rights were an important political argument in the French National Assembly, but not a legally enforceable claim. This is changing, however, both within the domestic realm through constitutional adjudication and also internationally through human rights conventions becoming binding international law, not only with regard to state to state relations but also for the individual person, offering her both domestic and international recourse. Initially, the preferred solution for the implementation of viable human rights protection was to have rights guaranteed by a nation-state. International obligations of states—if existing at all—have insufficient credibility. Consider the example of Israel: after World War II, Jews could not, and did not, expect protection from international documents and international-law induced goodwill, and in fact, needed a state of their own in order to ensure the protection of their fundamental rights.[13] The human rights problem remains acute for those groups who have not and will not have their own state: the physically challenged, abused children, or even those minorities for whom statehood is impracticable. Where statehood is seen as the intermediary for universalistic protection, the need for rule of law emerges as the practical system of actual protection.

International human rights as a concept is not best understood as a collection of rules in the legal sense. Even if interpreted as "rules," human rights

13. Cf. Ignatieff, *op. cit.*, note 1.

would still have to be perceived as a flexible set of rules that are very much dependent on specific context. The Universal Declaration talks about standards, not rules. The drafters of the Universal Declaration were content with a declaration that would raise consciousness, that would match the intention behind the French Declaration in serving as an authoritative reminder, a yardstick for the mind.[14] The French Declaration is understood to be a set of principles or a yardstick—a mark of reference that could be used to check any legislation against. Neither of the declarations is absolutist, though in fact, however, they are context-conscious in the sense of expressly authorizing restrictions. Restrictions are clearly permitted in the name of morality or public order in a democratic society (Universal Declaration). A kind of relativism has been built into human rights in the form of restrictions, which are, however, bounded. Limitations of rights are permissible under the Universal Declaration within what befits democracy. Of course, the French Declaration did not refer to democracy, although it did provide safeguards for political participation and envisioned, or even mandated, a representative system. On the other hand, with the inclusion of the "restrictions by law," and with the limits of liberty defined by the benchmark of harm as well as by other people's liberty, the French Declaration offers a functional map of the approach used in the Universal Declaration. Needless to say, even such formulations of human rights that on the surface may well appear unrestricted in nature, like the prohibition of cruel and unusual punishment, are context bound.[15]

Human rights universalism does not suggest that human rights are unconditionally applicable. If human rights are not perceived as imperative moral commands, but instead are understood as imperfect standards or mere guidance, then there is no difficulty in taking into consideration the circumstances and consequences of the guided action, even if one is not a consequentialist. Consider the following line of argument from Professor Korsgaard:[16]

---

14. *Ibid.* Osiatynski's chapter points to the pragmatic ambitions of the Universal Declaration.
15. Some of the provisions of the Universal Declaration consider the rights holder as if she were an object of a protective prohibition. This is the case with the prohibition of slavery and torture. Because these are not presented as a right (of action), rather as a freedom from something, the limits of Article 20 regarding the exercise of rights and freedoms seem not to apply. In contrast, could it be a valid argument that freedom from torture is limited to the extent torture is required to maintain public order in a democracy? The answer seems to be no, and this is also the position of the 1987 Convention against Torture. Yet this answer is not so self-evident to many since September 11, 2001.
16. Christine M. Korsgaard, Self-Constitution: Action, Identity, and Integrity. Lecture Five: The Constitutional Model and Bad Action. The John Locke Lectures, Oxford. www.people.fas.harvard.edu/~korsgaar/Korsgaard.LL5.

> Perhaps you may now be tempted to say that what makes the procedures normative is the usual quality of their outcomes, the fact that they get it right most of the time. After all, even if we do stand by the outcomes of our procedures though in this or that case they are bad, we would certainly change those procedures if their outcomes were bad too often. But this cannot be the whole answer, not only because it isn't always true—think of the jury system—but also because, as act utilitarians have been telling us for years, it is irrational to follow a procedure merely because it usually gets a good outcome, when you know that this time it will get a bad one. So perhaps we should say instead that the normativity of the procedures comes from the usual quality of their outcomes combined with the fact that we must have some such procedures, and we must stand by their results. But why must we have some such procedures? Because without them collective action is impossible.

If we replace Korsgaard's procedures with human rights we may conclude the following:

a. Human rights are to be observed because we have historical evidence regarding the quality of their usual outcome. The usual quality is good; Habeas Corpus generally helps prevent abuse. Human rights are a historical consequentialist formula comprised of specific negative political experiences and known ways to avoid their repetition.
b. We have to accept, however, that a given human rights action (intervention) might have a negative outcome "this time," and the usual procedures might not work in a particular application. It follows that we have to be aware of the circumstances which are likely to increase the chance of bad outcomes. For example, the person who insists on the application of human rights-based policies for women should be aware of the likelihood that a traditional community will be up in arms because of a deep-rooted opposition to the modern phenomenon of women's liberation.
c. We should follow human rights procedure to the extent that its observance is dictated by the need for collective action. However, because the impact of collective action is rather conjectural and has certain obvious consequent harms, the departure from the obvious dictates of human rights is likely. The contemporary problem of human rights is that their broad application has reduced the percentile of good outcomes, and yet, within the context of a particular action or application, they do not offer practical techniques that can be used to predict with sufficient precision if negative effects may be in store.

One would expect that with regard to universality there are two diametrically opposed positions: one either claims that human rights are universal or that they are not. In truth, this is not such a black and white issue. Remember Pierre Bourdieu's warning: "If you meet a dichotomy when thinking, be brave:

try to escape."[17] Even if there is a universal element in human rights, this does not necessarily deny local and contextual considerations. Universality is not always setting priorities:

We often do better to ask how the two sides of a dichotomy, in our case universal and local, might—and do—combine and connect, and how best they might be made to combine and connect. That way we might relieve, on the one hand, the abstraction and arrogance that can go with single-minded insistence on purported universals (which have all *originated* somewhere in particular) and, on the other, the parochialism and relativism that can flow from excessive devotion to the local. (Krygier)

When it comes to human rights, if the authors of this volume cannot escape taking sides, they tend to gravitate to one position while qualifying their position as often as possible. Here are some of the strategies:

- Perhaps what we have now is not universal human rights but one can certainly work successfully to develop it. (Mutua)
- The relentless effort to universalize—through Western intellectual crusades—what is essentially a European corpus of human rights cannot succeed. Nor will it advance the cause to demonize those who resist the corpus. The multifaceted critique of the corpus from Africans, Asians, Moslems, Hindus, and a host of critical thinkers from around the world are in fact valuable resources which, if used right, can be *the* way for human rights to be redeemed and truly universalized.
- "Multiculturalization" of the human rights corpus could be attempted in a number of areas: balancing between individual and group rights, giving more substance to social and economic rights, relating rights to duties, and addressing the relationship between the corpus and the particularities of various economic systems.
- Universalism is irrefutable but it may have differing sources, meanings, implications, and consequences.
- Human rights universalism is not the 180 degree opposite of particularism or localism.
- We should resist the temptation (or assumed obligation) to take sides. The task is to seek the best combination of components even if they originate in competing theorems. (Krygier)
- Human rights universalism is of the kind that allows for taking contextual matters into account. For Brems and Sadurski universality is contextual, at the same time they deny that particularism is relevant to the status of human rights universalism. Sadurski in particular finds the particularist claim unacceptable.

---

17. Quoted in Dominique Memmi, "Public-Private Opposition and Biopolitics: A Response to Judit Sándor," 69, 1 *Social Research* (2002) 143.

Sadurski's position exemplifies "weak cultural relativism," to use Jack Donnelly's old category.[18] However, if one realizes that human rights are standards, and not rules or commands, then the particularized applications do not amount to a switch from some abstract universality or to concessions to local culture: paper standards simply come alive in particular contexts. How one approximates the standard is left to the combinations offered by and within the rule of law. Further, context does not change identity, not even imaginary identities.

Is not this doctrine of "inborn" flexibility simply an easy way out of the difficulties of local application for universalists? After all, how do we determine that a (general) standard has been violated if local practice supports the activity? It is argued that the standard will remain identifiable, notwithstanding local practices. The commonly used example relates to torture and cruel punishment (clearly a historically changing concept). Is the stoning to death of a raped mother not cruel if justified by a local interpretation of *Shari'ah* (an interpretation dismissed by many respectable scholars of Islam)? Ask the victim. But what if the victim too knows that stoning is the law and finds the institution respectable? She may well not perceive the same degree of extraordinary cruelty as I do. I assume that there can be a rational discussion based on empirical facts regarding the nature of stoning. In the context-bound human rights discussion the currently practiced, socially viable, and affordable forms or systems of punishment are compared. Contextualizing human rights means, at least to me, that locally affordable solutions are selected from a general set of solutions which satisfy the standard in question. Personally, I find most forms of incarceration cruel, yet I would not argue against incarceration on human rights grounds; for, in the case of most societies, I can offer no socially convincing or affordable alternatives to incarceration. I can, however, argue against the unnecessary infliction of pain. We can expect local institutions of punishment not to resort to the infliction of unnecessary pain. The death penalty per se is unnecessary according to most contemporary standards; but it is without a doubt that those forms of punishment that cause *extra* pain are unacceptable, including malfunctioning electric chairs, and so on. Let me clarify: the fact that not every prison cell comes equipped with a television would not qualify as a problem in the above global comparison, whereas the fact that a prison cannot protect inmates against rape is definitely a human rights issue.

The remarkable flexibility in opening up the universal approach to local and particular considerations corresponds to various strategies and bases deployed to maintain the relevance of human rights as a universal concept

18. Jack Donnelly, "Cultural Relativism and Universal Human Rights," 6 *Human Rights Quarterly* (1984) 401.

and standard. Inoue relies on Rawls (of the nineties) and Saul Kriepke's interpretative theory to prove that contextual differences, or historical contextualism, are in need of "philosophical arguments with universal validity." Inoue intends to reconstruct the foundations of universalism along a route that would allow for reflexive universalism.

"Enforcement of the universal demands of morality without imposing one's own cultural conception of things on others" is a possibility for Shweder. "It requires a good deal of ethnographic and historical work aimed at understanding local social, political, and economic contexts and the goals, values, and pictures of the world held by 'others.'" In other words, the problem with universalism is not an intrinsic one; the problem is simply that activists use universalism as a pretext to imposing their own vision of "good life." Note Brems' position: she refuses to accept a formulation of human rights as a moral vision of good life. While Shweder has a rather thick moral vision of human rights. Western activists might be overzealous in imposing their own vision of a good life, but this is not a sufficient argument against the value of good life as a standard. The idea of human rights is first and foremost rooted in "righteous behavior." Without good life or righteous behavior, the outsider will have no reasonable grounds for criticism, nor can intervention by cosmopolitan, "outsider," observers be meaningfully criticized. There can be no critical dialogue and meaningful interaction of any sort without the acceptance of universalism.

An alternative to this is offered by—among others—Judge Richard Posner, as discussed in Shweder's chapter. Posner does not accept universalism and proposes that the claims of human rights be valid exclusively in Western culture. All cultures are for themselves. Particularism, however, comes at a price. According to this logic, no culture has any obligation to respect another, and it might as well dismiss the other if it can afford to do so. Further, in the context of his analysis of the radically anti-universalist position of Judge Posner, Shweder points out that if no universal moral obligation is understood to exist, unrestrained power is then the only player to chart the course of history, both locally and globally. Those who see only the menace of imperialism masquerading as (phony) universalism have no grounds to object to unjustified intervention. Without the moral obligation to tolerate another culture equipped with a set of ethics different in some or many aspects from ours, there would be no theoretical barrier to a real drive to eradicate that which is (or perceived as being) different. There would be no need to justify intervention. And it would be natural for any set of local social norms to strive for global domination.

Of course, just how restrained such tolerance should render context-sensitive human rights remains to be determined. After all, we are presented with an asymmetry that was identified by Stuart Hampshire, which reads, "liberal democratic societies...permit...a plurality of conceptions of good life" while the various "experts in the will of God maintain a single conception of the good which determines the way of life of the society as a whole."[19]

The chapters dealing with the rule of law offer contradictory views on the practical difficulties of human rights implementation through the rule of law and court-centered positive law as it is known in the West. Rule of law practices restrict the universal application of human rights, though not necessarily its universal validity. The practical tool for enforcing individual human rights is the individualistic rule of law. Distortions inevitably occur due to the insufficient social reach of the rule of law. In Krygier's analysis the rule of law fails to reach exactly those parts of society where victimization might be the most blatant. Sadurski finds the legal adaptations of human rights to contingencies much less problematic. In his view, the judicial handling of discriminatory practices and of the historically evolved restrictions on speech is successful, especially if these adaptations for the local context are also legally controlled. Brems is much more willing to consider human rights within a "dialogical generation" process, and has in mind a partly different set of actors in determining the dialogue. She comes rather close to Sadurski in setting the limits of contextualism: "Flexibility only comes into play when human rights discourse attains a certain level of sophistication. A very substantial part of human rights discourse, especially at the level of public opinion, concerns gross violations: torture, arbitrary arrest, the prohibition of a religion, the destruction of crops and houses, slavery-like labor conditions, etc. These cannot be justified in any context." What we have is a convergence of the various Western positions, and even where different methodologies or styles are applied they still all bear the same mark of a single core of human rights values.

An argument has also been made that the sensitivity to context, which is arguably present in the actual legal enforcement of human rights standards, might even prove an illusion or altogether irrelevant. Upham's chapter points out the resource constraints in developing countries. He sees the rule of law as counterproductive and destructive for developing countries. If he is right, in many countries there are insufficient resources to implement human rights through the rule of law, and, to the extent the rule of law is operative, it will be meaningless or even oppressive and human rights compromised. Upham writes, "the training of Chinese judges by American law professors does not prevent the detention of political dissidents—or, perversely, enables judges to provide plausible legal reasons for their detention—political leaders on all

19. Stuart Hampshire, "Justice is Strife," Presidential Address delivered before the Sixty-fifth Annual Pacific Division Meeting of the American Philosophical Association in San Francisco, California, March 29, 1991.

sides may turn away from law completely and miss the modest role that law can play in political and economic development."

3. Human Rights Politics

Human rights influence power, hence they, too, are a matter of politics, and their application is politicized. Human rights politics is a factor in international politics. The political dimensions are an underlying concern for most authors of this volume, and human rights politics is directly confronted in both Shweder's and Petrova's chapters. Human rights protection and (generally belated) international intervention may have destabilizing effects on the targeted country under criticism for its human rights record. Some international intervention may actually undermine stability and can result in inadvertent yet very real additional suffering. Consider the following account from Anne Itto, a Sudanese aid worker (with a British Ph.D.): "The gender agenda of aid agencies in Sudan demonstrates the naiveté of donors who have prioritized the needs of women and children without regard for the context of the emergency. For example, World Food Program (WFP) started distributing food aid to local women's groups, which, although efficient, has made women targets for looting and other abuses."[20] As mentioned above, the recent criminalization of FGM in a number of African countries has contributed to a growth in self-awareness and self-confidence, and a consequent sense of liberation among many young women. As a result of their choice not to undergo the traditional operation, however, they instead become subjects of persecution and consequently live in danger. Moreover, their family relations tend to deteriorate due to more pronounced generational conflict, leading to further isolation.

Human rights politics (i.e., choices influencing political action) need be aware of these considerations. Interventionists need to be cognizant of the moral obligations that accompany their blanket insistence on the observation of human rights. If no efficient protection is in place for those who are encouraged to make human rights claims (*in situ*) on their own behalf, then any claim made by outsiders on behalf of those directly involved may well be morally questionable. Once human rights enforcement is found wanting and intervention determined to be legitimate and necessary, intervention is permissible only if it is efficient, meaning that it will result in effective and sustainable human rights protection. Intervention has to satisfy the precautionary principle: it must prevent intervention-induced suffering to the

20. Anne Itto, "An Insider's View of Humanitarian Assistance," *Fletcher Forum of World Affairs* (Spring 2000) 26.

greatest extent possible. Even if there is efficient protection internally (within the country involved), or internationally, the bystander who advocates intervention must consider the entire range of circumstantial problems that can result from external intervention—such as the infringement of sovereignty (in the case of international intervention), an effect that is often judged to be almost as gross a violation as outright occupation or colonization in the eyes of many in the affected country or community. These local perceptions might be wrong, but even so, wrong perceptions are to be taken into consideration. Nevertheless, the caveats regarding intervention should not apply to the act of identifying and disclosing human rights violations, or at least it is not generally thought that criticism in and of itself is destabilizing to such a degree that it could cause additional suffering.

The diversity found among the various approaches to our problem—both among those who are forced to give a more complex and sophisticated account of universalism, as well as among those who cannot be satisfied with universal answers—has to do with the current political development of human rights and the rule of law. "The idea of universal human rights is in itself a highly contested *political* idea" (Sadurski, emphasis added). The contested standards emerge within the framework of political action and are in the hands of powerful actors, although these actors are neither unified (nor are they universal players). The taming of and the dissatisfaction with universalism are both critical reflections on this politics. As Petrova indicates, universal and local positions are equivalent in the political dimension: both can be used in support of, or against the established order. Petrova and Teitel (addressing the issue of international criminal courts dealing with gross violations) document various dimensions of the political interaction that have the (combined) effect of restructuring the rule of law and human rights.

Petrova observes the transformation of the political function of human rights from criticism of the political regime to the defense of the global order. The point is corroborated in Osiatynski's chapter: "Twentieth-century human rights are international, which means that they were designed for claims against abusive governments by other governments." Thus governments became the paramount users of human rights (rhetoric), including governments that are themselves of an oppressive leaning.

The international politics of human rights moves increasingly toward interventionism. Such interventionism remains a selective one (apparently inconsistent when examined on purely moral grounds), because the final word in all these matters is ultimately uttered by *Realpolitik*. Underneath the emerging international universalism of universal jurisdiction there are local limits that often contradict the normative consensus. Contemporary developments, "while universal in aspiration, continue by and large to reflect continued adherence to traditional principles of state consent, nationality, and territoriality" (Teitel). But Haarscher, notwithstanding the double standard, finds progress even in these developments. The present "results are quite imperfect, and one may even fear here and there a deterioration of the human rights protections for some groups... . Nevertheless, nobody can reasonably defend Saddam Hussein, or Milosevic, or mullah Omar: their fall is a victory for human rights, even when it is partial, precarious, or ambiguous."

The importance of understanding the political dimension of the debate surrounding the "universal applicability of human rights" is clearly documented in the post-9/11 (2001) discourse. The issue is this: are religions—and as far as the contemporary world is concerned, Islam—an obstacle to human rights?[21] Part of the concern is that Islam and other community-based traditions require a different approach to human rights, one that is non-Western and non-individualistic. This idea is raised in Mutua's chapter. Therefore, we wonder whether it is possible to structure human rights in such a fundamentally different way? Another issue of concern is whether certain forms or "distortions" of Islam are simply incompatible with human rights. Avineri argues that there are certain structural elements in Islam—namely, the absence of a church—that explain the vulnerability of Islamic countries to the rule of despotic regimes, which use the Qur'an to justify violations of human rights, including systematic violations of the rights of women deemed heretics, etc. It is hard to maintain the compatibility of the "theology" of human rights with that of Islam when the religious doctrine is a source of power. Consider the impact of religion on the administration of justice, for example, with regard to the systematic persecution of the Ahmadis in Pakistan (a rule of law country, at least according to her Constitution).[22]

---

21. Intellectually, I find it problematic that "Islam" is singled out without mentioning the history of Catholicism, or the fate of Michel Servet in Geneva, or contemporary Hindutva, or "majority church" intolerance irrespective of the religion's location and context.

22. Consider the following letter that appeared in the Pakistani daily *Dawn* (4 October 2002):

 "Blasphemy Law Essential

 There have been many incidents where people punished the blasphemy accused by themselves. This should never have happened. However, such a situation arises when authorities don't take a serious view of the most sensitive issue of sacrilege by someone publicly.

 Muslims are extremely sensitive about the honour of the Holy Prophet (PBUH) and care for it more than their own lives because it is the basis of their faith. Even the Quaid-i-Azam, who was also a great constitutional lawyer, had defended an accused who had killed a blasphemer. However, there are some NGOs which claim to represent human rights, but factually they maintain no contacts with the common people. Their spokespersons have neither been raised nor educated in local conditions.

 ...

 The law of the land should be invoked as per the historic perspective, tradition, culture and aspirations of the people. The blasphemy law is very much in accordance with

However, not unlike other religions, Islam is not unified. It reacts to human rights and related modernization pressures in very complex ways, with changing historical fortune. Human rights and the rule of law, whether universal or not, are negotiated in a local political process—with the involvement of many outside parties, and with local actors jumping on the universal bandwagon and even stepping onto the international stage. These complexities are evident in the past and current reactions of Islamic Iran, as described in two respective chapters of this volume: the first by Shiva Balaghi regarding the 1905–11 Constitutional Revolution, and the other by Ann Elizabeth Mayer regarding the present Khameini period.

"The grossly inadequate human rights protections in the 1979 Iranian Constitution [of the Islamic Republic of Iran] had already signaled that Islam would be the pretext for restricting rights, if not nullifying them altogether.... But, did Islam in and of itself compel this outcome?" Mayer answers her question with a resounding *no*, and portrays the complex mentalities that determined the Iranian position; one that is constantly subject to renegotiation, due—among others—to the theological position which granted women political participation rights. She concludes that "it is not religion and culture that independently create obstacles in the way of international human rights law, but rather, factors associated with particular historical trends and circumstances as well as an interplay between domestic politics and global developments." Avineri's position on the same problem is that although religion is a crucial determinant, Iran has an ambiguous heritage of religious tradition. In Iran specific historical circumstances diminish or reshape the negative influence of religion.

4. Imperialism with Sensitivity or Dialogic Co-existence?

However complex the dynamic of internationally influenced human rights politics (as part of political and cultural struggles), the normative question does not go away: If one subscribes to a core normative concept of universal human rights to what extent are cultural-religious practices to be respected? Sometimes scholars prefer not to take sides on this issue. They identify the enormous tension between religious/cultural dictates and universalist human

---

these conditions.

...

We need peace and harmony in our beloved country and for this purpose the law of blasphemy is essential.
Dr Abdur Razzaq Sikendar
Chancellor, Jamia Islamia, Binnori Town, Karachi"

rights claims, and limit their exposition to elaboration on the theoretical foundations of a possible multidisciplinary paradigm that can address the problem of the local. Stacy (who implicitly finds certain religion-induced practices to be in violation of human rights), for example, is very keen on maintaining this scholarly position: "Under the conditions of globalization, the philosophy of rights is confronted more than ever with the tension that has been apparent since the Silk Road—that there is a disconnect between its roots in the Western intellectual tradition and the centrality of the individual within that tradition on the one hand, and human rights claims that derive from a group or collective identity on the other."

For others taking a position cannot be avoided. If an alternative particularistic set of standards is developed, it must first of all be supplied with sufficient supporting arguments to fit the definition of human rights. The challenge cannot be met. The only way out of this mousetrap is the radical denial of human rights, but given the current domination of the human rights language this option is not very attractive. Globality is decisive in the form of international and superpower reactions, and even if double standards apply, isolation or self-exclusion has not proven efficient.

While particularist programs denying the uniform applicability of Western human rights run the risk of self-exclusion from the family of human rights claims, human rights absolutism runs the serious risk of arrogance and hubris. Irrespective of its inherent moral legitimacy it will run into resistance, will be inefficient and even destructive.

Today, universalists are concerned about the alleged rigidity of abstract, commandeering universalism. Generalized notions (agendas bordering on detached ideology) have the unfortunate tendency to become insensitive, and, once an attempt is made to implement them, to be perceived as misplaced goodwill or erroneous imperialistic ambition. In order to avoid the pitfalls of a structurally predetermined human rights imperialism, I wish to propose a strategy of *respectful engagement*, which is above all characterized by a conscious modesty. All grounds for accusations of imperialism are to be avoided. There is already more than enough evidence of unintended bad consequences resulting from human rights dictates that, rather than being carefully implemented, were imposed on actors and victims. As mentioned above, human rights are not precepts or commands, and hence the injection of human rights as a set of strict rules into the organism of traditional cultures might be a recipe for disaster. Human rights, when used properly, help to generate certain broad patterns that allow for local considerations—whatever "local" means; but are not *the* magic potion to cure all specific problems. Yet it must also be understood that the inconsiderate application of norms in the name of universality should not be automatic cause for the oft-cited criticism directed against universalism. Overreaching application of norms should really only be grounds for criticism of what they in fact are: the erroneously extended application of universalism, and not for criticism of the underlying concept of universalism itself.

Where are the points of engagement enabling mutually meaningful interaction? Stacy elevates "the struggle to comprehend cultural [etc.] incommensurability" to a moral obligation. Human rights ought not be the predetermined sets of standards of the Enlightenment, but actual reformulations of the original program of enhancing human agency. Dialogue is the hope of those who are culturally bound to respect the Western preference of individual choice. But why should others engage in this dialogue when they are the only ones that have something to lose? Changes in local practices desired (and even required) by the West are the consequences of Western globalization of the material world, an irresistible development that has little to do with mutual understanding and human rights cultures. *Shari'ah* law has been proposed as a subject for discussion, for it is allegedly fit to be the focus of meaningful dialogue—but why not choose instead the Catholic position on abortion? Any implicated culture will claim the right not to participate in the unequal dialogue.[23]

In 1990 Deng and An-Na'im stated that there is "controversy surrounding cross-cultural perspectives on human rights, and the debate has just begun and that its parameters are still to be defined and its course is still to be charted. The central issue in this debate is whether looking at human rights from the various cultural perspectives that now coexist and interact in the world community promotes or undermines international standards."[24]

"Cultures can converge in support of human rights"[25] was the hopeful answer of Amy Gutmann. Yes, certainly, but what if they don't? The practical differences are quite considerable. It might be true, as Gutmann claims, that there are plural foundations, some of which do not directly compete with one another. If the pragmatic application resulting from the differing foundations is acceptable, for example, in light of a common second-order standard behind human rights (e.g., that harm and suffering are to be reduced), the dictates of the different foundations might then be acceptable. The differences might be empirically limited; similarities might point towards a core meaning. But if all cultural foundations are equally valid, who

23. Professor An-Na'im and others argue in the context of African proselytization that vulnerable religious and other cultures should be granted special protection against the unfair competition of resource-rich Western religions.

24. Abdullahi Ahmed An-Na'im and Francis M. Deng, (eds.), *Human Rights in Africa: Cross-Cultural Perspectives*, Washington, D.C.: Brookings Institution (1990) 9.

25. Amy Gutmann, introduction to Ignatieff, *op. cit.*, note 1, XX. She argues that a universal regime of human rights should be compatible with moral pluralism, although not necessarily with any given moral system.

will be charged with determining what the core meaning is? A precondition for such commensurability is that all foundations allow for rational pragmatism. If, for example, a human rights "foundation" interprets human suffering to be divinely imposed, then the overlaps with other "foundations" advocating the eradication of suffering will remain superficial. If human rights are supported on more than one ground, then what is the guarantee that more than nominal agreement can be reached? After all, in terms of equivalency of foundations, very different approaches may yield similar provisions—but only to a point. For example, Judaism's focus on communal duty provides that universal rights pertain to all of humankind through the universal, interpersonal, human obligations of the *Noahide* law.[26] Is this to say that a universally satisfactory human rights system is in the offing *within* Judaism or another communal-duty based system?

Inoue has a preference for human rights developed through dialogue. Brems proposes "inclusive universality" that takes into consideration the particularist critique. "If human rights are valid for all people in all societies, they must then reflect in an equal manner the needs and values of all human beings." This position contrasts interestingly with that of the other Belgian author in the volume, Haarscher. In his view, human rights are not about the common needs of all humans. For Brems, on the other hand, Haarscher's position is representative of those critiques of relativism which ignore that the particularist critique "accepts the worldwide validity of human rights as a matter of principle." Does it? Not even all universalists accept such validity, in the sense that for many universalists universal validity does not follow from principles.

To accept the human rights of particularism is not without risks. If we accept that every culture has its distinctive formulation of human rights, the "central project" may collapse. This is the real dividing line between two distinct groups of tame universalists in this volume: some authors like Sadurski and Haarscher are not ready to run the risk of giving up on the core program of universal and uniform liberation that began with the Enlightenment. Others seem to accept the need for a universalistic claim without being specific as to its implications: this is a "wait and see" attitude that allows the seeds of human rights to take root and mature in the environment of dialogue, context, and culture. To flower, bear fruit—or dry out and disappear completely.

The expansion of the multicultural dimension may have increased sensitivity to human rights values in some cultures, but has not resulted in a more robust international human rights regime: humanitarian intervention,

26. Suzanne Last Stone, "Sinaitic and Noahide Law: Legal Pluralism in Jewish Law," 12 *Cardozo Law Review* (1991) 1157.

taken as a sign of a more robust operational system, develops from international interaction but nonetheless is not the result of intercultural consensus. The failures of humanitarian and human rights-guided intervention point to the shortcomings of culturally insensitive human rights politics. Human rights and the rule of law share the same shortcoming identified by Krygier: these institutions tend to self-perpetuation which can be contagious when offered up for export. The institutional claim is that "institutions initially introduced...come to be reified as the best and ... only way to fulfill" the given goals. The more we encounter problems arising from the terminology of human rights, the more likely it is that uniform and thus increasingly inadequate means will be used to address very different sorts of social problems and relations. Human rights inefficiencies and fiascos have forced advocates to be more humble, and humility has forced them to see the limits and parameters of their actions.

Considering the above, the theoretical reflection in this volume is part of a healthy process of developing rational techniques for handling the difficulties and consequences of the universalist approach to human rights. The new strategy is based on humility and modesty. Human rights have become increasingly sensitive to local contingencies, partly because of known failures and unintended consequences. Some authors, like Stacy, locate human rights between contingency and certainty. The relativist challenge has also generated increased interest in constructing useful mechanisms of internal review of human rights policies and procedures, which have for some time now suffered from a counterproductive attitude marked by arrogance and a lack of internal consistency. These same policies and procedures have been further hindered by the their patchwork makeup—an assortment of ideas and poorly coordinated practices. The way out is through humility, critical review (and better yet, preview) of consequences, and moral and practical accountability of human rights actors. This critical position of restraint, however, comes at a price. The constant reevaluation of human rights with the emphasis on context and contingencies undermines the self-assuredness and unambiguous assertiveness of human rights. Universalism and its relatively straightforward, non-nuanced standards of human rights are an unsurpassed litmus test for the quick evaluation of situations and actions in a complex and poorly comprehended world. Human rights prejudice is an efficient mental tool within its limits. The commonly shared understanding that there are limitations on just what is to be included in the arsenal of realistic options at hand in any given situation is "key to cooperative encounters with others." The costs and delays of renegotiations and justifications through participation might be prohibitive.

Part I
Universality in Context

Chapter 1

Wiktor Osiatynski

On the Universality of the Universal Declaration of Human Rights

In 1948 the leaders of the world hailed the Universal Declaration of Human Rights as a set of standards to guide humankind. The Declaration gave a new meaning to the very word "universalism." Instead of a universality of colonial allegiance or of faith imposed by swords and religious symbols, humankind was to be bound by a set of universal standards that were agreed upon by the leaders of free nations and that gave hope to leaders of those people striving for independence and self-determination.

Fifty years later, the very universality of human rights has been fiercely challenged. Human rights were often presented as the ideology of the West, as a secular "Western religion," as a tool of Western imperialism, or as a Western neocolonial "ideology."[1] Such challenges originate from various quarters in the West, East, and South. Their common denominator is skepticism towards an understanding of human rights as universal standards.

1. The notion of a "human rights religion" was often used by the conservative opponents of the bills of rights in constitutional debates in postcommunist countries. For a description of human rights as a neocolonial ideology, see Makau Mutua, "The Ideology of Human Rights" in Makau Mutua and Robert Howse (eds.), *Trading in Human Rights: The Human Rights Obligations of the World Trade Organization* (2000). Also see Mutua in this volume, chapter 2.

András Sajó (ed.), Human Rights with Modesty: The Problem of Universalism, *33-50.*

The most common challenge is that the idea of human rights is essentially Western, and not universal. It has developed in the West and was imposed by the West on the rest of the world, first in 1948, and later by the United Nations system and other means of global domination, not excluding force. In a less drastic formulation, a claim is made that the West uses force to impose human rights. In its more radical version the West is accused of using force to impose the philosophy of human rights, and human rights is the new tool in the Western crusade against the South.

A related challenge is that the idea of human rights does not help to solve the most important problems of non-Western societies. The extreme of which is that the idea of human rights is seen to be in conflict with important developmental goals of non-Western nations.

Finally, the critics say that despite the formulations of the Universal Declaration of Human Rights the idea of human rights is not only alien to non-Western nations and their people, but it is even incompatible with traditional cultures, religions, and societies outside the West.

This chapter deals with the first challenges to the idea of human rights and their history. It also discusses the Universal Declaration of Human Rights from the perspective of the origins of different ideas and values that were synthesized in the document. I hope that recalling some basic facts from more than fifty years ago and analyzing the sources of human rights will be helpful, particularly in the discussion of economic and social dimensions of human rights.

1. The Origins of Human Rights

First, we need to distinguish between the eighteenth-century idea of individual rights and the twentieth-century concept of human rights. The former was the result of a long train of thought and of institutions that were in existence before the Magna Carta of liberties in 1215; which then assumed the form of liberties and freedoms acknowledged during the Renaissance; received impetus as a reaction against absolutism; to find their final formulation during the Enlightenment. The idea of individual rights was thus definitely Western, and even though some philosophers, like Immanuel Kant and Thomas Paine, talked about the rights of all men, no one attributed universality to eighteenth-century individual rights. They were the rights of white males, to be further limited to white male property owners. The rest, including white women and workers as well as the people of the colonized world outside Europe, were treated, at best, as the objects of white men's benevolent paternalism, at worst, as simply objects and slaves. Concepts of progress, evolution, Darwinism, and eventually racism provided justification for the superiority of white males.

The West did not try to impose the idea of individual rights on the rest of humankind. To the contrary, it positively acted to prevent other people from enjoying the rights and freedoms restricted for itself as master. In the nineteenth century even the West turned its back on this idea and replaced it with utilitarianism and majoritarian democracy or with such collectivist ideologies as nationalism and socialism.[2] Outside Europe, the West ruthlessly violated the rights of indigenous populations, the victims of colonialism and imperialism. Within the West, it violated people's rights in genocidal wars and in the Holocaust.

The idea of rights reemerged during World War II, reformulated, however, in terms of human rights. The term *human rights* first appeared in the Atlantic Charter issued by the leading Western powers at the beginning of 1942. The Allies stated the purposes of the war to be the defense of "life, liberty, and religious freedoms" as well as the worldwide preservation of human rights. The Charter was aimed at the world, i.e., it was directed to potential members of a worldwide coalition that was to join the Allies in the war against the countries of the Axis, primarily Germany and Japan. The Charter's usage of the term "human rights" could be perceived as a promise by the West to extend the benefits of "Western" liberty to the non-Western allies. From the point of view of the emerging concept of human rights, of crucial importance was the fact that World War II was *the world* war, and a number of non-Western nations were fighting together with Western democracies for liberty against fascism and its allies.

The idea of human rights was upheld in the Charter of the United Nations. Along with the Convention on genocide, human rights were to codify natural law that was used, with some reluctance, to try top Nazi leaders at the Nuremberg trials. Human rights were also to protect people as individuals from abuses by nationalist or collectivist nation-states. They were to limit the risk that legitimately elected, i.e., formally democratic, governments might commit crimes and cruelties in the name of majority rule, as was the case with Germany under Hitler. While the works in the Economic and Social Council focused on enshrining in human rights documents at least some of the progressive labor legislation that had been developed by welfare-state reformers and accepted by the International Labor Organization (ILO) between the two wars.

All these rights had undoubtedly Western origins. However, now, they were to be treated as truly human, i.e., extended to all people of the world.

---

2. See Louis Henkin, "The Nineteenth Century Anti-Thesis," in *The Age of Rights*, New York: Columbia University Press (1990) 13 ff.

This "universalization" of rights was later cited by critics who claimed that, already in 1948, rights were imposed by the West on the rest of the world. The defenders of human rights rebut by pointing to the good intentions of the drafters who wanted to prevent the repetition of its own practices, for there had been all too many atrocities committed by the Western powers against non-Western people. In this sense human rights were to be seen as the self-limitation of dominant powers, similar to the way a constitution can be perceived as the self-limitation of those who wield power within a state. It has also been suggested that the drafters of the UDHR wanted to protect the rest of the world from committing atrocities similar to those which had been recently committed by the Europeans.[3]

A closer look at the origins of human rights shows an even more complex picture. While the idea of human rights was attractive to Western intellectuals, preparatory work on human rights was not strongly supported by their governments, particularly the Great Powers.[4] Each of which had a record which diverged from the proclaimed standards: the Soviet Union had domestic terror and the Gulag; England and France had colonies; and the United States had racism. The Great Powers also wanted to protect their supremacy in the post-World War II world and used the concepts of domestic jurisdiction and state sovereignty to preclude possible interventions in their affairs by less powerful nations. Therefore, for the Great Powers, "The human rights project was peripheral, launched as a concession to small countries and in response to demands of numerous religious and humanitarian associations that the Allies live up to their war rhetoric."[5]

In Dumbarton Oaks, in the summer of 1944, the Great Powers made plans for the future international organization that would serve peace, security, and international cooperation. They "agreed to their opposition to any meaningful provisions concerning international human rights."[6] While the United States wanted to include human rights into the general principles of the Charter of the United Nations, the Soviets claimed that such provisions are "not ger-

3. Michael Ignatieff writes that "a consciousness of European savagery is built into the very language of the Declaration's preamble" and further that "human rights norms are not so much a declaration of superiority of European civilization as a warning by Europeans that the rest of the world should not reproduce their mistakes." Michael Ignatieff, "The Attack on Human Rights," 80:6 *Foreign Affairs* (November/December 2001) 107.

4. See Paul G. Lauren, *The Evolution of International Human Rights: Visions Seen*, Philadelphia: University of Pennsylvania Press (1998) 165-171 and Mary Ann Glendon, *A World Made New: Eleanor Roosevelt and the Universal Declaration of Human Rights*, New York: Random House (2001) 4-20. For the details of the creation of the UDHR, see also Johannes Morsink, *The Universal Declaration of Human Rights: Origins, Drafting, and Intent*, Philadelphia: University of Pennsylvania Press (1999).

5. Glendon, *op. cit.*, note 4, XV.

6. Lauren, *op. cit.*, note 4, 166.

mane to the main tasks of an international security organization."[7] It was China that emphasized the need for the international organization "to be able to enforce justice in the world" and agreed "to cede as much of its sovereign power as may be required."[8] Wellington Koo, a Chinese representative, also raised issues concerning the right of all people to equality and non-discrimination, as well as the need to secure social welfare in the future world order. The Soviet Union and Great Britain outright rejected the Chinese proposals and all three powers (the United States included) "shared a deep concern over 'the equality of races question' specifically and the larger issue of human rights in general."[9] The United States still insisted on a general statement about human rights, but agreed that it be mentioned in the context of social and economic cooperation. The Chinese proposal about racial equality was completely deleted from the Dumbarton Oaks document which was written in the language of state powers rather than the rights of individuals.

At the beginning of the San Francisco conference in April 1945, it was obvious that the Great Powers will not foster the idea of human rights.[10] During the conference, however, they realized "that crusades once unleashed are not easily reined in or halted. Expectations had been raised, promises made, and proposals issued during this 'people's war' that were not about to be denied. Countless men and women, including those among minority groups, smaller nations, and colonial peoples, had been led to believe that their personal sacrifices in war and their witness to genocide would bring certain results to the world."[11]

Such sentiments were voiced by the representatives of the smaller nations who managed to subvert the plans agreed upon by the Great Powers. The organizers invited to San Francisco all the states that had declared war on Germany and Japan by 1 March 1945 (including Argentina that declared war in March). The largest bloc was formed by the independent states of Latin America. The non-Western countries represented were China, the Philippine Commonwealth, India, Iraq, Iran, Syria, Lebanon, Saudi Arabia, Turkey, Egypt, Ethiopia, Liberia, and South Africa. Most of these countries found their spokesman in the person of Carlos Romulo of the Philippines, a journalist who had received the Pulitzer Prize for a series of articles about the coming of colonialism. Romulo succeeded in inserting in the UN Charter's

7. *Ibid.*, 169.

8. *Ibid.*, 166.

9. *Ibid.*, 167.

10 . On the eve of the San Francisco conference of 1945, one thing was clear: The Great Powers were not going to take the initiative in making human rights a centerpiece of their postwar arrangements. It was not in their interest to do so." Glendon, *op. cit.*, note 4, 10.

11. Lauren, *op. cit.*, note 4, 171.

Preamble the formulation on the "self-determination of peoples" as one of the purposes of the United Nations. He also pressed for anti-discrimination provisions—supported by representatives from Brazil, Egypt, India, Panama, Uruguay, Mexico, the Dominican Republic, Cuba, and Venezuela.

The human rights cause was supported by the more than forty non-governmental organizations, mostly from the United States, who were invited to San Francisco as consultants and observers. In early May representatives of some of these organizations met with Edward Stettinius, the U.S. secretary of state, who agreed to press for the formation of the Human Rights Comission.[12] At the insistence of the coalition of NGOs and smaller countries, references to human rights were incorporated into the Charter of the United Nations—among the discussion of the purposes of the UN in the Preamble and in an additional six articles.[13] Art. 68 assigned to the Economic and Social Council the task of establishing a commission for the promotion of human rights.

The work in the Commission was dominated by a small number of leading participants that included Peng-Chun Chang, a Chinese philosopher, playwright, and diplomat; René Cassin, French Nobel Peace Prize laureate, who lost twenty-nine close relatives in Nazi death camps; Charles Malik, an existentialist philosopher and student of Alfred North Whitehead and Martin Heidegger, who turned diplomat when his homeland Lebanon received independence and served as a main spokesman for the Arab League; and Mrs. Eleanor Roosevelt who brought to the entire effort the commitment of her late husband and her own dedication to humanitarian causes. Other active participants included John P. Humphrey, Canadian director of the United Nations Human Rights Division, who prepared the preliminary draft of the Declaration; Carlos Romulo; Hansa Mehta of India, who helped bring the issue of women's rights into the Declaration; and Hernan Santa Cruz, Chilean leftist, who brought to the committee the Latin American dedication to social and economic rights.

Among official representatives of the states, Latin American governments were the most dedicated advocates of the adoption of the Declaration. Besides this bloc in the third committee, where the discussion of the final draft took place toward the end of 1948, there were representatives from a number of predominantly Islamic states (Afghanistan, Egypt, Iran, Iraq, Pakistan, Saudi Arabia, Syria, Turkey, Yemen, as well as India and Lebanon, where Islam has many adherents); largely Buddhist China, Burma, and Siam;

---

12. This was the single exception to the firm opposition to naming any special commission in the UN Charter agreed upon by the Great Powers. Mary Ann Glendon claims that this meeting "marked a crucial turning point." Glendon, *op. cit.*, note 4, 17.

13. Arts. 1, 13, 55, 62, 68, and 76.

Hindu India; as well as Ethiopia and Liberia from sub-Saharan Africa. This coalition of states and individuals pressed for the adoption of the UDHR and influenced its content. The character of this coalition disproves the accusation that, in 1948, human rights were imposed on the rest of the world by the West. Instead, it would be more accurate to say that, at the time, "the mightiest nations on earth bowed to the demands of smaller countries for recognition of common standards by which the rights and wrongs of every nation's behavior could be measured."[14]

The imposition thesis appeared much later and was unheard of during the preparatory work on the Declaration. The document was unanimously adopted by the UN General Assembly on 10 December 1948.[15] It is true that in 1948 many colonial nations of Asia, and particularly of sub-Saharan Africa, were not represented in the United Nations. Nevertheless, the new states subsequently signed and ratified the Declaration and re-confirmed dedication to the idea of human rights by then signing the human rights Covenants, after they were adopted in 1966.[16] One hundred seventy-one states sent their delegates to the 1993 Vienna Conference on Human Rights. UDHR served as a model for some ninety constitutions, including the nineteen constitutions of new post-colonial countries, mainly from Africa, that included specific references to the Declaration.[17]

The advocates of the imposition thesis are not persuaded by facts and numbers. They claim that non-Western drafters, like Professors Chang and Malik were themselves adherents of Western values, that the signing of the human rights documents was demanded by colonial powers as a prerequisite for independence, and that even though the elites of newly independent states signed such documents, they did not consult beforehand with the people. These arguments deserve attention.

Mary Ann Glendon showed recently that non-Western drafters did contribute significant insights from their own cultures. Moreover, their mastery of European tradition helped them "to understand other cultures and to 'translate' concepts from one frame of reference to another."[18] Other non-Western philosophers, asked by UNESCO to reflect on human rights from

---

14. Glendon, *op. cit.*, note 4, XV.
15. The Soviet Union and her five satellites as well as South Africa and Saudi Arabia abstained from voting.
16. As of 15 May 2000, 144 states signed the Covenant on Civil and Political Rights (CCPR) and 142—the Covenant on Economic, Social, and Cultural Rights (CESCR).
17. For a full list, see Glendon, *op. cit.*, note 4, 228, from which all the data in this paragraph were taken.
18. Glendon claims that those skills, "indispensable for effective cross-cultural collaboration, were key to the successful adoption of the Declaration without a single dissenting vote." Glendon, *op. cit.*, note 4, 226.

the perspective of their cultures, tried to find in their cultures values supportive of human rights even though the notion of rights was absent.[19] Generally, UNESCO philosophers concluded that "a few basic practical concepts of human rights are so widely shared that they 'may be viewed as implicit in man's nature as a member of society.'"[20] Similarly, Wellington Koo, a Chinese delegate to the Dumbarton Oaks conference, did not justify the right of all people to equality and non-discrimination in Western terms, but "went on to speak out about the influence of Confucius, Mo Zi, and Sun Yat-sen, explaining that 'the thought of universal brotherhood had been deeply rooted in the minds of the Chinese for more than two thousand years.'"[21]

While the philosophers in the Human Rights Commission, or those asked to reflect on their own culture by UNESCO, could be accused of "internationalism," a similar claim cannot be held against government representatives who were bound by the principle of state sovereignty and were responsive to local elites and hierarchical institutions based on traditions in their own countries. It is noteworthy, however, that during the drafting period only Saudi Arabia made a claim that the freedom to marry and a right to change one's religion were purely Western, rather than universal. There were no other objections on cultural grounds to any other provision of the UDHR.

This brings us to the thesis that the adoption of human rights documents and language were the conditions of independence. There is no proof that Western colonial powers did exert such pressure, particularly taking into account their own skepticism toward human rights. It was not only the newly independent states who failed to consult with the people. In no country was participation in the United Nations and the subsequent signing and ratification of human rights documents preceded by specific referenda or consultations with an aim to assess public opinion. The leaders of state assumed that they have a mandate to sign. Since human rights were in effect a limiting of state power, it could be argued that such self-limitations did not call for expressions of popular support, as should be the case when new pacts grant new powers to state authorities or impose new duties on citizens. Nevertheless, in the Third World there is a strong need for broad participation in the renegotiation of state constitutions and human rights documents.[22] This fact, however, supports rather than contradicts the universality of human rights, for rights embrace and elevate the right to participation in public affairs.

---

19. For the results of the UNESCO inquiry, see *Human Rights: Comments and Interpretations*, UNESCO (1949).
20. Quoted in Glendon, *op. cit.*, note 4, 226.
21. Lauren, *op. cit.*, note 4, 167.
22. This author made such an observation on the basis of personal experience at a number of meetings concerning human rights and constitutions in Africa and South America.

Many politicians and philosophers in the Third World say that it is time to renegotiate the idea of human rights. The fact is that the idea they want to renegotiate is not the one embodied in the 1948 Declaration—they want to renegotiate a different idea of human rights that came to prominence after 1975.

2. Individual Rights and Human Rights

The argument that the ideas upheld by the UDHR are of Western origin is common and obvious. However, many social and political institutions also have European roots, such as constitutions, parliaments, organization of governments, etc. Similarly, many scientific theories and technological achievements have originated in Europe which does not prevent their being used to benefit non-Europeans. The West itself does not reject non-Western inventions, if they are useful, simply on the basis of their origin. Jack Donnelly has convincingly demonstrated that, despite its Western origin, the idea of human rights can be very useful in all contexts where the modern state has invaded traditional societies.[23]

To claim that human rights originated from Western ideas is not to say much, for there are at least two Western European traditions of rights. One emphasized the inherent rights of an individual and natural social groups against authorities of a state. This tradition, best elaborated by John Locke, was relevant in seventeenth-century England and, particularly, during the eighteenth century in the American colonies which struggled against the British state. Even though England has made incremental departures from this tradition ever since the eighteenth century, it is referred to as the Anglo-American tradition. On the European continent another tradition of rights prevailed. There, rights were perceived as a sort of grant given by an enlightened state in the fulfillment of its obligations to society.[24] Among these obligations was the duty of rulers to protect citizens and to care for them in times of need or deprivation. Rights understood in this way were not to protect individuals *from* the government, but to be realized *through* the government of an active rather than passive state. This vision of rights was embodied in the French revolutionary constitution of 1790 as well as in the second

23. See Jack Donnelly, *Universal Human Rights in Theory and Practice*, Ithaca: Cornell University Press (1989) 57-63.

24. Horst Dippel in his study of the influence of the American Declaration of Independence in Germany has demonstrated that the concept of inalienable rights preceding government was simply incomprehensible for a majority of educated and enlightened Europeans in the late eighteenth century. Horst Dippel, *Germany and the American Revolution 1770-1800*, Chapel Hill: University of North Carolina Press (1977) 163-167.

Declaration of the Rights of Man and Citizen of 1793.[25] It was also present in the General Code of Prussia of 1794, the constitution of Norway of 1815, and in the social legislation that spread throughout Europe, including England, in the late nineteenth century.

Louis Henkin defines the two traditions in the following way. According to the first one, "Individual rights protect autonomy and freedom, limit government, and provide immunity from undue, unreasonable exercise of authority...But in the nineteenth century there began to grow *another sense of rights*, rooted not in individual autonomy but in community, adding to liberty and equality the implications of fraternity." It implies "a broader view of the obligations of society and the purposes of government—not only to maintain security and protect life, liberty, and property, but also to guarantee and if necessary provide basic human needs."[26]

Mary Ann Glendon distinguishes between an individualistic Anglo-American tradition of rights that emphasized individual liberty without much attention to constraints and responsibilities, and a "dignitarian" tradition prevailing on the European continent. The latter put more emphasis on family, communities, and on citizens' duties. While the first tradition found little support in Asia or Africa, the second one was more compatible with traditions of non-Western countries. According to Glendon the Declaration embodies the spirit of the second tradition.[27] Undoubtedly, the obligation of a state to guarantee the rights of citizens rather than just protect their autonomy is derived from the continental tradition.

While the UDHR has its roots primarily in the European traditions of individual rights, this tradition, however, was further changed, and one major element of that change was the very dynamics of the preparatory work that led to the formulation of the Declaration and the document itself. For the very mode of the adoption of the UDHR precluded that it could only be a broad compromise between and synthesis of various traditions, values, and

25. The 1789 Declaration, however, belonged to the Anglo-American rather than to the continental tradition, this may explain why it was muted a year later and replaced in 1793.

26. Louis Henkin, Gerald L. Neuman, Diane F. Orentlichter, David W. Leebron, *Human Rights*, New York: Foundation Press (1999) 280.

27. "In the spirit of the latter vision, the Declaration's 'Everyone' is an individual who is constituted, in important ways, by and through relationships with others. 'Everyone' is envisioned as uniquely valuable in himself (there are three separate references to the free development of one's personality), but 'Everyone' is expected to act toward others 'in a spirit of brotherhood.' 'Everyone' is depicted as situated in a variety of specifically named, real-life relationships of mutual dependency: families, communities, religious groups, workplaces, associations, societies, cultures, nations, and an emerging international order. Though its main body is devoted to basic individual freedoms, the Declaration begins with an exhortation to act in 'a spirit of brotherhood' and ends with community, order, and society." Glendon, *op. cit.*, note 4, 227.

needs, many of which had never been articulated before in the language of rights. Most of these traditions had their roots in European social and philosophical thought, but these roots were diverse. The very concept of individual rights and liberties as well as their inalienability (mentioned in the Preamble) comes from the liberal Anglo-American tradition. Civil and political rights included in the Declaration originate from the same source. A crucial notion of dignity, however, was brought in from Christian thought, particularly from the philosophy of personalism represented by Jacques Maritain. The philosophical source was the same for the notion of the free or full development of personality that runs through the Declaration.[28]

Although free development of human potential could be seen as a form of the "pursuit of happiness" from the Declaration of Independence, it is much closer to the hearts of Marxists for whom the full development of everyone's potential had been an essential element of Marx's concept of freedom.[29]

European conservatives could join Christian philosophers as well as Marxists in support of the duties to the community emphasized in Art. 29. The inclusion of duties into the Declaration was welcomed by the Asians for whom duties rather than rights have been essential elements of dignity. It also satisfied the representatives of Latin America who had just adopted, in May 1948, the American Declaration of Rights and Duties. While accepting duties, the Marxists—as well as liberals—were more reluctant in the acceptance of a number of provisions urged by a conservative Christian coalition, i.e., that the family is "the natural and fundamental group unit of society and is entitled to protection by society and the State," or that "parents have a prior right to choose the kind of education that shall be given to their children," and a right to "special care and assistance" during motherhood and childhood.[30] In Art. 17 which granted everyone "the right to own property" Marxists and socialists were satisfied with the addition of the qualification: "alone as well as in association with others."

Finally, there was a broad coalition of Christians, Marxists, socialists, and social-democrats who supported the idea of "social progress and better standards of living in greater freedom" as mentioned in the Preamble. They were supported by American New Dealers, who remembered the freedoms from fear and freedom from want declared by President Franklin Delano Roosevelt in 1941. The same coalition was supportive of social and economic rights, elaborated in detail in Arts. 22-26; they were joined by the intelligentsia and intellectuals in advocating the right to participate in culture and

28. See Arts. 22; 26.2; and 29.
29. See Andrzej Walicki, "Marx and Freedom," *The New York Review of Books* (24 November 1983).
30. Arts. 17; 26.3; and 25.2, respectively.

science. Those who believed in a classical individualistic concept of rights conceded on all of these provisions, but welcomed the provision on the protection of the intellectual property of authors provided in Art. 27.2.[31] At the same time, no single participant challenged civil and political rights that are at the core of the liberal concept. The entire project was led in the spirit of cooperation and mutual enrichment. Mary Ann Glendon notes that "there was remarkably little disagreement regarding its basic substance, despite intense wrangling over some specifics. At every stage, even the Communist bloc and Saudi Arabia voted in favor of most of the articles when they were taken up one by one. "*The 'traditional' political and civil rights—the ones now most often labeled 'Western'—were the least controversial of all.*"[32]

All of the Declaration's provisions (except the right to free marriage and to change one's religion, challenged by Saudi Arabia) had the strong support of a great majority of non-Western participants who hoped to take from various European traditions such principles and values which seemed important for their own people. Therefore, we can see the Declaration not merely as a compromise, but as a unique synthesis of various concept of rights that had been formulated and advocated hitherto. An important element of this synthesis was the combination of freedom and economic security. Civil liberties and political rights, together with social and economic rights, were equally important in light of the main goal of the Declaration, i.e., the preservation of world peace.[33]

There were many reasons why social and economic rights found an important place in the Declaration. One was the fact that, in their attempt to dilute the entire idea of human rights, the Great Powers in Dumbarton Oaks reluctantly agreed to incorporate human rights provisions into the UN Charter but only in the area of "international cooperation in social and economic matters."[34] The Human Rights Commission was consequently created within the Economic and Social Council which by its nature dealt with economic and social matters. Not without importance was the fact that the ILO was the single effective element of the system of international cooperation created after World War I. It was created in 1919, by the Treaty of Versailles, to deal with the issues of social justice and working conditions, and thus, to pre-

31. The most far-reaching departure from the liberal concept of rights was a right to "periodic holidays with pay" (Art. 24) which later prompted Maurice Cranston to reject the entire concept of social and economic rights as "lofty ideas." See Maurice William Cranston, *What Are Human Rights?*, New York: Basic Books (1962) 65-71.

32. Glendon, *op. cit.*, note 4, 226. (Emphasis added, W.O.)

33. The Declaration, however, did not take a stand on two issues that later became very controversial: that social and economic rights may be contingent upon civil and political rights, or that personal freedom depends on social security.

34. Lauren, *op. cit.*, note 4, 169.

vent revolution. Between the two wars, ILO adopted close to one hundred international conventions dealing, among others, with the issues of working conditions, social security, and trade unions.[35] In 1946, ILO became a specialized agency on the United Nations. Its positive experience influenced the framers of the UDHR.

Social and economic rights had also been adopted in a number of post-World War II constitutions. Many of these rights were also acknowledged, on the statutory level, by the New Deal legislation, and were then strongly emphasized in the American Declaration of Rights adopted in Bogota in May 1948. In fact, the representatives of Latin American states were the strongest advocates of social and economic rights during the preparatory work on the Declaration. Coming from poor countries—often governed by authoritarian regimes—they did not emphasize civil and political rights but rather the right to social security, health care, pensions, financial relief, and other social benefits. They were backed, among others, by Peng-Chun Chang of China who emphasized that "economic and social justice, far from being an entirely modern notion, was a 2500-year-old Confucian idea."[36] Another supporter of the inclusion of the provisions on economic and social justice and full employment was Foreign Minister Herbert V. Evatt of Australia.

Many Western European intellectuals, still shaken by the Great Depression of the thirties that paved the way for fascism, also craved guarantees for social rights. For them, democracy meant primarily social democracy, i.e., workers' rights, social security rights, rights to health care, education, and broad participation in culture. Labor leaders and American New Dealers, Christian philosophers, social-democrats, socialists, and communists, as well as the representatives of the non-Western nations—all agreed about the paramount importance of these rights.

But in the ruins and poverty that followed the war and persisted among colonized nations, no government could afford to commit itself to granting such rights enforceability in courts.[37] Therefore, the inclusion of social rights in the Declaration predetermined the character of the entire document. The Declaration did not include means for its own enforcement; it was a col-

---

35. Scott Davidson claims that ILO "may be seen as the precursor of the system of the protection of economic, social, and cultural rights." See Scott Davidson, *Human Rights*, Buckingham: Open University Press (1993) 9.

36. See Glendon, *op. cit.*, note 4, 185.

37. In her speech to the General Assembly on 9 December 1948, Eleanor Roosevelt said that the U.S. government gave its "wholehearted support" to the articles on social and economic rights but did not consider them to "imply an obligation on governments to assure the enjoyment of these rights by direct governmental action." Quoted in Glendon, *op. cit.*, note 4, 186.

lection of standards and a call to national governments of states-parties to implement them.[38]

The Declaration went beyond mere aspirations by creating the moral grounds for claim rights.[39] It even went a step further in setting grounds for civic and political action, toward changing the social and international order in congruence with rights.[40] Its primary goal, however, was educational. The framers of the Declaration emphasized its cultural significance. They did not deal with enforcement mechanisms, with criminal courts for the perpetrators of abuses, nor with military interventions to stop such abuses, not only because such mechanisms were left for other agencies, notably for the Security Council, but also because they believed that "culture is prior to law."[41] This spirit of the framers in 1948 was best encapsulated in Art. 26.2 of the Declaration:

> Education shall be directed to the full development of the human personality and to the strengthening of respect for human rights and fundamental freedoms. It shall promote understanding, tolerance and friendship among all nations, racial and religious groups, and shall further the activities of the United Nations for the maintenance of peace.

Human rights and the underlying theory were to become educational subjects and taught, which, in the minds of the framers, would bring the world closer to the standards and aspirations declared in the document.

3. The Eighteenth and the Twentieth-Century Theories of Rights

This underlying theory is worth summarizing, primarily because it differs significantly from the original Western concepts of individual rights formulated during the Enlightenment.[42] While the eighteenth-century, primarily theo-

38. The Preamble stated that "human rights should be protected by the rule of law," while Art. 8 called for "the rights to an effective remedy by the competent national tribunal" but only "for acts violating fundamental rights granted him by the constitution or by law."
39. Art. 2: "Everyone is entitled to all the rights and freedoms set forth in this declaration."
40. "Everyone is entitled to a social and international order in which the rights and freedoms set forth in this Declaration can be fully realized." (Art. 28)
41. Glendon, *op. cit.*, note 4, 238. Glendon quotes some framers on that subject: René Cassin said that the "respect for human rights depends on the mentalities of individuals and social groups"; Charles Malik suggested that before the aspirations are implemented "men, cultures, and nations must first mature inwardly"; and Peng-Chun Chang considered as the UDHR's main goal "to build up better human beings, and not merely to punish those who violate human rights." (Glendon, *op. cit.*, note 4, 239.)
42. The following comparison expands the ideas first presented by Henkin, *op. cit.*, note 26, 280-284.

retical concept of individual rights was created by philosophers, the twentieth-century idea of human rights was formulated by politicians and involved citizens. The theoretical bases for individual rights were theories of natural law, natural rights and social contract; right originated in a contract or—in a continental mutation—they were granted by a benevolent ruler. Human rights lack underlying theory and are focused on political practice. They spring from dignity rather than originate in contract, therefore no grant of rights is needed; and consequently they are inherent rather than inalienable. The contractual basis for individual rights is replaced by the notion of popular sovereignty underlying human rights.

The goal of individual rights, to protect freedom and prevent tyranny, was expanded on in human rights: which are meant to protect not only freedom but also peace and justice, and foster friendly relations between individuals and states. They are to prevent rebellion rather than tyranny.

The principal value protected by twentieth-century rights theory is human dignity rather than individual autonomy, as was the case in the eighteenth century. Individual rights were closely linked to economic principles of market economy; human rights are not linked to any economic theory or system. Individual rights were a political principle which had vertical application between individual citizens and the state. Human rights are not only political but also moral principles, the implementation of which depends primarily on education of citizens and state elites alike. The application of human rights goes beyond relations between citizens and the state and are horizontally applicable to relations between individuals and private parties. This horizontal aspect of human rights goes beyond mere claim-rights, but also encompasses duties that individuals may have toward others and toward society as whole.

While individual rights were limited to white male property owners, human rights are universal, in the sense that they belong to every human being. They are also more broadly defined than individual rights which were limited to civil liberties and political rights with a strong emphasis on property. Human rights differ in that they also include social and economic benefits as well as other solidarity rights—and they give much weaker protection to property.[43] In the International Covenant on Civil and Political Rights there is no provision on property rights, while the UDHR endorses collective property.[44] In regard to future developments, new claims for the so-called third generation rights, which include some group rights, will also be formulated in terms

43. In classical liberal theory property is the foundation of all other civil liberties, see Cranston, *op. cit.*, note 31, 47-50.

44. "Everyone has the right to own property alone as well as in association with others." (Art. 17.1.)

of human rights. The protection and implementation of these positive rights implies a new role for the state. Consequently, while the eighteenth-century concept focused primarily on freedoms from the state and assumed a passive (protective) state, the idea of human rights implies a much more active state with many obligations to fulfill towards its citizens.

Individual rights were domestic. Ideally, they were to be enshrined in enforceable constitutions or bills of rights. They were to be protected by a number of internal measures, beginning with petitions, through court cases, all the way to the right to resist as a last resort. In cases where rights were continuously violated, resistance was justified; this element of Lockean theory was used by Thomas Jefferson and his collaborators to justify the American claim to independence. The twentieth-century concept of human rights does not grant such right for it could not be reconciled with the principle of state sovereignty which dominated post-World War II arrangements.[45] It accepts the principle of state sovereignty over its citizens and the resulting international relevance of human rights. Human rights form a code of conduct for states and imply that when a given state violates this code other states will exert pressure to bring the perpetrators to order.[46]

4. Conclusion: Human Rights as the Language of the Oppressed and the Language of Power

The most significant difference between the two concepts is the audience to whom the language of rights is addressed. Eighteenth-century individual rights were a matter between individuals and groups of individuals—i.e., a civil society—and the state. Rights were claimed by citizens against their own governments.[47] Twentieth-century human rights are international,

45. The Preamble to UDHR talks about "rebellion against tyranny and oppression" as the recourse of "last resort" to which people may be compelled. It is based, however, on the premise that if human rights are protected by the rule of law, people will not need to rebel. There exists no explicit or implicit right to resist in the catalogue of human rights.

46. Human rights only very slightly weakened the principle of state sovereignty by granting the extremely limited and ineffective right to individual complaint in the First Optional Protocol to ICCPR. At their inception human rights were formulated as moral standards and aspirations, therefore, the framers did not pay much attention to the way in which such international pressure will take place. Military intervention or the criminal responsibility of heads of states were not even discussed during the preparation of the UDHR.

47. Although in the nineteenth century, quite often citizens in a given country were helped through international campaigns in their support. It is important to note, however, that such international humanitarian campaigns were usually launched by citizens and civil societies abroad rather than by foreign governments. (The most notable exception was the British war against the slave trade in the nineteenth century.)

which means that they were designed for claims against abusive governments by other governments.

This difference has two consequences. One is that, within this concept, a way is paved for some governments to claim positive benefit-rights from other governments, as is the case with the so-called right to development. Second, by making state governments parties to human rights agreements and covenants, the new concept inevitably led to the use of human rights as the language of power rather than of the oppressed.

The result is that human rights are used by governments in seeking and defending power. As the language of international relations, human rights provide support to arguments in international conflicts between Great Powers of the West, East, and South. The rhetoric of rights still serves oppressed individuals and societies, but it also serves governments, including oppressive governments.

It was in this new application of human rights that they were first "Westernized" and limited to their eighteenth-century roots. This tendency found its clearest expression during the Cold War, particularly in the 1970s when human rights had become a foreign policy instrument of the Western bloc in the confrontation with Communism. The Helsinki Agreement petrified this "Westernized" concept of human rights and made it the main objective of the international human rights movement. From now on, for the West, human rights were identified with civil and political rights. The objectives of the international human rights movement—created by a growing number of human rights- oriented NGOs—were defined in a similar manner.

After the end of the Cold War, human rights were "Southernized" by the governments and other representatives of the Third World countries that had, by then, acquired a numeric majority in the United Nations. In turn, civil and political rights were truncated from the UDHR synthesis, and social and economic as well as solidarity rights were given prominence. This development found its expression in the Vienna Declaration and Programme of Action of the World Conference on Human Rights held in 1993.[48]

It is primarily in the context of international conflicts between state powers that the issues of cultural relativism were raised. In these debates, cultural relativism is being used primarily toward political ends, most often to protect oppressive regimes; and the entire idea of human rights is losing its original meaning and significance.

Therefore, it is vitally important to distinguish between the political usage of cultural relativism and those cultural differences that need to be acknowl-

48. For an analysis of the rewriting of human rights before and during the Vienna Conference, see Adamantia Pollis, "Cultural Relativism Revisited: Through a State Prism," 18 *Human Rights Quarterly* (1996) 316-344.

edged and reconciled if the idea of human rights is to become truly universal.

Chapter 2

Makau Mutua

The Complexity of Universalism in Human Rights

I want to suggest, at the outset, that we must approach all claims of universality with caution and trepidation. There can be little doubt that visions of universality and predestination have been intertwined throughout modern history, and have been deployed as the linchpin for advancing narrow, sectarian, and exclusionary ideas and practices. At the purely theoretical level, therefore, we are chastised to look not once, but twice, and again, at universalizing creeds, messages, ideas, and phenomena. This is not to suggest that universality is always wrong-headed, or devious, but it is rather to assume that universality is not a natural phenomenon. In other words, universality is always constructed by an interest for a specific purpose, with a definite intent.

Second, I want to suggest that all truths are local—they are contextual, cultural, historical, and time-bound. Again, this is not to say that local truths cannot become universal truths—they can, but the question is how one gets there. If we do not understand this basic admonition, we risk repeating the colossal inhumanities and incalculable mistakes which were wrought by the evils of slavery (in pursuit of the universalization of the market); Christianity and Islam (in the quest for the spiritual conquest of non-European and non-Arabic peoples and the destruction of their cosmologies); and colonization (in search of the imposition of commerce and Eurocentrism).

András Sajó (ed.), Human Rights with Modesty: The Problem of Universalism, *51-64.*

The question therefore is how local truths are legitimately transformed into universal creeds—what value judgments are made, who makes those judgments, how they are made, and for what purpose. Ultimately, we must ask ourselves what good is intended by universal creeds—and whether they redound to the benefits of peoples everywhere. For me these questions are non-negotiable because they must be answered before we can declare a particular creed universal, in effect a glimpse of eternity, or an inflexible truth. This is crucial because once we confer such status on a creed or truth, then that truth becomes transhistorical, universally valid, and urgent. The failure to comply with it denotes a fundamental breach of civilization, for which the direst consequences might be borne by the violator.

1. The Forcible Embrace of Human Rights

In 1998, amid much fanfare and pageantry, many important personalities and institutions, including numerous governments, celebrated the fiftieth anniversary of the Universal Declaration of Human Rights. That seminal document launched human rights internationally, an idea that has arguably given expression to one of the most important developments of our times. But largely lost in those celebrations were the voices that problematize the idea of human rights and point to its difficulties from normative, institutional, and multicultural perspectives. Perhaps there should have been wrenching, soul-searching, and probing inquiries into the phenomenon known as the human rights movement. But it was not to be. Was it because the human rights movement is an unqualified good, or were critical voices muffled and silenced? What could have accounted for the universally near-total approval and unbridled joy that marked the moment of the UDHR milestone?

It is a virtual certainty that the human rights corpus, if fully implemented, would alter the fundamental character of any state, its cultures, and society. On that basis alone, without even judging its appropriateness, the doctrine of human rights bears close scrutiny. It is true that there are emergent debates and disagreements between scholars, policymakers, and advocates about the character and purposes to which the human rights corpus should be put. Some of these debates focus on questions of normativity, the need for a cultural consensus and legitimacy, and the problems of effective and consistent enforcement. Others suggest a radical reformulation of human rights. These are the vexing problems that we must urgently address.

Since the human rights corpus has profound implications for all human societies, particularly those that are non-Western, there is a need to openly discuss the political agenda of the human rights movement. The movement's apoliticization obscures its true character and the cultural identity of the norms that it seeks to universalize. While many cultures and peoples of all political and historical traditions around the world have accepted the idea of human rights, many have wanted to couple their embrace with a degree of originality. This ranges from marginal contributions, on the one hand, to radical reformulations on the other. Thinkers who are non-Western resist the idea that the official UN-sanctioned human rights movement is the final answer and should not be subject to attack or scrutiny. I reject this assertion of a final truth and suggest in this chapter its limitations.

Emergent research and scholarship have opened huge vistas of doubt about blind faith in the officially constructed human rights movement. While my work has focused on the relationship between the state and the language of rights as an avenue for protecting human dignity, it questions the official formulations of the corpus and the purposes they serve. This view constitutes a philosophy that seeks to expand the scope of human rights and pleads for alternative understandings of the human rights movement. There is a paucity of scholarship by non-Westerners like myself in this idiom, although there is a dire need to speak across cultures and identities in human rights. My work fits in this category and will hopefully serve the purpose of enriching dialogue in human rights. The outcome is an attempt that advances critical approaches to human rights.

This piece presents a view of human rights that questions the assumptions of the major actors in the human rights movement. It attempts to make an explicit link between human rights norms and the fundamental characteristics of liberal democracy as practiced in the West, and to question the mythical elevation of the human rights corpus beyond politics and political ideology. It questions the deployment of human rights to advance or protect norms and practices that may be detrimental to societies in the Third World. In other words, the work presents a series of critical lenses and approaches through which human rights should be viewed.

2. The Need for Probing Critiques

The main authors of the human rights discourse have thus far been reluctant to be critical of the human rights movement. There are several reasons for this trepidation of critical analysis. First, I suspect that many of the movement's authors sincerely doubt that an honest inquiry could pin the human rights movement down to a specific political structure or deconstruct it in a way that bares its biases and politics. The Cold War, which pitted the capitalist West against the Socialist and Communist bloc, deeply perverted the philosophies of states towards human rights. The West purported to champion civil and political rights, whereas the Soviet bloc posed as the sole guarantors of economic, social, and cultural rights. At that time, to engage in probing critiques would have been an admission against interest in the context of the Cold War, amidst states only too eager to exploit cultural and political excuses to justify or continue repressive policies and practices. Whatever the case, it now seems imperative that we no longer circumvent probing inquiries about the philosophical and political raison d'être of the human rights regime; in fact, they must be encouraged and welcomed.

While I do not think that the human rights movement is a Western conspiracy to deepen its cultural stranglehold over the globe, I do believe that its abstraction and apoliticization obscure the political character of the norms that it seeks to universalize. As I see it, the purportedly universal is at its core and in many of its details, liberal and European. The continued reluctance to openly identify human rights with liberal democracy delays the reformation, reconstruction, and the multiculturalization of human rights. Defining those who seek to reopen or continue the debate about the cultural nature and the raw political purposes of the human rights regime as "outsiders" or even as "enemies" of the movement is the greatest obstacle to the efforts to bring about true universalization.

Just over half a century after the Universal Declaration of Human Rights laid the foundation for the human rights movement, diverse peoples have embraced those ideas across the earth. That fact is undeniable. But it is only part of the story. Those same people who have embraced that corpus also seek to contribute to it, at times by radically reformulating it, at others by tinkering at the margins. The human rights movement must not be closed to the idea of change or believe that it is the "final" answer. It is not. This belief, which is religious in the evangelical sense, invites "end of history" conclusions and leaves humanity stuck at the doors of liberalism, unable to go forward or imagine a postliberal society. As an assertion of a final truth, it must be rejected.

As a philosophy that seeks the diffusion of liberalism and its primacy around the globe, ironically, the human rights corpus can be said to be favorable to political and cultural homogenization while hostile to difference and diversity, the two variables that are at the heart of the vitality of the world today. Yet, strangely, many human rights instruments explicitly encourage diversity through the norm of equal protection, which Henry Steiner, for instance, sees as the cardinal human rights norm. As he correctly notes:

> Other rights declared in basic human rights instruments complement the ideal of equal respect and confirm the value placed on diversity. Everyone has a right to adopt "a religion or belief of his choice" and has freedom "either individually or in community with others and in public or private" to manifest belief or religion in practice and teaching. Rights to "peaceful assembly" and "freedom of association with others," in each case qualified by typical

grounds for limitation like public order or national security, further commit the human rights movement to the protection of people's ongoing capacity to form, develop, and preserve different types of groups.[1]

The paradox of the corpus is that it seeks to foster diversity and difference but does so only under the rubric of Western political democracy. In other words, it says that diversity is good so long as it is exercised within the liberal paradigm, a construct that for the purposes of the corpus is not negotiable. The door to difference appears to be open while in reality it is closed shut. This inelasticity and cultural parochialism of the human rights corpus needs urgent revision so that the ideals of difference and diversity can be realized. The long-term interests of the human rights movement are not likely to be served by the pious and righteous advocacy of human rights norms as frozen and fixed principles whose content and cultural relevance is unquestionable.

Based on this premise, the human rights movement needs to alter its orientation, which until now has been an orientation of moral, political, and legal certitude. There needs to be a realization that the movement is young and that its youth gives it an experimental status, not that of a final truth. The major authors of the human rights discourse seem to believe that all the most important human rights standards and norms have already been set and that what remains of the project is elaboration and implementation. This attitude is at the heart of the push to prematurely cut off debate about the political and philosophical roots, nature, and relevance of the human rights corpus.

Debates about the universality of the corpus between the industrialized West and the South should not be viewed with alarm or as necessarily symptomatic of a lack of commitment to human rights by those in the Third World. Attempts to question the normative framework of human rights, their cultural relevance, and the need for a cross-cultural recreation of norms will not be silenced or wished away by universalists who are unwilling to engage in the debate. As Deng and An-Na'im argued in a volume exploring these issues, the debate is just beginning:

> Whatever the reason for the controversy surrounding cross-cultural perspectives on human rights, the essays in this volume clearly demonstrate that the debate has just begun and that its parameters are still to be defined and its course is still to be charted. The central issue in this debate is whether looking at human rights from the various cultural perspectives that now coexist and interact in the world community promotes or undermines international standards.[2]

1. Henry J. Steiner, "Ideals and Counter-Ideals in the Struggle Over Autonomy Regimes for Minorities," 66 *Notre Dame Law Review* (1991) 1539, 1548.
2. Abdullahi Ahmed An-Na'im and Francis M. Deng, "Chapter One, Introduction," in Abdullahi Ahmed An-Na'im and Francis M. Deng, (eds.), *Human Rights in Africa: Cross-Cultural Perspectives*, Washington, D.C.: Brookings Institution (1990) 9.

There is little doubt that certain states and governments will hide behind the veil of culture to perpetuate practices that are harmful to their populations. That cynicism, however, must not be confused with genuine attempts to bequeath cross-cultural legitimacy to a universal human rights corpus. Deng and An-Nai'm ask a series of biting questions that leave little doubt about the indispensability of cross-culturalism.[3] Richard Schwartz affirms this point of view: he sees the necessity of a cross-fertilization of cultures if a universal human rights corpus is to emerge. According to him:

> Every culture will have its distinctive ways of formulating and supporting human rights. Every society can learn from other societies more effective ways to implement human rights. While honoring the diversity of cultures, we can also build toward common principles that all can support. As agreement is reached on the substance, we may begin to trust international law to provide a salutary and acceptable safeguard to ensure that all people can count on a minimum standard of human rights.[4]

The failure of most universalists—particularly the most conventional thinkers and activists among them—to positively engage in this debate unnecessarily antagonizes Third World cultural pluralists and lends credence to charges of cultural imperialism. This is particularly the case if the human rights corpus is seen purely as a liberal project with the overriding, though not explicitly stated, goal of imposing a Western-style liberal democracy, complete with its condiments. The forceful rejection of dialogue also leads to the inevitable conclusion that there is a hierarchy of cultures, an assumption that is not only detrimental to the human rights project but is also inconsistent with the human rights corpus' commitment to equality, diversity, and difference. Ultimately, the unrelenting universalist push seeks to destroy difference by creating the rationale for various forms of intervention and penetration of other cultures with the intent of transforming them into the liberal model. This view legitimizes intervention and leaves open only the mode, that is,

3. *Ibid.*, 10-11. What follows is a list of several of the questions the editors ask: "Is this [cross-cultural approach to creating a universal corpus] a fanciful ideal or an achievable objective? Are we being romantic and are we unnecessarily complicating the process of universalizing the cause of human rights, or are we presenting a cultural challenge for all members of the human family and their respective cultures that can help shape the lofty ideals of universal human rights? And could such worldwide involvement in itself lead to a realization of the universality of human dignity, which is the cornerstone of international human rights? Or would it be more practical to assume that some cultures are just not blessed with these human ideals, and that the sooner they recognize this and try to adjust and live up to the challenge presented by the pioneering leadership of those more endowed with these lofty values, the better for their own good and for the good of humanity?"
4. Richard D. Schwartz, "Human Rights in an Evolving Culture," in Abdullahi Ahmed An-Na'im and Francis M. Deng (eds.), *op. cit.*, note 2, 368-382.

whether intervention takes the form of military force; sanction systems, bilateral or multilateral; a cultural package bound in one or another form of exchange; or trade and aid.

What should not be at stake in conversations about human rights is the singular obsession with the universalization of one or another cultural model. Rather, the overriding objective of actors ought to be to envisage norms and political models whose experimental purpose is the reduction, if not the elimination, of conditions that perpetuate human indignity, violence, poverty, and powerlessness. For that to be possible, and to resonate in different corners of the earth, societies at their grassroots have to participate in the construction of principles and structures that enhance the human dignity of all, big and small, male and female, believer and unbeliever, this race and that community. But those norms and structures must be grown at home, and must utilize the cultural tools familiar to the people at the grassroots. Even if they turn out to resemble the ideas and institutions of political democracy, or borrow from it, they will belong to the people. What the human rights movement must not do is to close all doors, turn away other cultures, and impose itself in its current form and structure on the world. A postliberal society, however that will look, cannot be constructed by freezing liberalism in time.

3. The Third World and Human Rights

The human rights promise to the Third World is containment—if not elimination—of cruel living conditions, state instability, and other social crises through the rule of law, granting of individual rights, and a state based on constitutionalism. The Third World is asked to follow a particular script of history for this promise to mature. That script holds that the future of the international community lies in liberal nationalism and democratic internal self-determination. The impression given is that a unitary international community is possible within this template if only the Third World follows suit by climbing up the civilizational ladder. It is my argument, however, that this historical model, as now diffused through human rights, cannot respond to the needs of the Third World absent some radical rethinking and restructuring of the international order.

Today the presence of the United States—which has succeeded France and the United Kingdom as the major global cultural, military, and political power—is ubiquitous. This became especially true after the collapse of the Soviet Union and Communism a decade ago. There is virtually no conflict or issue of importance today in which the United States does not seek, and often play, the crucial role whether by omission or commission. From the conflicts in central Africa to crises of the former Yugoslavia to the corridors of the United Nations, the United States is the single most important actor in the world today. In a sense the U.S. chief executive sits atop a global empire. It is an empire governed by the cultures, traditions, and norms of the European West. The European colonial powers of yesteryear have, as it were, passed the torch to the United States. The United States has renewed and revitalized the Age of Europe. The domination of the globe exercised by European powers for the last several centuries has been assumed by the United States. The United States is now the major determinant for international peace and security and the spokesperson for the welfare of humanity. Never before has one state wielded so much power and influence over so vast a population. A global policeman, the United States now plays the central civilizing role through the export of markets, culture, and human rights.

Increasingly, the human rights movement has come to be openly identified with the United States, whose chief executive now invokes human rights virtually every time he addresses a non-European nation.[5] In fact, former President Bill Clinton's international speeches had come to resemble lectures and sermons, very much in the savior mode.[6] This is the wrong course. The human rights movement, and its ally the American state, must abandon the pathology of the savior mentality if there is to be any real hope in a genuine international discourse on rights. The relentless efforts to universalize an essentially European corpus of human rights through Western crusades cannot succeed. Nor will demonizing those who resist it. The critiques of the corpus from Africans, Asians, Moslems, Hindus, and a host of critical thinkers from around the world are the avenues through which human rights can be redeemed and truly universalized. This multiculturalization of the corpus could be attempted in a number of areas: balancing between individual and group rights, giving more substance to social and economic rights, relating rights to duties, and addressing the relationship between the corpus and economic systems. This article does not develop those substantive critiques. That calls for another project. Further work must be done on these questions—and on the corrupting influences of the individualism of the human rights corpus—to chart out how such a vision affects or distorts non-European societies.

Ultimately, a new theory of internationalism and human rights that responds to diverse cultures must confront the inequities of the international order. In this respect, human rights must break from the historical continuum expressed in its grand narrative that keeps intact the hierarchical relationships between European and non-European populations. Nathaniel Berman is right in his prognosis of what has to be done:

5. Laura Myers, "Clinton Talk at University Prods China on Freedom," *Buffalo News* (29 June 1998) A1.
6. Charles Babington, "Improve Rights Record, Clinton Tells Turkey," *Washington Post* (15 November 1999) A21.

> The contradictions between commitments to sovereign equality, stunning political and economic imbalances, and paternalistic humanitarianism cannot be definitively resolved logically, doctrinally, or institutionally; rather, they must be confronted in ongoing struggle in all legal, political, economic, and cultural arenas. Projections of a unitary international community, even in the guise of the inclusive UN, or a unified civilizational consensus, even in the guise of human rights discourse, may be provisionally useful and important but cannot indefinitely defer the need to confront these contradictions.[7]

The approach in this chapter views the human rights text and its discourse as requiring that typology of state which is based on the ethos of constitutionalism and political democracy.[8] The logic of the human rights text is that political democracy is the only political system that can guarantee or realize the fundamental rights it encodes.[9] As Henry Steiner points out, the basic human rights texts, such as the ICCPR, should be understood not as imposing a universal blueprint of the myriad details of democratic government, but rather as creating a minimum framework for popular participation, individual security, and non-violent change.[10] Fair enough. The point then is that if this were a game or sport, its essence would have been decided, leaving those who adopt the sport only the option of tweaking or revising the rules governing it without transforming its purpose. In other words, genuine universality is not possible if the core content of the human rights corpus is exclusively decided, leaving non-European cultures with the possibility to make only minor contributions at the margins, and only in its form.

Using political democracy as one medium through which the human rights culture is conveyed, one is able to capture the imperial project at work. First, the choice of a political ideology that is necessary for human rights is an exclusionary act. Thus cultures that fall outside that ideological box immediately wear the label of the savage. To be redeemed from their culture and history, which may be thousands of years old, a people must then deny themselves or continue to churn out victims. The savior in this case

---

7. Nathaniel Berman, "Beyond Colonialism and Nationalism? Ethiopia, Czechoslovakia, and a Peaceful Change," 65 *Nordic Journal of International Law* (1996) 421, 478.
8. See Henry J. Steiner, "Do Human Rights Require a Particular Form of Democracy," in Eugene Cotran and Abdel Omar Sherif (eds.), *Democracy, the Rule of Law and Islam*, The Hague: Kluwer Law International (1999) 193.
9. *Ibid.*, 200. Steiner, for example, does not dispute that the human rights text requires a political democracy. He argues that it in fact does impose just such a model. But he correctly points out that the model envisaged is not "detailed and complete." The "essential elements" of a democratic government that the human rights instruments impose do not constitute a complete blueprint but rather "leave a great deal open for invention, for political variation, for progressive development of the very notion of democracy."
10. *Ibid.*, 200-201.

becomes the norms of democratic government, however those are transmitted or imposed on the offending cultures. Institutions and other media like the United Nations that purports to have a universalist warrant, or others, like the United States Agency for International Development, an obvious instrument of U.S. interests and foreign policy, are critical to the realization of the grand script of human rights explored in this chapter. It has, however, been my argument that the imposition of the current dogma of human rights on non-European societies flies in the face of conceptions of human dignity, and rejects the contributions of other cultures in efforts to create a universal corpus of human rights. Proponents of human rights should accept the limitations of working within this official script. Then they must reject it and seek a truly universal platform.

The purpose of this chapter is not to raise or validate the idea of an original, pure, or superior Third World society or culture. Nor is it to provide a normative blueprint for another human rights corpus, although that project must be pursued with urgency. It did not set out to provide a substantive critique of the Eurocentric human rights corpus, although doing so is necessary and must be part of making a complete case against the dominant Western human rights project. The chapter is rather a plea for genuine cross-contamination of cultures to create a new multicultural human rights corpus. What is advocated here is the need for the human rights movement to rethink and reorient its hierarchized binary view of the world in which the European West leads the way and the rest of the globe follows in a structure that resembles a child-parent relationship. Nor do I mean to suggest that all human rights communities in the West believe and work to ratify that hierarchy. Human rights can play a major role in changing the unjust international order, particularly in correcting the imbalances between the West and the Third World—but it will not do so unless it stops working within its rigid script. Ultimately, the quest must be one for the construction of a human rights movement that wins.

4. Eurocentrism and Human Rights

The adoption in 1948 by the United Nations of the Universal Declaration of Human Rights, the foundational document of the human rights movement, sought to give universal legitimacy to a doctrine that is fundamentally Eurocentric in its construction. Sanctimonious to a fault, the UDHR underscored its arrogance by proclaiming itself the common standard of achievement for all peoples and nations. The fact that a half-century later human rights have become a central norm of global civilization does not vindicate their universality. It is rather a telling testament to the conceptual, cultural, economic, military, and philosophical domination of the European West over non-European peoples and traditions.

The fundamental texts of international human rights law are derived from bodies of domestic jurisprudence developed over several centuries in Western Europe and the United States. The dominant influence of Western liberal thought and philosophies are unmistakable. No one familiar with Western liberal traditions of political democracy and free market capitalism would find international human rights law unusual. Its emphasis on the individual egoist as the center of the moral universe underlines its European orientation. The basic human rights texts drew heavily from the American Bill of Rights and the French Declaration of the Rights of Man. There is virtually no evidence to suggest that they drew inspiration from Asian, Islamic, Buddhist, Hindu, African, or any other non-European traditions.

Many fair-minded observers have acknowledged that the West was able to impose its philosophy of human rights on the rest of the world because in 1948 it dominated the United Nations. Non-Western philosophies and traditions particularly on the nature of man and the purposes for political society were either unrepresented or marginalized during the early formulation of human rights. Most Asian and African societies were European colonies and not participants in the making of human rights law. Professor Mary Ann Glendon of Harvard Law School has emphasized in a recent book the important role played by Charles Malik of Lebanon and Peng-chun Chang of China in the drafting of the UDHR.[11] Although non-Westerners, both Malik and Chang were educated in the United States and were firmly rooted in the European intellectual traditions of the day. The contributions of these two prominent non-Westerners were not steeped in the philosophies or the intellectual and cultural traditions from which they hailed.

There is no doubt that the current human rights corpus is well meaning. But that is beside the point. Human rights suffer from several basic and interdependent flaws. International human rights fall within the historical continuum of the European colonial project in which whites pose as the saviors of a benighted and savage non-European world. The white human rights zealot joins the unbroken chain that connects her to the colonial administrator, the Bible-wielding missionary, and the merchant of free enterprise. Salvation in the modern world is presented as only possible through the holy trinity of human rights, political democracy, and free markets.

Thus human rights reject the cross-fertilization of cultures and instead seek the transformation of non-Western cultures by Western cultures. To the official guardians and custodians of human rights—the United Nations,

11. Mary Ann Glendon, *A World Made New: Eleanor Roosevelt and the Universal Declaration of Rights*, New York: Random House (2001).

Western governments, senior Western scholars, and human rights activists—calls by non-Westerners for the multicultural reconstruction of human rights are blasphemous. Such calls are demonized as the hypocritical cries of cultural relativists, an evil species of humans who are apologists for savage cultures. What the guardians and custodians seek is the remaking of non-Europeans into little dark, brown, and yellow Europeans, in effect dumb copies of the original. This view of human rights reentrenches and revitalizes the international hierarchy of race and color in which whites, who are privileged globally as a race, are the models and saviors of non-whites, who are victims and savages.

Perhaps in no other area in human rights is the cultural arrogance of the European West more poignant than in the advocacy over the practice labeled in the West as female genital mutilation (FGM). Mutilation implies the willful, savage, and sadistic infliction of pain on a hapless victim. It is language that stigmatizes as barbaric cultures that condone the practice and dehumanizes the women who are subjected to it. This formulation decontextualizes the cultural foundation of the practice and promotes the stereotype of barbaric machete-wielding natives only too eager to inflict pain on women in their own societies. It is a view that is racist.

There is an urgent need for the human rights movement to step back from this arrogant approach. It should respect cultural pluralism as a basis for finding common universality on some issues. In the FGM example, a new approach would first excavate the social meaning and purposes of the practice, as well as its effects, and then investigate the conflicting positions over the practice in that society. Rather than demonizing and finger pointing under the tutelage of outsiders and their local collaborators, solutions to the issue could be found through intracultural dialogue and introspection. Such solutions might range from modifying the practice to discarding it.

In the area of political governance and in particular on the rights to political participation and religious freedom, the practices of Western states are used as the yardstick. Political democracy may be inevitable but non-Western political traditions must be allowed to evolve their own distinctive systems conducive to their demographic, historical, and cultural traditions. On religious freedom, it is wrong-headed to simply protect the right of missionary Christianity to proselytize and decimate non-Western spiritual traditions and cultures at will. Western knee-jerk reactions to restrictions on Christians in non-Western countries such as China or India must be balanced against the duty of those societies to protect their spiritual heritages from the swarming, imperial faiths bent on total domination of the spiritual universe.

Like earlier crusades, the human rights movement lacks the monopoly of virtue that its advocates claim. If human rights are to represent a higher human intelligence—that I believe they ought—they must overcome the seemingly incurable virus to universalize Eurocentric norms and values by demonizing, repudiating, and recreating that which is different and non-European. Human rights are not a problem per se, nor is the human rights corpus irredeemable. But we must realize that the current human rights represent just one tradition, that of Europe. And even in European or Eurocentric political and philosophical universes, which include Europe, the dominant traditions in the Americas, Australia, and New Zealand, the human rights corpus is an expression of only one European tradition. It will remain incomplete and illegitimate in non-European societies unless it is reconstructed to create a truly multicultural mosaic. The universalization of human rights cannot succeed unless the corpus is moored in all the cultures of the world. Ideas do not become universal merely because powerful interests declare them to be so. Inclusion not exclusion is the key to legitimacy.

5. Conclusion

This chapter represents an attempt by a scholar from the Third World to respond at the level of critique to the human rights corpus. It is based partly on my long and deep commitment to the construction of decent, ethical, fair, and humane political societies. But it also springs from my resistance to a doctrine that I view as part of the colonial project in which I am a subject not a citizen. The chapter therefore is not an attempt to launch a new blueprint for a competing or even a more universal human rights corpus. I think that the construction of a cross-culturally legitimate and genuinely universal creed of human dignity is urgently needed, and that this work will in its modest way make the case and pave the way for just such a corpus.

Finally, I hope that this scholarship serves as a footprint, a signpost for the work which must be done to reconstruct the human rights corpus by constructing normatively a more inclusive doctrine for human dignity. The world is literally in a state of emergency. Ruthless, hedonistic, and relentlessly individualistic and deeply exploitative beliefs and systems have in the last decade been given universal legitimacy by economic and cultural globalization. The current official human rights corpus does not have the analytical or normative tools—or even the desire and gumption—to unpack the complex oppressions which globalization now wreaks on individuals and communities. Constructed primarily as the moral guardian of global capitalism and liberal internationalism, the human rights corpus is simply unable to confront structurally and in a meaningful way the deep-seated imbalances of power and privilege which bedevil our world.

A new human rights corpus must first lay a comprehensive framework for what constitutes the building blocks of an ethical, humane, and just society. In this conception, the new corpus must address in a fundamental way not only the political dimensions—which the present official human rights doctrine preoccupies itself with—of human societies but also the economic prerequisites for an ethical society. As such, the new corpus must discard the false premises of the current corpus and reject its excesses, while building on those of its notions which have the potential for genuine universality. Scholars must spend less time worrying about or imagining more effective formulae for the implementation of the current human rights corpus. What is needed is groundbreaking and soul-searching work that will enable us to construct a society free of the daily avalanche of cruelties and oppressions. Such work must point us to a place that rejects colonialist and exploitative doctrines, no matter their origins. This is a project that must be pursued with urgency.

Chapter 3

Richard A. Shweder

Moral Realism without the Ethnocentrism: Is It Just a List of Empty Truisms?

What are the universal ideals of morality? Is it possible to enforce them without imposing one's own parochial conception of things on others? And precisely how is that to be done?

President George W. Bush of the United States expressed his own views on some of the above questions in his first post-September 11 State of the Union address to Congress and the nation (29 January 2002). He spoke as follows:

> America will lead by defending liberty and justice because they are right and true and unchanging for all people everywhere. No nation owns these aspirations and no nation is exempt from them. We have no intention of imposing our culture, but America will always stand firm for the non-negotiable demands of human dignity, the rule of law, limits on the power of the state, respect for women, private property, free speech, equal justice and religious tolerance.

Mr. Bush's words will seem incontestable and perhaps even inspiring to some; for others they will cry out for analysis, specification, and critique. For example, when it comes to claims about moral ideals that are "right and true," and

András Sajó (ed.), Human Rights with Modesty: The Problem of Universalism, *65-102.*

hence universally binding, consider the views expressed by Richard Posner, U.S. appellate judge and University of Chicago senior lecturer, who is the most widely cited contemporary American legal scholar. In the remarks quoted below, which come from Posner's 1997 Oliver Wendell Holmes Lectures at Harvard University entitled "The Problematic of Moral and Legal Theory," he uses the word "morality" descriptively (rather than normatively) to refer to an existing social consensus about what in particular counts as acceptable behavior. He states:

> First, morality is local. There are no interesting moral universals. There are tautological ones, such as "Murder is wrong" where "murder" means "wrongful killing," and there are a few rudimentary principles of social cooperation—such as "Don't lie all the time" or "Don't break promises without any reason" or "Don't kill your relatives or neighbors indiscriminately"—that may be common to all human societies. If one wants to call these rudimentary principles the universal moral law, fine; but as a practical matter, no moral code can be criticized by appealing to norms that are valid across cultures, norms to which the code of a particular culture is a better or worse approximation. These norms, the rudimentary principles of social cooperation that I have mentioned, are too abstract to serve as standards for moral judgment. Any meaningful moral realism is therefore out, and moral relativism (or at least a form of moral relativism, an important qualification to which I shall return shortly) is in. Relativism suggests an adaptationist conception of morality, in which morality is judged nonmorally—in the way a hammer might be judged well or poorly adapted to its function of hammering nails—by its contribution to the survival, or other goals, of a society. My analysis also suggests that no useful meaning can be given to the expression "moral progress" and that no such progress can be demonstrated.[1]

In his Harvard University lectures Judge Posner offered a sustained attack on moral realism, a critique of precisely the type of intellectual stance whose validity is presupposed in President Bush's State of the Union address. The Judge, who is a relativist and an anti-realist, is quite distrustful of the idea that there are right and true universal moral facts that can be usefully applied by leaders to resolve moral disputes between groups. He not only suggests that "many moral claims are just the gift wrapping of theoretically ungrounded (and ungroundable) preferences and aversions."[2] He also argues that if any nonlocal moral facts exist at all, they are completely useless for resolving any actual real world moral issue.

1. Richard Posner, "The Oliver Wendell Holmes Lectures: The Problematics of Moral and Legal Theory," 111 *Harvard Law Review* (1998) 1637 ff.
2. *Ibid.*

In this chapter I plan to selectively analyze Mr. Bush's universalistic conception of moral realism and Richard Posner's relativistic, anti-realist (and I might add, positivistic) conception of social norms. I partially examine and critique each approach so as to draw some lessons and benefits from both. My aim is to sketch the broad outlines of an approach to the moral evaluation (critique and justification) of cultural practices that is grounded in moral realism, acknowledges the existence of many universal moral ideals, yet avoids the hazards of cultural parochialism and ethnocentrism in making judgments about concrete cases.

The chapter is in four parts. First, there is a specification of the intellectual stance known as moral realism, with special attention to some of the questions raised by President Bush's State of the Union address. Second, I acknowledge some of the important truths contained in Richard Posner's relativistic critique of moral realism, while attending to some of the limitations of his anti-realist, positive science analysis. Third, a summary description is given of what I think social scientists know about the folk or everyday psychology of morality around the world; and a consideration of the implications of that research for our understanding of the intellectual foundations of moral judgments?

The latter part of the chapter includes a discussion of the tension between the folk psychology of moral judgment and the way moral judgments are analyzed within the theoretical framework of "modernist" discourse about persons, society, and nature. A "modernist" theoretical framework has two distinctive intellectual features. The first is a (thin) metaphysics according to which the "real" world (equated with the idea of the "objective world") is understood to be a material world, and hence devoid of all non-material things (such as normative values). The second feature is a (thin) notion of rational justification, which is restricted in modernist thinking to some combination of deductive and/or inductive logic, pure formalism, and direct sense-experience (no divine revelations, revealed truths, or scriptural narratives). That modernist contraction or reduction of what counts as real and as rational has led some scholars to the dismal conclusion that there is no such thing as moral truth. Moral claims are thus sometimes analyzed by modernists (such as Posner) in ways that contrast with how judgments of right and wrong or good and bad are understood in the moral psychology of everyday life, where they are assumed to be truth claims about a moral reality. Instead, as Posner notes, moral claims are interpreted (by modernists) in terms of their consequences; and they are merely viewed as instrumental moves in the self-interested service of other types of ends.

Fourth and finally, speaking as a moral realist of sorts, I suggest that while in principle it should be possible to morally evaluate (criticize or justify) the social norms of "others" from a non-ethnocentric moral perspective, it can be quite difficult to do so in practice. One of the constant hazards for moral realists in general (and for human rights activists in particular) is the danger of provincialism. In practice our own local, culturally socialized "gut reactions" are readily available, and they can be emotionally insistent and intellectually presumptive, thereby making it all too easy for us to rush to moral judgment about unfamiliar "others," and to get things very wrong.

I illustrate the problem and risks of provincialism (and its corollaries, parochialism and ethnocentrism) with a brief examination of the cultural practice of genital modifications for African youth.[3] I sketch a critique of the global human rights discourse that describes African parents as "mutilators" or "torturers" of their own children, a discourse, which wittingly or unwittingly, represents African adults as either monsters or as ignoramuses who do not appreciate the welfare consequences of their own child-rearing customs.

The customary practice of cosmetic genital surgery for both males and females is socially endorsed by healthy majorities of women and men in many East and West African ethnic groups. The surgery is aimed at several recognizable goals, including (e.g.) promoting "normal" gender identity, improving one's looks, and promoting a sense of belonging and solidarity with one's ethnic group. Yet the practice of female (although not male) genital modification has been condemned as a moral outrage and a human rights violation by First World feminists and by several international organizations, including the World Health Organization. I suggest that a properly applied moral realism, one that is free of ethnocentrism, must be grounded on accurate and valid cultural and scientific knowledge. I critique the global discourse condemning cosmetic genital modifications in Africa for its factual errors, overheated rhetoric, and lurid sensational depictions of Third World "others." A properly applied moral realism must be intellectually cautious and protect itself against the inclination to express, promote, or celebrate one's own local tastes and parochial prejudices under the banner of universal human rights.

Thus, in the final section of the chapter I undertake a moral assessment of the social norms of African parents with regard to the practice of cosmetic genital surgeries for sons and daughters. I suggest that a normative moral realism is not necessarily hostile to the existence of diversity in social norms concerning gender identity and physical appearance across human groups.

---

3. For a much more complete discussion of the practice, see Richard A. Shweder, "What About 'Female Genital Mutiliation'?: And Why Culture Matters in the First Place," in Richard A. Shweder, Martha Minow and Hazel Markus (eds.), *Engaging Cultural Differences: The Multicultural Challenge in Liberal Democracies*, New York: Russell Sage Foundation Press (2002) and also Bettina Shell-Duncan and Ylva Hernlund (eds.), *Female "Circumcision" in Africa: Culture, Change and Controversy*, Boulder, Colo.: Lynne Rienner (2000).

The case of African genital surgeries is, of course, provocative and challenging, both intellectually and emotionally; and not simply because my conclusions are bound to be discordant with the prior assumptions of many First World readers. Non-ethnocentric moral evaluation requires the disciplined bracketing of one's own culturally formed preferences and aversions, and the setting aside of personal political agendas. And, in this instance, it requires the acquisition of a good deal of non-intuitive knowledge about health outcomes, human sexuality, local cultural contexts, and alternative points of view concerning gender development and physical beauty. I cite the current global campaign aimed at the "eradication" of female genital modifications on the Africa continent as an example of some of the hazards of cultural provincialism and ethnocentrism that arise in making condemnatory moral claims about unfamiliar culturally endorsed practices.

The moral critique of the cultural practice of female genital surgeries in Africa that has been developed by the anti-"FGM" human rights movement is itself highly vulnerable to criticism. Not only is it lurid, sensational, and emotionally preemptive in its rhetorical representation of the practice. It is also inconsistent with the best medical and ethnographic evidence available on the health consequences and local meanings of these genital modifications in Africa.[4] I shall argue that the widely circulated, horrifying, and utterly damning claim that African parents routinely maim, torture, oppress, mutilate, or murder their daughters and deprive them of a capacity for sexual response is as ill-informed, baseless, and fanciful as it is condemnatory and nightmarish.

The chapter thus begins with a defense of the idea of a non-ethnocentric moral realism. It ends, however, with an examination of a tragedy in moralistic high-minded parochialism—namely, with a critique of the false construction, invidious labeling, and misrepresentation of customary African cosmetic surgery as "female genital mutilation." An ethnocentric moral realism—namely, a moral realism that succumbs to the temptation to presumptively project, reify, and universalize one's own local cultural tastes and homegrown political agendas as essential truths—is perhaps far worse than no moral realism at all.

---

4. See, e.g., Fuambai Ahmadu, "Rites and Wrongs: Excision and Power among Kono Women of Sierra Leone," in Shell-Duncan and Hernlund, *ibid.*; Ulla Larsen and Sharon Yan, "Does Female Circumcision Affect Infertility and Fertility?: A Study of the Central African Republic, Côte d'Ivoire and Tanzania," 37, 3 *Demography* (2000) 313-321; Linda Morison, Caroline Scherf, Gloria Ekpo, Katie Pain, Beryl West, Roseland Coleman, and Gijs Walraven, "The Long-Term Reproductive Health Consequences of Female Genital Cutting in Rural Gambia: A Community-Bases Survey," 6 *Tropical Medicine and International Health* (2001) 643-653; and Carla M. Obermeyer, "Female Genital Surgeries: The Known, the Unknown, and the Unknowable," 13 *Medical Anthropology Quarterly* (1999) 79-106.

1. George W. Bush: Moral Realist

President Bush was not invited to the Central European University conference in Budapest at which the essays published in this book were initially circulated. Under the title "Universalism in Law: Human Rights and the Rule of Law" the conferees were invited to cross-examine the movement to globalize human rights, assessing its degree of historical particularism, and scrutinizing it as a putative form of cultural imperialism. Nevertheless, the President's State of the Union address before the Congress of the United States and the American people raises issues that are directly relevant to our proceedings. I want to focus on three of his central assertions. First, that there are "non-negotiable demands" for the design of any decent society. Second, that those demands are non-negotiable precisely because they are grounded on matters of fact concerning universal moral truths; and not simply because the President or the people of the most powerful nation in the world happen to like them or embrace them as their ideals. Third, his suggestion that it is actually possible to define those non-negotiable ideals in ways that are (a) substantial enough to allow the United States to lead the world in the direction of progressive social and cultural reform and also (b) universally valid enough to avoid the hazards of ethnocentrism.

That third proposition—the claim of progressive political (and military?) leadership free of ethnocentrism—is perhaps the most ambiguous of President Bush's pronouncements. It is possible that when he says, "we have no intention of imposing our culture," he really and truly is speaking as a cultural pluralist. In general, American neo-conservatives such as Mr. Bush are ideologically committed to such values as individual liberty, the decentralization of authority, an anti-monopolistic preference for the small over the big, a balance of power, deregulation and local control, and the expansion of private enterprise for the sake of creative innovation. Facially, those values would appear to be incompatible with monistic imperial visions of a single best way of life to be enforced or promoted by well-financed, well-connected or powerful, global or national institutions.

So it is possible that Mr. Bush really does not believe that the whole world should be encouraged or reshaped to resemble the United States in its social, political, family and gender norms. It is quite possible that he fully recognizes that the ideals of free speech, equal justice, religious tolerance, respect for women (and so forth) may take very different forms in different historical traditions. It is possible that he would readily acknowledge that those ideals are often in conflict with each other, and that they might be weighed and balanced differently and valued in different degrees by rational and morally decent people in other societies.

Thus, for example, it is not entirely clear from his statement whether he really believes current interpretations of the right to freedom of expression in the United States should be universally binding. In the United States the right to freedom of speech allows public expressions of hatred or loathing for ethnic, racial, and religious groups. That is not true in India or many other parts of the world where ethnic conflict is a potential threat to social order, and hence communal "hate speech" is against the law. Perhaps President Bush would accept that other nations might legitimately interpret the right to free speech more restrictively. Perhaps he might tolerate the government of China's population control policies and laws restricting the number of children allowed per family, rather than condemn that country to overpopulation in the name of a non-negotiable constitutional right to family privacy in decisions about reproduction. Perhaps he might accept that the ideal of respect for women is compatible with Islamic and Hindu traditions and "family values" in which women are guardians of the home, and in which public displays of sexually suggestive or "immodest" modes of dress are disapproved of or socially prohibited.

In other words it is possible that Mr. Bush is more of a cultural pluralist than I have supposed. It is conceivable that he is far less eager to give any specific face (for example, the face of bourgeois liberal feminism or the face of middle-class Judeo-Christian family life in the United States today) to his moral vision than I have imagined. Nevertheless, whatever the precise implication of Mr. Bush's expressed disinclination to impose his culture on others, his comments were surely designed to join politics and power with some image of a supposed universal moral truth, and his speech raises the following critical question. Is it really possible to enforce the universal demands of morality without imposing one's own cultural conception of things on others, and precisely how is that to be done? I think it can be done, but it requires a good deal of ethnographic and historical work aimed at understanding local social, political, and economic contexts and the goals, values, and pictures of the world held by "others." And the results of that intellectual work may surprise some human rights activists who often seem to think their own (all-too-readily available) subjective vision of the good life ought to be good for everyone, and provides an obvious gold standard for judging the quality of life of "others."

In any case, any thoughtful response to Mr. Bush's rousing speech must address several questions. First and foremost, are there in fact universally binding moral ideals, such that it would be intellectually defensible for the United States (or any other nation-state or international organization) to use their power (should they have it) to uphold those ideals everywhere in the world?

In this regard, President Bush's State of the Union address is a clear example of the intellectual stance of moral realism, which is associated with the notion of "universally binding moral ideals," by which I mean, borrowing Mr. Bush's words, goods and values that are "right and true." It is also a philosophically controversial stance. As we shall see, the controversy arises in part because moral universalism is a hazardous concept, especially when linked to the idea of moral realism or moral truth. It is one thing to assert that there are universal objective truths about the physical world, for example, that force equals mass times acceleration everywhere you go on the globe. It is quite another to assert that one's moral judgments about what is good or bad, or right or wrong, and the existing social norms of one's own group, are not just matters of local preference or taste but accurate representations of universal moral facts. Or, that what one morally desires is desired primarily because it is objectively "desirable," and thus, is the kind of thing that any morally decent and fully rational human being, whether a Hottentot, an Hasidic Jew, or the president of the United States ought to "desire."

The intellectual stance of universalistic moral realism of the type presupposed by George W. Bush has three features. First, the stance is prescriptive or normative in intent. It tells people how they ought to behave, with regard to the management and development of the self, with regard to other members of society, and with regard to nature (including the world of imagined spirits and gods). Second, it tries to derive its prescriptions from either "reason" or "facts about what is right and good." Potentially that includes imagined facts about the divine or divinely revealed (and hence, if truly divine, reasonable) nature of things. Third, the stance implies or presupposes that in one way or another the world of human beings (and perhaps even the universe in general) is reigned over by a transcendental moral force. The moral force is thought to be transcendental in the sense that its moral principles are authoritative and binding whether or not they happen to be cognized and understood by the contingent (and merely human mind) of particular living beings or leaders of particular nations. Hence, President Bush's notion that no nation is exempt from the moral law.

It is imperative that I note at this point that the universalistic moral realist stance of which I speak is not a descriptive claim about what people here or there happen to believe, value, desire, or do. It is a claim about what they ought to believe, value, desire, and do in order to be moral human beings. Thus, a universalistic moral realist might readily grant that the existence of universal moral ideals (e.g., putatively, a right to privacy in decisions about childbirth, or a right to educate one's children in a religion of one's choice) is no guarantee that everyone will discover them, although conceivably everyone might. The existence of universal moral goods, the sensible universalistic moral realist will readily grant, is no guarantee that such moral goods have in fact played a part in the life of any particular person or people.

These points are especially relevant in evaluating Richard Posner's observation that from a descriptive point of view there is in fact relatively little universal social consensus about what is acceptable behavior, that the social norms of different groups are not the same around the world. Even if Judge Posner's observation is more or less true, it may not be germane in debates about moral realism because universalistic moral realism is not necessarily meant to be a claim about a universal social consensus.

Sir William Blackstone, the eighteenth-century English jurist, depicts quite beautifully the intellectual stance of the universalistic moral realist. When evaluating the difference between the laws of gravity and the Ten Commandments he states the following: "This then is the general signification of law, a rule of action dictated by some superior being; and in those creatures that have neither the power to think, nor to will, such laws must be invariably obeyed... [L]aws in their more confined sense... denote the rules... by which man, the noblest of all sublunary beings... is commanded to make use of those faculties in the general regulation of his behaviour."[5] Any sensible universalistic moral realist would have a ready and powerful response to any positivist or empiricist who thinks that the core truths of a universalistic moral realism turn on ethnographic evidence or on facts about what people in far away places happen to believe, value, or do. That ready and powerful response is this:

1. That the doctrine of universalistic moral realism is a theory about what is desirable, not what is desired. In other words, universalistic moral realism does not claim that everywhere one goes in the world one will discover that all (or any) objective moral principles have in fact been cognized, understood, or put into practice.
2. That the having of preferences and desires per se, even pan human preferences and desires, for example lust, envy and greed, does not make them preference-worthy or desirable. Which is why, if there are right and true moral universals, their desirability or positive value must be derived from either reason or from facts about the divine (and hence) reasonable origins of one's ideas about what is right and/or good.
3. That it is not the case that moral judgments become more right and true or more authoritative by virtue of the sheer number of people who share those judgments or put them into practice. Simply declaring that something is right does not make it right. Consensus does not produce either mathematical or moral truth, no matter how many people, nations, or

5. William Blackstone, *Commentaries on the Laws of England*, Chicago: University Chicago Press (1979), Book 1. 39.

powerful institutions, or elite members of society say it is true. It is not by majority vote, but rather through reference to reason and/or divine origin that a genuine universalistic moral realist stance demands justification.

Thus in the context of scholarship in the normative moral arena, the idea of universalistic moral realism (or indeed the very idea of a moral "universal") does not imply "uniformly found everywhere." The idea has far more to do with the idea of universally binding standards or ideals for dignified or righteous behavior (the objectively desirable) and rather less to do with the empirical distribution of human practices, perspectives, aversions, preferences, and desires.

One very good reason for being interested in defining universally binding moral ideals is the following. If there are non-negotiable demands of the political and/or social order (derived from right and true moral ideals) this makes it possible for "outsiders" to reasonably evaluate (criticize, condemn, or justify) the cultural practices of "insiders"? It makes it possible for "minority" groups to reasonably evaluate (criticize, condemn or justify) the behavior of "majority" groups (and one might add, vice versa, it makes it possible for majority groups to reasonably evaluate the conduct of minority groups)? Indeed, it also makes it possible for local groups (the cultural "insiders") to reasonably criticize or condemn the attempts of internationalists or cosmopolitan human rights activists (the "outsiders") to intervene in and alter local culturally endorsed ways of life? All that critique, cast in all those directions, becomes justifiable if it can be done in the name of what is right and true.

Given the potential for social critique that is made possible by a credible universalistic moral realism, the question arises again in full force: How is it possible to formulate a meaningful statement about moral rights, goods, duties, and values that is free of ethnocentrism? The fear, of course, is that the whole enterprise is a form of high-minded ethnocentric imperial domination by those who are powerful or well-connected enough to mandate that everyone should see and value the world in only one way, namely, according to the dominant group's culturally preferred set of terms. That anxiety was made quite explicit in 1948 when the Executive Board of the American Anthropological Association refused to endorse the United Nations Declaration on the Rights of Man on the grounds that it was an ethnocentric document projecting "First World" values on everyone everywhere.[6]

6. Sally Engle Merry, "Ethnography in the Archives," in June Starr and Mark Goodale (eds.), *Practicing Ethnography in Law: New Dialogues, Enduring Practices*, New York: Palgrave/St. Martin's (2002); Richard A. Shweder, "The View from Manywheres," *Anthropology Newsletter*, American Anthropological Association (December 1996).

If one looks at the most active moral proselytizers in the world today—secular egalitarian "liberationists," Christian missionaries, and Islamic fundamentalists—there are those who believe that the American Constitution and its Bill of Rights, preferably as interpreted by the "Warren Court," is an accurate expression of "natural" moral law. Alternatively, there are those who believe that the goods and values set forth in the Qur'an are accurate or perfect representations of tablets containing moral laws and ideals housed in heaven. There are those who think that the Ten Commandments or perhaps the New Testament is the place to look for objective values. There may even be a few ecumenists or humanists who want to look beyond ideological and secular/religious divides. They may actually believe that the American Constitution, the Qur'an, and the "sacred texts" of the major world religions express the same values, and that they do so precisely because those values are "right and true." In all such cases those who make such claims would presumably assure us that they are not being ethnocentric or parochial, but merely speaking the truth. But whatever they happen to believe about what is really real, right, and true in the moral domain, are they correct in their beliefs when they speak in the name of "the truth"? And how do they actually know, other than by simply inspecting their own culturally socialized ethical intuitions? Is there more to moral judgment than just culturally socialized ethical intuition? If so, what is the mandatory or "non-negotiable" part of morality and what is the discretionary or "negotiable" part; and is that distinction between the mandatory and discretionary aspects of morality of any use in arriving at a non-ethnocentric moral assessment of cultural practices?

2. Judge Richard Posner: The Voice of the Anti-Realist

I have just described what I take to be the character or nature of universalistic moral realism. I now turn to a discussion of Richard Posner's "anti-universalistic anti-realist" critique. Allow me to begin this section with two more quotations from Judge Posner's Oliver Wendell Holmes Lectures, which you will find published not in the *Congressional Record* but in the *Harvard Law Review*.[7]

> Every society, and every subculture within a society, past or present, has had a moral code, but a code shaped by the exigencies of life in that society or that subculture rather than by a glimpse of some overarching source of moral obligations. To the extent it is adaptive to those exigencies, the code cannot be

7. Posner, *op. cit.*, note 1.

> criticized convincingly by outsiders. Infanticide is abhorred in our culture, but routine in societies that lack the resources to feed all children that are born. Slavery is routine when the victors in war cannot afford to feed or free their captives, so that the alternative to slavery is death. Are infanticide and slavery "wrong" in these circumstances? It is provincial to say that "we are right about slavery," for example, "and the Greeks wrong," so different was slavery in the ancient world from racial enslavement, as practiced, for example, in the United States until the end of the Civil War, and so different were the material conditions that nurtured these different forms of slavery. To call infanticide or slavery presumptively bad would be almost as provincial as to condemn them without qualification. The inhabitants of an infanticidal or slave society would say with equal plausibility that infanticide or slavery is presumptively good, though they might allow that the presumption could be rebutted in peaceable, wealthy, technologically complex societies.

And just in case your eyes are not yet wide-open, the Judge offers the following illustration of the limits of universalistic moral realism.

> A contemporary example of a practice that outrages most Americans is female genital mutilation, which is common among African (including Egyptian) Muslims. Defenders of the practice claim that it is indispensable to maintaining the integrity of the family in those communities. The claim is arguable, though I do not know whether it is correct. If it is correct, the moral critic is disarmed, for there is no lever for exalting individual choice or sexual pleasure over family values. It is vacuous to complain that the mutilated girls are often too young to be able to make a responsible choice (assuming they are even given a choice) whether to undergo the procedure, for the moral code of their communities is not founded on principles of freedom or autonomy. It is equally beside the point to show that many people in these societies are opposed to female genital mutilation. That just means there are competing moralities within these societies, as there are within our society. As there is no basis for choosing on moral grounds between a dominant and a dissenting morality, moral pluralism provides no leverage for moral critique; indeed it tends to reinforce the lesson of relativism. Yet we should not think it a disaster that moral pluralism renders some moral issues indeterminate, for we shall see that moral diversity can be a source of social strength.

Later I will have more to say about the socially endorsed practice of cosmetic genital modifications in Africa. Here I would note, however, that the practice is not limited to Muslim populations in Africa and is customary for many ethnic groups in East and West Africa. I would also note that among ethnic groups where genital modifications are customary they are rarely done only to girls, and those who defend or support the practice in Africa are just as likely to be women as men. In the case of both boys and girls the modifications in question are viewed as aesthetic improvements of the human body, not as "mutilations." Moreover, as I shall suggest later, the anti-"FGM" arguments made by human rights activists are factually inaccurate and do not stand up well to critical examination. The rapid spread and popularization of the lurid claim that African parents routinely maim and murder their female children and deprive them of a sexual capacity should be distressing to anyone who cares about the fairness and accuracy of cultural representations in our public policy debates. The invidious verbal labeling of a customary form of body modification (which, from the point of view of African mothers, is aimed at promoting the well-being—gender identity and physical attractiveness—of their children) as "genital mutilation" ought to be experienced as an embarrassment for the human rights movement. The best and most recent evidence available suggests that such claims and representations are fundamentally misleading. Judge Posner's provocative illustration is thus an apt and useful one for discussing the promise, hazards, and limits of moralizing about other peoples' culturally endorsed practices.

Three features of Posner's position with regard to this and other cases are especially worthy of note. First, he describes himself as a moral relativist. He believes "that the criteria for pronouncing a moral claim valid are local, that is, are relative to the moral code of the particular culture in which the claim is advanced, so that we cannot call another 'immoral' unless we add 'by our lights.'"[8]

Second, he also allows that he is a moral subjectivist in the sense that he believes that there are no "reasonably concrete transcultural moral truths." In effect he argues that there is no independent or transcendent or objective domain of the right and the true (no "objective order of goodness") to which one might appeal, as the legitimate source for one's particular judgments about what is right or wrong, good or bad.

Third, he claims that he is not a strong moral skeptic. There are moral truths worth knowing, he argues. But they are facts about what is right and wrong in one's own society, for example, the existing social norms and laws of one's own land. These local norms and laws are knowable, he argues, and he is quite prepared to make parochial judgments about what is right and wrong for members of his parish or community. In that "weak" sense he labels himself a "local moral realist."

Of course it should be noted that Posner's concept of "realism" in his description of himself as a "weak local moral realist" is not the kind of "realism" that "moral realists" have in mind when they speak of inalienable rights or natural moral laws. Posner's "weak local moral realism" is the "realism" of a

8. *Ibid.*, 1642.

descriptivist or positivist. He uses the term mainly to acknowledge the reality or existence of consequential social norms, social control processes, and systems of punishment within groups.

What the Judge is not prepared to do is pretend that his judgments about the practices of other societies are anything more than reactions based on feelings of personal disgust. Perhaps as a result of personal temperament or cultural taste he might feel revolted by some practice (such as infanticide or suttee) and even feel inclined to intervene to stop the practice with the power at his command. Nevertheless he argues, in keeping with his positivistic approach, "moral emotions" (shame, guilt, disgust, indignation) have no universal concrete moral content or objective foundation or source in some transcendental domain of the moral good.

Not surprisingly he also rejects the idea that there is a universal moral obligation to tolerate cultures that have social norms different from one's own. He comes close to saying that the experience of a negative feeling state may result in the exercise of power to eradicate the practices of others, and that it is misguided to even ask whether such an intervention is justifiable or not. The moral domain by Richard Posner's account is simply a natural scene in which different groups, each with their own distinctive social norms and equipped (in varying degrees) with powers and resources to dominate the local or global scene, compete with each other to perpetuate their own way of life. Some will succeed better than others. Some will adapt or surrender their social norms under pressure to do so. But none of this social norm competition or social norm replacement represents moral progress, and there are no rational discussions or arguments to be had about what the outcome of the competition or conflict ought to be. Why? Because, according to Posner, there is no objective moral standard against which divergent claims about what is right and good can be assessed. All that matters is power and the struggle to carry forward one's way of life efficiently, and to survive in the competition with other groups.

In a moment I plan to raise some criticisms of Judge Posner's approach to the analysis of local social norms. I will also highlight some of the points in his analysis that I take to be well-established truths, which have implications, I believe, for the proper development of a normative (rather than merely descriptive) theory of "local moral realism." First, however, I want to locate his position in a broader and older philosophical and intellectual context, then discuss certain basic findings about the character of moral judgments in everyday life around the world.

3. The Modern "Fictionalization" of Moral Truth

Perhaps the most hoary and hotly contested philosophical question concerning the nature of morality asks whether (and in what sense) "goodness" and "badness" are real or objective properties that particular actions possess in varying degrees. Philosophical "cognitivists" of various stripes (Plato and Kant being the most famous) answer the question in the affirmative. The "cognitivists" conclude that any particular moral judgment (e.g., that "it is bad to kill large mammals for the sake of food consumption") must thus be either true or false (rather than neither true nor false). When George W. Bush mentions "non-negotiable demands" that are right and true he is speaking the language of moral "cognitivism."

In contrast, philosophical "emotivists" of various stripes (Sir David Hume and the Greek Sophists are perhaps the most famous; and, at least in this regard, Judge Posner is a Humean) argue that "goodness" and "badness" are not objective properties. They argue that there really is no real or natural property "out there" to be represented or described with such terms as "good" or "bad." According to the philosophical "emotivist," moral judgments are neither true nor false; they are merely expressions of personal or collective choice. According to the philosophical "emotivist," the only thing worth talking about on the subject of human moral judgments is not whether they are valid, but rather the way moral language (or more accurately moral "rhetoric") gets used to further pragmatic ends. Examples of such furthered ends include: to voice preferences, serve self-interest, command or commend others, maintain power and position, or reinforce some local cultural consensus about socially acceptable behavior.

Either way ("cognitivism" vs. "emotivism"; Plato vs. the Sophists; Kant vs. Hume; Bush vs. Posner) the central philosophical question that arises about the nature of morality is whether a moral judgment is the kind of judgment where it is relevant to ask about its objective validity. "Is it morally bad for Americans to circumcise male babies?" "Is it morally good that abortions are legally available in Russia as a method of birth control?" Do such judgments entail propositions and modes of reasoning which could (at least in principle, if not in practice) be evaluated and cross-examined for their degree of accuracy in representing some real domain of moral truth? The philosophical "cognitivist" says "yes": moral judgments, like scientific judgments, are either true or false; and moral competence amounts to discovering the truth of the matter (by means of either secular or theological modes of knowledge production). The philosophical "emotivist" says "no": judgments of good and bad only express likes and dislikes, positive and negative feeling states, collective tastes and aversions. You can, of course, trace the origins of those subjective elements (in history or individual socialization) and record their consequences (for example, for group survival). But what you cannot do, says the "emotivist," is ask whether likes, preferences, or tastes are accurate estimations of what is truly "good" (or "bad"), because those highfalutin moral terms are just projections or reified labels for our feelings.

Posner's anti-realism also represents an important stream of modernist thought in the "West." From roughly the seventeenth century onwards, among the philosophers and scientists who have mattered most in defining the character of secular thought and society in Western Europe and the United States, a materialist conception of what is really real was constructed in which there was no space for objective values. At about the same time a conception of rational justification was developed in which rational justification was reduced to some combination of deductive and inductive logic, form and direct sense-experience (no revelations or deniable presuppositions, no scriptural narratives or authoritative voices from on high). Given this narrowing of the metaphysical imagination to physical nature, and the restrictions on what counts as rational justification, it is hardly surprising that many modernists began to feel theoretical queasy about the very idea of a natural or objective obligation such as a "natural right." For, given the modernist's conception of what is real and of how justifications must be given, the idea of the good and the right are metaphysically deprived of natural or objective status. Only physical objects exist in the objective world and everything else is only a thought in someone's head.

One consequence of the radical modernist denaturing of values and morality is that modernists who have undertaken a systematic examination of conscientious human judgments about what is right and good tend to fall into one of two camps. On the one hand, there are the skeptics (such as Posner, who in this regard *is* a strong skeptic) who think that our moral sense has nothing to do with the discovery of "some overarching source of moral obligations," because moral obligations (goodness, rightness) are not objective things. On the other hand, not every modernist is a skeptic about the intellectual foundations of morality. Some struggle on, trying desperately (and unsuccessfully, as I think Posner rightly points out) to justify our judgments of obligation within the modernist's limiting framework for rational justification. Given this fairly dismal state of the art it is perhaps not surprising that (at least in my limited experience in forums in which there are "declarations" of universal rights) the rational basis for the claim that there exist "inalienable rights" is rarely addressed. There is rarely a clear distinction made between "natural rights" and "positive law" assertions of rights. Nor are distinctions typically made between "rights" per se and other (non-rights based) ways of talking about things (goals, ends, or actions) that are thought to be "good" or of "value." This of course does not stop the cosmopolitan elites who attend such meetings from gathering together and making declarations or pronouncements about all the many "rights" that are true (natural or objective), non-negotiable (inalienable) and hence universally binding!

4. Five Facts Concerning Moral Judgments in Everyday Life

I now want to react to Posner's anti-realist critique of moral reasoning from the point of view of research findings on the moral psychology of everyday life.[9] This research will not settle the metaphysical debates about whether the "goodncss" or "rightness" of an act exists independently of our believing it so. Nor will it tell us whether human beings are correct in thinking that values such as efficiency, fairness, or loyalty are right and true, or whether, alternatively, they are just thought to be right and true. Nevertheless, any discussion of the possibility of making non-ethnocentric moral evaluations across cultures must take seriously the tentative discovery of something like a universal perception or recognition of the goodness or inherent value of certain abstract moral ideals; ideals such as loyalty to friends, gratitude for gifts, treating like cases alike and different cases differently, and many others. Much more research needs to be done on moral psychology across cultures. Nevertheless one is tempted to say we now know enough to consider that there is an abstract moral psychology available to "normal" human beings (a sense of conscience) intuitively grounded on those abstract moral ideals.

The psychology of morality is the study of everyday judgments about the kinds of actions and practices that are said to be loathsome, outrageous, disgusting, shameful or otherwise bad, evil, or wrong. On the basis of the ethnographic record and work in cultural psychology we now know at least five things about these judgments. Here I more or less recapitulate things I have described in other contexts.[10]

1. Moral judgments are ubiquitous. Members of every cultural community assume that they are parties to an agreement to uphold a certain way of life, praise or permit certain kinds of actions and practices, and condemn and prohibit others. In this regard both Emile Durkheim and Richard

9. Richard A. Shweder, Manamohan Mahapatra and Joan G. Miller, "Culture and Moral Development," in Jerome Kagan and Sharon Lamb (eds.), *The Emergence of Morality in Young Children*, Chicago: University of Chicago Press (1987) 1-83; Richard A. Shweder, Nancy C. Much, Manamohan Mahapatra, and Lawrence Park, "The 'Big Three' of Morality (Autonomy, Community, Divinity), and the 'Big Three' Explanations of Suffering," in Paul Rozin and Allan Brandt (eds.), *Morality and Health*, New York: Routledge (1998) 119-169; and James Q. Wilson, *The Moral Sense*, New York: Free Press (1993).

10. Shweder, *op. cit.*, note 6, and Richard A. Shweder, *Why do Men Barbecue? Recipes for Cultural Psychology*, Cambridge, Mass.: Harvard University Press (2003).

Posner are right. The social order is experienced as a moral order, and it is vigilantly and incessantly sustained by small and large judgments about right and wrong, good and bad, virtue and vice. For example, I have conducted research in a Hindu temple town in India. Local social norms in that community produce strong feeling of moral disapproval for each of the following actions: a widow eating fish; a man talking to his younger brother's wife; a mother refusing to sleep in the same bed with her children.[11]

2. Moral judgments do not spontaneously converge over time. Actions and practices that are a source of moral approbation in one community are frequently the source of moral opprobrium in another, and moral disagreements can persist over generations, if not centuries. For example, the current "Western" or "First World" alarm over the practice of female genital modifications in Africa is nothing new. Indeed, it is very much a replay of the moral indignation expressed in the 1920s by Christian missionaries and British colonial administrators as they embraced what they took to be their "white man's burden" to uplift the peoples of the "dark continent" from error, ignorance, barbarism, and confusion. Then as now majority populations in numerous African ethnic groups held the practice of both male and female "circumcision" in high regard. They believed the surgery made their children more beautiful, civilized, mature and marriageable, and bestowed on them an appropriate gender and ethnic group identity which was thought to be an essential condition for their well-being and development. Then as now many African mothers resented the implication that they are either monsters or ignoramuses for engaging in what they think of as an honorable and morally motivated custom. In this regard Judge Posner is surely right. From a purely descriptive point of view there is a large local or non-universal component to social norms. When it comes to specific practices or concrete cases, people around the world do not tend to agree about what is morally acceptable behavior.
3. Nevertheless, despite the fact that concrete moral judgments do not converge over time or across societies, *at an intuitive level* "normal" human beings are "naturally" inclined in the direction of moral realism. Thus, the moral judgments of everyday life are widely, perhaps universally, experi-

11. Richard A. Shweder, Manamohan Mahapatra, and Joan G. Miller, "Culture and Moral Development," in James W. Stigler, Richard A. Shweder and Gilbert Herdt (eds.), *Cultural Psychology: Essays on Comparative Human Development*, Cambridge: Cambridge University Press (1990) 130-145; Richard A. Shweder, Lene Jensen and William Goldstein, "Who Sleeps By Whom Revisited: A Method for Extracting the Moral 'Goods' Implicit in Praxis," in Jacqueline Goodnow, Peggy Miller and Frank Kessel (eds.), *Cultural Practices as Contexts for Development*, San Francisco, California: Jossey-Bass (1995); and Shweder, Much, Mahapatra, and Park, *op. cit.*, note 9.

enced as cognitive judgments and not solely as aesthetic or emotive judgments. The philosopher Arthur Lovejoy has noted this truth. He points out that when people say: "It is wrong to oppress the helpless" or "the conduct of Adolph Hitler was wicked," they "do not in fact conceive of themselves merely to be reporting on the state of their own emotions" and mean to be saying something more than "I am very unpleasantly affected when I think of it."[12] On a worldwide scale it appears that when everyday folk make a moral judgment, they themselves implicitly believe there are matters of objective fact to which their judgment refers. When everyday folk make such judgments as "circumcision is an outrage," "abortion is evil," or "it is wrong for Americans to put their elderly parents in a nursing home" they believe that they are making a truthful claim about some domain of moral reality. That is what makes a moral judgment "cognitive." It is precisely because we are all intuitive "cognitivists" in everyday life that we normally feel we should be able to justify (give good reasons for) our moral judgments, if called upon to do so by others, or by our own conscience. Or else we feel we should control our feelings of (e.g.) disgust or outrage, rather than allow them to dominate our actions, when and if our moral judgments turn out to be unjustified. It takes a good deal of counter-intuitive theoretical reasoning to arrive at the emotivist's stance that judgments of right and wrong or of good and bad are (from an ontological point of view) nothing more than tastes or preferences. It takes a good deal more deliberation and theorizing to arrive at the Posner-like conclusion that there are no true and good objective moral reasons to regulate one's own conduct or to tolerate group differences in social norms, aside, perhaps, from fear—of disapproval, retaliation, punishment, etc.

4. At the same time moral judgments are also widely, perhaps universally, processed in awareness as aesthetic and emotive judgments and not solely as cognitive judgments. Despite the fact that moral judgments ("that's good," "that's wrong") are thought to be judgments about some domain of moral truth, such judgments resemble aesthetic and emotive judgments ("that's ugly," "that's disgusting"). They occur rapidly and without the assistance of deliberative reason, indeed without much need for conscious reflection at all. Moreover, moral judgments are powerful motivators of action largely because they produce in people powerful feelings of ugliness, repugnance, guilt, indignation, or shame. This feature of everyday moral judgments, that they are not only non-convergent but also aesthetic and emotive is a profound fact of life. And it is a fact of life that plays a part in what the philosopher Stuart Hampshire (writing many years prior to

12. Arthur Lovejoy, *Reflections on Human Nature*, Baltimore: Johns Hopkins University Press (1961) 253, 255.

September 11) has described as "the outstanding political problem of our time."[13] The political problem, as Hampshire perceives it, is the relation between "self-consciously traditional societies" and "liberal democratic societies." In self-consciously traditional societies, he suggests, "priests of the church, or rabbis or imans or mullahs, and other experts in the will of God maintain a single conception of the good which determines the way of life of the society as a whole." Liberal democratic societies, in contrast, "permit, or encourage, a plurality of conceptions of the good." Hampshire notes that "The severity of this problem was for a long time concealed by the belief in a positivist theory of modernization, a theory that is traceable to the French Enlightenment. The positivists believed that all societies across the globe will gradually discard their traditional attachments to supernatural forces because of the need for rational, scientific and experimental methods of thought which a modern industrial economy involves. This is the old faith, widespread in the nineteenth century, that there must be a step-by-step convergence on liberal values, on 'our values.' We now know that there is no 'must' about it and that all such theories of human history have a predictive value of zero." Hampshire goes on to say:

> In fact, it is not only possible but, on the present evidence, probable that most conceptions of the good, and most ways of life, which are typical of commercial, liberal, industrialized societies will often seem altogether hateful to substantial minorities within these societies and even more hateful to most of the populations within traditional societies in other continents. As a liberal by philosophical conviction, I think I ought to expect to be hated, and to be found to be superficial and contemptible, by a large part of mankind. In looking for principles of minimum justice, one needs to see that one's way of life and habits of speech and of thought, not only seem wrong to large populations [but] can be repugnant in very much the same way in which alien habits of eating, or alien sexual customs, can be repugnant.

If Hampshire is right, that sense of repugnance is likely to be mutual. Witness, for example, the utter contempt with which human rights activists—mostly hailing from liberal commercial industrialized societies and from descendents of Westernized elite populations in former colonies—react to the beliefs and practices concerning gender, discipline, sexuality, modesty, dress, reproduction, and family life (etc.) of majority populations in Africa or Asia.

5. Finally, and quite crucially for this discussion of moral realism, the imagined truths or posited objective "goods" that are the supposed cogni-

13. Stuart Hampshire, "Justice is Conflict," *The Tanner Lectures on Human Values*, delivered at Harvard University (30-31 October 1996) 14.

tive grounds for moral judgments around the world are many, not one. The moral character of an action or practice (e.g., voluntarily ending a pregnancy) is typically established by connecting that action through a chain of factual, means-ends, and causal reasoning to some argument-ending "terminal good," such as personal freedom, family privacy, the avoidance of physical or psychological harm to others. On a worldwide scale the argument-ending "terminal goods" or "moral ideals" of deliberative moral judgments privileged in this or that cultural community are rich and diverse. They include such "noble ends" as autonomy, justice, harm avoidance (including self-defense), loyalty, benevolence, piety, duty, respect, gratitude, sympathy, chastity, purity, sanctity ("cleanliness" in the spiritual sense), and others. Several proposals have been advanced in the social sciences for classifying these goods into a smaller set, such as the four core and irreducible virtues noted by James Q. Wilson in his book on *The Moral Sense*:[14] fairness, duty, self-control, and sympathy. My associates and I have also proposed that on a worldwide scale there is a "big three" of morality. There is an "ethics of autonomy" based on moral concepts such as harm, rights and justice, which is designed to protect individuals in pursuit of the gratification of their wants. There is an "ethics of community" based on moral concepts such as duty (including self-sacrifice), hierarchy and interdependency, which is designed to help individuals achieve dignity by virtue of their role and position in a particular group or society. There is an "ethics of divinity" based on moral concepts such as natural order, sacred order, sanctity, sin and pollution, which is designed to maintain the integrity of the spiritual side of human nature. These ethics, however, vary in their centrality and distribution both across and within groups, although to some degree and in some way everyone has got all of them.[15] It is crucial, however, to recognize that these "terminal goods" are "argument-ending" only in a contingent sense. Namely in the sense that those who happen to disagree about whether an action is good or bad are led to see its moral point (the "terminal good") and thus to end their argument because they have become convinced that in that instance no further rational justification is necessary. Of course, if moral goods (such as liberty versus fairness, or "choice" versus "family values"; or for that matter "limited government" versus the use of the coercive power of the state to enforce "right and true" moral demands) are in fact plural

14. Wilson, *op. cit.*, note 9.
15. See Lene Jensen, "Habits of the Heart Revisited: Autonomy, Community and Divinity in Adult's Moral Language," 18 *Qualitative Sociology* (1995) 71-86; J. Haidt, S. Koller and M. Diaz, "Affect, Culture, and Morality, or Is It Wrong to Eat Your Dog?," 65 *Journal of Personality and Social Psychology* (1993) 613-625; Shweder, Mahapatra, and Miller, *op. cit.*, note 11; Shweder, Much, Mahapatra and Park, *op. cit.*, note 9.

and irreducible, then any argument or disagreement over which of the many moral goods should take precedence has no general rational resolution. As Posner notes, there will be "no lever for exalting" one terminal or ultimate good over another. That means that even if values are objective or real there will always be room for disputes about which moral goods should have precedence in any particular case. The recognition that a particular action or practice serves some previously unrecognized good (for example, self-defense) may bring an argument about the moral value of the action or practice to an end. But if the terminal goods of morality are many and not one, they cannot settle all possible moral disputes; in particular, as Judge Posner notes in his remarks about "family values" versus "freedom of choice," they cannot settle disagreements about which "goods" ought to take precedence in any particular case.

5. Some Thoughts About the Five Qualities of Moral Judgments

Thus we know that everyday moral judgments around the world have five qualities: they are ubiquitous, passionate, motivating, truth asserting, and divergent. This particular package of features is suggestive.

For one thing, the historical and cross-cultural persistence of passionate yet non-convergent moral truth claims raises questions about the cognitive basis of moral diversity. It is tempting to suggest that fully rational, morally decent people from different ethnic groups or cultural communities may have divergent moral responses to particular cases for at least the following reason. It is because universal values, even if they could be established as objective goods, are universal only to the extent they are abstract (some, such as Judge Posner, would say "empty"). They cannot in and of themselves determine in general and across all contexts whether (e.g.) it is right or wrong to arrange a marriage. Whether it is good or bad to sacrifice and/or butcher large mammals such as goats or sheep. Whether it is savory or unsavory to put your parents in an old-age home. Whether it is vicious or virtuous to have a large family. Whether it is moral or immoral to abort a fetus. Whether it is commendable or contemptible to encourage girls as well as boys to enter into a covenant with God (or to become full members of their society) by means of a ritual initiation involving genital modifications or circumcision. It all depends. Morally decent and fully rational people can disagree about such things, even in the face of a plentitude of shared objective values.

One is also tempted to suggest that it is precisely because moral reactions are ubiquitous, passionate, motivating, truth asserting, and divergent that secrecy, separation, and local control (including local self-determination) have been characteristic adaptations when two or more moral communities passionately disagree about the virtue of some particular customary action. Under such circumstances it makes sense to "live and let live" and keep out of each other's way or seek to preserve a balance of power so as to maintain a state of peaceful coexistence. In our technologically "wired" post-Cold War cosmopolitan world which values the free flow of everything, it has become increasingly difficult for communities with divergent moral judgments to maintain distance, hide from each other's gaze or retain sufficient power to keep their judgments private or local. The "immoral," the "barbaric" or the "evil" "other" is made readily available by CNN or the New York Times and sensational depictions of "difference" are now "in your face." Even as you rest in your living room you may be incited by words and images to react emotionally and negatively against someone or some practice you know little about on the other side of the globe.

Given such conditions, under which censorious misunderstandings of cultural differences are readily disseminated, wisdom urges caution in arriving at moral judgments about other people's socially endorsed practices. Given such conditions, one hopes, at the very least, that the social science disciplines such as anthropology and sociology will supply us with a much fuller exegesis of local meanings and indigenous points of view. One looks for the development of a critical moral theory that might enable us to see validity and virtue in the beliefs and practices of others, who may disagree with us about what is right and wrong. But how can a sympathetic understanding of those who differ from us actually be achieved? And why should we even try to perceive validity and virtue in the beliefs and practices of others?

6. Towards a Normative Local Moral Realism

One approach to answering such questions can be found in Isaiah Berlin's theory of "value pluralism," as described and systematized in an important book by John Gray.[16] Berlin's moral theory is associated with the idea that "human values are objective but irreducibly diverse." And it is linked to an intellectual stance which affirms the "reality, validity and human intelligibility of values and forms of life very different from our own." One basic claim of the theory is that "fundamental human values are many, that they are often in conflict and rarely, if ever, necessarily harmonious, and that some at least of these conflicts are among incommensurables—conflicts among values for which there is no single, common standard of measurement or arbitration."[17] In other

16. John Gray, *Isaiah Berlin*, Princeton, New Jersey: Princeton University Press (1996).
17. *Ibid.*, 1, 3, 6, 8.

words some moral dilemmas are insolvable or undecidable by rational reflection—to which one might comment "just as Richard Posner has argued."

Posner and Berlin are both pluralists, and their critiques of moral theory are similar in several ways. Both reject the idea that it is possible to rationally settle all moral disputes. Both argue that people around the world do not universally agree on what particular behaviors are right or wrong. Both argue that moral judgments depend on circumstances. One can easily imagine Berlin accepting Posner's argument that even the presumption that infanticide is immoral is too presumptive and provincial to count as a moral universal. Both would agree that most of the universal maxims of morality (for example, the injunction to be fair-minded in the sense of treating like cases alike and different cases differently) cannot in and of themselves resolve real world moral disputes. Both are eager to point out that there is no determinate or universal way to choose between various alternative moral claims, for example claims of autonomy versus community, or liberty versus equality.

Nevertheless, in contrast to Judge Posner, I believe Berlin's version of value pluralism would hold that fundamental human values are not just empty truisms and that they play an essential part in the reasonable construction and intelligibility of any moral system. But what part? In trying to answer that question I can only speak for myself.

Let us consider one of the findings of the research on everyday moral reasoning, as summarized above (points 3 and 5). I have suggested that it can be argued that within human moral psychology there is a base set of "terminal goods," which appear to function almost like "revealed truths." Once someone truly understands the moral good or worthy end (e.g., self-defense, reduction of physical harm, fair distribution of burdens) served by a particular behavior they do not go on to say "so who cares about the reduction of harm or about self-defense or about the reasonable distribution of costs." This type of revelatory recognition of ultimate moral validity—the argumentative equivalent of a revealed moral truth—can even be witnessed in Posner's exposition of his anti-realist critique, where at least three such examples can be found in the quoted sections of his Oliver Wendell Holmes Lectures. The first occurs in his illustration of "female genital mutilation"—why should or why would a moral critic be (as Posner puts it) "disarmed" at all by the invocation of "family values" over "individual choice," unless it were the case that both types of values were already universally recognized as valid or objective goods? Second, Judge Posner constructs and interprets both infanticide and slavery (in ancient Greece, but not in the nineteenth-century United States) as cases that are intelligible as morally valid practices. He does this by representing each practice as a means to a universally recognized moral good—namely the reduction of physical harm (to already born children and to the slaves themselves, respectively). His argument succeeds precisely to the extent that he can count on us all sharing in the revelation of a base set of objective goods, from which one of those goods flows from the application of the moral maxim "do less harm rather than more." Third, he distinguishes "racial enslavement" (in the United States) from slavery in the ancient world. In doing so, he implies that "racial enslavement" (as it existed for some time in the United States) is not as easily connected to a recognizable moral end, and thus, unlike slavery in ancient Greece, ought to be viewed as a contemptible social norm. In all three cases Posner's argument is potentially persuasive because he is able to direct our attention to the moral integrity of local contexts; and those local contexts become morally intelligible precisely because he can presuppose and thus trade on our common sense revelation of a base set of moral truths. In other words, in all three instances Judge Posner is in fact normatively evaluating the practices of "others" in universally recognizable terms. When it comes to human moral psychology it appears that some lights are not just "our lights" but are "everyone's lights."

In citing these three examples I am simply drawing attention to the implicit normative moral structure to some of Judge Posner's arguments about the diversity of social norms. He implies that if we knew enough about the local context of cultures in which infanticide or slavery is permissible, any rational person would conclude that there are good reasons for the practices. And what are the reasons that would convince any rational person not to condemn infanticide or slavery outright in such cases? Well, in the examples given, infanticide and slavery are represented as ways to save lives, in particular the lives of either children who are older or of the slaves themselves. And what makes saving those lives a good reason for the practices? Does not the argument count on us recognizing aggregate harm reduction as a worthy end, as an objective moral good, as a potential virtue? The correctness of a moral judgment may well be relative to circumstances. Nevertheless, implicit in Posner's argument is the idea that under certain correct descriptions of the circumstances there are certain moral judgments that are universally true. Thus, if infanticide or slavery ought to be judged acceptable at some time and in some place (even if the moral reason is nothing other than collective self-defense), it ought to be judged so by any fully informed, rational human being, and not just "by our lights." And it will be so judged because with an informed understanding of the local scene any rational person should be able to recognize those practices, in those instances and under those circumstances, as local instantiations of some universal moral ideal (e.g., "do less harm rather than more").

The "revealed truths" or abstract moral goods (such as harm reduction) of human moral psychology also appear in another guise. We learn from the study of human psychology that an understanding of the cognitive side of moral judgment is a necessary precondition for a full understanding of the psychology of human emotions. As noted earlier, if one participates in philosophical arguments about the nature of morality, one will be pigeonholed as either a cognitivist or an emotivist. If you are a philosophical emotivist you will argue, as does Judge Posner, that the emotions are devoid of moral content, and that they are expressions of will or preference, and can provide no rational justification for an action. If you are a philosophical cognitivist you will not necessarily disagree; indeed, you may have no philosophical interest in the emotions precisely because you will care only about the "good reasons" for undertaking this or that action, and you may assume that emotions are not reasons. But is this exactly right?

It seems noteworthy that ordinary adult human beings experience their moral judgments as both "cognitive" judgments and "emotive" judgments, and that both reason and feeling play such major roles in moral psychology around the world. And it is also worth noting I think that there appears to be a universal moral content to many human emotions, even if that moral content basically references abstract moral goods. Thus upon analysis many human emotions seem to contain within themselves a moral core. "Fear," for example, is associated with issues of safety and harm and motivates us to eliminate the conditions that produce it. "Anger" and "indignation" are associated with issues of fairness, equity and just desert, and motivate us to eliminate injustice from the world. "Love" and "compassion" are associated with protection of the vulnerable and motivate us to take care of others. In each case our emotional reactions can be justified or intellectually warranted by the good reasons (the "cognitive" conditions, e.g., the threat to safety, the injustice, the vulnerability) that produced them. They cannot be justified by pointing only to the motivating feeling states (e.g., the heat or tension or uncertainty) that "drive" us to act, because feelings per se are not "cognitive" and make no truth claims. And, of course, it would be quite insufficient to translate "I am angry at him" as only meaning "I have been unfairly treated by him." "I have been unfairly treated by him" is in the domain of reason. It is a proposition about a state of the world that can be judged true or false. If it is false one should not be angry, assuming you are a reasonable person. And yes, "anger" is more than just its "cognitive" core. It is also the feeling state that motivates or pushes us to action. Yet it must be associated with a correct cognitive appraisal (e.g., someone was truly unfairly treated) if it is to move us to act in a moral sort of way. One thing all this suggests is that abstract moral goods do have an essential role to play in moral evaluations of cultural practices. They are not trivial, even if they are devoid of specific behavioral content. Indeed, one might argue that they are essential for the very construction of social norms.

Let us take the abstract moral ideal that "one should treat like cases alike and different cases differently." This is a formal principle of justice, which, if formulated so abstractly, is devoid of determinant content. In and of itself it would not help in settling a moral dispute, because any actual moral dispute about what is just will require that one come forward with a substantive theory about what makes cases alike and what makes them different. Stated abstractly the formal ideal of justice comes close to being a self-evident truth; and is one of the "revealed truths" of human psychology. It is hard to even imagine someone asserting its denial as a general moral ideal ("You should treat like cases differently and different cases alike"!), without wondering about that person's sincerity, seriousness, or "normalcy."

Nevertheless, even though it is an empty abstraction, the formal ideal of justice is not trivial or dispensable. Quite the contrary, the abstraction has a dynamic and almost dialectical relationship to our culturally grounded experiences. On the one hand, the formalism ("treat like cases alike and different cases differently") makes it possible for us to order and record our experiences; because of the force of the formal principle of justice particular experiences get classified and are given definition as we experience them. On the other hand, the formalism gets interpreted as we classify and order those experiences. We give substantive meaning to the abstraction by deciding what things are alike, and why. Yes, the formalism by itself is empty; and yes, how we end up classifying and ordering things as alike or different is underdetermined by the abstraction. Yet it is indispensable all the same, because it enables us to construct a substantive theory of which features of similarity and difference actually matter, make sense, or are functional, in this or that just society. Without it we would be lost in a social world with no normative categories or definition. The process seems almost Kantian: concepts without percepts are empty, percepts without concepts are blind.

In sum, what I think we learn from the study of moral psychology is that "normal" human beings respond to situations as if there are universally binding objective values, just too many of them (for example, justice, beneficence, autonomy, sacrifice, liberty, loyalty, sanctity, duty, and so forth, as indicated earlier). Those taken-for-objective and universally valued ends of life are diverse, heterogeneous, irreducible to some common denominator such as "utility" or "pleasure," and inherently in conflict with each other. That means that all the things thought to be good in life cannot be simultaneously maximized. When it comes to implementing such values there are always trade-offs, which is why there are different traditions of values (i.e., cultures) and why no one cultural tradition has ever been able to honor everything that is good. That fact alone is reason enough to place some value on "tolerance" as an objective virtue, because "tolerance" can be justified as a way of acknowledging a truth about the inherent incompleteness or partiality of one's own way of life. If the theory of value pluralism is correct, there are inevitably both losses and gains associated with one's commitment to any one way of life.

Value pluralism of the type proposed implies that it should be possible, from a strictly moral point of view, to be a moral realist while acknowledging the legitimacy of different ways of life. A normative local moral realism based on an Isaiah Berlin-like theory of value does not imply that social norms must be the same wherever you go. Such an approach might ground itself, as I have tried to do, on the discovery of universally acknowledged abstract values. Such an approach might be prepared to apply those abstract values as the psychological equivalents of "revealed truths." It might hold that having access to those "revealed truths" (the abstract virtues or goods of morality) is partly definitive of what it means to be a "normal" human being or to have a "conscience." It might hold that having access to those "revealed truths" is what makes the very different social norms of "others" morally intelligible. The list of "revealed truths" or universally binding values is likely to include diverse concepts, related to formal or structural aspects of human sociality. Examples include the notion that cruelty is evil (one should not hurt others without a reason), that you should treat like cases alike and different cases differently, that highly vulnerable members of one's group are entitled to protection from harm, and so forth.

This particular type of moral realism can alternatively be labeled "value pluralism" (following Berlin), or "normative local moral realism" (borrowing some of that phrase from Posner) or "moral universalism without the uniformity." That last phrase expresses the way I prefer to conceptualize pluralism, by showing due respect for both the universal and the local. One implication of the approach is that any cultural system or system of "social norms" that is entitled to respect should be capable of being represented as a moral order recognizable to all human beings. (Earlier I have argued that that is precisely what Judge Posner succeeds in doing with his examples of infanticide and ancient Greek slavery). Indeed, one might argue that any cultural system entitled to respect should, if pressed to justify itself, be able to provide its members with "good reasons" for their practices, such that those practices can be understood and experienced as a concrete instance of some abstract moral standard. It is worth noting that one of the ways a cultural anthropologist tries to achieve a charitable or sympathetic understanding of unfamiliar or even alien "others" is to try to reconstruct and make explicit the connections between a concrete instance of some customary behavior and some universally recognizable "terminal good." This is what I shall try to do below, with regards to the case of cosmetic genital surgeries in East and West Africa.

This process of filling in with "good reasons" the gap between abstract universal moral standards and concrete local actions may involve many local or parochial concepts and beliefs, and there is much room for discretion, given the ultimate limits of human reason. Choices must be made about which "goods" take precedence, which apply in this case but not in that case, and so forth. However, this process of filling in the gap can be very "cognitive" (the arguments and disagreement are about what is right and what true), both in its assumptions and in its effects.

If the theory of value pluralism is true, a global convergence in moral judgments about particular social norms is unlikely to occur. Of course it is quite possible, as Stuart Hampshire (see above) implies, that morally decent and fully rational peoples, each feeling at home in their own way of life, will reciprocally feel disgusted by the social norms of the "other." But feelings of astonishment, interest, fascination and appreciation are equally possible in a world populated by diverse cultures. I would also suggest that in many instances (certainly not all, but many) our initial feelings of disgust or disapproval are lacking in validity, if only because we initially or automatically react to unfamiliar things as if they were familiar. If and when such feelings are in fact invalid, they are likely to become attenuated or held in abeyance once the connection of the practice to some recognizable abstract universal moral ideal can be demonstrated in a convincing way. Indeed, one of the main reasons for doing cultural anthropology is to see whether it is possible to provide the necessary exegesis of local context and "native point of view," so as to render "others" intelligible not as monsters, innocents or fools, but as recognizably reasonable and moral human beings. This may not always be possible, though it often is, despite initial impressions to the contrary.

I now turn to the practice of cosmetic genital surgery in East and West Africa, which is a useful if challenging test case for the relevance of a theory of normative local moral realism for understanding the unfamiliar practices of others. Although these surgeries are almost always customary for both boys and girls in societies where girls are "circumcised," the very idea of a culturally expected cosmetic genital surgery for female youth may, at first blush, offend the reader's moral/emotional sense. One aim of this volume is to examine the use and abuse of moral discourse (i.e., "human rights" discourse) in making judgments across cultural communities. With regard to that aim it is relevant to ask whether an offense to the culturally shaped emotional sensibilities of one group is a *sufficient* reason to justify the eradication of a practice that is socially endorsed by another group? Given that the answer to that question is (and ought to) be "no," I evaluate the non-emotive reasons put forward by anti-"FGM" activists in defense of their "eradication campaigns," and suggest that they are all quite vulnerable to criticism.

7. Which is the Human Rights Violation? African Cosmetic Genital Surgeries or the First World Campaign to Eradicate Them?

Unless you are an anthropologist who knows a good deal about East and West African gender identity and coming of age ceremonies, you may have a hard time thinking about African genital modifications with an open mind. This is largely because of the way the practice has been represented in a global discourse that bears little relationship to informed anthropological accounts or to the existing corpus of scientifically credible medical studies. I believe it is important for those interested in developing a non-ethnocentric discourse for cultural critique to conscientiously critique the global discourse that has grown up around this topic, and to have a close look at the evolution of the anti-"FGM" activist movement. This is a case where the human rights movement has been insufficiently attentive to the hazards of provincialism, parochialism, and ethnocentrism. There has been a rush to moral judgment by activists who think of themselves as "good guys" liberating the oppressed and educating the ignorant. At the same time there has been too little scientifically respectable fact-gathering and insufficient contextual and cultural analysis.

If you read and believe the literature put out by anti-"FGM" activists[18] then what African peoples are said to be doing is indeed horrifying. For what you must believe is that Africa is indeed a "Dark Continent" where for hundreds, if not thousands of years, African parents have been murdering and maiming their daughters and depriving them of the capacity for a sexual response. You must believe that African women are under the thumb of African men and that they are either monsters ("mutilators" of their children, torturers who disrespect the bodily integrity of their offspring) or very ignorant of health consequences and the best interests and fundamental rights of their children. Or alternatively, that African women are so oppressed, beaten down, indoctrinated, or passive as to have lost all sense of moral responsibility and agency.

There is a powerful impulse within some First World liberal democracies to leave people free to live their lives according to their own views of what

18. See, e.g., Asma El Dareer, *Women, Why Do You Weep?: Circumcision and Its Consequences*, London: Zed Press (1982); Franziska P. Hosken, *The Hosken Report: Genital and Sexual Mutilation of Females*, Lexington, Mass.: Women's International Network News (1993); Olayinka Koso-Thomas, *The Circumcision of Women: A Strategy for Eradication*, London: Zed Books Ltd. (1987); Susan Rich and Stephanie Joyce, *Eradicating Female Genital Mutiliation: Lessons for Donors*, Washington, D.C.: Wallace Global Fund for a Sustainable Future (1996).

is good, true, beautiful, or effective. But not if in choosing what to do, they do great harm to those who are innocent, vulnerable, and not in a position to make choices for themselves. If such representations were accurate who would not want to "save the children" and bring the practice of female genital surgery to an end. But are they accurate? Compare such horrifying representations of the African "other" with the accounts of four anthropologists who know something about either Africa, the practice, or both.[19]

This is what Robert Edgerton,[20] an expert on East African history and contemporary society, says about the practice of female circumcision in Kenya in the 1920s and 1930s, at a time of British colonial rule when Christian missionaries and colonial administrators tried unsuccessfully to wipe it out. Then as now, about half of all Kenyan ethnic groups circumcised both girls and boys. Edgerton remarks that the operation was performed without anesthesia and hence was very painful "yet most girls bore it bravely and few suffered serious infection or injury as a result. Circumcised women did not lose their ability to enjoy sexual relations, nor was their child-bearing capacity diminished. Nevertheless the practice offended Christian sensibilities."

This is what Sandra Lane and Robert Rubinstein say about the practice in Egypt today, where approximately 85–90% of females and males are circumcised.

> An important caveat, however, is that many members of societies that practice traditional female genital surgeries do not view the result as mutilation. Among these groups, in fact, the resulting appearance is considered an improvement over female genitalia in their natural state. Indeed, to call a woman uncircumcised, or to call a man the son of an uncircumcised mother, is a terrible insult and noncircumcised adult female genitalia are often considered disgusting. In interviews we conducted in rural and urban Egypt and in studies conducted by faculty of the High Institute of Nursing, Zagazig University, Egypt, the overwhelming majority of circumcised women planned to have the procedure performed on their daughters. In discussions with some fifty women we found only two who resent and are angry at having been circumcised. Even these women do not think that female circumcision is one of the most critical problems facing Egyptian women and girls. In the rural Egyptian hamlet where we have conducted fieldwork some women were not familiar with groups that did not circumcise their girls. When they learned that the female researcher was not circumcised their response was disgust mixed with joking laughter.

19. I have recounted these ethnographic reports in other articles, including Richard A. Shweder, "The Moral Challenge in Cultural Migration," in Nancy Foner (ed.), *Anthropology and Contemporary Migration*, Santa Fe, N. Mex.: School for American Research Press (in press).

20. Robert B. Edgerton, *Mau Mau: An African Crucible*, New York: The Free Press (1989) 40.

> They wondered how she could have thus gotten married and questioned how her mother could have neglected such an important part of her preparation for womanhood.[21]

This is what Carla Obermeyer, an epidemiologist and medical anthropologist at Harvard University, says after a recent comprehensive review of the medical and demographic literature on the health consequences of the cultural practice.

> On the basis of the vast literature on the harmful effects of genital surgeries, one might have anticipated finding a wealth of studies that document considerable increases in mortality and morbidity. This review could find no incontrovertible evidence on mortality, and the rate of medical complications suggest that they are the exception rather than the rule.... In fact, studies that systematically investigate the sexual feelings of women and men in societies where genital surgeries are found are rare, and the scant information that is available calls into question the assertion that female genital surgeries are fundamentally antithetical to women's sexuality and incompatible with sexual enjoyment.[22]

Obermeyer's conclusions converge with the findings of the very recent large-scale Medical Research Council study of the long-term reproductive health consequences of female circumcision.[23] The study, conducted in the Gambia, compared circumcised women with those who were uncircumcised. In the Gambia the surgery most often involves a full clitoridectomy and either partial or complete excision of the labia minora. More than 1,100 women (ages fifteen to fifty-four) from three ethnic groups (Mandinka, Wolof, and Fula) were interviewed and also given gynecological examinations and laboratory tests. Very few differences were discovered in the reproductive health status of circumcised versus uncircumcised women. As noted in the research report, the supposed morbidities (such as infertility, painful sex, vulval tumors, menstrual problems, incontinence, and most endogenous infections), often cited by anti-"FGM" advocacy groups as common long-term problems of female circumcision, did not distinguish between circumcised and uncircumcised women. The authors of the report caution anti-"FGM" activists against exaggerating the morbidity and mortality risks of the practice.

This is what Fuambai Ahmadu, an anthropologist at the London School of Economics and Political Science, says about her own ritual initiation in Sierra Leone:

---

21. Sandra D. Lane and Robert A. Rubinstein, "Judging the Other: Responding to Traditional Female Genital Surgeries," 26 *Hastings Center Report* (1996) 35.

22. Obermeyer, *op. cit.*, note 4, 92-95.

23. Morison et al., *op. cit.*, note 4.

> It is difficult for me—considering the number of ceremonies I have observed, including my own—to accept that what appears to be expressions of joy and ecstatic celebrations of womanhood in actuality disguise hidden experiences of coercion and subjugation. Indeed, I offer that the bulk of Kono women who uphold these rituals do so because they want to—they relish in the supernatural powers of their ritual leaders over and against men in society, and they embrace the legitimacy of female authority and particularly, the authority of their mothers and grandmothers.[24]

Ms. Ahmadu grew up in the United States, after her parents migrated there when she was five years old. As a young adult, at age twenty-two, she returned to Sierra Leone to be initiated just like all other Kono women. Speaking at the American Anthropological Association[25] meetings in Chicago three years ago, she remarked:

> I also share with feminist scholars and activists campaigning against the practice a concern for women's physical, psychological and sexual well-being, as well as with the implications of these traditional rituals for women's status and power in society. Coming from an ethnic group [the Kono of Eastern Sierra Leone] in which female (and male) initiation and circumcision are institutionalized and a central feature of culture and society and having myself undergone this traditional process of becoming a "woman," I find it increasingly challenging to reconcile my own experiences with prevailing global discourses on female circumcision.

From the point of view of a "normative local moral realist" or "value-pluralist," the social norms of another cultural community can be different from one's own and yet be morally defensible at the same time. For this to be so, however, it must be possible to draw a plausible connection between the unfamiliar social norm of others and one or more recognizable goods, taking into account local beliefs and points of view that are not obvious examples of error, ignorance, confusion, or illogicality. To engage in cultural criticism or cultural justification in this way one must guard against one's initial ethnocentric moral judgments, be slow to morally judge others, and be willing to collect systematic information about the perspectives and beliefs of "others." At the end of the day one may find that one's initial reactions were valid, but not necessarily always, or even often.

---

24. Ahmadu, *op. cit.*, note 4.
25. Ahmadu also presented her "Rights and Wrongs" in the panel on "Female Genital Cutting: Local Dynamics of a Global Debate" at the 98th Annual Meeting of the American Anthropological Association (Chicago, Illinois, 18 November 1999).

For example, this is what I discovered in my research for a recent essay addressing the question (among others) whether both female and male circumcision should be tolerated in a multicultural society such as the United States,[26] on grounds of gender equity, family privacy, and freedom of religion. For one thing, the discourse constructing the practice as "female genital mutilation," "torture," or "oppression of women" is not a global or universal discourse. It is primarily a rhetoric embraced by those who are shocked to discover that there are actually peoples in the world who believe that not just the male body but also the female body needs to be surgically altered for the sake of normal individual development. The rhetoric is neither objective nor value neutral. It is certainly not the rhetoric used by those who live in communities where cosmetic genital surgeries for boys and girls are socially endorsed. So how should we fairly and accurately describe and represent the things that are done in these communities?

It turns out that in places where the practice of female circumcision is popular, it is widely believed by women that these genital alterations improve their bodies and make them more beautiful, more feminine, more civilized, and more honorable. In other words, there is a cultural aesthetics in play among circumcising ethnic groups, an ideal of the human sexual region as smooth, cleansed and refined, which supports the view that the genitals of both women and men are unsightly, misshapen and rather unappealing, if left in their "natural" state. Thus these genital surgeries are thought to have a positive cosmetic function; they are thought to beautify because the body is made smooth and a protrusion or "fleshy encumbrance" removed that is thought to be ugly and odious to both sight and touch.[27] "Mutilating" their sons and daughters is the last thing on the minds of African parents. Thus, the question arises: isn't the world big enough to accommodate cultural differences in judgments about what is beautiful and what is ugly? How does one justify imposing a uniform aesthetic standard for the human body on everyone in the world?

African parents in circumcising cultures also believe that these surgical genital modifications make their sons more masculine and their daughters more feminine. In many East and West African communities unmodified genitals (in both males and females) are seen as sexually ambiguous. The foreskin of the penis is perceived as a feminine element in the male and boys are thought to attain mature sexual identity by its removal. The clitoris is viewed as an unwelcome vestige of the male sexual organ; and its external attenu-

26. Shweder, *op. cit.*, note 3.

27. See, e.g., Koso-Thomas, *op. cit.*, note 18, 7; Lane and Rubinstein, *op. cit.*, note 21; Otto Meinardus, "Mythological, Historical and Sociological Aspects of the Practice of Female Circumcision Among the Egyptians," 16 *Acta Ethnographica*, Academiae Scientiarum Hungaricae (1967) 387-397; El Dareer *op. cit.*, note 18.

ation (much of the tissue structure of the clitoris is internal and is never removed) is positively associated with several good things. These include attainment of full female identity, induction into a social network and support group of powerful adult women, and ultimately marriage and motherhood.[28] Many women who uphold these traditions of female initiation seek to empower themselves by getting rid of what they perceive as an unbidden yet dispensable visible trace of unwanted male anatomy.

Genital surgeries for both boys and girls are also thought to lift children out of a state of nature and render them civilized. In part this is because a genital alteration is locally viewed in some parts of Africa as a symbolic action that says something about one's willingness to exercise restraint over feelings of lust and self-control over the anti-social desire for sexual pleasure. Many African women and men view the practice as honorable because the surgery announces one's commitment to perpetuate the lineage and value the womb as the source of social reproduction.[29]

Thus, in striking contrast to the claims made in the anti-"FGM" advocacy literature, in places where female genital alterations are commonplace, they are not only popular, but also fashionable. As hard as it may be for "us" to believe (and I recognize that for some of "us" this really is hard to believe), many women in places such as Mali, Somalia, Egypt, Kenya, or Chad are repulsed by the idea of unmodified female genitals. They view unmodified genitals as ugly, unrefined and undignified, and hence not fully human. They associate unmodified genitals with life outside of or at the bottom of civilized society.

A full critique of the discourse of the anti-"FGM" activist movement is not possible here.[30] Minimally however, in addition to the evidence on health

28. Ahmadu, *op. cit.*, note 4; Meinardus, *ibid.*, 389.

29. See, e.g., Janice Boddy, "Womb as Oasis: The Symbolic Context of Pharaonic Circumcision in Rural Northern Sudan," 9 *American Ethnologist* (1982) 682-698 and *Wombs and Alien spirits: Women, Men and the Zar Cult in Northern Sudan*, Madison: University of Wisconsin Press (1989) and "Violence Embodied? Circumcision, Gender Politics, and Cultural Aesthetics," in R. Emerson Dobash and Russell P. Dobash (eds.), *Rethinking Violence Against Women*, London: Sage (1996) 77-110.

30. See, e.g., Rogaia Mustafa Abusharaf, "Virtuous Cuts: Female Genital Circumcision in an African Ontology," 12 *Differences: A Journal of Feminist Cultural Studies* (2001) 112-139; Ahmadu, *op. cit.*, note 4; Jomo Kenyatta, *Facing Mount Kenya: The Tribal Life of the Gikuyu*, London: Secker and Warburg (1938); the two publications by Corinne Kratz: *Affecting Performance: Meaning, Movement and Experience in Okiek Women's Initiation*, Washington, D.C.: Smithsonian Institute Press (1994) and "Contexts, Controversies, Dilemmas: Teaching Circumcision," in Misty Bastian and Jane Parpart (eds.), *Teaching Africa: African Studies in the New Millenium*, Boulder, Colo.: Lynne Rienner (1999); Obermeyer, *op. cit.*, note 4; Leslye A. Obiora, "Rethinking Polemics and Intransigence in the Campaign Against Female Circumcision," 47 *Case Western Reserve Law Review* (1997) 275; Morison et

consequences mentioned earlier, the following points need to be addressed and debated, if there is to be a serious evenhanded non-ethnocentric discussion of the topic.

1. Despite claims to the contrary, the practice of genital alteration is a rather poor example of gender inequality or of society picking on women. If one surveys the cultures of the world, one finds very few cultures where genital surgeries are done to girls but not to boys, although there are many cultures where they are done only to boys or to both sexes. The male genital alterations often take place in adolescence and they can involve major modifications (including sub-incision, in which the penis is split along the line of the urethra). Viewed on a worldwide scale, and looked at from the point of view of the prevalence, timing, and intensity of the relevant initiation rites, one is hard pressed to argue that this is an obvious instance of a gender inequity disfavoring girls. Quite the contrary, social recognition for both boys and girls of their ritual transformation into a more mature status as empowered men and women is not infrequently a major point of the ceremony. In other words, female circumcision, when and where it occurs in Africa, is much more a case of society treating boys and girls equally before the common law and inducting them into responsible adulthood in parallel ways.
2. The practice is also a rather poor example of patriarchal domination. Many patriarchal cultures in Europe and Asia do not engage in genital alterations at all or (as in the case of Jews, many non-African Muslims, and many African ethnic groups) exclude girls from participation in the practice and do it only to boys. Moreover, the African ethnic groups that circumcise both females and males are very different from each other in kinship, religion, economy, family life, ceremonial practice, and so forth. Some are Islamic, some are not. Some are patriarchal, some (such as the Kono, a matrilineal society) are not. Some link the genital alteration to formal initiation into well-established and powerful women's organizations, but some do not.[31] Some are concerned with female purity, sexual restraint outside of marriage and the social regulation of desire, while others are more relaxed about premarital sexual play and are not puritanical.
3. When it comes to female initiation and genital alterations the practice is almost always controlled, performed, and most strongly upheld by

al., *op. cit.*, note 4; Shweder, *op. cit.*, note 3; C. J. Walley, "Searching for 'Voices': Feminism, Anthropology, and the Global Debate over Female Genital Operations," 12 *Cultural Anthropology* (1997) 405-438.

31. On the connection between circumcision and entrance into "women's secret societies" in Sierra Leone, see Ahmadu, *op. cit.*, note 4.

women, although male kin often do provide material and moral support. Typically, however, men have rather little to do with these female operations, may not know very much about them and may feel it is not really their business to butt in or tell their wives, mothers, aunts, and grandmothers what to do. It is the women of the society who are the cultural experts in this intimate feminine domain, and they are not particularly inclined to give up their powers or share their secrets. I have lived and taught in Kenya, where the practice is routine for some ethnic groups.[32] There the adolescent girls who undergo the ritual initiation generally look forward to it. It is an ordeal and it can be painful (especially if done "naturally" and without anesthesia) but it is viewed as a test of courage. It is an event organized and controlled by women, who have their own view of the aesthetics of the body—a different view from ours about what is civilized, dignified and beautiful. The girl's parents are not trying to be cruel to their daughter—African parents love their children too. No one is tortured. In fact there is typically a celebration surrounding the event.

4. Imagine an African mother living in the United States who holds the following convictions. She believes that her daughters as well as her sons should be able to improve their looks and their marriage prospects, enter into a covenant with God, and be honored as adult members of the community via circumcision. Imagine that her proposed surgical procedure (for example, a cut in the prepuce that covers the clitoris) is no more substantial from a medical point of view than the customary American male circumcision operation. Why should we not extend that option to (e.g.) the Kono parents of daughters as well as to (e.g.) the Jewish parents of sons? Principles of gender equity, due process before the law, religious and cultural freedom, and family privacy would seem to support the option. Or is one going to argue that gender equity requires that male circumcision be criminalized as well, thereby attempting (as anti-male circumcision activists in Canada and the United States are attempting) to eradicate a practice that has been central to Judaism and Islam for thousands of years?
5. Or imagine a sixteen-year-old female Somali teenager living in the United States who believes that a genital alteration would be "something very great." She likes the look of her mother's body and her recently circumcised cousin's body far better than she likes the look of her own. She wants to be a mature and beautiful women, Somali style. She wants to marry a Somali man or at least a man who appreciates the intimate appearances of an initiated woman's body. She wants to show solidarity with other African women who express their sense of beauty, civility,

32. See Kenyatta, *op. cit.*; Kratz *op. cit.*; Walley, *op. cit.*; see all at note 30.

and feminine dignity in this way; and she shares their sense of aesthetics and seemliness. She reviews the medical literature and discovers that the surgery can be done safely, hygienically and with no great effect on her sexual capacities. After consultation with her parents and the full support of other members of her community she elects to carry on the tradition. In a society that endorses sex change operations, breast enhancements, nose jobs and a vast array of cosmetic surgeries, what principle of justice demands that her cultural heritage and ideals for the human body should be criminalized and brought to an end? I wonder what a human rights perspective has to say in this instance.

8. Conclusion

I have argued that any universalistic moral realism or fundamental human rights perspective that truly seeks to avoid the accusation of ethnocentrism ought to be critical of the overheated rhetoric of the anti-"FGM" advocacy movement. I have recounted some medical and ethnographic evidence concerning the consequences and significance of the practice of genital modifications in Africa. It appears to be possible to give an account of this practice that makes it morally intelligible to us, while taking proper account of local context and indigenous meanings. In conclusion, I see no inherent reason that a moral realism must be ethnocentric. Indeed, I have suggested that a normative local moral realism is not only possible, given the nature of human moral psychology, but is indispensable for understanding the social norms of "others." Nevertheless, the risks of ethnocentrism are not insubstantial when unfamiliar cultures collide. Indeed, given the current imbalance of power in the world and the increasing popularity of the idea that "the West is best," ethnocentrism may be very difficult to overcome. It is, of course, one of the moral ideals of anthropology that it should seek to counter ethnocentrism. Whether it will succeed remains to be seen. "FGM" is a challenging test case, in which one's ultimate willingness to tolerate differences in social norms turns on one's ability to connect those norms to some recognizable universal moral ideals, to guard against lurid, sensational, and ultimately insufficiently informed depictions of "others," and to resist the temptation to use human rights discourse as a way to universalize the cultural preferences of one's own group. Whether or not I have succeeded in taking a small step in those directions I leave it to the reader to judge, by his or her own lights, or even, perhaps, by lights that all human beings ought to be able to recognize, and may already share.

Chapter 4

Guy Haarscher

Can Human Rights Be "Contextualized"?

1. Introduction: Globalization and Human Rights

There is today a globalization of constitutional values, in particular human rights and the rule of law.[1] Globalization is more than financial deregulation (capital can be found everywhere in the world: it can circulate, enter countries—and also "leave" them, which is a condition for a safe "entrance"); and more than the globalization of communications through television (cable and satellite), mobile phones, the new technologies, the Internet. There is

1. In French, one can translate the phrase "rule of law" either by État (*State*) de droit or by état (*situation*) de droit. It might be reasonable to adopt the latter translation inasmuch as today the rule of law is much broader than the realm of the State *sensu stricto*. It is interesting to note that, in the seventeenth and eighteenth centuries, the States (at least in Continental Europe) tried to absorb the various sources of law by imposing the primacy, or even the monopoly, of the statutes. Today the State, and thus the domestic statute, has been enfeebled by globalization (but also by the emergence of sub-State entities). On this problem, see François Ost and Michaël van de Kerkhove, *De la pyramide au réseau*, Bruxelles: Publications des Facultés universitaires Saint-Louis (2002). "Republicans," like the philosopher Pierre-André Taguieff and the politician Jean-Pierre Chevènement (who recently ran for president in France), strongly criticize such a process: for them there is no real rule of law without a State (a "republic") composed of free and equal citizens—no *état de droit* without *État*.

András Sajó (ed.), Human Rights with Modesty: The Problem of Universalism, *103-120.*

a cultural globalization and an economic-industrial globalization characterized by the domination of the United States through entertainment, the way of informing people, of eating (McDonald's), etc. To say the least, these two processes of globalization are often considered (with resentment) the export of a dominant "Western" paradigm.

But there is also a *globalization of human rights*.[2] Basically, this phenomenon is not that recent: the very notion of human rights that emerged in Europe in Modern Times implies universality in that these rights are, by definition, valid for all human beings (as is stated, for instance, in the American Declaration of Independence) as opposed to context-dependent, more relative—thus less important—rights. Until the Second World War international law was rather alien to human rights. Even the League of Nations, in the framework of which a sophisticated system of minority protection had been elaborated, did not impose on member states the respect of human rights. It was only after the Second World War and the reaction to Nazism that the international state of nature (to use Hobbes' terminology) was, at least to some extent, weakened in favor of universal human rights. Now, from 1945 on to the beginning of the 1990s, the proclamation of human rights as a worldwide concern was affected by a formidable ambiguity: in 1948 the United Nations adopted the Universal Declaration of Human Rights without a single negative vote.[3] This resolution would be followed by many UN declarations and conventions, most notably the 1966 Covenants: the first on civil and political rights, and the second on economic, social, and cultural rights.[4] Notwithstanding, the Security Council, which has a monopoly on the legitimate use of violence within the UN system, had, already in 1948, a permanent member (the Soviet Union) that was a totalitarian regime—China would become communist in 1949, with well-known consequences.[5] In sum, since 1945 human rights constitute at least in principle the very basis of the international order. After the collapse of the Soviet Union and the beginning of the globalization process, the universality of human rights was progressively reaffirmed (with much resistance, of course) at the world level, in particular in the domain of criminal law: the struggle against impunity concerning the

2. See Benoit Frydman and Guy Haarscher, *Philosophie du droit*, 2d ed., Paris: Dalloz (2001) 138.
3. The vote for the declaration was unanimous (48 votes, plus 8 abstentions coming from South Africa, Saudi Arabia, the USSR and its satellites).
4. Out of 185 members of the UN, 144 have so far ratified the first Covenant, 142 the second. Approximately half the member states (95) have ratified the Optional Protocol (which opens, among other things, a right to individual petition to the Committee of Human Rights).
5. See Jean Pasqualini, *Prisonnier de Mao. Sept ans de travail dans un camp en Chine*, Paris: Gallimard, coll. "Témoins" (1974).

most serious violations of human rights (war crimes, crimes against humanity, genocide) acquired a new momentum and led to the creation of ad hoc international tribunals (for the former Yugoslavia and Rwanda), then to an International Criminal Court that will begin to function in 2003.[6]

Today—and this is the very topic of this volume—this globalization (universalization) is sometimes challenged. In order to avoid conceptual confusion (which only benefits tyrants), let us distinguish between various types of attacks against the universality of human rights.

2. Frontal Attacks

The primacy of universal human rights is challenged from many points of view. Frontal attacks are explicit clashes between human rights and other values. Let us quickly give some important examples of such a strategy.

2.1 The European extreme right: xenophobia and racism

In France the extreme right has been the subject of much recent discussion because of Le Pen's strong showing in the first round of the presidential elections in May 2002 (he severely lost the second round to Chirac). The *Front national* has a history of racism, anti-Semitism, hatred of foreigners, and discriminatory policies called "*préférence nationale.*" In brief: Le Pen strives to promote values that are blatantly at odds with universal human rights. But we shall see later that he also attempts to acquire a sort of respectability by paying lip service to (and distorting the very notion of) human rights. Hitler also alternated violently anti-Semitic discourse with more moderate speech dedicated in particular to winning the favor of the Junkers and Hindenburg.[7] But as nationalism, provided it was not expressed with the brutality of the SA, it was palatable, and he did not have to go so far as Le Pen[8] in defending democratic values.

---

6. Belgium has even passed a statute in 1999 giving its jurisdictions "universal competence" on these crimes. Many controversies arose about such a generous idea and its potential perverse effects, see Guy Haarscher, "La loi de compétence universelle n'arrêtera pas la regression," in *Le Soir*, Brussels (5 December 2001).
7. See Georges Goriely, *Hitler prend le pouvoir*, 2d ed., Bruxelles: Editions Complexe (1999).
8. But even if Le Pen now pays tribute to republican values and "regrets" what he said notably on the "detail" of history (the Shoah), he still defends the *préférence nationale*, that is, official discrimination. The justification for such a policy is rather sophisticated: I prefer my daughter to my cousin, he says, then my cousin to my neighbor, etc. So, by analogy, I prefer the French to the "Others," even if they work in France, pay taxes, etc.

2.2 "Asian" or other values against Western ethnocentrism

In 1993, at the Second World Conference on Human Rights organized under the auspices of the UN, the Chinese representatives attacked human rights as being, at least in some respects, in opposition to "Asian values." Singapore (and also Malaysia) made the same point, although, as we shall see hereunder, the violation of certain first generation human rights was justified in the name of development—that is, broadly speaking, social rights.

2.3 Islamism

Since the September 11 attacks, the positions taken by the Al Qaeda group have been aired on CNN and Al Jazeera. Beyond the classical critiques of the American policy concerning Israel and Iraq, Bin Laden made a point that is worth closer inspection: he attacked *secularization*. The word is complex. Generally speaking, it means that in Modern Times increasingly more spheres of social life are experienced without any reference to—or intrusion by—a church. So the "eternal" or its self-proclaimed representatives are less able to rule in secular (that is: temporal, "in the world"[9]) matters. Secularism in *this* sense means: the State does not intervene in non-secular ("celestial") matters, which are the prerogative of conscience, that is, liberty and autonomy of the individual. The concept of secularism is not against religion per se: it is against the political domination of a certain church over individuals who do not accept its authority; it is against a State that serves as the secular arm of a denomination. Of course, secularism has also meant that *only secular matters exist, the rest is an illusion*. This is a (protected) opinion in open societies, but of course not the official "opinion" of the government, which has to remain perfectly neutral in these matters. Now one could consider that religion is not only an illusion, but that it is a *dangerous* illusion, preventing people from attacking their true oppressors and inciting them to accept reality as it is (the product of the unfathomable ways of Providence). So it is that Marx labeled religion "the opium of the people." Of course, the latter opinion is also permitted (and protected) in liberal States. But what would definitely make secularism an unacceptable political attitude is if religion would be considered (1) an illusion, (2) a dangerous illusion, and (3) a dangerous illusion that the State should extirpate by force. This is precisely what the Communist parties did on the basis of Marx's thesis. The *latter* kind of secularization (there is nothing beyond the "secular," and people who think differently will be persecuted) is of course not only aggressively anti-religious: it

9. The French language has retained the link between "secular" (*séculier*) and "century" (*le siècle*).

also runs counter to the first (legitimate) idea of secularism; that is, the State does not intervene in non-secular matters, and so doing liberates a space for conscience and autonomy.

The Islamists attack *both* kinds of secularization, the "bad" version as well as the "good." There is then, on their part, a frontal attack on freedom of conscience (which presupposes the "good" secularization process and the neutrality of the State in spiritual matters)—on what is perhaps the most fundamental of all human rights.[10]

2.4 "African values" (Mobutu and "authenticity")

A very common argument against colonialism and, after 1960, against neocolonialism is the following: the critiques coming from the West and addressed to African postcolonial leaders are supposed to reflect European ethnocentrism and to subordinate "African values" to alien principles of behavior. President Mobutu of Zaire was particularly apt at playing such a game: when the Belgians (former colonial ruler) or the Americans, or NGOs, criticized blatant violations of human rights on the part of his regime, he answered by invoking traditional African authority, thus rejecting a critique originating from "outside" the culture he was supposed to embody. This is a very perverse argument. As for China invoking "Asian values," we could retort that the Mobutu (or the Chinese) regime is a product of what was the *worst* of the Western political ideologies in the nineteenth and twentieth centuries: fascism and bolshevism—both being very popular in some parts of the Third World. Instead of a debate between Western values (human rights) and African or Asian values, we have very often, as a matter of fact, a confrontation between "bad" Western values (the ideology of the unitary party, use of modern propaganda tools, etc.) and "good" Western values (human rights). This confrontation drastically weakens the "authenticity" argument ("our" values vs. "your" values) by substantially, and not peripherally, transforming the debate into a discussion about the validity of different Western political philosophies.

2.5 Provisional conclusions about "frontal attacks"

Frontal attacks are difficult from an intellectual perspective: they run counter to the official ideology of the international community, that is, human

10. See Jellinek's thesis on the fundamental character of freedom of conscience in the history of human rights. In particular, see his controversy with Boutmy, in 1902 in "La Déclaration des droits de l'homme et du citoyen et Mr. Jellinek," *Annales de l'École Libre des Sciences Politiques* (1902) 415.

rights.[11] As it were, proponents of these positions will not have access to the normal public space, having not paid the "entrance fee" (the acceptance of human rights as *the* fundamental political value). For this reason these attacks are not often made by States (official members of the United Nations), but by more informal groups, assisted by some governments in a more or less clandestine way.[12]

A frontal attack can also be partial. Muslim States have strongly objected to a right to *change* religion (which is of course fundamental for freedom of conscience) because, according to their interpretation of Islam, abandoning the religion of the Prophet would be equivalent to an act of *treason*. In response, it has been argued that changing religion today no longer entails changing political loyalties and rallying hostile Christian States, "crusaders," etc.[13]

3. Non-Frontal Attacks

3.1 The problem: the application

The non-frontal attack is different. We are not, as was the case before, confronted with a clash of values. On the contrary, in the present situation the value of human rights is supposedly accepted, but the problem is related to application: particular circumstances make the respect of human rights (or part of them) *unaffordable*.

The "affordability argument" is, strictly speaking, only compatible with an "internal" perspective: it is based on premises that are, at least prima facie, compatible with the value of human rights. "We cannot afford it" means: we

11. Actually, the argument is also valid for a national community: this was shown in a dramatic way by the rejection of Le Pen in the second round of the French presidential election on 5 May 2002. His *half*-watered-down discourse did not reassure the French: his past is known (particularly the documented use of torture in Algeria, which, curiously enough, was not often mentioned in the campaign), as is his present (his support of "national preference," that is, official legal discrimination).

12. In the majority of cases, the Islamists have failed in their attempted "re-islamization from the top," see Gilles Kepel, *La revanche de Dieu. Chrétiens, juifs et musulmans à la reconquête du monde*, Paris: Editions du Seuil (1991) 56-81. Only Iran is a relatively successful product of such a process, that is, seizing State power (the Taliban lost power in Afghanistan after September 11 and the American military action). Iraq acts in a more perverse way on Islam, invoking sovereignty in order to argue against foreign intervention. (Saddam Hussein violently crushed Islamist revolts that took place in the south of the country.)

13. See the discussions on this topic during the preparatory phase of the 1981 Declaration Against Intolerance and Discrimination Based on Religion or Belief, in Natan Lerner, *Group Rights and Discrimination in International Law*, Dordrecht: Kluwer (1991) 75-98.

fully accept the validity of these principles, but the circumstances prevent us from concretely applying them *hic and nunc* (here and now). Sometimes such an argument is sound, sometimes it is only an excuse. There is an interesting example of such an uncertainty in the domain of minority protection, a special and very problematic category of human rights. At the Paris Conference of 1919, President Woodrow Wilson wanted to introduce into the Draft Covenant of the League of Nations a general minority protection clause. After many debates, this proposal was finally rejected. The opposition to the clause can, generally speaking, be interpreted in two different ways. Either, which was very often the case, governments wanted to protect ethnic majorities and thought that such a provision would require them to appease their minorities. Or, the delegates who finally discarded the proposal acted out of an ethics of responsibility (in a Weberian sense): that is, they were not motivated by ethnic bigotry; on the contrary, they found that protecting all minorities in the world was, as such, a legitimate and commendable goal. But they did not want to blindly apply the principle *fiat justitia, pereat mundus*. In other words, they took into account the consequences of their political choices: a responsible leader or actor accords a definite importance to the *feasibility* (or "affordability") of the policies he promotes or supports. If a policy will predictably create uncontrollable phenomena, then the ethics of responsibility will "advise" them *not to apply* a principle they might fundamentally agree with, because the consequences might be worse than the present situation.

Another example, borrowed from the same domain, derives from the question of the borders of the newly decolonized countries in Africa after 1960. Many African intellectuals had long concluded that these borders, drawn at the end of the nineteenth century by the colonial powers, did not create (in any sense) the conditions for the emancipation of the people. Around 1960, the conventional wisdom was that the liberated should rid themselves of these colonial remnants. A few years later, the Organization of African Unity adopted the principle of the intangibility of frontiers. Why such a radical change of position? Again, for the two above-mentioned reasons: interests, of dictators in preserving "their" political territory; and an ethics of responsibility, related to the awareness of the potential chain reaction that would be set into motion by the altering of frontiers in a single place, even if such modifications created a situation more favorable to ethnic minorities.

As an end to these preliminary remarks, it only makes sense to speak of "affordability" in the context of *internal* arguments ("We would like to do so, but we cannot"). "External" arguments, based on different values, Asian or others, which are not subordinate to a "Western" value system, are independent of any idea of affordability: *"Even if we could afford it, we would not do it."*

3.2 The argument (excuse?) of economic development

Socio-economic development is a good example of the "internal" argument. Lee Kuan Yew used it to try to justify his authoritarian regime in Singapore (although he also invoked Asian values, an "external" argument). The idea that economic development and the promotion of social rights presuppose the "temporary" non-respect of first generation human rights has been defended many times and in various forms in the Third World. The argument cites (second generation) human rights to justify the limitation or sometimes blatant violation of basic liberties. Therefore the argument of development is clearly different from the "values" argument: it is prima facie compatible with an affirmation of human rights, but "later," when the economy will permit it.[14] Of course, this kind of political attitude can often be interpreted as a sort of "escape route": it allows a political leader to win on all planes by paying lip service, without real commitment, to the value of human rights and by delaying their effective application to a future that will never be realized (the *lendemains qui chantent* will never come). Such a tribute paid by vice to virtue would of course reduce human rights to a vague abstract ideal that has no meaning at all in the present experience. In the Soviet system, the primacy of social rights had similarly perverse effects: contrary to first generation rights (which involve freedom of political criticism), second generation ones can be reassuring for a despotic power. Indeed, *panem et circenses*, as the Romans conceived them, satisfy the people at least in a certain way, making claims to freedom less pressing.[15] To summarize the argument: the future against the present, and social rights[16] against liberties. These two rhetorical strategies allow political leaders to neglect (or suppress) liberties in the name of human rights themselves or, as in the case of communism, in the name of a bright future that will be even more liberating than "simple" human rights: the disappearance of the State and of the market, with the advent of an egalitarian community free of alienation). In other terms: such a legitimizing discourse allows the violators of (first generation) rights to pretend that they have paid the "entrance ticket" to the international community. Now in *certain* cases the argument might be valid (although very dangerous). But it remains that development without transparency and good governance, without the rule of

14. John Rawls, the liberal thinker par excellence, uses this argument in *A Theory of Justice*, Cambridge, Mass.: Harvard University Press (1971).

15. But we know that the guarantee of social rights in the context of a closed and firmly State-controlled society leads to economic absurdities (the skyrocketing of subsidies, and, eventually, the collapse of the whole system: this was one of the reasons for the implosion of the Soviet Union at the end of the 1980s and the beginning of the 1990s).

16. When "third generation" rights will be invoked, the confusion will substantially increase.

law and the respect of at least "some" first generation rights, is almost always doomed to failure.

3.3 The argument of emergency

Regardless of the problems accompanying the process of economic development, there are other ways of professing a *wish* to defend human rights, only to then argue that one *cannot* due to the consequences of such a policy. One such instance is the situation of emergency that is covered by Art. 15 of the European Convention on Human Rights. Everyone knows that invoking emergency allows rulers to violate human rights because the very existence of the political community is (or is supposed to be) in danger. In *some* cases, it is true that defending the security of the people and the nation cannot be done efficiently while strictly respecting certain basic liberties. We have seen after September 11 how problematic the struggle against an elusive enemy who threatens the very lives of innocent people can be. As far as human rights are concerned: how is it possible to eradicate terrorism without using methods that are less "liberal" than in normal times? In the beginning of 2002, American intellectuals wrote a "letter" in which they conditionally defended the war led by the United States against Al Qaeda in Afghanistan. By invoking the theory of a just war,[17] they accepted that military action could be a legitimate response to prevent other acts of terrorism, even if such a war would involve recourse to "violence," and particularly the unavoidable, and hotly debated, "collateral damage." Situations of emergency have very often been used as the "internal" argument par excellence: a temporary violation of human rights is supposed to be indispensable for the reaffirmation of a society guaranteeing...human rights. Many checks have been imagined in order to limit the scope of such violence and avoid the catastrophe of the French revolutionary *Terreur*, or the worst periods of Stalinism, or, until recently, the dictatorships in Latin America, or ethnic cleansing in former Yugoslavia. Art. 15 of the European Convention on Human Rights allows governments, in certain circumstances and with the exception of some rights that should not be *derogated* from, to limit or suppress some human rights that are guaranteed in the treaty itself. Similarly, humanitarian law ascribes some limits to the use of violence in war.[18] We shall see in the next section how complex the question of human rights is in the post-September 11 emergency situation.

---

17. This argument has been mainly influenced by one of the signatories, Michael Walzer, author of *Just and Unjust Wars: A Moral Argument with Historical Illustrations*, 2d ed., New York: Basic Books (1992). See also my reaction to the letter: Guy Haarscher, "La guerre d'Afghanistan est-elle juste?" *Le Soir*, Brussels (25 February 2002).

18. On this notion of limit and the correlative problems, see Guy Haarscher, *Les démocraties survivront-elles au terrorisme?*, Bruxelles: Editions Labor (2002) *passim*.

3.4 Double standards in international politics: some reflections on the struggle against Al Qaeda

It is worth posing again the question of human rights in the light of the events of September 11.[19] One typically hears: politics is much too realist to take charge of the human rights ideal in a coherent way. States are immersed in the world of force relationships, that is, they live in what Hobbes called a "state of nature," even if some progress toward a "cosmopolitan order" in the Kantian sense has been recently realized. In brief: if a political leader is faithful to some rules of conduct, these rules will be based on an ethics of responsibility, in the sense that the great sociologist Max Weber gave to this phrase in the beginning of the twentieth century. Thus the leader will accept having dirty hands, will not necessarily respect *hic and nunc* the principles (human rights), but will, in a strategic way, try to realize them in the future of a better world. We know that if this discourse that puts the emphasis on consequences (for which the leader feels "responsible") is pushed to the extremes, the application of accepted principles will be indefinitely delayed, that is, put off until the bright promised distant future. Even in a democratic State, where the exercise of power is checked by the rule of law and civil liberties, international politics presuppose very problematic choices concerning human rights. How is it possible to reconcile national egoism on the one hand, together with the geopolitical, military, and economic strategies of States; the legitimate interests of their citizens; and, on the other hand, the intransigent defense of human rights everywhere in the world? Are not these incompatible aims doomed to clash? Hence the attempt to invest the judiciary with the task of prosecuting and judging the most serious violations of human rights law (war crimes, crimes against humanity, genocide). But in the absence of a real *political* international order, the action of prosecutors and judges will be dependent on the goodwill of governments. And even if, as we have seen in the introduction, the International Criminal Court offers hope that in the long run the culture of impunity will disappear, there are still emergencies that impose on political power an immediate (or short-term) reaction.

3.4.1 "Classical" double standard

Let us consider for a moment the situation of human rights in the world just before the attacks against New York and Washington on September 11. Let us begin with some meaningful examples: brutal repression of the Chechens by the Russian army; planned "ethnocide" of the Sinkiang Uighurs and the Tibetans by the Chinese government; dictatorships (sometimes on the verge

19. *Ibid.*, 21 ff.

of madness) in the former Soviet republics of Central Asia (Turkmenistan, Uzbekistan, Tajikistan, Kazakhstan, Kyrgyzstan); and the second Intifada in Israel (suicide attacks and brutal repression). Violations of human rights everywhere (with notable differences from one place to another, and some relative exceptions) in the Arab countries. Worrisome status of human rights in the non-Arab Muslim countries (Iran, Afghanistan, Pakistan, with Indonesia on the verge of dismantling and chaos). These endemic and sometimes trivialized human rights abuses are known by all the specialized international organizations; they are tolerated while trying to institute change here and there. Sometimes, progress in certain human rights is a consequence (but not necessarily an aim) of an international action: war against Saddam Hussein to liberate Kuwait; NATO intervention in Bosnia to stop ethnic cleansing on the part—essentially, but not only—of the Serbs; war in Kosovo against Milosevic to end the oppression of the Albanian population. In these particular cases, each time the protection of universal human rights had to be supplemented, so to speak, by other geostrategic or economic motives, that is, linked to the particular interests of the intervening States. We can ironically call "happy" those people whose rights have been violated when such violation is an embarrassment, in one way or another, to the outside world, and better, if possible, to the powerful: the world then takes interest in their predicament and they benefit from strong, possibly military, action. The violation of their rights alone surely would not have triggered such a move.

Of course, impenitent idealists will draw from this the most radical consequences: human rights do not count, only the sordid interests of the Great Powers (today, the United States) are important—all this is only *Realpolitik*. Such criticism of course reappears, sometimes in an intensified form, in relation the war against Al Qaeda and the Taliban who supported Bin Laden. It is worthwhile then to analyze the argument in a somewhat deeper manner. Kuwait, Bosnia, Kosovo, and Afghanistan: in each case vigorous military action effected progress, even partial, for human rights. It liberated the Kuwaiti people from foreign occupation and protects the Kurds in the North and the Shiites in the South from Iraqi war planes. For the Bosnians, it ended the continual shelling of Sarajevo and the unbearable policy that Mladic and Karadzic implemented with the support of Belgrade—but it does not spare Srebrenica the horror. It frees the Albanian Kosovars from terrible Serbian oppression and puts Kosovo under international protection. And it ends for the Afghans (in particular for the women) the merciless repression on the part of the "students in religion," while (maybe) helping to prevent new terrorist attacks in the West (or elsewhere). Now these results are quite imperfect, and one may even fear here and there a deterioration of human rights protections for some groups—I think of the Serbian minority in Kosovo (but the fall of Milosevic will probably solve many problems) or of the fate of the Iraqi people who are victims of an embargo that has become absurd and of ruthless repression by the Baghdad regime, or maybe also of the people in the West who might suffer from a certain radicalization of the law-and-order ideology after September 11 and the war in Afghanistan. Nevertheless, nobody can reasonably defend Saddam Hussein, or Milosevic, or mullah Omar: their fall is a victory for human rights, even when it is partial, precarious, or ambiguous.

Let us suppose that the good anti-American soul accepts these arguments. He or she will rightly add another reason to suspect the purity of such a struggle: double standard. A political struggle is *never* pure. If one tries to measure relative progress in human rights against an inaccessible moral ideal (*fiat justitia, pereat mundus*), one risks underestimating the real advances that create rights, e.g., a new sense of freedom or a fragile possibility of happiness. But let us confront the "double standard" argument, which is by no means negligible: at the time of the military operations against Iraq (in the early 1990s), an atrocious civil war was tearing Liberia apart. The massacres that resulted from this "domestic" war left the international community largely indifferent: the horrible crimes that were committed in that "grey" area in Africa would anyway not have the least repercussion in our countries; they would not put us in danger. Actually, they would not have the least impact on our way of life. This war continues on in the region (today in neighboring Sierra Leone[20]) and is intensified by the traffic of gems. But who in the international community takes a real interest? Africa today is what is called, in a derogatory way, a *backwater*: that is, a continent almost totally deprived of strategic interest. It *had* great strategic interest when the Soviet Union used it in order to advance its pawns in the geopolitical game of the Cold War. At that time, human rights did not really count: any dictator, provided he was able to "hold" his country, even by using the most unacceptable means (for instance, Mobutu in former Zaire), became a potential ally in the struggle against Communism. Today, Africa does not interest us any longer—even the atrocious Rwandan genocide did not have any influence on us (this country "counts" so little on the strategic map of the world...). Africa seems always to be on the losing side as far as the international defense of human rights is concerned: either (as during the Cold War) one did not criticize overly the allied governments out of fear that they would easily change sides and strengthen the position of the Soviet Union; or (post-1989) one has no more interest in it (what would be the "use" of struggling for human rights in a region devoid of any major strategic stakes?).

Anyway, after the Soviet retreat in the 1990s, Afghanistan itself had become a backwater. Except for courageous representatives of NGOs (when

20. Recently, the British sent troops there under the aegis of the UN.

the Taliban allowed them to work in the field or did not prosecute them for proselytism), who was really moved by the terrible predicament of the women? Afghanistan was no longer a strategic area, human rights violations did not count anymore—or so little... The "double standard" argument is thus quite powerful: if some human rights violations generate attention and effective response while others, as serious as the former, are simply "forgotten," sometimes in a quite deliberate—quite "political"—way, is this not irrefutable proof that human rights are only a cover hiding completely different goals related to *Realpolitik* and the interests of the Great Powers? But such an argument only creates an imbalance in the analysis I have just presented. Indeed, it would certainly be absurd to try to deny the famous "double standard," which means that human rights will be defended only if *other factors* motivate political leaders to action. One must, however, keep in mind the fact that more often than not democracies, first of all the United States, did intervene, in particular during the Cold War, *against* human rights (in Vietnam, in Chile, etc.). When an "impure" policy (as is always the case) improves a human rights situation, even locally and in a relative way, why be fussy? Actually, there is a missing factor in such argumentation, namely, *public opinion*. Let us never forget that, in a democracy, public opinion is crucial for political leaders, first of all—and this is the most immediate reason—because they must be reelected. What could prevent civil society from critically and vigilantly supporting such actions by making sure that the goal (human rights) is not opportunely forgotten—this happens—but above all that *one does not lose in one place what one has won in another one?* Indeed, such a "localism" would be a particularly devious way of weakening universal human rights protection.

3.4.2 Radical double standard

The double standard has a more radical dimension which cannot be reduced to the opposition between strategic countries or regions and backwaters. In certain cases, there is a risk of *degradation* of human rights protection in one place at the very time when, somewhere else, there is hope that an *improvement* will take place. International action presupposes the building of a coalition: even the very isolationist Bush administration has had to resort to it in the war against Al Qaeda. Now, one chooses allies in order to make action more efficient. Let us take a very famous example: during the Gulf War Syria's support was crucial. But Hafez el Assad's regime was catastrophic as far as the respect of the most elementary liberties is concerned. Saddam was first to be forced out of Kuwait, while Saudi Arabia had to be protected against invasion (concerning human rights, the latter regime recently beheaded homosexuals...). If Saddam had succeeded, the outside (in particular: Western) world would have become dependent for its oil supply on an unpredictable and unscrupulous dictator (in 1988 he used chemical weapons in Halabja against Kurdish civilians). This strategic alliance weakened criticism of Damascus' human rights violations and—not negligible in the post-September 11 context—its support of international terrorism. But considering human rights only from the strategic perspective of political (and military) leaders is a perverted view: supporting Assad was ipso facto aggravating the already blatant abandonment of his people or prisoners to his arbitrary power. One does not criticize overly a precious ally in an eminently risky international action.

The situation is very similar in the recently built coalition that is aimed at destroying Al Qaeda by toppling the Taliban regime, which has protected Al Qaeda or fallen hostage to it. The United States, the European Union, Russia, and China were for the first time in the same camp. But unanimity in the struggle against terrorism can be misleading. The Russians wage a barbarous war in Chechnya, which has been criticized as such by all human rights organizations. Nothing, not even Chechen terrorism, can justify such atrocities, especially against civilians. But the alliance between the United States and Russia in the legitimate struggle against international terrorism might—will—have the perverse effect of further silencing the already cautious criticism of Putin's colonial war in the Caucasus. Silence on Grozny (or what remains of it) in the name of the eradication of Al Qaeda? One could reason in the same way about China: repression and ethnocide of the Uighurs in Sinkiang and of the Tibetans are now less likely to be denounced for what they are.

3.4.3 Radical and perverse double standard

We must make a further distinction between Chechnya and Sinkiang on the one hand, and Tibet on the other. In the latter case, a people with a millenary Buddhist tradition suffer the worst human rights violations without a terrorist response: the Dalai Lama is himself an apostle of non-violence. But in the Caucasus and Sinkiang where the repressed population is Muslim, the absurd repressive policies of, respectively, the Russians and the Chinese *feed* Islamist terrorism and strengthen Al Qaeda. Here we are not in the presence of a *simple*, as it were, double standard, be it "normal" or radical. In the case of Tibet, the focus on anti-terrorism will probably lead to a softening of the criticism of the ethnocide in the Himalaya. Here, in this zero-sum game, what is won on one side will be lost on the other: help us (the United States) to liberate the Afghans from the Taliban and you (the Chinese) will have still more leverage in Tibet. In the case of the Uighurs and the Chechens, the situation is still more complex: the human rights situation will not only become even worse than it was before September 11 (one dares not embarrass such complacent allies), but giving a free hand to the despots in Moscow and Beijing can strengthen terrorism because these governments will be able to pursue a policy that literally besieges despised populations. Here, one could say that human rights might lose on all sides: the situation in Chechnya and Sinkiang could deteriorate, which could then encourage terrorism (only the Afghan women would maybe "win" something).

The situation is eminently paradoxical: terrorism will be weakened "here" (in Afghanistan) and strengthened "there" (in lawless regions where befriended tyrants will be able to exploit freely without risking international pressure). If we were to summarize the situation in a few words we could say that the Gulf War that took place "elsewhere" did not alter the disastrous human rights situation in Liberia, while the war did help to improve that of the Kuwaitis (but the Americans spoiled the opportunity for an improvement of the situation of the Iraqi people). In the case of Tibet, the situation is *aggravated* by the necessary alliance against terrorism. Finally, in the case of Chechnya and Sinkiang, human rights has become more or less "taboo" (as in Tibet), but this silence *feeds terrorism itself*. In the latter case, one can *truly* affirm that the struggle against terrorism contradicts the proclaimed goal: guaranteeing human rights.

Not only Russia and China put the coalition in such an awkward position: Central Asian republics like Turkmenistan, Uzbekistan, Tajikistan and Kazakhstan play a strategic role in the anti-terrorist struggle. The dictators of these republics also feed, because of their short-sighted policies, the networks that are supposed to be eradicated.

And there are also the Arab—generally Muslim—allies. In such a context, one is accustomed to label *moderate* the "friendly" States. This is a particularly misleading term: these regimes are moderate only from the point of view of the West and its interests (a more appropriate label would be "docile"). As far as their domestic policy is concerned, they are corrupt and dictatorial and therefore considered illegitimate by populations which are influenced more by fundamentalists than by liberals. The *real moderates* are, so to speak, squeezed between corrupt powers and Islamists who would win (as the Algerian case showed) non-rigged general elections. Here again, supporting these regimes might backlash by indirectly feeding terrorism.

4. Counterattacking by Accusing

4.1 The argument of tolerance: setting the fox to mind the geese

The argument reads: universalism does not take into account the sensitivities of religious majorities (for instance, by outlawing gender discrimination although it may be prescribed by some religions). This is, as it were, an inversion of the reasoning. The "accused" is no longer saying: *we* cannot be faithful to the principle of human rights because we have other values, or because we cannot apply them here and now (for instance, for the sake of socio-economic development; or because of a situation of emergency; or because no politics—in particular international—can exist without "dirty hands"). On the contrary, the accusation is now simply reversed:[21] *you* are not loyal to *your* values by criticizing *us*. One of these celebrated Enlightenment values is tolerance: does it not play a central role in human rights culture? Now, by not accepting *our* "difference," you are *yourself intolerant.*

In my opinion this is a particularly perverse interpretation of the idea of tolerance. Indeed, the latter consists of protecting the "different" *individual* who believes in something other than the imposed orthodoxy (the "theologico-political"); the accomplishment of tolerance is freedom of conscience. Here, the notion of tolerance is used to prove *exactly the contrary*: that freedom of conscience (or individual autonomy, or gender equality, etc.) must be limited. It often happens that the adversary, instead of clearly referring to other values (see "Asian values" for the Chinese, or fascism, or the contemporary extreme Right—at least when it does not seek "respectability"—or Islamism), apparently invokes human rights by *subtly distorting them at their very intellectual core*. So we have here a *third* situation: neither the values themselves nor their application are at issue; the *language* of human rights is perverted, the fox is set to mind the geese.

Even the European Court of Human Rights, which is the most efficient guarantor of human rights in a regional order, sometimes uses the word "tolerance" in a distorted sense (that is, in relation to the respect of values and collective practices instead of individual liberty).[22] We might also mention the often debated notion of Muslim tolerance in the past: referring to the *millet* system of struggle against Western arrogance is one thing (for instance, the declaration made shortly after September 11 by Prime Minister Silvio

---

21. I have analyzed such a phenomenon, which Albert Camus called "inversion of the positions of the hangman and the victim," in Haarscher, *op. cit.*, note 18.
22. See my comment on *Otto-Preminger v. Austria* (1994) in Guy Haarscher, "Tolerance of the Intolerant?" *Ratio Juris*, 10 (2) (1997) 236-46.

Berlusconi of Italy, in which he referred to Islam as a "medieval" and per se intolerant religion); considering it a solution to contemporary problems of religious pluralism would be another. This would amount to progress in many Muslim countries but would not be *enough*: freedom of conscience is "more" than simple "tolerance."

4.2 Imperialism and neocolonialism

Can universalism of law (and particularly human rights) be considered an instrument of *imperialist* or *neocolonialist* intervention? Here again, the counterattack consists of an accusation: *you* are incoherent, you do not respect your *own* values at the very moment when you try to impose them. The well-known right of intervention is, of course, the focus of such an attack. It can be criticized in various ways. First, by saying: "*We* do not have to respect human rights because these are not *our* values"; second by saying: "Yes, we must respect them, they are our values as they are yours, but imposing them on us is none of your business, especially if you use (military) violence." Third, by saying: "Yes, we accept human rights as a fundamental standard of political conduct. Yes, an international instance with a legitimate power of coercion should impose them on everyone, but *you* are not entitled to do that yourselves (United States; humanitarian interventions, notably by France in the nineteenth century, etc.) because of your "normal" geopolitical interests (every government is accountable to its people before being accountable to the rest of the world), or because of your hidden, shameful—imperialist, neocolonialist—strategies."

5. Provisional Conclusion: Are Human Rights an Ethnocentric Notion?

Human rights are *proclaimed* to be universal in character. We do not have the space here to enter into the details of the philosophical and theological debate about the justification of such a radical, supposedly transcultural, claim. But let us outline some brief elements of the problem. Philosophy first. Is there a rational defense of human rights that would make them acceptable to any reasonable and "in good faith" interlocutor? Hume questioned the very possibility of rationalizing norms (or of intellectually "jumping" from facts to norms).[23]

23 . It is not contrary to reason to prefer the destruction of the whole world to the scratching of my finger. It is not contrary to reason for me to choose my total ruin, to prevent the least uneasiness of an Indian or person wholly unknown to me." David Hume, *A Treatise of Human Nature*, London: Fontana-Collins (1972) II:157.

Jefferson's God, in the Declaration of Independence of 1776, played a supplementary role: God gave men the natural rights to life, liberty, and the pursuit of happiness (rights from which the whole ensemble of human rights law can easily be deduced). And we *know* these rights in a self-evident way. So God and reason, supernatural light and natural light are, as it were, united to give human rights a "transcendental" foundation. But such a philosopher's God, who transcends the various denominations and is supposedly "valid" for them all, is quite abstract; moreover, it is not at all certain that believers will always easily accept it: such a liberal Protestant conception of religion is unlikely to generate a universal consensus. At the time when the philosopher's God was at the center of Descartes' argumentation, Pascal opposed to it the God of Abraham, Isaac, and Jacob; that is, a *concrete* God, and not an abstract intellectual construct. It is probable then that the God of theism has not the intellectual power for rebutting Hume's "scratching of my finger" argument. Now the more God becomes related to a concrete community, a particular liturgy, etc., the more universalism is in danger: Muslims will be loyal to the God of Muhammad (the most radical will only be loyal to the *Shari'ah*), Jews to the Torah, and Christians to their particular "denominations."

The liberalization of religion is very often considered a Western phenomenon. Pluralism, democracy, and human rights have "won" in the context of—and against—a religion that, at least in principle, contained the notion of the separation between God and Caesar. But such an assumption may be quite misleading. Everything depends on the choice of the *interlocutor*. It has been argued that the reference to specific values (Asian, African, ethno-national, religious) is very often an excuse on the part of dictators to avoid intervention from outside. The right of people to self-determination often boils down to the right of a dictator to "dispose" of his "own" people. So the argument of "cultural specificity" has a very different meaning when it is adhered to by the oppressed than when it is invoked by the oppressor. Now one can argue that no human being wants to be arbitrarily deprived of life, to be tortured, to be exploited or despised. Such a core of human dignity is probably universal. It is true that the *interpretation* of such a basic notion will vary from culture to culture (in particular, a notion of freedom of expression that includes—as stated in the famous *Handyside* decision by the European Court of Human Rights (1976)—speech "that offends, shocks or disturbs the State or any sector of the population" will not be easily accepted all over the world). But there are always liberal elements in a culture, which is a complex ensemble that evolves in various ways. Showing that the universality of human rights does not come from a Western ethnocentrism, but is, so to speak, the patrimony of humanity as a whole is a very difficult—but not impossible—task. Above all, it will have to avoid the dangers inherent in "localizing" human rights in the ways I have briefly summarized above.

Chapter 5

Tatsuo Inoue

Reinstating the Universal in the Discourse of Human Rights and Justice

Human rights and justice are the most typical of universalistic values. What are claimed to be human rights are universally attributed to all human beings simply by virtue of their being human. Justice excludes particularistic discriminations and requires us to give others universalizable reasons (i.e., reasons that are acceptable both to us and them, irrespective of *who* we and they happen to be) when we are responsible for differentiated treatments that are to their detriment. Justice in this universalistic sense underlies both human rights and the idea of the rule of law (as opposed to the rule of personal will). The universalistic nature of human rights and justice has been a source of their strong moral appeal. But as the universalistic language comes to sound more and more naïve and even dangerous to the sophisticated and disenchanted contemporary spirit, this feature of human rights and justice now seems to have become a chief source of skepticism and reservation.

The end of the Cold War briefly heightened faith in universal values partly because it brought about a euphoric feeling that liberal democracy with its own conception of human rights and justice won a final victory over its chief ideological rivals, Marxism and other variants of communism, and partly because it seemed to have removed the obstacles (such as the rampant

András Sajó (ed.), Human Rights with Modesty: The Problem of Universalism, *121-139.*

uses of veto in the Security Council) to UN-backed international cooperation to implement shared international norms. But this faith did not prevail long. Another acute ideological rivalry was stirred up by the proponents of "Asian values" who denied the universal validity of the "Western conception of human rights." Discontent with the Western politico-ideological hegemony has been fomented in the Islamic world. Trust has been undermined in the fairness of the collective operations initiated by the major powerful Western countries in enforcing international norms and implementing human rights, to the extent that cynicism about these norms and rights has been engendered by the blatant double standards, callous indifference to "collateral" civilian casualties, and lack of sincere and sustained commitment to humanitarian aid.[1]

Whatever may be the background political conditions for the skepticism and cynicism about universal values, it has become a dominant tendency in contemporary legal and political philosophy to attack or abandon universalism in favor of a contextualist justification and interpretation of political values. On the one hand, this tendency can be found in the contemporary critics of liberalism that was once a stronghold of universalistic conceptions of human rights and justice. Communitarians reject liberal universalism as too thin to give us a morally effective identity and erosive of more specific and richer conceptions of the common good embedded in the traditions of specific political communities. Civic republicans reject it as giving individual rights philosophical priority over democratic deliberation and popular sovereignty and undermining our civic virtue that is based on our sharing a sense of special responsibility for the particular intermediary and national communities to which we belong. Multiculturalists reject it as blind to the importance of cultural identity for human dignity and hostile to group-specific rights that ethnic and national minorities need to overcome the assimilationist pressures generated in particular historical and socio-economic contexts. Feminists reject it as covering up and rationalizing the patriarchal dominance of men over women pervading the particular contexts of everyday "private" life, or as the privileging of the ethics of rights over the ethics of care that require us to understand and respond to the particular needs of individuals in their close personal relationships.

On the other hand, liberalism itself has come to show the tendency to turn its back on universalism. To give a most remarkable example, John Rawls abandoned the claim to philosophical justifiability and universal validity that his liberal theory of justice used to rest on and turned to the "overlap-

1. For searching criticisms of such hypocrisy, see Noam Chomsky, *9-11*, New York: Seven Stories Press (2001), and Thomas Pogge, "Priorities of Global Justice," in Thomas Pogge (ed.), *Global Justice*, Oxford: Blackwell Publishers (2001) 6-23.

ping consensus" embedded in the political culture of Western constitutional democracies for the basis of what he calls political conceptions of justice or political liberalism.[2] Rawls' contextualist conversion was welcomed by Richard Rorty, a neo-pragmatic deconstructionist critic of philosophical universalism and a defender of the postmodern "ethno-centric" version of liberal politics.[3] John Gray presented a blunter formulation of contextualized liberalism with his manifesto of post-liberalism in which he declared the death of liberalism as philosophical doctrine and claimed that its viable substance can be rescued as constitutive of the way of life in Western civil societies.[4]

These moves in contemporary thought can be summed up as a retreat from the philosophical search for the universal to the contextualization of human values into historical and social particularities. In this chapter I aim to rescue philosophical universalism from the current contextualist attack and abandonment by identifying and defending the indispensable functions it has as an epistemological and moral basis for human rights and justice. In the next section I will criticize historical contextualism shared by some communitarians and post-philosophical political liberals, which I think the most important and problematic of the current contextualist turn of political and legal philosophy. In the third section I will present a perspective of context-sensitive critical universalism which shows that we need philosophical universalism just to overcome the vices ascribed to it by contextualists and that the contextualism unmediated by philosophical universalism will reinforce rather than remove these vices.

1. What's Wrong with Historical Contextualism?

Communitarians turn to the historically shaped tradition of their specific political community for the source of values guiding its political practice. Rawls' conversion to political liberalism and other exponents of post-philosophical liberalism share the same metatheory of political values that may be called historical contextualism, but they identify different (liberal rather than communitarian) values as permeated in the tradition of the same political community (typically, the United States) that both they and communitarians are concerned with. This shows that the historical context of the community

2. Cf. John Rawls, *Political Liberalism*, New York: Columbia University Press (1993).
3. Cf. Richard Rorty, "The Priority of Democracy to Philosophy," in *Objectivity, Relativism and Truth*, Cambridge: Cambridge University Press (1991) 175-196 and *id.*, *Contingency, Irony and Solidarity*, Cambridge: Cambridge University Press (1989) 44-69.
4. Cf. John Gray, Post-Liberalism: *Studies in Political Thought*, New York: Routledge (1993).

they resort to is not pre-philosophical data but a product of philosophical reconstruction. They hide their own controversial philosophical commitments in the shade of history; this is unavoidable because history cannot reveal its meaning without the light of philosophy.

The starting point of my argument for this claim is the undeniable fact that the historical context of our society—tradition, political culture, or whatever you may call it—is open to competing interpretations. Given the fact of interpretive rivalry, historical contextualists have two options: interpretive relativism or interpretive rationalism. Interpretive relativists assert that we can choose whatever interpretation we like because no one interpretation is better than another. Interpretive rationalists hold that we have to choose the best of all the competing interpretations because we can distinguish between good and bad (or better and worse) interpretations. Whichever option may be taken, historical contextualism will prove to be self-defeating.

Interpretive relativism is not a negation of philosophical universalism but its most arrogant and inadequate version. An interpretive relativist locates herself in the heights inhabited by the neutral spectator who transcends the interpretive conflicts and passes on all the participants in the conflicts a sweepingly universal meta-interpretive judgment that all of their interpretive claims are equally good (or equally arbitrary or incommensurable), so that there is nothing to distinguish them from one another. The contenders in the interpretive conflicts disagree with each other about which interpretation is correct and ipso facto agree in rejecting this universal meta-interpretive judgment. The relativist spectator claims to *know* that all of the contenders are wrong in rejecting her judgment. She claims that only she is in a privileged position free from the epistemological illusion shared by all the contenders. How can she obtain this privileged knowledge? It is *not* rooted in any given historical context because it goes beyond all the interpretive claims related to such a context. It *is* a very controversial, transcendent, and decontextualized piece of philosophical epistemology. Historical relativism defeats itself if it is based on such an epistemological claim. Moreover, this claim is itself self-defeating if it is based on a further epistemological thesis that no proposition can be true if it lacks a decision procedure for resolving controversy regarding its truth. This thesis implies that interpretive relativism cannot be true because it lacks such a decision procedure.

Interpretive rationalism is better fitted for the standpoint of the participants in the interpretive conflicts. If a historical contextualist takes this option, he has to provide a reason for holding that his interpretation is superior. He may resort to the claim that his interpretation succeeds in digging up "the true fundamental meaning" of the community's tradition buried deep under historical bedrock, as some communitarians do when they claim that interpretive conflicts about derivative meanings of a tradition can be resolved by appealing to the common understanding of its more fundamental meaning or configuration of meanings that they assume, by a postulate, to be out there.[5] If the historical contextualist with a rationalist temper chooses this defense, he is subject to the criticism that he commits the same error as the Platonic hypostatization of meaning that has been castigated as a delusion of philosophical universalism. A Platonic contemplator of the Ideas or the Forms shining in the highest sphere of the universe and a contextualist excavator of a deposit of shared meanings believed to lie in the depths of the down-to-earth human historical practices differ only in that the one loves the metaphor of ascent while the other prefers that of descent. They share the realist theory of meaning which assumes that meanings are some sort of preexistent reality independent of interpretive reconstruction. If we call Platonism "celestial realism," this kind of historical contextualism can be called "terrestrial realism." Terrestrial realism is an inverted Platonism. It subverted the Platonic regime of the Forms but has revived its epistemic authoritarianism in a secularized form.

If historical contextualism is to dissociate itself from terrestrial realism without going back to interpretive relativism, it has to be based on an alternative theory that can explain and guide both the reconstructive function and the validity-claim of interpretation. The philosophical groundwork for such a theory was provided by Willard Quine's theory of "radical translation" that showed factual indeterminacy of meaning[6] and Donald Davidson's theory of interpretation that presented "the principle of charity"—according to which we should choose a linguistic theory that makes true more statements of the object of our interpretation than do any other competing theories equally fitted to the factual linguistic data—as a guide for rational reconstruction of meaning under the unavoidable condition of factual indeterminacy.[7] Ronald Dworkin's theory of "law as integrity" can be seen as a further step to build up these philosophical insights into a general theory of interpretive reconstruction in law and other human practices.[8] We can extract and reformulate the essentials of these theoretical developments as follows:

An interpretation cannot be a description of meanings that exist as given social facts because meanings cannot be determined by factual data of the

5. For an elaboration of this approach, see Michael Walzer, *Interpretation and Social Criticism*, Cambridge, Mass.: Harvard University Press (1987) and *id.*, *Spheres of Justice: A Defense of Pluralism and Equality*, New York: Basic Books (1983).
6. Cf. Willard Quine, *Word and Object*, Cambridge, Mass.: MIT Press (1960).
7. Cf. Donald Davidson, *Inquiries into Truth and Interpretation*, Oxford: Oxford University Press (1986).
8. Cf. Ronald Dworkin, *Law's Empire*, Cambridge, Mass.: Belknap Press of Harvard University Press (1986).

practice to be interpreted. Several competing interpretive schemes can have an adequate level of overall fit with the factual data while some schemes are rejected as failing to do so. Since several schemes enable us to make sense of the facts, we have to choose the one that enables us to make a *better* sense of them than the others. That is to say, an interpretation of a human practice is better not because it discovers the substratum of meaning that is given out there, but because it is supported by the interpretive scheme that enables us to see the settled historical data of the given practice as based on more intelligible, more consistent, more acceptable, and more viable principles than the other schemes framing the competing interpretations.

This theory may be called interpretive reconstructivism. It shows historical contextualists a way out of the impasses of interpretive relativism and terrestrial realism. But if they take this way out, they have to abandon their doctrine because it leads beyond the historical context. According to this theory, identification of meaning depends on our normative or evaluative judgment about which interpretive scheme enables us to see the given practice as the most respectable. The value judgment involved in interpretation is not about the best shape that the practice could take if it started afresh with a clean slate but about the best profile in which its history can be seen. Interpretation is neither a factual description nor moral idealization, but factually bounded moral optimization of the given practice. Even if it is a bounded optimization, it requires us to assume an evaluative scale on which the competing interpretive schemes that pass the test of factual fit are further rated. Such a scale is certainly very controversial, but that is the point. It is not given in the historical context of the practice as shared understanding or overlapping consensus or the like. It depends on each interpreter's own philosophical perspective. When an interpreter claims that her interpretation is better than the competing ones, she is committed to a very controversial philosophical claim that her evaluative scale is superior to those of her interpretive competitors. Hence she cannot avoid being involved in the debates about which evaluative scale is philosophically valid. She has to show philosophical reasons, reasons that she claims to be universally valid, to justify her interpretation. All this means that historical context cannot reveal its meaning without being illuminated by the light of philosophy as search for the universal.

To exemplify and clarify this point, let us think about "the tradition of constitutional democracy" in the United States which is unmistakably a paradigmatic source for Rawlsian political liberalism (and other versions of post-philosophical liberalism). The overlapping consensus as the basis of political liberalism expresses the idea that there exists a cohesive set of constitutional essentials embedded in the public political culture of a constitutional democracy like the United States which is shared by different reasonable comprehensive doctrines prospering in that culture (such as Kantian liberalism of autonomy, J.S. Mill's utilitarian and partly Romantic liberalism, liberal Catholicism after the second Vatican Council, Rawls' earlier theory of justice as fairness), each of which accepts and supports the essentials on its own distinct philosophical ground. Rawls claims that his political conception of justice is freestanding in the sense that it is based only on the shared principles in this overlapping consensus without being committed to any of the specific competing philosophical grounds of these comprehensive doctrines. This claim is untenable for two reasons. First, we identify different sets of principles as the constitutional essentials depending on our different philosophical standpoints. Liberals want to expand them to cover the right to privacy and other "unenumerated rights," while conservatives want to cut them off. There is no philosophically neutral way to identify the essentials. Minimalism is not a shared answer but a commitment to a very controversial politico-philosophical standpoint. Second, even when we appear to accept the same constitutional principles, our interpretations of their implications differ greatly if we have different justifications for them on our different philosophical grounds. Liberals, conservatives, deliberative democrats, and feminists interpret the meaning of free speech in a significantly different and competing way because their justifications for protecting it are different. Meaning is not an independently existing substance, but rather, is dependent on the justifications we construct as evinced by interpretive reconstructivism.

The lack of shared understanding of the constitutional essentials is attested by the conflicts in (and *about*) the American constitutional practices. The stronghold of rugged individualism is defended and reinforced by libertarians who identify and interpret the constitutional essentials on a basis of Lockean natural rights of self-ownership or economic efficiency of market competition. Liberals in the American sense have been promoting a competing egalitarian conception of the constitutional essentials to defend the activist welfare state after the New Deal and to develop the cause of anti-racism and anti-discrimination of the civil rights movement. The so-called republican reinterpretation of the constitutional essentials has also been set forward by civic republicans and some communitarians who criticize both libertarians and liberals as undermining the civic virtue cultivated in a variety of intermediary communities toward which they look as the cornerstone of American democracy. Some multiculturalists, such as James Tully, who develop the politics of cultural recognition in the constitutional setting go even as far as to criticize as a colonialist legacy the dominant assumption that the Constitution of the United States of America has the exclusive authority as the source of the constitutional essentials, and propose to revive "treaty constitutionalism" that respects the spirit of mutual recognition and consensus formation at an intercultural level that can be traced back to the treaties between the indigenous peoples and settlers.[9]

These radical conflicts lead us to ask the following question of Rawls and other contextualists who believe that the constitutional tradition or political culture can replace philosophy: "Whose tradition? Whose culture?" They cannot answer, "*Our* tradition, *our* culture." For this answer simply begs the question or even suppresses it because there are such deeply conflicting interpretations of "our culture" and "our tradition." Rawls attempts to tame this conflict by "the strategy of avoidance," by dissociating himself from controversial principles. But this strategy is not workable because it is impossible. For example, his earlier theory of justice as fairness, his own comprehensive doctrine, includes the difference principle which conditions the distributive differentiation on the optimization of the lot of the worst-off. Because this principle is controverted by libertarians while favored by egalitarians, he excludes it from the constitutional essentials in his political liberalism, to which he admits only the principle of social minimum that can be accepted by those libertarians who approve of the safety net.[10] Can he obtain overlapping consensus this way? The answer is clearly no. This move is welcomed by libertarians, but rejected as a betrayal by those egalitarians who supported his conception of "justice as fairness" as a theoretical crystallization of the spirit of the New Deal and the civil rights movement. As is said above, minimalism is not a shared answer but just another way of taking sides. This strategy of avoidance is an attempt to avoid what is unavoidable.

My point is not just that we cannot please everybody—which even Rawls is ready to admit. With the idea of overlapping consensus he tries to accommodate not unlimited diversity but *reasonable* pluralism, and thus, he excludes the intolerant doctrines of moral or religious fundamentalism as unreasonable. But the above-mentioned fact of radical conflicts shows that there is no shared conception of the constitutional essentials even among those comprehensive doctrines that Rawls regards as reasonable. When he identifies the constitutional essentials, he cannot avoid committing himself to one of the competing interpretations of the constitutional tradition. So he is forced to make arguments which show that his interpretation illuminates "our constitutional tradition" in a better philosophical light than other competing interpretations. To turn to the fiction of overlapping consensus for support of his standpoint is a maneuver to avoid the philosophical burden of proof while making a very controversial philosophical claim.

9. Cf. James Tully, *Strange Multiplicity: Constitutionalism in an Age of Diversity*, Cambridge: Cambridge University Press (1995).

10. Rawls, *op. cit.*, note 2, 228-229.

Moreover, he has to provide philosophical justification for the exclusion of fundamentalism as unreasonable. We should recall that fundamentalism is a deeply rooted tradition in the United States that has been handed down from the early Puritan communities to the Moral Majority and other contemporary populist movements of religious politics. American fundamentalists celebrated their judicial victory in 1986 when the Supreme Court upheld anti-sodomy law as constitutional in *Bowers v. Hardwick*.[11] They claim that their standpoint is not the denial, but the best conception of the constitutional essentials because American democracy depends on the civic virtue cultivated in the kind of moral and religious communities that they strive to protect against the corrosive influences of the libertine vices. Rawls cannot reject their doctrines just by saying that they are alien to "our constitutional tradition" or "unreasonable." They are undeniably part of the American political and constitutional tradition and understand themselves as reasonable participants in its interpretive conflict. Rawls has to make some philosophical arguments, say, about the relationships between human freedom and virtue, to show that his liberal conception of the constitutional essentials sets off that tradition as more respectable than the fundamentalist interpretation.

I have argued that historical contextualists are trapped in a trilemma. They would either lapse into interpretive relativism as an arrogant and untenable version of universalism, or into terrestrial realism as dogmatic as celestial realism without the help of interpretive reconstructivism that is a better alternative theory of interpretation. They would then be subject to the same criticisms that they directed against philosophical universalism. If they turn to interpretive reconstructivism, however, they would have to abandon their own basic tenet. By arguing this way I have tried to show that we can reveal the meaning of our historical practice only by joining in the philosophical debates on general issues about human values, with universal validity-claim irreducible to the particular shared understanding in a given historical context. In the next section I will develop my attempt to rehabilitate the discredited universalist thinking by presenting a perspective of critical universalism in which we can correct and overcome the conventional misunderstandings and criticisms of philosophical universalism.

11. For discussions of this case in the light of legal and political philosophy, see Ronald Dworkin, "Liberal Community," 77 *California Law Review* (1989) 479-504 and Michael Sandel, "Moral Argument and Liberal Toleration," 77 *California Law Review* (1989) 521-538.

2. Toward a Critical Universalism

The current trend to retreat from philosophy into history or from the universal into the contextual is motivated by several distorted images of universalism. Here I will take up four such images that I think are the most influential in discrediting the universalistic perspective: hegemony, homogenizing standardization, rule-determinism, and foundationalism. All of these features constitute what used to be called dogmatism. I would like to show that an adequately conceived universalism is not only noncommittal with respect to them, but in fact, indispensable for the critical thinking that overcomes these dogmatic mindsets. Hence this perspective may be called critical universalism.

2.1 Universalism as critique of hegemony

Universalism is often castigated as hegemonic. The prevalent form of this denunciation is that universalism is a West-centrism, which imposes specifically Western values on non-Western societies through claims to universal validity and rationalizes the hegemonic dominance of the West over the world. Recently this attack has been vehemently mounted by the proponents of "Asian values" who reject Western criticism of human rights violations in some authoritarian Asian societies as cultural imperialism.

Some defend universalism against this attack by asserting that if we are to go beyond pseudo-universal Western values, we have to explore the genuinely universal principles that offer us a fair basis for intercultural or intercivilizational cooperation and cohabitation in the global human society. Other universalists indicate that even if the *genesis* of human rights, constitutionalism, and the rule of law are traced to Western traditions, it does not follow that the *validity* of these values is limited to Western societies. These responses are correct in delimiting the logical impact of the Asian values discourse, but they are not sufficiently thoroughgoing to challenge the problematic claim and assumption of its proponents. The first response avoids challenging their claim that the validity of civil and political rights is limited to Western societies; the second leaves intact their assumption that these values have prospered in the Western traditions. I have developed a critique of the "Asian values" discourse from a different perspective that rejects both the claim and the assumption in another work of mine.[12] Here I will present only the gist of my argument.

12. Cf. Tatsuo Inoue, "Liberal Democracy and Asian Orientalism," in Joanne Bauer and Daniel A. Bell (eds.), *The East Asian Challenge for Human Rights*, Cambridge: Cambridge University Press (1999) 27-59.

The underlying fallacy of the Asian values discourse is that its proponents are dominated by the West-centrism that they claim to overcome. The proponents are in fact entrapped in Orientalism as the intellectual device of Western hegemony. The core of Orientalism is the deep-seated drive to construct a self-identity for Western "Civil Society" around the embodiment of human rights and democracy as "historical fate." To set forth this self-portrait as a positive figure, there must be a negative ground that it is contrasted against. The Orient, which includes Islamic *Umma* and authoritarian developmentalist Asian countries, is thus stipulated or invented as the *Other* that has a heterogeneous cultural essence incompatible with these values of Civil Society. This Orientalist identity-constitution purifies Western societies from the negative legacies in their human rights record, such as racism, slavery, colonialism, religious intolerance, anti-Semitism, class discriminations, patriarchy and the like, and at the same time it dumps some of these wastes remaining from Western self-purification into the territory assigned for the identity of the Other. The Orientalist dichotomy thereby denies the internal diversity and transformative potentials of Asian societies and reproduces the Hegelian prejudice of Asian historical stagnancy in the form of a revised belief that the Asian economy is capable of development although Asian politics is not.[13]

The Asian values proponents accept the distorted perceptions of Western and Asian societies invented by the Orientalist identity polarization, although they change the negative evaluative connotation of the stereotype imposed on Asia into a positive one. They take advantage of the Orientalist stereotype of Asia to suppress the different multiple voices within their societies and ipso facto support and promote the Western self-sanctification internally coupled with this prejudiced stereotype of Asia. Actually, they receive intellectual support from some of the above-mentioned Western contextualist liberals who reproduce the Orientalist dichotomous identity by making the fundamental principles of constitutional democracy and Civil Society disclaim philosophical and universal validity, i.e., arguing that they are not applicable to non-Western societies, while defending them as deeply and firmly embedded in the tradition of Western societies. Rawls thus defends what he calls well-ordered or decent hierarchies, which subsume contemporary Asian authoritarian regimes, as legitimate members of international society governed by his conception of "the law of peoples"—an internationalized version of his political conception of justice;[14] and Gray joins the Asian values proponents

13. The Orientalist drive as presented here is revealingly exemplified by Ernest Gellner in one of his late works. Cf. Ernest Gellner, *Conditions of Liberty: Civil Society and Its Rivals*, London: Hamish Hamilton (1994) esp. 200, 213-214. For a criticism of his view, see *ibid.*, 48-49.

14. Cf. John Rawls, *The Law of Peoples with "The Idea of Public Reason Revisited,"* Cambridge, Mass.: Harvard University Press (1999) esp. 59-78.

in denouncing criticism of the violations of civil and political rights in these authoritarian regimes as Western cultural imperialism.[15] Here we can clearly see an intellectual partnership or complicity between the Asian values discourse and Orientalism as Western self-sanctification.

We can expose and overcome this complicity only if we sincerely accept human rights values and democracy as universal normative principles that are *critically* applicable both to the Western and Asian societies. Asian societies are far from the stereotype of a culturally monolithic and collectively cohesive community. They have their own internal religious and cultural diversity comparable to, and in many cases even greater, than that of Western societies. The tensions between individualism and communitarianism run *through* not *between* Asian and Western societies because they are universal dilemmas of human society. Accordingly, Asian societies have their own needs to develop constitutional democracy that combines democratic self-governance with the protection of fundamental human rights of individuals and minorities to accommodate the conflicts generated by these diversities and tensions in a fair manner.

On the other hand, Western societies should take human rights and democracy seriously and not self-complacently claim to have already achieved both, but rather as principles for their ongoing self-critical enterprise of revealing and transforming the darker half of their historical ego suppressed by the Orientalist mentality. We should recall that interpretive reconstruction of the political practice of a given society, as defended in the last section, is not a moral idealization of its history, but its factually bounded optimization to be conducted on the basis of frank recognition of the existence of conflicting and ambivalent forces in its history. An interpreter is required not to suppress the darker aspects of its history under the disguise of shared understanding or overlapping consensus, but to confront them and identify a better set of latent justificatory principles for the self-critical reexamination and selective adoption of its historical legacies for its future successive development. Moreover, what is presented as the best of the competing interpretive schemes must be acknowledged to be less than morally ideal. I have emphasized that the evaluative scale for interpretive reconstruction must have a philosophical claim to universal validity simply because it must not be tailored down to idealize the given practice, but be set as a larger scale that shows both the moral potentials and limits of the given practice.

All this then means that universalism of human rights and democracy is far from a rationalization of Western hegemony, but shows us how to go beyond the complicity of the Orientalist reproduction of this hegemony and the professedly "anti-hegemonic" Asian values discourse, and to acknowledge

15. Gray, *op. cit.*, note 4, 317.

and cope with the internal diversities and tensions within both Western and Asian societies that are concealed by this complicity.

2.2 Universalization as critique of standardization and homogenization

The second source of anti-universalism is the confusion of universalization required by justice and human rights with standardization and homogenization. A classic form of such criticism is based on the opposition of equity to justice. It is often said that justice requires us to subsume particular cases each with its own unique features under abstract general categories and thereby prevents us from reaching adequate resolution of concrete human conflicts with sufficient concern for their particular circumstances, while equity enables us to be sensitive to the concrete adequacy of conflict resolution. The multiculturalist defense of group-specific rights can be reformulated as a variant of such criticism that is directed against the universalization implicated in the idea of human rights. The idea of universal human rights assumes, so goes this criticism, that the holders of *human* rights are abstract individuals deprived of their cultural and ethnic particularities, and therefore, it fails to capture or even rejects group-specific minority rights that are possessed exclusively by members of specific minority groups to protect their cultural bases of personal identity and self-respect; moreover, human rights press cultural and ethnic minorities to assimilate into the mainstream majority culture by imposing on them the normalized model of "a human being."

Against the equity-based criticism we can defend justice by distinguishing its requirement of universalizability from that of generalization. Justice does not prohibit us from taking particular circumstances of each case into full consideration. It only prohibits us from using our power to make such a discrimination against others that cannot be justified without resorting to non-universalizable reasons, namely, reasons that depend on the difference between each of us and the others in terms of our individual identity. To put it another way, justice requires us to justify our claims (rights-claims and power-claims) on others with *reversible* reasons, reasons that would be acceptable both to us and them even if our situations and theirs were reversed. Since our situations involve our viewpoints, justice also requires us to give others *public* justification for our claims on them, justification by reasons that would be acceptable not just from our idiosyncratic viewpoint but also from that of others. Reasons that would be acceptable even from the viewpoints of others are not simply the reasons that they are likely to accept, but the ones that they would not be able to reject as unfair if they accept the requirement of public justification. Counter-factuality here involves normative constraint. The public justification requirement, therefore, is not a requirement for actual consensus but a test to be used in critically examining whether actual consensus is the rationalization of dominance, of those parties with greater powers and transaction resources over those with lesser ones.

Justice conceived in this way requires the majority to imagine themselves in the shoes of the cultural minorities and to examine whether the political institutions and decisions that the majority take for granted or defend in the name of general consensus would be acceptable even if they were in the plight of minorities. Far from rationalizing the assimilationist pressures on the minorities, justice offers multiculturalists an indispensable moral basis for negotiating with the majority about fair terms of cohabitation. Group-specific rights can be justified in terms of universalistic justice if it is shown that preferential treatment for minority groups secured by such rights are necessary to counterbalance the structural disadvantage that "the free market of cultures" places on cultural and ethnic minorities regarding opportunities in education, employment, business, media access, etc. Justice can also restrain minority groups from abusing their group-specific rights to repress their own internal sub-minorities because such abuse involves the same irreversible discriminations that the majority is prohibited from making against the minorities.[16]

Since human rights are based on justice, they also require public justification. The principle of universal human rights has an element of "abstraction" in the sense that it requires that individuals should be enabled to enjoy human rights irrespective of their cultural or ethnic backgrounds. But this abstraction has nothing to do with normalization or homogenization of minorities. It rather requires that members of the majority detach themselves from their own ethno-cultural background and place themselves in the shoes of minorities so that they can understand the latter's special need to have their human dignity protected against homogenizing pressures. This is not an anthropological abstraction of individuals but a moral abstraction that reflects the requirement of public justification through counterfactual moral thought experiment. Human rights and justice restrain both the majority and minorities from dogmatizing their own specific cultural perspective as the absolute frame of reference from which their moral imagination can never take a step back. A step back is necessary if we are not to deny the right to

16. The justification and limitation of group-specific minority rights that are presented in the text as derivable from a universalistic concept of justice roughly correspond to the legitimate "external protection" and illegitimate "internal restriction" that Will Kymlicka distinguished in terms of the functions of minority rights. Cf. Will Kymlicka, *Multicultural Citizenship*, Oxford: Clarendon Press (1995).

cultural difference and reach a fair accommodation of the competing rights claims to cultural difference advanced by various ethno-cultural groups.

2.3 Universalism as rule-indeterminism

The third form of anti-universalism criticizes universalism as making the same error as the realist (anti-nominalist) theory of meaning due to its commitment to rule-determinism, which holds that all human actions and judgments can and should be univocally governed by preexisting articulate rules. Rule-determinists are depicted as having a desire to deprive others of the freedom to interpret rules in a creative way, while concealing the arbitrariness of their own interpretation. In Jurisprudence a radical criticism of rule-determinism is provided within the tradition of attacking the faith in legal certainty that has evolved from legal realism to the critical legal studies (CLS) movement. The most sophisticated and destructive philosophical argument for rule-determinism is given by Saul Kripke who interpreted Ludwig Wittgenstein's paradox of rule-following to have proved the radical indeterminacy of rule as a normative guide for its applications.[17]

Kripke argued that the Wittgensteinian rule-following paradox shows that there are an infinite number of descriptions of a rule (or a system of rules) that are compatible with the totality of facts (psychological as well as physical) about its past uses. This argument is nothing new. It has a structural similarity to Humean refutation of Induction. Another isomorphic argument is given by the above-mentioned Quine's theory of radical translation. All that arguments of this type show is that our interpretive conflict about the meaning of a rule cannot be decided by the factual data about its usage. This factual indeterminacy of rules does not refute the universalist perspective but rather leads us to take such a perspective. As is shown by the interpretive reconstructivism discussed in the last section, the factual indeterminacy of rules implies that we have to depend on our normative judgment in deciding which interpretive scheme enables us to see the past facts in the best light. To justify such normative judgment, we have to resort to an evaluative scale that has a philosophical claim to universal validity. This perspective applies not only to interpretation of legal and linguistic rules but also to that of human historical practice in general. In my criticism of historical contextualism in the last section, I tried to show that we need a light of philosophical universalism to illuminate the meaning of historical particularity.

Some CLS proponents reject interpretive reconstructivism in the context of law on the ground that legal practice is so schizophrenic or so full of

17. Cf. Saul Kripke, *Wittgenstein on Rules and Private Language: An Elementary Exposition*, Oxford: Blackwell Publishers (1982).

radical contradictions in their justificatory principles that there is no coherent interpretive scheme that can make it intelligible.[18] This criticism misses the point of interpretive reconstructivism, which is that the more confusing the factual data are, the greater our need to make normative reconstruction of them. Justificatory principles are not the actual cause of the interpersonal conflict involved in legislation and adjudication given as historical facts, but the reconstructed purports that interpreters ascribe to legal data in order to make them intelligible and defensible. The CLS criticism assumes that one part of legal data univocally determines one set of justificatory principles, while another part also univocally determines another contradictory set, and that the meanings of these sets of principles are so rigidly and independently fixed that there is no way to interpret them coherently. This is actually the claim of *overdeterminacy* rather than *indeterminacy* of law and can be rejected as making a pre-Kripkean (or pre-Quinean and pre-Davidsonian) error of assuming the factual determinability of meaning.

The CLS criticism can be reformulated as the claim that there is no distinction between moral idealization and factually bounded interpretive optimization of law, so that interpretive conflicts in law are reduced to the conflicts of political ideologies that set forth competing social ideals. This is not a rejection of interpretive reconstructivism, but an attempt to radicalize it because it pushes the reconstructivist assumption of factual underdeterminacy of meaning to its logical limit: complete indeterminacy. Although I think the claim of complete indeterminacy goes too far, we need not go into this issue. The point to be made here is that if this CLS claim is tenable, the participants in legal practice have a greater need and a stronger reason to make philosophical arguments using universal validity-claim transcending the historical context to justify their political ideology. Although the deconstructionist branch of CLS distances itself from philosophical universalism, its followers cannot escape from philosophy by retreating into historical contextualism as is shown in the last section. Nor can relativism be their way out because, as I have shown with reference to interpretive relativism, it is the most arrogant and self-defeating version of philosophical universalism.

2.4 Universalism as anti-foundationalist dialogue

The last source of anti-universalism to be discussed here is the confusion of universalism with foundationalism. Those captured by this confusion hold that universalism stipulates consent by the universal audience as the condition for our judgments being justified and thus requires indisputable proof

18. For a standard formulation of this view, see Roberto Unger, *The Critical Legal Studies Movement*, Harvard University Press (1986).

of the same nature as that demanded by foundationalism. They reject universalism because such foundationalist justification is impossible. Since Gödel's incompleteness theorem proves that this axiomatic approach fails even in mathematics, we should *a fortiori* reject foundationalism for our empirical and evaluative judgments. However, universalism need not be equated with foundationalism; it can be coupled with the following anti-foundationalist theory of justification that may be called dialogicalism.

Let me start by giving an example. While I am writing this paper, I believe that the floor of my study will not collapse at any moment. Do I have to justify this belief of mine? The answer is a definite no, for there is no one who challenges it. The mere logical possibility of the belief being false does not require me to justify it. We could not function if we were not able to depend on non-justified beliefs. Imagine the following situation in contrast: my landlord warns me to leave my room immediately because the props supporting the floor have been found to be gravely rotten. But I insist on staying in my study to finish my overdue paper, arguing that it will not collapse quickly. He tells me that I am too negligent. Must I now justify my optimistic belief (or wishful thinking)? Yes, of course. As this example shows, justification is not a logical or mathematical demonstration to be conducted indiscriminately on every assumption or belief. Justification is instead an act of responding to another who expresses an objection and as such is a form of dialogue. Justification as a dialogue does not involve demonstrating the soundness of our belief system as a whole, in such a way that every logically possible objection from every rational agent is a priori resolved, but to respond to a particular person who raises a concrete objection to a specific part of our belief system by providing reasons for our holding this particular belief that she can understand and accept. I hasten to add that imposed silence does not mean the absence of objections, for there is a greater dialogical need to supply justification for suppressed objections. The basic features of justification as a dialogue can be formulated in the following way.

1. We do not have to justify all of our beliefs. We have to justify only that belief of ours to which someone has raised an objection. (By "someone has raised an objection," I mean, "She has raised an objection or would have raised it if she were not silenced." The same shall apply hereinafter.)
2. We do not have to justify our beliefs to everyone. We have to give justification only to the particular persons who have raised objections.
3. The objector has to show specific reasons why she objects to that particular belief of ours. She must have her own belief system on which her objection is based. In other words, we need not address our justification to the comprehensive skeptic who refuses to be committed to any belief, because such a skeptic cannot show any specific reason for objecting to our beliefs.

4. Because the objector has her own belief system and objects only to a particular part of our belief system, there is then a common part of the two belief systems that we share. Let us call this part a dialogical background. We can resort to the shared dialogical background as a source of reasons that we can adduce to her.
5. The dialogical backgrounds are dialogically context-dependent in the sense that what constitutes them varies depending on who objects to which part of our belief system and for what reasons. There is no overarching background belief system that is privileged to govern all the justificatory dialogues. Any part of the dialogical background given in the context of a specific justificatory dialogue is open to criticism in another dialogical context that involves a different objector or a new objection from the same objector.
6. Justification is dialogically context-dependent in the sense that the same judgment which is justifiable in one context of justificatory dialogue can be refuted in another. Justification is always tentative.

Dialogicalism as presented above rejects foundationalism in that it does not prevent us from depending on non-demonstrated beliefs and makes justification context-dependent. On the other hand, it rejects historical contextualism or conventionalism in that it denies that there is any dominant tradition or convention that transcends political controversy and constitutes the common basis for all the justificatory dialogues in a given society. It also rejects relativism in that it makes justification not agent-relative but context-dependent, and acknowledges the inter-subjective justifiability of our judgment. Moreover, it rejects all of these competing theories of justification in that it makes universal validity the *regulative idea*, not the *criterion*, for justification.

From the perspective of dialogicalism, justification is context-dependent and so distinguished from the attainment of universal validity. For that very reason, however, universal validity is set as the regulative idea which context-dependent justification is always seen as falling short of and which requires us to reexamine a judgment, justified in a given dialogical context, by responding to new dialogical challenges from different agents and from different perspectives. If we abandon this regulative idea which makes us aware of the partiality and tentativeness of our justification, we would fall into a dogmatic fixation on a specific justificatory context shared with our familiar dialogical partners and close our spiritual door to the disturbing and disquieting new dialogical challenges from those others whose cultural, experiential, and intellectual backgrounds are very different from ours. We would then lose sight of the contextual limits of our justification and absolutize it. Universal validity as the regulative idea is an essential condition for the contextuality and critical open-endedness of our justification.

I would like to add that the universalistic concept of justice as presented above provides a normative basis for dialogicalism. The public justification requirement implied by this conception tells us to transcend our idiosyncratic beliefs and to turn to the dialogical background we share with our dialogical partners for reasons intelligible and acceptable both for them and us. Furthermore, it also requires us to reexamine the same dialogical background if it is challenged by others outside that context for comprising non-universalizable (irreversible) discrimination. The critically open-ended contextuality of justification is also supported by the universalism immanent in the idea of justice.

3. Conclusion

In this chapter I have criticized historical contextualism and tried to defend an alternative perspective of critical universalism against four major forms of anti-universalism. I hope I have made it clear that the quest for the universal enables us to recognize and respond to the diversity of particular contexts of human life in a fair way. Let me conclude this paper by summing up the points I have made to show this:

1. The universal principles of human rights and democracy enable us to go beyond the Orientalist dichotomy that suppresses the internal diversity within both Western and Asian societies, and to accommodate fairly the tensions generated by this diversity.
2. The multiculturalists' insight into the need for group-specific rights of minorities can be adequately developed if subjected to the public justification requirement and the moral abstraction requirement inherent in the universalistic ideas of justice and human rights.
3. The factual indeterminacy of the meaning of law and human practices in general implies that we need an evaluative scale with philosophical claim to universal validity to assess the competing reconstructive interpretations about the contextual meaning of these practices.
4. Universal validity, as the regulative idea, and the universalistic concept of justice are the epistemological and normative bases for the dialogical contextualization of justification open to ongoing critical reexamination from diverse perspectives.

In a nutshell, the quest for the universal is indispensable to the dissolution of the hegemonic suppression of genuine diversity, to the fair accommodation of cultural diversity, to the illumination of contextual meanings, and to open contextual justification.

Chapter 6

Wojciech Sadurski

Universalism, Localism and Paternalism in Human Rights Discourse

The idea of universal human rights is in itself a highly contested political idea, and some of its purported beneficiaries reject it vigorously. This is neither paradoxical nor conclusively damaging to the universalist idea: there is no contradiction between a theory's aspiration to universal implementation and its being local in its pedigree and even reach. Whether such a conception is rendered in these circumstances "intolerant" (because we propose to displace the values of the people with whom we disagree), or "paternalistic" (because we attempt to impart it upon those who visibly do not espouse it, and we claim to do it for their own good), and further, whether such "intolerance" or "paternalism" is a bad thing, is a matter of substantive moral argument which I will attempt in the first part of this chapter. But even if we dispel (as I will try to) the charges of an objectionable form of intolerance or paternalism leveled at a universalist project of human rights, we do not thereby satisfy ourselves about the feasibility of such a project, and its feasibility will be discussed in the second part of this chapter. I will claim, rather unoriginally, that there are clear limits to the feasibility of the universalist project, and that the structure of human rights discourse is such that certain factual factors which are built into this discourse are crucially context dependent. I will try to identify

András Sajó (ed.), Human Rights with Modesty: The Problem of Universalism, *141-160.*

the main categories of such factors, and provide illustrations for these categories by different case studies culled from our conventional human rights discourse.

I take it to be uncontroversial that there is a presumption, built into human rights liberalism, in favor of universalism—a presumption which can be overcome only by very weighty arguments. Diversity, as an allegedly inherent value of a good society, does not in itself figure among such arguments. Unless, that is, it can be further reduced to the good of the individual subjects for whom departures from the universal liberal freedoms are proposed. "True" liberalism is therefore reluctant to easily accept the arguments for cultural exceptionalism, group rights, membership-based particularities, and for community- and citizenship-conscious claims, as it suspects that all such arguments, exceptions, and claims have a potential for exclusion, discrimination, and intergroup oppression. As noted by the author who has recently made by far the most eloquent and passionate defense of such liberal universalism:

> [I]t seems overwhelmingly plausible that some groups will operate in ways that are severely inimical to the interests of at any rate some of their members. To the extent that they do, cultural diversity cannot be an unqualified good. In fact, once we follow the path opened up by that thought, we shall soon arrive at the conclusion that diversity is desirable to the degree, and only to the degree, that each of the diverse groups functions in a way that is well adapted to advance the welfare and secure the rights of its members.[1]

One does not have to endorse all the polemical excesses contained in Brian Barry's recent book to agree that, in the project of "political liberalism" which is tolerant of moral and cultural diversity, there is something deeply troubling to a person committed to the value of liberty—the price of which is paid by the most vulnerable and powerless members of illiberal groups and states.

1. Intolerance, Paternalism, and Human Rights Universalism

Our frequent reticence in making universalistic human rights claims—that apply to a society different from ours, which seemingly does not value the same rights as we—is usually grounded in an attempt to avoid hubris, a moral or intellectual arrogance. Indeed, we do not want to be seen as "imposing" our values on those who do not seem to espouse them. Hence, the celebrated Rawls's plea for the law of peoples—the plea which can be read as a warning against the (alleged) intolerance inherent in the missionary zeal of liberals:

1. Brian Barry, *Culture and Equality*, Cambridge: Polity (2001) 134.

"If all societies were required to be liberal, then the idea of political liberalism would fail to express due toleration for other acceptable ways (if such there are, as I assume) of ordering society."[2]

In this part of my chapter I will claim that it is *unlikely*, as a practical matter, that an intolerant attitude might move someone to postulate universalist conceptions of human rights. Rather, if there is a prima facie objectionable attitude which is likely to trigger a universalist conception of human rights, it is paternalism and not intolerance. This point needs to be explored in more detail (part 1.2), but first a digression about the political context of the intolerance objection to human rights universalism must be made (part 1.1).

1.1 The problem of defective representation

The political context in which universalistic claims of human rights are most often made (and refuted) in the modern world suggests that, more often than not, the universalistic claims are neither paternalistic nor intolerant but aim at displacing the claims of non-democratic governments to represent the true values and preferences of their people—claims which are rarely credible. This is, politically speaking, the most usual situation in which universalistic human rights claims meet the resistance of "other" societies which seemingly do not share those values. In reality, the "resistance" comes from a despotic elite of this other society and has nothing to do with the actual preferences and desires of the people who would often be delighted by some form of "interference." Anti-universalistic objections are then usually merely a rhetoric used by a non-democratic power elite who wants to keep its grip on society—*vide* the ideology of "Asian values" which should be properly seen as part of the legitimation strategy of authoritarian regimes.[3] As an ex-deputy prime minister of Malaysia said: "[I]t is altogether shameful, if ingenious, to cite Asian values as an excuse for autocratic practices and denial of basic rights and liberties."[4] The call to "respect local values" is then based on a mistaken assumption as to the genuine spokesperson for the society in question. Our universalistic claims are therefore, of course, based on *anything but* paternalism (much less, intolerance).

The ambiguity about how to ascertain the actual preferences of a distant people, and in particular, how representative of those preferences their governments are, may be seen as underlying some of the critiques of Rawls'

2. John Rawls, *The Law of Peoples*, Cambridge, Mass.: Harvard University Press (1999) 59, 84.
3. See Mark R. Thompson, "Whatever Happened to 'Asian Values'?", 12 *Journal of Democracy* (2001) 154-65.
4. Anwar Ibrahim, quoted in "What Would Confucius Say Now?", *The Economist* (25 July 1998) 25.

Law of Peoples.[5] The book caused a degree of dismay among those who had long postulated an extension of Rawls' conception of justice as fairness on an international scale, and who thought that Rawls has now turned out to be inexplicably solicitous of various non-liberal regimes in his *Law of Peoples*. Putting the questions of economic justice to one side, we may say that the extension of the first principle of justice (as announced in *A Theory of Justice*) would result in a global human rights principle (going much beyond the human rights minimum established by Rawls as a yardstick for "decent" but hierarchical societies). This solicitousness is based, I believe, on a question-begging connection between moral judgments and practical "feasibility" in Rawls. Responding to those who would like to ground the global principles of justice on a sort of "global original position," Rawls observes that "peoples as corporate bodies organized by their governments now exist in some form all over the world."[6] From this statement of fact (which, in itself, need not carry any moral significance) Rawls immediately proceeds to conclude that: "Historically speaking, all principles and standards proposed for the law of peoples must, *to be feasible*, prove acceptable to the considered and reflective public opinion of peoples *and their governments*."[7]

The status of this "feasibility" proviso is unclear. Why must the principles also be acceptable to governments, in addition to the peoples, in order to pass the constructivist test of justification? After all, the law of peoples is determined in the same constructivist way as principles of justice in the conception of justice-as-fairness; hence, only the "appropriate reasons" guiding the specification of the Law of Peoples under "fair conditions" count.[8] True, principles *un*acceptable to governments (while acceptable to their peoples) have little chance of being universally followed, but then we face the issue of noncompliance, and hence of nonideal theory, while the principles for the law of peoples belong to ideal theory, which aims to describe the world "in which all peoples *accept and follow* the (ideal of the) Law of Peoples."[9] Rawls explicitly announces that the extension of the law of peoples from liberal to hierarchical societies belongs to the ideal theory;[10] it is therefore not a step triggered by noncompliance, unfavorable conditions, etc., and as such, is subject to the same justification procedure as within liberal societies. The feasibility test demanding an additional acceptance of principles by government,

5. Ibid.
6. John Rawls, "The Law of Peoples," in Stephen Shute & Susan Hurley (eds.), *On Human Rights: The Oxford Amnesty Lectures*, New York: Basic Books (1993) 50.
7. *Ibid.*, 50, emphases added.
8. Rawls, *op. cit.*, note 2, 32.
9. *Ibid.*, 89, emphasis added.
10. *Ibid.*, 5.

over and above that of their people, presupposes that they are not the accurate spokespersons for their peoples' preferences—that they are not democratic, in other words—but this seems to put them beyond the range of societies which are "well-ordered and just." Rawls explains that, while there is no fully-fledged democratic system required of those societies, there nevertheless must be "a decent consultation hierarchy" and public officials must be guided by a common-good conception of justice.[11] Since he explicitly contrasts a "consultation hierarchy" and a "paternalistic regime"[12] (with the implication that the latter would not pass the test of a well-ordered society), it follows that such a regime must track the avowed preferences of its people (otherwise a common-good conception would be purely paternalistic: the only factor that stands between the common-good test and paternalism is the tracking of the avowed preferences). Either way, there seems to be no reason for those governments to be included in the reflective equilibrium on the law of peoples: either they are so non-democratic as to place themselves beyond the pale of well-ordered societies, or they do track the preferences of their people in which case they need not be included because they are treated, in the theory of justification, merely as a mouthpiece for their people. The "global original position" does not need, therefore, to invite the governments into its constituency.

1.2 Intolerance and paternalism

But now let us put the case of defective representation of preferences to one side. Let us consider a situation in which our universalistic claims indeed meet a genuine resistance by the community upon which we would like to extend our conception of rights, and the ruling elite is at one with a large majority of the community. Under such circumstances, is it really *intolerance* that is implicated by a universalist discourse of human rights? The distinction between intolerance and paternalism may be obscure in real life, but is quite sharp and clear when stated in abstract terms. I will define here intolerance as an interference with other people's behavior based on our moral disagreement with their values. (Note that it is a maximally neutral, and perhaps somewhat artificial, concept of intolerance: under this definition, intolerance has no necessarily negative connotation because if you agree with me that the values with which I interfere are morally repugnant, then you are likely to approve of my intolerance, as in an intolerance for thieves or plagiarists). Paternalism is defined as an interference with other people's behavior on the basis that their values, when pursued, are (in the opinion of the interferer) harmful to them, and that the overall consequences of the interference will

11. *Ibid.*, 71-2.
12. *Ibid.*, 72.

be to their benefit. So the criterion which distinguishes intolerance from paternalism is whether it is relevant for an interference that, in the eyes of the interferer, the interference benefits those upon whom values are imposed. Such a judgment of benefit is irrelevant for intolerance but crucial to (indeed, defining of) paternalism.

If we are careful to respect this standard distinction, it becomes clear, I believe, that paternalism is a less objectionable basis of universalism of human rights (if there is to be one) than intolerance. Human rights identify the standards which, in the eyes of those who propound them, confer benefits upon the right-holders. They are not independent of the good of the right-holders; rather, their justification holds insofar as we believe that they are good for those upon whom we would like to extend them. It simply makes no moral sense to say: "Everyone ought to have a human right *x*, whether it benefits them or not." Rather, one may say: "Everyone ought to have a human right *x* because it benefits everyone, whether they actually realize it or not." And *this* is paternalism (subject to the provisos below). It may still be an objectionable attitude but it is *differently* (and, arguably, *less*) objectionable than the attitude of intolerance. What is the significance of this distinction?

I certainly do not want to make a general claim that intolerance, *in abstracto*, is more objectionable than paternalism.[13] But I believe that in the present context, that is, in the context of the discussion of universalism/localism of human rights discourse, paternalism is an attitude which has some redeeming virtues. In such context, our "paternalism" is most likely to be of a moderate version, that is, to be based on a plausible conviction that the resistance by members of distant societies to the rights which we would like to extend upon them results from ignorance and oppression, and that this ignorance and oppression is often deliberately supported by the power elite—so, in the end, the situation is not totally unlike the one that we have discussed in part 1.1, namely, that "local values" merely serve as an excuse for the ruling elite's oppressive policies.

Consider the issue of gender equality and the resistance of some Muslim societies to our insistence that women should be offered equal legal status and equal professional and educational opportunities as men. The resistance of *women* themselves to such an extension of human rights raises the issue of paternalism. The most plausible explanation of their resistance, if genuine, is that they are not given the necessary information and the necessary political freedom to form a considered judgment on the issue. It is not the case that we (*qua* universalistic human rights proponents) will keep insisting upon their rights to equality despite their resistance, but rather that we insist that

13. More on this distinction in the context of freedom of speech, see Wojciech Sadurski, *Freedom of Speech and Its Limits*, Dordrecht: Kluwer (1999) 173-78.

they should have an opportunity to know the full range of options, to understand the issues at stake, and to decide freely on the matter. But, of course, once we have reached that point we have extended at least some of the "universalistic" rights upon them in the process. Another, very likely explanation for the endorsement of such oppressive practices by women is that the process of non-autonomous preferences is at work, described by Jon Elster as a "sour grapes" syndrome, which consists of the adaptation of our preferences to what is seen as possible to achieve under existing constraints.[14] The phenomenon by which victims of discrimination or oppression accept their fate and convince themselves that they are actually well-off is psychologically understandable (reduction of "cognitive dissonance") and reasonably well explored; and surely it is an instance of a *pathology* of preference formation. These "adaptive preferences" do not fit the scheme of respect-deserving preferences which figure in traditional liberal critiques of paternalism.

Paternalism conceived as a response to ignorance and defects in preference formation is not particularly objectionable as long as it is present in proportion to the defect it proposes to remedy; indeed, it may be *more* objectionable to take at face value the expressed preferences without looking into the preference formation process. If we do the latter, we are likely to cheat ourselves, and end up producing comforting rationalizations for not taking action against oppression elsewhere: we hypocritically satisfy ourselves, for example, that those Muslim women do not want equality of access to education or employment, or that Asian peasants really do not want freedom of the press, etc. Perhaps they indeed do not want such rights at present, and if that is the case, our relentless insistence upon these rights for them is paternalistic; but if their not wanting such rights is a result of a state of ignorance in which they have been kept so that they never had an opportunity to consider that there may be a different way of living one's life, then our paternalism is actually less objectionable than our avoidance of interference.

But there is yet another, even less objectionable, version of paternalism which is likely to accompany many universalistic conceptions of human rights. Consider again the case of "our" (that is, enlightened liberals in the developed democracies) attitude to the subordination of women in some Muslim countries. The ignorance removing paternalism may be a likely motive for proselytizing gender equality to *women* who seem to be content with their condition in these countries. But what about the subordinating *men*? One answer is that the voice of oppressors should not count in moral argument, but this is to proceed too quickly. For their persistence in maintaining the pattern of women's

14. Jon Elster, *Sour Grapes*, Cambridge: Cambridge University Press (1983), esp. chapter III. See also Cass R. Sunstein, "Legal Interference with Private Preferences," 53 *University of Chicago Law Review* (1986) 1146-50.

rights violations may result from a sort of collective action dilemma: no one is prepared to unilaterally interrupt the state of affairs which benefits everyone so long as everyone else practices the norms contained in this pattern, nevertheless everyone (or, let us say modestly, a majority) would prefer a system of gender equality, with the condition that others play by the rules of this new system. (This is, of course, a sheer and perhaps fantastic speculation provided here only *arguendo.*) The subordinating men might have this preference for all sorts of reasons: because they do not want to look like barbarians to their Western counterparts (for example, business partners) in a globalized world; because they do not want to feel a sense of guilt toward the women they encounter; because they want to provide their wives and daughters with fair life opportunities; because they may realize that their religion, properly articulated, does not mandate a system of oppression of women, etc. In this case, the "imposition" of the system of gender equality by human rights universalists is a rational solution to a Prisoner's Dilemma: it identifies an optimal solution (optimal in the eyes of those to whom it applies, not just by *our* standards), and it selects the most effective means to achieve this preferred solution.

In one simplistic way, it *is* still paternalistic: it is an imposition of a system of rules in the best interests of those upon whom it is being imposed. However, it is a shallow notion of paternalism because it is not based on an identification of the central moral wrong (of paternalism), which is the "I know better what is really good for you" attitude. Such an attitude may or may not be present in an imposition of coercive rules based on a people's best interests. One recalls Isaiah Berlin's emphatic attack on paternalism:

> Paternalism is despotic, not because it is more oppressive than naked, brutal, unenlightened tyranny...but because it is an insult to my conception of myself as a human being, determined to make my own life in accordance with my own (not necessarily rational or benevolent) purposes, and, above all, entitled to be recognized as such by others.[15]

No such insult is evident in the "paternalistic" solution to the Prisoner's Dilemma. So in this *deeper* sense, the practice just described is *not* paternalistic because it does not involve displacing the actual preferences of the agents upon whom the system of rules is being imposed: rather, their motivations (as in any Prisoner's Dilemma situation) do not match their avowed preferences, and this distance between motivations and preferences needs to be bridged by the imposition of a rule with which everyone has to conform (and crucially, too, a rule which everyone *knows* all others have to conform with). Now if this form of paternalism may be plausibly attributed to some universalistic human rights pursuit in the modern world, then this is

15. Isaiah Berlin, *Four Essays on Liberty*, Oxford: Oxford University Press (1969) 157.

even less objectionable than the paternalism based on ignorance and other defects in preference formation because the most objectionable ingredient of paternalism, which renders it such an unwholesome attitude, is missing here: namely, the breach of the actual preferences of agents on the basis of an allegedly better insight into their true interests on the part of the imposer. To use Berlin's words, there is no "insult to [one's] conception of [oneself] as a human being" implicated by such paternalism.

2. Universalism Mediated by Contingency

Nothing said so far addresses the issue of the *feasibility* of the universalistic project of human rights. The contention which I would like to put forward, and defend in the remainder of this chapter, is that in the very structure of human rights there are some clear limits to the feasibility of universalism: not because of any "external" reasons, such as our possible concern about tolerance and avoidance of arrogance, but rather for "internal" reasons—because, *at a certain point*, universalism ceases to make good moral sense. "At a certain point" is a crucial proviso, and I will attempt below to identify some of these "points." To put it in a simplistic and only preliminary way, the normative weight of universal human rights depends crucially, for its justification, upon certain factual factors which obtain differently in different circumstances.

Roughly speaking, I identify two main versions of such mediation: empirical and justificatory. I will provide a case study to illustrate each of these two types of mediation. The first case study will be of the right to equal treatment; the second, the right to freedom of political speech and one particular, very specific but controversial issue, namely, to what extent people should have a right to freely express such repugnant propositions as those denying the fact of the Holocaust. I am not trying to say that we *should* not be universalistic in our human rights aspirations; rather, I suggest that, to a certain degree, we *cannot* be so. There is a point at which we need to blend, so to speak, some local justificatory or empirical factors with our universal human rights, and the results will be different in different societies. One and the same right will manifest differently in different societies, or its concrete articulation will or will not be justified in different societies, or its institutional articulation will have to take different forms.

2.1 The right not to be discriminated against

Perhaps the most important "universal" human right is the right not to be discriminated against: a right to equality. It is tempting to say that criteria of "discrimination" differ from culture to culture but this would be glib—to state that there is a right not to be discriminated against and then suggest that the criteria of discrimination are supplied by local cultures would be to render the whole principle of non-discrimination meaningless. For these are precisely those local cultures which often inflict discriminatory burdens upon its minorities and dissidents, and if the right to equal protection is to have an effective edge, it must provide those minorities with protection against discrimination perpetrated, or approved, by majorities. So the point at which the *universal* right of equality blends with the *contingent* facts must be located at a somewhat deeper level of theory of equality.

The most difficult task of an equal protection theory is to establish the workable and morally plausible criteria of non-discriminatory classifications: the criteria of what renders a classification permissible, and what taints it as violating legal equality. The most popular approach to identifying such criteria (if popularity is to be judged by the influence on judicial case law and on constitutional drafting) is by identifying certain types of classificatory properties as discriminatory per se, and thus either absolutely impermissible, or at least triggering a much stricter than usual standard of scrutiny of classification. The idea is that certain traits of individuals can never serve as grounds of legal classifications in impositions of legal burdens or in conferral of legal benefits (or, in a weaker version, that when they do serve as such grounds, they call for a much stronger defense than other types of classification).

This theory—which, for brevity, may be called a "per se theory of discrimination"—is as legally influential as it is philosophically implausible. Indeed, if one tries to give the best possible justification to this theory, its implausibility becomes apparent. The most likely candidates for "impermissible" traits are those which are immutable, such as race or gender. But if one tries to provide a coherent justification for what is wrong per se in drawing legal classifications on grounds which are immutable, then the theory breaks down. The most obvious reason which springs to one's mind is connected to an intuitive feeling that there is something particularly wrong in classifying people who are selected on the basis of characteristics which are beyond their control. There may be two ways of making this general intuition more specific. One such reason would be to say that immutable characteristics are, by their very nature, much more tightly linked to the *identity* of an individual than are the alterable characteristics which are more defining of a person's changeable *roles* in society. But, unless this equivalence is a matter of definition, so that anything that is immutable is *defined* as identity-constituting (in which case the argument is circular), immutability is a very imperfect proxy for identity. There are some characteristics which are immutable but which do not define anything particularly significant about an individual's identity (for example, freckles on one's back), and there are also characteristics which *may* define an individual to a great degree but which are alterable (for example, membership of a political party). But even if it were true that immutability properly captures identity-constituting characteristics, it would still be question-begging to say that legal classifications based on identity-defining characteristics are necessarily more suspicious than classifications based on more contingent properties.

A second (and probably better) reason why one might consider "immutability" as an impermissible criterion of legal classification is on the basis of the argument that imposing legal burdens upon individuals defined by criteria which do not leave the bearers of those burdens any opportunity to escape a burdened group is unfair. The key feature which would disqualify immutable characteristics from serving as a basis for legal classifications is, therefore, that individuals so classified cannot, through acts of their own volition, escape burdensome classifications. But again, the very articulation of this reason is sufficient to discredit it. It is analogous to an argument that hate speech addressed against a racial minority would be considered less harmful if members of that minority could easily change their skin color. Or to saying that persecution of members of a particular religion is not wrong as long as the adherents to this religion can convert to another faith.

So the theory of legal equality must work a little harder if it wants to identify the criteria for non-discriminatory classification—the criteria which would be both philosophically respectable (that is, would engage an explanation about the link between such criteria and that which confers moral odium upon discrimination), and also which would match our intuitive line drawn between discriminatory and non-discriminatory classifications. Such a theory most likely will refer to some legislative *motives* for classification as impermissible, and as tainting the classification with discriminatory character. But of course, to end the matter there would render the theory of discrimination largely unworkable because we need some more precise signposts for identifying the contempt (or hostility, or prejudice, etc.) behind a given classification. In order to make a theory workable, we need some indicia of classification which would serve as reliable indicators of contempt as a likely source of a given classification. As often is the case, we need to infer about the legislator's motive from the outcome—this is not something peculiar to a conception of legal *equality*. But we certainly cannot content ourselves with saying: people have a universal right not to be subject to classifications triggered by legislators' contempt, hostility, or prejudice. Because the disagreement about whether a given classification actually does express contempt largely replicates a more fundamental disagreement about whether such a classification is unjust, and the right against unjust classifications, without more, is meaningless as a universal standard—that is, as a standard of human rights that we would like to recommend to societies other than our own. We need more workable indicia than some vague standard.

What might serve as such indicia? A prior question to be answered should be, "how do we go about searching for such indicia?" The answer I provide appeals to a familiar method of trying to match general principles with our intuitive convictions that some actual patterns are unqualifiedly immoral—a method of reflective equilibrium. Here, we need to match our intuitive responses to what is wrong about some undoubtedly odious discriminations with our general theory that discrimination is a legislative expression of contempt. In Rawls's explanation, "reflective equilibrium" consists of achieving a rough coherence between our "considered convictions of justice" (understood as specific and intuitive moral responses to situations lending themselves to evaluations in terms of justice) and our "principles of justice" (understood as general and abstract moral maxims).[16] This methodology seems to be particularly well suited to our purposes here. In the area of anti-discrimination law, many of us are relatively uncertain about whether remedial racial preferences or protective bans upon the employment of women in some positions or the exclusion of women from combat duty are discriminatory or not. Furthermore, even if some of us have strong views about these matters, we face a disagreement among rational people arguing in good faith about the acceptability of those regulations. But we do not have similar doubts, and we do not face a similar disagreement in our societies, about whether racial segregation in public transport is wrong, whether refusal of voting rights to women is wrong, or whether religious tests for public office are wrong. The point is to elaborate the test of prejudice, hostility, and other wrongful motives using the latter (unquestionable) cases of discrimination as a starting point and then apply them to those actual moral disagreements and dilemmas which we face in our societies.

I have three such candidates for indicia of contempt which may emerge from such a process of reflective equilibrium: three indicia which are present in indubitable discriminations, which connect with contempt, and yet give more traction than contempt itself. The first indicium found in all indubitably objectionable discriminations is the fact that they impose legal burdens upon those who (before the law under scrutiny) had already been in a legally and socially disadvantageous situation—the law in question did not reverse, but added to, the preexisting (that is, present before the law under consideration) pattern of disadvantage. It has the effect of perpetrating, strengthening, or freezing the existing pattern of disadvantage. The second indicium is that truly objectionable discriminations can be characterized as the imposition of burdens by those who enjoy better access to lawmaking (either through numerical strength or for other reasons) upon those at a disadvantage in this classification. It can be therefore characterized as exploitation of access

16. John Rawls, *A Theory of Justice*, Cambridge, Mass.: Harvard University Press (1972) 19-20.

to lawmaking power in order to improve one's own position. Third, all truly odious discriminations have a stigmatizing function. Apart from all other burdens, they also place on its victims the stamp of inferiority, whether moral, intellectual, or both. The burden placed by a classification upon the losers also carries the symbolic message that a particular group is unworthy or incapable of performing certain social tasks, or enjoying certain social benefits, to an equal degree as other groups.

Now it would take a long argument to defend the use of these three indicia (a task I have attempted elsewhere)[17] and all that I can do here is assert that they fare quite well in a reflective equilibrium test. If one thinks of some paradigmatically invidious discriminations, such as the exclusion of women from education or work, or denial of voting rights to members of racial minorities, one finds all three features prominently present in these classifications. And not just present but also functionally related to the contempt, prejudice, or hostility underlying the lawmaker's attitude towards the victims of classification. To confirm this insight, consider why "reverse discrimination"—affirmative action based often on the same criteria of classification as those which have featured in more paradigmatic discrimination—is so much less obvious a candidate for objectionable discrimination. It is because it lacks some of the three (often, all three) indicia proposed above. Affirmative action is not a classification which adds to the already existing pattern of disadvantage. It is not an act of imposing burdens upon others by those who have privileged access to lawmaking. Nor does it carry (at least, it is not supposed to carry) a message of inferiority of those disadvantaged by the classification (here, the non-beneficiaries of affirmative action schemes). To the degree to which any of these indicia are present in a purported affirmative action, its benign (and morally unproblematic) character is correspondingly reduced.

It is now time to connect this argument with the "universalism of human rights" discourse. Suppose one claims that all should benefit from a legally recognized protection against discrimination, and that the state should not discriminate (or condone discrimination) against any group or individual. If my argument about a plausible conception of non-discrimination is correct, then it translates into the claim that those legal classifications which carry the three indicia just described should be struck down, or (in a weaker version) should be treated with the utmost suspicion, and be allowed to stand only if absolutely necessary to achieve particularly pressing goals. But of course each of the three indicia listed above is, in an important sense, "local," and responds to patterns and factors which are context dependent rather than universal. The first indicium relies upon a baseline of a preexisting pat-

17. Wojciech Sadurski, "The Concept of Legal Equality and an Underlying Theory of Discrimination," *Saint Louis-Warsaw Transatlantic Law Journal* (1998) 93-102.

tern of disadvantage in a given society; a pattern which may or may not be replicated in a different society. The second indicium makes a reference to an actual distribution of opportunities consisting of access to and influence on the lawmaking process; it identifies the groups which are closer to the process and those which can be seen as "permanent minorities" (perhaps "discrete and insular minorities") whose voice on legislative proposals is rarely heard and rarely taken into account. The third indicium appeals to a cultural symbolic meaning conveyed by a classification: does the message imply, in the minds of those who receive it, that those burdened by the classification are somehow inferior, less worthy, undeserving of different treatment? Is the stigma attached—in a given society, at a given time—to the particular burden?

None of these indicia lends itself to a universalist articulation. Put together, they create a template which can be applied only if we infuse them with the factual circumstances of a given society, of its own patterns of disadvantage, the structure of its ruling elites, and its prevailing symbolic meanings of stigma. The *limits* of universalistic claims of a right to equal protection are reached when we try to articulate the morally plausible standards of non-discriminatory classification for a specific society.

We would not have that problem if the "per se theory" (or, to use Dworkin's language, a "banned sources" theory) was plausible. We would then be able to say, in a universalistic vein, that whenever and wherever legal classifications draw the legally significant distinctions between citizens along the lines of their race, or sex, or religion, or whatever other individual property—they violate a universal principle of non-discrimination. But such a "per se theory" is profoundly implausible, for the reasons indicated above, and so we are left with a theory which can claim strong moral plausibility, but which in the balance deprives us of the luxury of universalistic articulation. When asked, "Is a particular racial classification in a particular country consistent with the rule of non-discrimination?" we must answer "It depends." Fortunately, if we accept the theory outlined above, we know what it depends *on*. But to give a considered answer we need to look at the local circumstances through the lens of our three proposed indicia, and the answer will differ from place to place, from country to country, and from epoch to epoch.

2.2 A right to outrageous speech

My second case study concerns the universal human right to free speech. More specifically, it is about free political and academic speech, and even more particularly, about free speech the contents of which are likely to hurt deeply—and for understandable reasons[18]—many people who will likely

18. As opposed to the speech which hurts people because of their unusual, eccentric sensitivities.

consider it a deliberate and grave insult to their national, ethnic, or religious group. To focus the examination even more narrowly, I will consider just one example of such speech, namely, the case of Holocaust denial.[19]

My choice of the case study is dictated by several factors. First, it is a real and lively issue in a number of contemporary democracies (the so-called historic revisionists made themselves known and heard in countries as diverse as Poland, France, Germany, the United States, the United Kingdom, Canada, and Australia). Second, it is an issue which elicited diverse responses in those countries—with some (France, Germany, Austria) introducing formal legal sanctions for expressions of such views, and others (notably the United States) considering these expressions as belonging to the sphere of constitutionally protected speech. Hence, the case provides an interesting litmus test for universality: if the right in question is universal, and if it extends to this particular form of speech, then we have good reasons for remonstrating with those countries (such as France or Germany) which prohibit these expressions and for urging them to comply with the universal human right. Of course, it is important to remember that the Holocaust denial law is used here merely as an instantiation of a broader right, that is the right to unpopular or hurtful speech on public matters. To postulate a universal human right to deny the fact of Holocaust sounds bizarre, but to postulate a right to political speech which may hurt many of the listeners is not.

This particular case study is significant because it encapsulates at least two independently significant themes in traditional thinking about what makes free speech valuable even if it is deeply offensive and hurtful to some. First, that speech which aims at making an academic or scholarly finding (however misguided) should never be censored or penalized because the best way to pursue truth is by letting all the hypotheses and theories compete freely in a marketplace-like environment—a variation on the Millian anti-censorship theme.[20] Second, that speech which is about matters of public (and more specifically, political) interest deserves particularly stringent protection regardless of its contents and regardless of the hostility it may provoke because any attempt to censor some speakers in that domain reduces the sovereign position of the people exercised through democratic self-government. This may

19. For a good discussion of different legal approaches to Holocaust denial, see Jonathan Cooper and Adrian Marshall Williams, "Hate Speech, Holocaust Denial and International Human Rights Law," 6 *European Human Rights Law Review* (1999) 593-613.

20. Its *locus classicus* is of course the second chapter of John Stuart Mill's *On Liberty*. Perhaps the best-known modern judicial statement of this idea is the United States Supreme Court's assertion that "[e]ven a false statement may be deemed to make a valuable contribution to public debate," *New York Times v. Sullivan*, 376 U.S. 255, 279 n. 19 (1964). A modified recent restatement of the theory may be found in Cass R. Sunstein, *Democracy and the Problem of Free Speech*, New York: Free Press (1993).

be referred to as the Meiklejohnian theme.[21] The case study selected here seems to implicate both the Millian and Meiklejohnian themes because it is both about an alleged statement of a historical truth and an intended political position about the alleged exploitation by Jews today of the Holocaust. The fact that, to most of us, the denial of the Holocaust is an absolute historical nonsense does not make it any less worthy of protection under the Millian theory, and the fact that it is morally and politically abhorrent does not diminish its claim for protection under the Meiklejohnian thesis.

Suppose you believe (as I do) in the two themes of the free speech argument—the Millian and the Meiklejohnian themes—as providing good reasons for a robust protection of speech even if it is offensive, harmful, and patently untrue. Suppose you believe that it is a universal human right that, as a general proposition, all societies should tolerate speech on public and academic issues even if many people are upset by it, and even if most of us think the speech false. Or, to put it more moderately, and from a negative side, you believe that it should be at least a universally recognized part of the right to free speech that the very fact of its patent falsity and its strong offensiveness are *not* sufficiently good reasons for its suppression. No genuine right to freedom of speech (you believe) can survive the proviso that an act of speech, to enjoy protection, must be true and must be inoffensive. Further, let us assume for the sake of argument that since you believe that the right to free speech—at least as far as speech on public and academic matters—should be universally recognized, this proviso forms a part of your understanding of universal human rights.

But this still does not settle conclusively the question as to which legal regime of Holocaust denial conforms with the universal principle of freedom of speech. The proviso that offensiveness and falsity are not sufficient reasons for speech suppression does not imply that *any* offensive and/or false speech must be, in virtue of its offensiveness and/or falsity, legally protected. For the offensiveness may be of such magnitude that the presumption in favor of speech protection regardless of its marginal offensiveness will be rebutted here. And the harm incident to its falsity may be of such gravity that it will defeat all usual arguments for protection of harmful speech.[22] This is the proviso which Dworkin had expressly attached to his initial "rights as trumps" articulation: to say that rights trump utility considerations means only that a simple net disutility of a right-exercise is not a sufficient ground for preventing this exercise, but at a higher level of the scale of disutility, we may

21. See Alexander Meiklejohn, *Free Speech and Its Relation to Self-Government*, Port Washington, N.Y.: Kennikat Press (1948).

22. See Frederick Schauer, *Free Speech: A Philosophical Enquiry*, Cambridge: Cambridge University Press (1982) 7-10.

be authorized (indeed, obliged) to stop the exercise of a right without at the same time denying the trumping characteristic of this right.[23]

Where does this place us with respect to Holocaust denial laws? "It all depends," again, although this time it depends on factors that are somewhat different than those depicted in the case study of discrimination. Let me suggest an intuition with which to work through. Those who do not share the intuition will admittedly have no reason to follow me in the attempt to unpack it and provide rationalization for it—this will not be *their* reflective equilibrium.[24] But when I think about Holocaust denial (and even more generally, anti-Semitic and other hate speech) I have this intuition: I do not object to this type of speech being legal in the United States (where it is legal) or in Canada (where it is illegal), but I do object to such speech being protected in Germany (where it has been declared illegal) and perhaps in Austria (where it is also illegal).

Those who do not find this intuition outlandish might ask themselves a question about what accounts for the difference between the United States and Germany in this respect. One obvious reason is a matter of sensibility: one may be committed to a robust principle of free speech, and normally be prepared to tolerate even extremely unpalatable consequences, but one feels just *sickened* by the fact that the country which perpetrated the Holocaust on Jews in Europe only sixty years ago could now legally protect its own citizens who wish to deny that it actually happened. Such a feeling of nausea does not necessarily derive from the idea that offense to the memory of Holocaust victims, and to the sensitivities of their survivors, is greater when the lie is uttered in Berlin than in Boston—though this may be the case. It is simply a much greater violation of sensibility norms.

If that is all there is to the distinction between (say) the United States and Germany then it arguably gives us no mileage in providing a plausible rationalization to our initial intuition. But there may be more. There are different types of social harms which may result from speech, and some are disallowed from figuring as justifications for restrictions on speech (for example, "harm" associated with political satire which damages the reputations of politicians), while others are not (for example, harms which weaken national security resulting from the willful publication of military secrets). There are many harms which lie in between such obvious cases: they are not absolutely disallowed from figuring in justifications for speech suppression, but the threshold for demonstrating that harm is sufficiently severe and/or sufficiently likely is increased to a relatively high level. Something like a doctrine of "a clear or present danger" (or its equivalents) acts as a threshold-lifting device

23. Ronald Dworkin, *Taking Rights Seriously*, (rev. ed.), London: Duckworth (1978) 92.

24. As is clearly the case with Cooper and Marshall, *op. cit.*, note 19.

and places a high presumption (with varying chances of refutation in various cases) in favor of legal protection for speech.

An example of the sort of harm that lies between the two extremes just noted is the growth of extreme political movements. Such extreme movements are one type of evil which may result from certain types of speech and which may present a danger to the democratic system and to the peaceful stability of society. They may figure among the justifications for suppression of speech, but the threshold for demonstrating the reality of the threat must be relatively high. This proposition is, obviously, a mere assertion which calls for further argument but for the present purposes I will take this assertion to be plausible. And this may provide us with an explanation of our initial intuition about Holocaust denial laws. Holocaust denial is (as I would suggest without the risk of sounding eccentric) an expression of anti-Semitism masquerading as a historical theory. It is a part of a larger package of an ideology which maintains that Jews cannot be trusted in anything, even in regard to their own past. As such, it is not merely a veiled incitement to societal distrust toward an ethnic group.[25] It is also a useful symbolic rallying theme for extreme anti-Semitic movements. But the danger that such speech is likely to provoke is different in different countries. In Germany, with racist and other extreme right movements reaching a high point of political mobilization, there is a real threat that an unrestricted circulation of openly racist propaganda may undermine democratic stability to a point of crisis. In the United States, the groups which feed on literature such as "historical revisionism" are part of the political folklore, just as are flat-Earthers and Montana separatists: probably irritating and deeply offensive to many, but very unlikely to reach a capacity to challenge the democratic system.

The question about the applicability of this particular "universal human right"—the right to express publicly one's political opinions and one's scholarly findings—depends therefore upon some contingent local circumstances, in this case, whether the exercise of this right is likely to undermine the social stability of a democratic system. This boils down to a debate about "intolerant democracies." Some democracies have urgent reasons to be intolerant toward undemocratic movements if the integrity of their democratic institutions is at stake, while others can afford to be tolerant towards extreme anti-democratic movements.[26] This is not a matter of an intellectual choice of one theo-

25. As Michel Troper concludes, with respect to the French loi Gayssot: "En punissant la négation du génocide des mêmes peines que l'incitation à la haine raciale, [le Parlement] présume qu'elle est une acte équivalent parce qu'il est de même nature et qu'il porte comme lui atteinte à des intérets qui doivent être protégés," in Michel Troper, "La loi Gayssot et la Constitution," 54 *Annales* (1999) 1239-55 at 1252.

26. See Gregory H. Fox and Georg Nolte, "Intolerant Democracies," 36 *Harvard International Law Journal* (1995) 1-70.

retical conception of democracy as opposed to another, but rather a matter of political urgency which is of a contingent and local character. And so it is with human rights in general, and this particular human right in particular. To the question whether one should have a right to speak one's mind freely even if it may be seen as offensive or false, the answer is again, "It depends," and again, we have a rough idea of what it depends *on*. The factors which are decisive in this case take the form of empirical evidence regarding: the level of mobilization and the organizational capabilities of the extremist movements which use this form of speech as their tool; the amount of societal support for these organizations and the level of social frustration which feeds the social demand for these movements; the likelihood of these extremist groups to perpetrate acts of violence and ignite social instability; etc.

Of course, to an orthodox civil libertarian such criteria are anathema. The right to free speech, we will be told, cannot be guaranteed under the condition that this speech will be ineffective. But "effectiveness" of speech in terms of leading to social disturbances is an argument which fits the proportionality or necessity analysis in the European tradition (whether a restriction is necessary in a democratic society to avert certain, clearly specified social evils), or the "strict scrutiny" of restrictions of constitutional rights in U.S. constitutional parlance. The contingent factors affecting the likelihood of instability or danger, which a restriction of a right permissibly averts, enter the analysis of how a universal right blends with a local situation.

3. Conclusion

We have considered two different cases of how a universal human right blends with local conditions to different outcomes, as a function of different local variables. These two types of local variables belong to different categories. In the first case (the principle of anti-discrimination) an answer to the question about whether people have a right to be protected against certain types of official classifications depended upon certain facts which figured in the very justification of that right. They figured in the right only indirectly and negatively (the three factors which, as I suggested, were the plausible indicia of contempt in classification, provided us with good reasons for hostility towards certain classifications, and so grounded an individual's human right to be protected against them), but figured there nevertheless. They identified—as indicia, or if you like, as plausible symptoms—the presence of factors which justify our hostility towards certain classifications, and therefore justify our extension of the protection of individuals against these classifications. As this protection against contempt-based classifications is universally justified, we consider it a universal human right; but as the facts which suggest the presence of such factors (indicia) differ from place to place, the blending of a universal right with the local conditions will produce different local contours of that right.

The second type of variable is of a somewhat different character. The variables on which the existence of a certain human right depended were of an empirical character, just as in our first category, but they were not related to the justification of a right but rather to the outer boundaries of the right. They had to do with the important goods which collide with a given right, and which therefore argue for a more or less restrictive approach to the scope of a given right. They are not "justificatory" in the sense that these facts do not appertain to the reasons we have for protecting such a right in the first place, but rather they indicate the point of conflict between the right and other social goods which may enter into collision with the goods protected by that right.

One should not exaggerate the differences between these types of variables. "Justificatory" variables are of empirical character, while "empirical" variables may figure in the justification for the definition of a scope of a right. And they are not meant to be an exhaustive list. Put together, they provide an illustration for a proposition made at the outset: there is nothing intolerant (perhaps only paternalistic, but in an unobjectionable way) in formulating human rights with a universalistic aspiration—meant to apply to societies different from our own—but for their articulation; they will blend with local contingent circumstances in different ways, resulting in different local shapes of universal rights.

Chapter 7

Helen Stacy*

International Human Rights in a Fragmenting World

There is a conceptual *contretemps* in international human rights. And just as this crisis is troubling to those who write about legal institutions, it poses a conundrum for those who write in philosophy, in comparative political and international studies, and in all academic areas that deal with identity, values, and human belief. It troubles those engaged in policy development, in social justice advocacy, and in NGOs. Across these disciplinary and professional fields scholars are asking the same question, as between radically different forms of human existence: how are "we" to decide whose values ought to trump when human values conflict on the international stage? Can human rights only be defended from within a set of foundational beliefs that are particular to specific Western ideological and cultural commitments? These questions about the universality of human rights have given rise to a vigorous debate about cultural relativism.

But while the philosophical debate about universalism and particularization continues unsolved and is quite possibly unsolvable, violence and injustice continue. Thus the question becomes more urgent: faced with terrible human rights violations, what sort of understanding of human rights should

* My thanks go to Ryan McEntee and Allegra McLeod for their valuable research assistance.

András Sajó (ed.), Human Rights with Modesty: The Problem of Universalism, *161-183.*

resonate in international criminal court hearings about human rights allegations? What values do international human rights embrace and exclude, and do they have an ontological basis giving them a genuine legitimacy that can carry across profound cultural differences? Law as an institution that enforces core political and social values cannot sidestep this debate.

The drafters of the 1948 Universal Declaration of Human Rights placed hope in the idea that declaring rights as moral universals would foster a global rights consciousness in "the common people" around the globe. Religion in any overt sense was kept out of the Declaration as a practical inducement to the different cultures of the world to join together. Enunciating rights without explaining why people have them was also a philosophical response to two confounding chapters in history—the revelation that the Holocaust had been perpetrated under the name of the rule of law and the experience of Stalinism as a stifling of individual agency together galvanized philosophy to subvert the religious concept of truth and to replace it with the less metaphysical concept of freedom.[1] And now, even after history has showed that fascism was far worse than even the worst of liberalism's most egregious failures, Rwanda, Yugoslavia and East Timor are recent evidence of national religious and ethnic intolerance with violent consequences. The resurgence in the last decade of civil and military aggression justified on grounds of religious, ethnic, and cultural conviction has given rise to a new array of international legal institutions—the International Criminal Tribunals for Rwanda, the International Criminal Tribunal for the former Yugoslavia, and now the International Criminal Court. International approval for these institutions is high, though not universal. One of the objections raised is the question of whether international human rights are secularized morality, and whether this morality is inextricably Western, liberal, and individualist.

What are legal institutions to do when there is no consensus about which values ought to shape political and social relations? Put differently, how can decisions about the content of human rights be made without reenacting nineteenth-century cultural imperialism, this time in the name of the expansion of political and behavioral norms? The legitimation of international human rights presents an ethical dilemma that stands at the crossroads of universal values on the one hand, and diversity and pluralism on the other.

---

1. Hannah Arendt, for example, has made a strong attack on legal positivism; German Jews had refused to disobey laws that sent them by the millions to their deaths because they had identified them as "their" laws. In her account of the Eichmann trial, she also notes that Eichmann's defense of a Kantian morality to obey the law gives rise to the need to read Kant from the angle of freedom as reflective judgment, with a strong dose of the Heideggerian reading of freedom as also entailing responsibility, read by Arendt as the *sensus communis* originally proposed by Kant. See Hannah Arendt, *Eichmann in Jerusalem: A Report on the Banality of Evil*, New York: Viking Press (1964).

Whereas traditional Western liberal jurisprudence promotes a knowable and continuing construct of human identity as the basis of a legal system that is consistent and precedent-based, other philosophical and theoretical positions celebrate "difference" and human variety. The increasing trend is for scholars of all stripes—liberals who favor pluralism, communitarians who situate the encumbered self into her constitutive context, and the diverse groups that gather under the heading of "poststructuralists"—to stress the need for legal thinking to be liberated from assumptions of universal humanity.

The most fundamental challenge to the narrow legal liberalism of the relativistic approach lies in its insistence that there is no transcendental human sameness. Rather, the diversity argument insists that humanity is marked by difference and variety in human values and in conceptions of the individual, the group, and the state. This divided consciousness is the hallmark of human rights in the late twentieth century, as postcolonial critiques emphasize the philosophical conflict between "the West and the Rest." Placed together, these philosophical and political critiques have posed questions of indeterminacy, contingency, pluralism, judgment, and experience. All of these concepts are deeply implicated in law and legal judgment. In law, just as in society, it is now plain that a single unitary political, ethical, theoretical framework is too crude; it cannot contain the diversity of the groups and the subjects to whom our legal institutions must respond. These questions go to the heart of the legitimacy of international human rights claims.

This set of problems rests on the terrain of the social and political upheaval dating from the old millennium to the beginning of the new. The end of the Cold War in the late 1980s and new technologies in an increasingly borderless world together convey the contemporary motif of fragmenting nation-states and proliferating groups and social organizations. The use of human rights language as an all-purpose rhetoric of appeal to the nation-state and the international community reflects the pluralism of present-day politics. And while the concept of international human rights as it was originally conceived in the Universal Declaration of Human Rights may have been too much a product of the metanarratives of the Enlightenment—the economically rational individual living within a Kantian nation-state that is capable of neutral legal judgment premised upon principles that treat humans as ends in themselves—human rights as they have come to be articulated in postcolonial, post-Cold War times are less fettered by such Western-centric assumptions. In the contemporary world, the idea of human rights makes moral and legal claims even though its claim to universal morality is problematic.

In what follows, the post-World War II human rights era is divided into three phases: post-World War II to *perestroika*; the post-Cold War period; and the contemporary phase of internationalization. The contemporary phase is marked by the confluence of two issues: an exceptional engagement around the world with the idea of human rights, on the one hand, with an intense debate about the moral standing of cultural difference on the other. My approach here, in thinking through the justification for human rights despite cultural difference, is informed by several contemporary accounts of the justification of legal power that emerge from different philosophical trends that span the liberal/communitarian/poststructuralist divide. I divide the discussion into three different paradigms that offer alternate justifications for human rights in the internationalized era: a political paradigm, a linguistic paradigm, and a procedural paradigm. Each has a philosophical or theoretical analogue: the political paradigm corresponds to the liberal cosmopolitanism explicated recently by Rawls; the linguistic paradigm corresponds to the radical alterity explicated by Levinas and Derrida; and the procedural paradigm corresponds to the legal proceduralism described by Habermas. Each analogue has features that do, and that do not, contribute to a model for human rights under the conditions of globalization. Finally, I propose a framework—a fusion of radical alterity within a procedural approach to legal conflict in circumstances of cultural difference—that provides both a practical and an ethical dimension to the justification for human rights that emphasizes the capacity for individuals to exercise agency and autonomy, and the capacity for law and politics to ameliorate human conflict. Together, they suggest a legal theory that can conceptualize both cultural difference and international human rights norms.

1. The New Epoch of Human Rights Language

There were two distinctive phases in the legal development of human rights in the twentieth century: from 1948 to the mid-1980s, socialist and capitalist cultures pursued the human rights attributes of their political ideologies, one by emphasizing social and economic rights, the other by giving primacy to political and civil rights. The second phase began with *perestroika*, when the utopian goal of social and economic rights as the means to political and civil rights was consigned officially to the ideological dustbin of failed social experiments. After the Cold War, human rights discourse has focused less upon whether human rights ought to be either negative or positive, and more about states' legal, political, and economic capacity to supply enough of both to satisfy the basic needs of their populations. The collapse of socialism and the emergence of the global market elided the ideological divisions of human rights as one, rather than two, "rights" cultures; not least because markets break down traditional social structures and encourage competitive behavior. The association of markets with civil and political human rights, and communism with social and economic human rights has been broken.

A third phase of human rights has now emerged—the phase of internationalization, or what has become known as globalization. The focus of human rights in this contemporary phase is different; linguistic, ethnic, or religious groups in many nation-states are increasingly asserting demands for recognition of their identity through some kind of distinctive legal expression, or even relative regulatory autonomy. Today's discourse of human rights now encompasses the status and scope of group rights and cultural rights, giving rise to debates about their epistemological and ontological foundations and whether such rights derive from universal human characteristics or unique cultural differences.[2] Clearly, not all appeals to human rights are an appeal to Western perceptions of individual dignity; in some jurisdictions, human rights have aided appeals to certain "universal" prerogatives as traditional cultural roles based on community identity have continued. While human rights have "gone global" in this era of internationalization, they have also "gone local." Rights to a separate cultural identity assert themselves against the notion of universal human values. In comparative doctrinal legal studies, there is now an increasing search for understanding of legal cultures, not in the positivist tradition of learning another culture's legal rules, but as "a thick description of legally related *mentalities*—traditions, institutional and professional histories, cultural assumptions, outlooks, values, attitudes and preferences."[3] Increasing numbers of Western and non-Western judicial systems are struggling to incorporate indigenous perspectives in decisions ranging from land rights, intellectual property rights, and criminal sentencing.[4] The more complex realization in this third phase in the trajectory of human rights is that, just as non-Western societies have values outside the individualistic value system of traditional liberalism, Western societies contain immense cultural diversity and value difference.

There is an additional feature to the contemporary phase, one that has been present in philosophical and political discourse but which is now a component of human rights discourse in international law. Over the last several decades, the roping of human rights to the individual has come under increasing pressure from the postcolonial resurgence of nationalism. Nationalism

---

2. Henry J. Steiner and Philip Alston, *International Human Rights in Context: Law, Politics, Morals*, 2d ed., Oxford: Oxford University Press (2000) 4-5.
3. Roger Cotterell, *Law and Community in a Time of Fear: Sociolegal Studies and the Reshaping of the Social*, January 31, 2002, (paper on file with author) referring to the legal anthropology scholars: Pierre Legrand, *Fragments on Law-as-Culture*, Deventer: W. E. J. Tjeenk Willink (1999); Pierre Legrand, "What 'Legal Transplants'?," in David Nelken and Johannes Feest (eds.), *Adapting Legal Cultures*, Portland, Oreg.: Hart Publishing (2001) and Vivian Grosswald Curran, "Cultural Immersion, Difference and Categories in U.S. Comparative Law," 46 *American Journal of Comparative Law* (1998) 43.
4. Elizabeth Povinelli, *The Cunning of Recognition*, Durham and London: Duke University Press (2002).

not only places the nation-state in question; it also puts into question the nature of the "selves" that normative international theory and the theory of human rights seek to empower or limit.[5] This epistemic difference was graphically illustrated in the Bangkok Declaration of 1993, when the Singaporean, Malaysian, Indonesian, and Chinese governments declared that Asian cultures ascribe a different meaning to human rights from the individualistic West's. "Asian values," they argued, place the group over the individual, place harmony and consensus over adversariness and debate, and place deference to authority over individual self-expression and freedom. More problematically, "Asian values" have at times become the justification for authoritarian Asian leaders and governments who use the language of human rights as rhetoric in defense of authoritarian practices, such as the suppression of free speech in journalistic criticism of dubious government development projects allegedly carried out to the economic benefit of a town or a region. This justificatory package emphasizes economic development and political stability (both domestic and regional) at the expense of civil and political rights, all in the name of protecting Asian sensibilities from the ravages of the Western mindset. Ironically, human rights transgressions of free speech and freedom of association are thus ostensibly committed in the name of human rights of economic prosperity and regional self-determination.

The Asian values debate of the 1990s emphasized two points. First, that the creation and maintenance of the institutions of democracy do not necessarily deliver a recognizable culture of human rights at the level of the nation-state. If people have their personal liberty and security guaranteed by law, they also have the legal and political capacity to define their own commitments and their own projects. There is no reason to assume that they will use this freedom to craft a package of civil and political rights that mirrors the Western model. Second, caution is warranted with regard to self-confident assumptions of universal standards of proper human behavior. Clearly, there is no broad and deep international consensus on the meaning of human rights, simply because there is no broad and deep international consensus on the values to which people adhere. Just as the "human" at the heart of human rights can no longer be thought of as the voting white man of the Enlightenment tradition, "the values imputed to human rights are not universally held."[6] Rather, "local religious and cultural beliefs...constitute the values that people hold."[7]

---

5. Tom Hadden, "The Question of Self-Determination and its Implications for Normative International Theory," in Simon Caney and Peter Jones (eds.), *Human Rights in Global Diversity*, London: Frank Cass (2001) 95.
6. Anthony J. Langlois, *The Politics of Justice and Human Rights: Southeast Asia and Universalist Theory*, Cambridge: Cambridge University Press (2001) 5.
7. *Ibid.*

But the conceptual confusion is even more acute at the level of real people who exhibit cultural difference, as numerous recent human rights issues demonstrate. In Saudi Arabia, a convicted man who had his hand amputated for theft became the focus of attention as to whether that action placed the Saudis in contravention of the ban on "cruel punishment" under the UN Convention against Torture. The French refusal to extradite to the United States suspects in the September 11, 2002 attack on the World Trade towers, because the death penalty is still practiced in the United States raised questions about American exceptionalism from the predominant Western standard of abolition of the death penalty.[8] And the arrest of local Pakistani leaders by regional authorities for passing a sentence of gang rape on a woman because of her brother's breach of tribal etiquette with a woman from another tribe drew attention to the conflict between coexistent provincial and national legal standards.[9] Each one of these issues poses a dilemma for a human rights theory that rests upon shared values and shared convictions.

Some proponents of globalization optimistically argue that a growing awareness of shared humanity amidst great cultural difference carries a certain moral authority, and that this will eventually provide the rationale for human rights as powerful transnational norms and standards of conduct[10]—even if the human rights that form the corpus of international law are not fixed but expand, change, and contract over time. Within this optimistic group, some proponents claim that human rights have an overriding status *vis-à-vis* other moralities; that human rights simply should not have to compete for our allegiance from among other moral frameworks. An alternative and more pessimistic account of globalization points out that while the information and technological revolution wrought by globalization has sharply increased our awareness of human diversity, the benefits of the new world order are unevenly distributed. This gloomier account points out that the material conditions of the economically oppressed do not seem to have improved from a growing awareness of our shared humanity. The world seems a long way from the moral integration that a universal understanding of human rights would require. How, amid this disputed terrain, should human rights as the *lingua franca* of international request be justified?

The sharper awareness of the immense degree of human diversity both within and between nation-states raises the question of how global norms of human rights ought to be developed, especially when the governance of the global community is not a macroscopic analogue of the representative and

8. www.deathpenaltyinfo.org/Terr-APExtradition.html
9. http://hrw.org/press/2002/07/pak0712.htm
10. Ian Clark, *Globalization and International Relations Theory*, Oxford: Oxford University Press (1999).

accountable governance of the nation-state. For most human rights violations, there is no direct legal means by which these norms can be enforced as no transnational body, including the United Nations, enjoys forms of authority which parallel those of the domestic governments of states. Even if international economic integration is growing under the conditions of globalization, the claim that there is wide agreement about the nature and substance of human rights is not necessarily true. This means that assertions of human rights are generally made in a context in which others—often, the state—assert that either there is no such human right, or that the state has not violated that right.

But it is precisely because significant numbers have experienced globalization as an oppressive experience—through the loss of traditional markets and traditional ways of organizing social life—that they seek a political means of asserting their claim against the state, a multinational corporation, or a substate actor.[11] Human rights discourse provides them with the language to do this, precisely because of the political and moral edge that human rights discourse has acquired over the last sixty years. In short, human rights have gone global not just because "the West" seeks to homogenize "the rest." It is equally true to say that the rhetoric of human rights has been seized upon outside the West because the powerless find in that language the means to articulate their struggle against unjust states and oppressive social practices. Under the tumultuous conditions of globalization, this is increasingly important. The conditions of internationalism thus force a more rigorous analysis of the tension between universal human standards of behavior and respect for cultural variance from those standards.

2. Philosophical Concepts of Human Rights

Philosophy as a combination of metaphysics (in the social sciences, the science of the first principles of being and identity) and ethics (the science of human duty as a system of morals) has traditionally concerned itself with reason, truth, and representation. Metaphysics and ethics in traditional Western philosophy have always been interconnected in this way, and traditional philosophy has had an ethical commitment to justice and freedom. Legal theory, like most modern undertakings, has tended to emphasize objectivity and rationality. For the great philosophers of the eighteenth and nineteenth century, the struggle for self-recognition began with procuring and creating the means of subsistence. Drawing from Kant, legal philosophy has traditionally inves-

11. Michael Ignatieff, *Human Rights as Politics and Idolatry*, Princeton and Oxford: Princeton University Press (2001) 7.

tigated justice, freedom, and notions of "the good" based upon the idealized cities and citizens of the Enlightenment dream. But the implications of the international era are philosophically complex. The collapse of the Berlin Wall in 1989 and the former Soviet Union's fragmentation is a metaphor for an ideological fragmentation of intellectual differences dating from the 1980s, between philosophy and theory, liberalism and communitarianism, cultural studies, gender studies, and postcolonial studies.

Over this period, philosophy following Heidegger and Nietzsche has criticized the Kantian system of thinking which established "truth" as the goal.[12] Legal philosophy as a discipline these days develops theories of justice amid the equivocations between metaphysics and ethics, traversing the gaps and silences in traditional accounts of legal regulation of human conduct. Human rights discourse now occupies a no man's land between traditional philosophy and the Parthenon of plurality exhorted by postcolonial studies, cultural studies, and other avant-garde academic phenomena. The most avant-garde within this philosophical tussle paints an absolute opposition between liberal individualism and cultural pluralism. For the human rights traditionalists, this avant-gardism has become a tool in trade of freewheeling intellectuals and popularists who play fast and loose with legal doctrines and intellectual trends. Some even worry that the emergent disciplines threaten the credibility of hard-won human rights victories.[13] For others, the era of

12. Legal scholarship that is critical of the analytical methods of traditional legal approaches has deployed critical social theory, especially that originating with Michel Foucault and Jacques Derrida. Foucault's opaquely acknowledged capacity for human agency to mark out an identity *beyond* sameness has produced an undercurrent of fear among his critics. The fear is that to acknowledge difference and diversity is to slide instantly into the abyss of cultural relativism. This misses the point about Foucault, who instead aimed to remove the sting from the concept of indeterminacy *itself.* Rather than make out an argument for relativism, he wanted to defuse the idea that indeterminacy would inevitably incur a loss of identity. The Foucauldian project is neither apathy, nor Nietzschean nihilism. Rather, it is a hypersensitivity to the different claims of other cultures, and skepticism towards the liberal hope that it is possible to bridge those differences. Derrida's point is different, and more explicitly ethical. Like Foucault, he questions the assumed commonality of values and beliefs of Western logo centrism. His point is that these are imposed violently through language. His deconstructive inversion of speech and writing is a warning that even face-to-face communication cannot guarantee an escape from exclusionary tactics. Exclusions lie within language *itself.* Derrida draws on Levinas' argument about the radical incommensurable singularity (or "radical alterity") of the "Other" (Levinas' "Other" is marked by capitalization), and then extends Levinas further to show that there is something in common between "I" and "Other"; that they are not completely impenetrable to each other. See Helen Stacy, *Postmodernism and Law: Jurisprudence in a Fragmenting World*, Aldershot, England: Ashgate (2001).

13. Some feminists ask the question: "How am I to get legal recognition of the unique harms that are visited upon the female body, when cultural theorists tell me that my body, my very identity, is just an amalgam of effects created by my social world?" See Donna Landry and Gerald MacLean, *Materialist Feminisms*, Oxford: Blackwell (1993).

preeminence of grand legal-politico-economic theories is over. These critics argue that the Enlightenment pedigree has been revealed as the expression of false consciousness that misrepresents the social world as sharing a single view of human identity, when in fact there is little agreement in the world about anything. In light of this criticism of the orthodox liberal project, it is more difficult to believe that any *one* theory or point of view could possibly grasp the complexity and diversity of human existence.

The singular vision of human identity that is the foundational premise of the orthodox philosophical account of human rights has thus been placed in doubt, even if it has not been entirely erased. It is possible to discern that, for all their elegance, legal theory's grand narratives were, and remain, gross simplifications of the world and its inhabitants. The chronology of the Holocaust, the post-World War II era of human rights, the end of the Cold War, and now the new international politics have contributed to the sense that philosophy needs to declare new ideological commitments. This sense is that, even if the confident assumption of shared human identity can no longer be sustained, at least we can be clear upon what ethical grounds our disagreements are fought. But despite these cracks in the philosophical foundations of universal values, the idea of human rights and the ideal of judgment have not lost their rallying force. The spread of the rhetoric of human rights across the East/West and North/South divide attests to its ongoing grip on the human imagination.

Whereas most scholarship on human rights in the first two phases of human rights discourse took place within distinctively traditional disciplinary domains—principally law, philosophy, and political science—contemporary human rights analysis increasingly takes place in cultural studies, in contemporary social theory, and in humanities-based approaches to cultural anthropology. The approach in these latter fields is to cut across the traditional disciplines and extrapolate from them to produce a broader way of analyzing and understanding human rights. Within this contemporary grouping, three alternative ways of analyzing the dilemma of cultural relativism in human rights can be categorized as the *political* and the *linguistic* and the *proceduralist*. From this analysis, I derive a fourth model that combines aspects of proceduralism with the ethic of alterity proposed by the linguistic approach. Together, these provide both ethical and practical signposts for thinking through human rights and cultural difference in the globalized era.

3. Human Rights as Politics

The political response to cultural relativism suggests that there simply ought to be a pragmatic acceptance of the existence of human rights as a phenomenon of widely shared belief, even if it cannot be accepted that all who believe in human rights share the same normative basis for those human rights. For example, Anthony Langlois, an Australian political theorist, has recently argued that the only universal amongst peoples is their capacity to think and to act as moral agents, and "it is false philosophical method that human rights have ever been seen as other than political."[14] He suggests that the better alternative in a postrationalist world where philosophical foundationalism is no longer viable is:

> a rolling hegemony of different articulations of justice, of human rights values, which take their turn at being the common sense of a society; which are open to debate; which are contentious but are also just to the extent that they are revisable through the return of the political.[15]

Langlois' approach to the problem of human rights under the culturally diverse conditions of globalization sidesteps the thorny problems of shared normativity by emphasizing the pragmatic value of human rights, arguing that it is only when "human rights [are] centered around a particular non-universal tradition—western liberalism...— [that they] cannot be universal."[16] This sidestepping movement is intended to extract human rights from the necessity of agreement about the transcendent morality of certain values. Langlois wants to replace liberal universality with a rolling political consensus about values, burying any Archimedean fixed point beneath vigorous political debate that continually contests prior agreements. But this feature, intended to save human rights from an ineluctable connection to Western liberal political ideals, is itself a problem. If human rights are simply a product of a nation-state's political process, then ought we not be concerned with the means by which that process operates? How can it be assumed that participation in the political process is equal and fair? How can it be assumed that the rolling consensus-from-dissensus does not crush the minority under the feet of the (louder) majority? What guarantees are there that majoritarianism does not become cruelty? And even if these procedural concerns can be put to rest, it is still necessary to address the deeper question of whether human rights ought to be simply political rights. Namely, is it a political advance to give up *entirely* upon a somewhat fixed ideal of good human behavior? Do we think that unceasing contingency necessarily produces a moral outcome, even if it is a morality that is temporary? If the articulation of human rights is only political whim and no more, then what is to prevent a political whim

14. Langlois, *op. cit.*, note 7, 134.
15. *Ibid.*, 143.
16. *Ibid.*, 7.

that deems human rights unnecessary? There are clearly some troubling flaws in this argument.

Even though Langlois distinguishes his model in some important respects from Rawls' early work, the fact is that the less radical version of Langlois' political approach may be found in Rawls' more recent work on international law and politics. Rawls contemplates, in *The Law of Peoples*, that non-Western states will not necessarily be convinced of the self-evident distinction of the legal and political system that produced the template for universal human rights. Whereas in *A Theory of Justice*, it seemed that Rawls was close to Kant's position in advocating a system of international law based upon a federation of liberal states;[17] when, in fact, his work on international law proposes that non-liberal states are permissible in an international legal order.[18] In *The Law of Peoples* Rawls argues that liberal and "decent non-liberal hierarchical" societies have equivalent moral standing.[19] Decent illiberal societies "affirm human rights and [have] at least the features of a decent consultation hierarchy or its analogue."[20] Liberal and illiberal societies have a duty to tolerate one another, and together have a duty of intervention against outlaw states. The duty to intervene is expressed by Rawls as a "refusal to tolerate outlaw states (as) a consequence of liberalism and decency."[21]

While he sketches the human rights that liberal and decent non-liberal hierarchical states share[22] and the Principles of the Law of Peoples,[23] Rawls

17. In *A Theory of Justice* Rawls provided a powerful justification for liberal political philosophy and one might consider that his theory of international law would place liberal constraints upon the permissible conduct of states. John Rawls, *A Theory of Justice*, Oxford: Oxford University Press (1973).

18. This prima facie contradiction can easily be understood once one understands the theoretical distance Rawls has traveled from the original universalistic conclusions he drew in *A Theory of Justice*. He has diluted his views in a more recent work so that a number of comprehensive worldviews—some of which are not avowedly liberal—are permissible in a particular state and between particular states.

19. Though not in the sense of being symmetrically situated in the original position—only liberal societies are situated here in relation to both their domestic and their international status. Decent societies are situated in the original position in relation to their international status.

20. John Rawls, *The Law of Peoples*, Cambridge, Mass.: Harvard University Press (1999) 110.

21. *Ibid.*, 81.

22. These are the rights to life, to liberty, to personal property; and to formal equality as expressed by the rules of natural justice. *Ibid.*, 65.

23. The principles of his Law of Peoples are:
    1. Peoples are free and independent, and their freedom and independence are to be respected by other peoples.
    2. Peoples are to observe treaties and undertakings.
    3. Peoples are equal and are parties to the agreements that bind them.
    4. Peoples are to observe the duty of non-intervention.

does not argue that international justice ought to be grounded only in human rights adopted by liberal society. Nor does he agree with offering financial and other incentives to decent non-liberal societies to become liberal societies.[24] Significantly, he argues strongly for a people's attachment to culture:

> Leaving aside the deep question of whether some forms of culture and ways of life are good in themselves, as I believe they are, it is surely a good for individuals and associations to be attached to their particular culture and to take part in its common public and civic life....It argues for preserving significant room for the idea of a people's self-determination and for some kind of loose or confederative form of a Society of Peoples, provided the divisive hostilities of different cultures can be tamed, as it seems they can be, by a society of well-ordered regimes. We seek a world in which ethnic hatreds leading to nationalistic wars will have ceased. A proper patriotism is an attachment to one's people and one's country, and a willingness to defend its legitimate claims while fully respecting the legitimate claims of other peoples.[25]

Rawls does not give up entirely on the idea of "decency" as a central concern of all people, while at the same time acknowledging that cultural attachments may temper that idea somewhat. In other words, Langlois' approach of pure contingency of political outcome is tempered in Rawls' approach by a moderate dose of Kantian metaethics. While a metasystem will not necessarily provide the detailed content of human rights, it does at least give a distinctly *moral* claim to the political activism of human rights. But it leaves other questions unanswered: is the flavor of "decency" ineluctably roped to Kantian values? What might human rights coming from an il-liberal society look like, and how ought liberal societies respond to il-liberal human rights? If it is a human right in the signatory countries to the Cairo Declaration of 1990 to be governed by Islamic law, then how should a liberal society react to the amputation of a hand as a criminal sanction? Is this cruel punishment—a breach of human rights as they are articulated in the international torture convention? In other words, by what criteria are we to assess whether

---

5. Peoples have the right of self-defense but no right to instigate war for reasons other than self-defense.
6. Peoples are to honor human rights.
7. Peoples are to observe certain specified restrictions in the conduct of war.
8. Peoples have a duty to assist other peoples living under unfavorable conditions that prevent their having a just or decent political and social regime.

24. The duty of liberal and illiberal societies to intervene in "outlaw states" is Rawls' analogue to humanitarian intervention; and the duty not to use financial incentives to bring illiberal states to their liberal senses is an analogue to the protests of some developing nations at loans that are tied to specific political reforms.

25. Rawls, *op. cit.*, note 21, 111-112.

an "attachment to culture" is a human rights violation? What is left of liberal individualism's respect for individual choice and bodily integrity when it can be trumped by group allegiance to a cultural or a religious practice? Can this be called a human right?

4. Human Rights as Language

An alternative approach to the cultural difference dilemma of human rights in the age of internationalism is to emphasize the value of human rights vocabulary as a discourse—as an international language of claim against an oppressive state or an oppressive culture. This approach starts with the factual observation that human rights language is today used everywhere around the world to linguistically frame resistance to oppression.[26] Human rights language is used not only in those Western nations that originally framed the orthodox Western philosophical account of human rights, but everywhere else as well. Human rights language has become the global *lingua franca* of request. Human rights are not merely the blunt homogenizing tool of the West that replaces or overrides cultural forms outside the West. Rather, the language of human rights acts as a lightening rod in all communities because it is a way of framing a request—a demand—that oppression cease and desist. And because it is a universal language that can be heard—even if not always heeded—by the nation-state and the international community, human rights language has an especially strong claim to recognition. Far from being the incubus of Western liberalism that some claim, human rights in the linguistic paradigm become inflected with the values and culture of its speaker, no matter where the words are uttered. As Anthony Appiah notes "the spread of human rights culture and the growth of human rights NGOs all around the world do not amount to the diffusion of a metaphysics of Enlightenment liberalism. To the extent that it is right, we do not have to defend it against the charge of ethnocentrism."[27]

Just as human rights in the political model sketched above have a secular justification, so too does the linguistic model. The hope of both models is to avoid the charge of ethnocentrism—in other words, if repressed people *in situ* choose to use human rights concepts and human rights language, they have then picked up their own tools in aid of their cause and are not inhabiting any sensibility other than their own. They are driving their own agenda, directing it where they choose and shaping the outcomes. The counterargument to this is the concern that human rights are so indelibly stained with

26. K. Anthony Appiah "Grounding Human Rights," in Ignatieff, *op. cit.*, note 12, 109.
27. *Ibid.*

Eurocentrism that they cannot signify a non-Western cause without thereby subverting the non-Western culture. Indeed, there are examples where the use of human rights language in a non-Western context has led to cultural trouble: for example, Australian Aboriginal women who use human rights language to protest the incidence of domestic violence in their community are criticized by Aboriginal men for betraying the Aboriginal political cause through the public recognition of certain problems in the Aboriginal community. To use human rights language can invite criticism and charges of betrayal of a minority's *espirit de corps.* The concern is that the stain of individualism is too deeply etched in the fabric of the language of human rights to disaggregate the cause from the language describing it.[28]

A more philosophical version of the rationalization of human rights in the domain of language is found in Jacques Derrida. For Derrida, "living," writing, and speech reflect a continual process of movement that can never reach a stasis of meaning, no matter how much the speakers of language may try to inscribe a stable and permanent meaning. Rather, there is always another meaning in writing that hides behind the apparent meaning; "always something hiding behind that which is present."[29] Derrida's approach identifies every communication, whether textual or spoken, as subject to the mediated understanding of those who receive that communication. This makes interpretation of text—words, action, and behavior—conditional and temporary. Derrida labels his ethics of interpretation as "cosmopolitanism"—a practice of friendship towards others and to an openness and generous hospitality to their otherness. Derrida reads Heidegger against himself, self-consciously avoiding the metaphysical thinking that led Heidegger to reify the German nation and to embrace a form of racism.[30] Rather, Derrida sees the opposite of Heidegger's error as leading to a cosmopolitan ethic; namely, the recognition of difference and otherness in other people ought simultaneously to entail an inclusive conception of humanity.

Combining his poststructural critique of language and its interpretation with the philosophy of Emmanuel Levinas, Derrida proposes an ethical responsibility to reach out to others in a genuine gesture of wishing to understand our differences; the precondition of the practice of this ethical responsibility is a cosmopolitanism predicated on a minimal community and an openness to the radical "otherness" among people—or radical alterity.[31]

28. Aihwa Ong, *Flexible Citizenship: The Cultural Logics of Transnationality*, Durham, N.C.: Duke University Press (1999).

29. George Ritzer, *Postmodern Social Theory*, New York: McGraw Hill (1997) 121.

30. Mark Bevir, "Derrida and the Heidegger Controversy: Enforcing Human Rights in International Society," in Simon Caney and Peter Jones (eds.), *Human Rights and Global Diversity*, London: Frank Cass (2001) 135.

31. Jacques Derrida, *The Politics of Friendship*, trans. George Collins, London: Verso Books (1997).

Derrida here goes further than Kant and against the grain of Western thinking: he argues for an ethical responsibility to acknowledge the Other as *other*, rather than to appropriate the "Other" as oneself. This also establishes an ethical responsibility to avoid inauthentic exoticism when encountering the "Other." The challenge and the hope of this ethic is:

> Learning to live with the instability of plurality; learning to accept and to encounter radical plurality that fully acknowledges singularity—is always fragile and precarious. [Learning to live with this]...is the problem of human living.[32]

The motivation behind Derrida's use of Levinas' approach has the attractive feature of emphasizing our *ethical* commitment to fully understanding cultural differences. But it leaves the content of human rights unsatisfactorily open. If openness to the radical "otherness" of a different culture does not necessarily lead to resolution of conflicts between values among cultures, what is the justificatory basis of legal judgment? For example, when the Nigerian woman accused of adultery after bearing her brother-in-law's child is unable to produce four male witnesses to the rape she claims, how might the Levinas-inflected ethic of alterity inform a new understanding of her plight in being sentenced to death by stoning before a *Shari'ah* court? Does it mean that we walk a mile in her shoes, or that we struggle to understand the sanctity of religious sentencing practices? Even if a cosmopolitan ethic of reaching into another's sensibility can provide a means of understanding an alternative legal rationality, how might that inform a response to situations of an absolute clash between a *Shari'ah* court and a Western court of incompatible models of evidentiary weight? What are the markers of a more inclusive model of humanity that might prevail in these circumstances of value conflict?

Despite the questions they raise, both the political and the linguistic models have an important feature that fits with contemporary international conditions: namely, that justice in human rights need not derive from the wellspring of the Enlightenment, but may derive from the discursive process that forms and re-forms the substantive content of human rights. This approach makes it at least partly possible to make a case for human rights without engaging in a metaphysical debate. In other words, human rights need not be deduced by reference to a common humanity and shared values, but only by peoples *in situ* arguing for and against the human rights that provide the best fit for their community.

But this advantage may also be the disadvantage of these two models. Both justifications run dangerously close to radical cultural relativism. Each

32. *Ibid.*, 162.

seems to suggest that every perspective is equally valid and that there is a moral equivalence between values. How can we say that something is right if we are unable to say that something else is wrong? And the slippery slope of cultural relativism threatens "an arrogant universalism that [seems] to force its values on others, and amorally vacuous relativism that [seems] to flee from hard judgments and to justify non-democratic practices."[33] In other words, if human rights are completely evacuated of their moral valence, how can there be a decision in situations of conflicts between rights?

5. Human Rights as Procedure

The third approach—the procedural—seeks to suture the difficulties in both the political and the linguistic approaches. The procedural approach can be teased from a combination of philosophical and political science scholarship that focuses on the decision-making function of law and politics. Michael Ignatieff has suggested that international human rights norms will only have legitimacy if they are the product of "a commitment to respect the reasoned commitments of others and to submit disputes to adjudication";[34] an approach which resembles the argument put forward by U.S. political theory professors, Amy Gutman and Denis Thompson, that the moral authority of collective decisions depends upon the moral quality of the process by which those decisions are made.[35]

This third approach bears a strong resemblance to Jurgen Habermas' legal proceduralism sketched in *Between Facts and Norms*,[36] which has had considerable influence on neo-liberal thinkers seeking a normative approach that transcends postmodern contingencies. The discourse ethics that Habermas set out in *Theory of Communicative Action*[37] assumed that the world consists of plural and competing ideals and values, and that only some of these are publicly articulated. The very premise of language itself is the possibility of reaching agreement as autonomous and equal participants in speech. Law penalizes failures to keep the agreement to obey outcomes of rational discourse in the process of democracy.

33. Lynda Schaefer et al. (eds.), *Negotiating Culture and Human Rights*, New York: Columbia University Press (2001) 4.
34. *Ibid.*, 84.
35. Amy Gutman and Denis Thompson, *Democracy and Disagreement*, Cambridge, Mass.: Harvard University Press (1998) 4.
36. Jürgen Habermas, *Between Facts and Norms: Towards a Discourse Theory of Law and Democracy*, Cambridge: MIT Press (1996).
37. Jürgen Habermas, *Theory of Communicative Action*, Boston: Beacon Press (1984).

Most recently, Habermas has constructed a political theory that emphasizes the institutional aspects of democracy through law. In *Between Facts and Norms*, Habermas' solution to the intrusive role of law in the modern state is the proposition that regulation of the "life world" should instead take place by abstract, depersonalized law. Law ought to be established by mutual agreement and understanding, and should be safeguarded by the political force of the state. Habermas sees this as legitimate state action based on the rule of law.[38] Habermas' examination of law and the state in *Between Facts and Norms* brings together his Kantian approach of universal morality with his "textual" approach that prioritizes the cultural norms in forms of life through communicative ethics. *Between Facts and Norms* thus considers the implications of discourse ethics for a theory of law within the democratic state. In his previous works, Habermas had said (along with Kant) that law and morality are distinct, adding to this the twist that both moral and legal norms depend implicitly upon the intuition to rightness contained within the discourse principle, or "the ideal speech situation." In keeping with the political impulse of his discourse-based ethics, he argues that we are active participants in law rather than merely subjects of the law. He continues his theme of the implication of law in the organization of late capitalism, saying that in complex societies, "law is the only medium which can establish moral obligations of mutual respect even among strangers."[39] For Habermas, validity is not a function of certainty of outcome in legal conflicts, but rather the discursive clarification of the pertinent facts and legal questions so that:

> affected parties can be confident that in procedures issuing in judicial decisions only relevant reasons will be decisive, and not arbitrary ones.[40]

Habermas' rationalization of the law does not therefore predetermine its content, but rather reconstructs it through the discourse principle: he claims that the discourse principle under the proceduralist paradigm generates legal and factual equality. It ensures that the state's positive law is the outcome of joint deliberations by legal actors about their ethical differences with each

38. Habermas makes it clear in *Between Facts and Norms* that he views the relationships between morality, law, and political democracy as structural; there is "no autonomous law without realized democracy." Law can only legitimate itself in a democracy where procedural rationality has been institutionalized. For, legal and political rules must involve the input of those affected by them. Law is not legitimate per se, but both depend upon, and are reinforced by, support from the public sphere of legal and political community. Under Habermas' formulation, political democracy and the rule of law are mutually reinforcing. The extent to which morality, law, and political democracy are rational depends upon the level of discursive activity about them.

39. Habermas, *op. cit.*, note 37, 460.

40. *Ibid.*, 218.

other. Indeed, Habermas' emphasis upon the autonomy of each culture as a subset of a larger society is clear recognition of the lack of universality among people, even if he recommends a certain universality of response to bureaucratic processes.

But there is a troubling assumption in Habermas' argument—namely, the idea of a sufficient commonality of beliefs, values, commitments, and emotions to ground our agreement to be bound by *all* outcomes of the procedural model, even those to which we are vehemently opposed. This is the weak point of his procedural model. The evidence of endless human diversity in values has never been stronger. Rather, what we are left with is "a practical commitment to...communicative reason [as] the basis—perhaps the only honest basis—for hope."[41] Just as troubling are the many examples of democracy failing, producing laws that seem to arise from parliamentary processes but that are far more draconian than the collective views of the political community will actually support. Procedural safeguards need an ethical supplement or they risk becoming just a promise of formalism.

6. A Fourth Alternative: A Jurisprudence of Human Rights in a Globalized World

From the political, linguistic, and procedural approaches described above, it can be seen that human rights are a dynamic composite of legal, political, and moral justification. These three approaches each struggle with, and partially respond to, the human rights dilemma of our time: namely, how is deep legitimacy for international consensus on international human rights norms to be built across intellectual and cultural lines? There is one shared feature in all these accounts of human rights, despite their varied positions on the liberal-communitarian spectrum: namely, the ongoing wish to attribute authentic agency to the claimant to respond to, as much as possible, the claimant's subjectively experienced human rights transgression. An assertion that a human right has been trammeled is also a search for legitimacy that comes from wide participation in legal interpretation, from the sense of owning the law or regulation in some way and not merely being subject to it.[42] Although human rights require the legal fiat of the nation-states or groups of states, they assume a broader claim than just access to legal recognition. My point here is that the commitment to the ideal of an authentic, agentic subject can equally be a feature of the unitary framework of modern legal institutions as it can be of the conceptualization of the critically self-aware, citizen-subject

41. *Ibid.*, 133.
42. Cotterell, *op. cit.*, note 4.

within disparate cultural settings. People can desire better treatment from their state, or their community, irrespective of where they live and of their political culture.

The traditional explanation of human rights deriving from universal human identity has given way in the international era to a different idea—namely, that a fuller sense of the world is found in the expanse of local narratives rather than in a single grand narrative. The concern with "otherness" as exemplified by scholarship following Levinas within a framework akin to the Habermasian model provides both an ethic for interpreting cultural difference, and a place for the exercise of the ethic. This ethic—what I shall term the *ethic of listening*—is a normative injunction to apply a moral code, a set of rules, to see, to hear, to struggle to comprehend, cultural, ethnic, religious and political incommensurability; and to respond to it. As an attitude or bearing, an ethic of listening cannot portend the substantive content of human rights. Neither can Habermas' procedural rationality. But they can be placed together to offer enough of a procedural safeguard against the tyrannical majoritarianism that could emerge from Langlois' political model, and enough of an emphasis upon the act of decision-making that threatens to consign Appiah and Derrida's linguistic approach to the realms of abstract dreams.

The ethic of alterity requires us to understand cultural difference as a moral obligation. Proceduralism provides a framework for the operation of this moral obligation, while at the same time providing enough of an Archimedean fixed point for a decision to be reached and made. The terms of Habermas' proceduralism do not rule out the potential of human rights judgments to evolve in step with political sensibilities. Under the approach I describe, just as one's culture can never fully capture all the beliefs and values that are held to be internal to that culture, so one's culture can never fully capture one's future commitments and attitudes. This is not so much an incompletely theorized philosophy of human values, but rather a dialogic understanding of cultural difference.

In other words, if "understanding people across the world is not categorically different from understanding people across the street,"[43] then we do not really need to resort to a purely pragmatic acceptance of human rights as simply political speech. Rather, we must recognize that at some points it will be impossible to avoid a direct engagement with differing moral schemas between different cultural systems. If a cultural group has a value or practice that is irreducible and which has its own distinctive ethical valence, then it may simply be impossible to coexist peaceably without acknowledging an intractable disagreement with another's cultural commitment. For example,

43. *Ibid.*, 10.

the different emphasis upon bodily integrity and the capacity of individuals to exit their cultural group makes it unlikely that there will be an acceptance in the United States and Europe of the practice of female genital circumcision. On the other hand, the careful receptivity of arguments for the cultural valence of that practice, in a procedural context of the Habermasian type, may produce the possibility of contributing to circumstances in which young women can exercise their preference to either exit or remain within a community that practices circumcision. In other words, the right to a cultural practice is coupled with a right to refuse a cultural practice, which in turn may lend legitimacy to exit options.

Human rights thus inhabit the space between contingency and certainty. Contingency—in any event, part of life—is formalized as the recognition, and search for understanding of, cultural difference. Certainty—at least enough for peaceable living amongst cultural difference—arises from a procedural framework in which to articulate those differences. It seems unnecessary that we should all agree on the content of human rights, just as it seems unnecessary that we should all agree on our various religious preferences. On the other hand, not even the harshest critics of the monopoly that Western culture and political ideology seems to have on human rights discourse would necessarily want the content of human rights to be stripped of everything but cultural contingency. Part of the answer must surely lie in judging human rights norms and their attendant legal principles by their performance under moral criticism, and not merely by the degree of either consensus or dissensus about them. At some point, the range of human rights asserted by individuals, groups, or other states means that there will be a need to declare a value preference for the particular model of human rights that the state supports. Law's task of expressing and mediating values will become increasingly complex in the future, requiring explicit recognition and codification of value-pluralism in many contexts.

Looking at human rights in this way has two consequences. First, it implies greater democratization. The procedural model envisages political participation emerging from political agency that is experienced equally by each citizen. Under this approach, it is likely that there will be almost as many interpretations of how human rights claims are to be understood as there are human bearers of values. The likely proliferation of versions of human rights will occur both within and between nation-states, because while the language of human rights may be inherently based upon liberal individualism, it has not meant that people have jettisoned all of their cultural attachments. These cultural attachments—whether they are group practices of female genital "modification" or state practices of corporal punishment—have become the new generation of human rights claims. Human rights are the most prominent rhetoric for constituting or arguing over the "selves" at stake in political self-determination. It is thus implicated in the very idea of democracy, both as a claim about the internal integration of the political community and as a claim about its boundaries and relations to people and powers outside.

Second, it reinforces the role of moral choice, or judgment; for if each of these interpretations is inherently no better or worse than any others, there must be mechanisms for navigating around the massive proliferation of ideas. The age of pluralism becomes characterized as one of engagement with other cultures across apparently intractable lines of difference. And while the proliferation of "selves" and identities in the age of globalization makes it clear that *any* judgment may last only as long as the shifting patterns of interest and claim that preceded the conflict requiring judgment, this has not removed the moral conscience from each and every one of us. In summing up the moral lessons of the Holocaust, Hannah Arendt noted that:

> Those few who where still able to tell right from wrong went really by their own judgments, and they did so freely; there were no rules they abided by...because no rules existed for the unprecedented.[44]

There is no contradiction between skepticism towards socially conventionalized norms, and the insistence that it does matter, and matter morally, what we do and what we don't do. Moral responsibility, as the most personal and inalienable of human possessions, and the most precious of human rights, becomes the habitus and the field of differences amongst peoples.

7. Conclusion

In law, just as in society, it has become plain in the international era that a single unitary political, ethical, theoretical framework is too crude, and that a universal metaphysics of human identity cannot adequately describe the singularity of the groups and the subjects to whom our legal institutions wish to respond. The value system of moral individualism at the core of the Western discourse on human rights and international justice is not absolute, and our deep longing for justice can be pursued in ways that are not *necessarily* roped to every element of modern legal systems. What is needed are new ways of listening to better understand how differences among cultures affect value judgments made, and how different normative paradigms ought to affect the political decisions that flow from those judgments.

Under the conditions of globalization, the philosophy of rights is confronted more than ever with the tension that has been apparent since the Silk Road—that there is a disconnect between its roots in the Western intellectual

44. Arendt, *op. cit.*, note 2, 295.

tradition and the centrality of the individual within that tradition on the one hand, and human rights claims that derive from a group or collective identity on the other. The resurgence in the last decade of civil and military aggression justified on grounds of religious, ethnic, and cultural conviction underscores the continuing urgency in articulating a rationale for human rights that can withstand the claim of violence committed in the name of culture.

The cultural difference perspective in law questions the veracity of the modern understanding of the legal subject. Whether moral values best issue from the crucible of political argumentation or are best articulated by judges from legal and legislative precedent, they retain their quality of being a selection—a *moral* choice, of our values about human behavior, enacted in a new legal rationality that is open to multidisciplinary paradigms and different ways of seeing and hearing. Langlois' intuition that the content of human rights should be principally settled within the political domain requires the Habermasian corrective of proceduralism. But politics and procedure alone ignore an equally important intuition: namely, that the human desire for justice is a yearning as much of the spirit as it is of the mind and of history. Human rights frame this yearning in a language of request. Levina's and Derrida's exhortation of attention to the radical difference of others about whom we know little provides the necessary ethical dimension to the politics and proceduralism of human rights.

Part II
Human Rights Politics

Chapter 8

Dimitrina Petrova

Social and Economic Dimensions of Universal Rights

In this chapter I will comment on the social and economic dimensions of universal rights from the perspective of my concept of "human rights politics." I will argue that social and economic rights seem to add legitimacy to the embattled human rights discourse today. From the area of social and economic rights, and mainly in the context of globalization, new concerns and new advocacy agendas are integrated into the human rights movement. The legitimation crisis caused by attacks on universality can be better addressed if social and economic rights are absorbed into the core of fundamental rights. The consistent, integrated human rights approach to social and economic issues will thus be better equipped to compete with nonliberal approaches originating outside the human rights paradigm.

1. Introduction: What Is Human Rights Politics?

I propose the concept of *human rights politics* as a new and specific field of research on human rights—from the point of view of the role they play in world politics. This is a new attempt to make sense of old and even outdated problems, such as the infamous "double standards" complaint against human rights; an attempt to create a consistent theoretic vision on how human

András Sajó (ed.), Human Rights with Modesty: The Problem of Universalism, *187-212.*

rights participate in shaping the political processes of our time. The essentials of human rights politics include the following:

- The human rights politics point of view is located outside the human rights paradigm, or discourse[1]—leaving aside for now the differences between these two terms. It requires that we step out of the human rights discourse in order to take a look at "human rights" from an outsider political science position.
- "Human rights politics" is the converse of a "human rights policy" approach. In the latter we look at a given social, political, cultural, or other issue through the lens of human rights philosophy and provide rights-based policy on that issue. For example, it is possible to establish human rights policy positions on varied issues such as migration, minority education, race statistics, etc.—in which our positions may compete with policies that are not based on rights, but on other sets of values, e.g., human development, economic efficiency, national security, conflict resolution, etc.
- In the human rights politics analysis "human rights" is seen, in a non-assuming way, as just one phenomenon among others that are at work in the political universe. The human rights politics approach involves the systematic and exhaustive examination of the relationship of the human rights paradigm, movement, and discourse with other political and social paradigms, movements, and discourses.
- More precisely, in human rights politics we aim to explore the *political functioning* of human rights—how human rights "work," in whose favor, against whom, and how efficiently.
- Ultimately, and still more precisely, ***human rights politics is about the relation of human rights to power.***

Quite obviously, engaging in human rights politics, as constructed here, is the professional responsibility of human rights advocates. They are not just practitioners, experts, campaigners, etc., but above all, well-informed citizens in the sense articulated by Alfred Schutz.[2] Human rights politics is simultaneously

1. Stanley Cohen suggests that there exist several different human rights discourses, each with its distinct validity claims and norms of professionalism: the diplomatic, legal, social scientific, etc. See Stanley Cohen, *Denial and Acknowledgement*, Jerusalem: Hebrew University (1995) I-V, 1-17. For the sake of the simplicity of my argument, I will speak of one single human rights discourse, expecting that my main points would not change significantly if a plurality of human rights discourses was assumed.
2. Alfred Schutz, "The Well-Informed Citizen: An Essay on the Social Distribution of Knowledge," in Alfred Schutz, *Collected Papers, Vol. II*, The Hague: Martinus Nijhoff (1964) 120-134. Schutz distinguishes between the man in the street, the expert, and the well-informed citizen, each differing in their inclination to take things for granted. The

a reflection upon the meaning of being involved in human rights—whether as a professional or a volunteer. Through a human rights politics analysis one can see the big picture and ask tough questions such as: Where do my priorities and assignments come from? Who pays me and who is interested in the results? Are there possible contexts in which the results and implications of my work would be controversial? Can my work be hijacked by actors with different agendas? What can I do to make sure that my voice is heard in the boardrooms where intervention is planned and policy is adopted? How can my colleagues and I participate in politics while preserving strict impartiality and objectivity? This type of concern and the attitude it precipitates is apparently pervasive in the moral history of mankind, including that of science and technology. One might draw parallels with the discussion of the social responsibility of nuclear physicists, genetic biologists, etc.

2. The Political Functions of Human Rights

The political functions of human rights change over history time, as well as across countries and regions. These functions have a dynamics of their own. The relevant questions to be asked when describing the political functions of human rights include: How are human rights positions and strategies related to certain political interests? Which actors do they help? Whom do they undermine? What are the political consequences of a given human rights campaign or action? Whose concerns do NGOs represent? Why are there tensions between human rights norms and human rights *Realpolitik*? Is the human rights movement changing the balance of power in the world? How?

In our times, one can observe an increasing *multiplication of the political functions of the human rights discourse*, as well as the human rights movement. However, we can take this a step further and ask: Is there an observable tendency in this process of multiplication? We will return to this question later.

The debate on the universality of human rights is of central interest to human rights politics. It is not possible here to outline even briefly the status of the debate, among both academics and practitioners. The debates range from radical attacks on human rights as an "ideology" in a morally disapprov-

well-informed citizen does not try to be an expert on everything, and neither does she accept the fundamental vagueness of simple perceptive knowledge or the irrationality of her own passions. She is able to form reasonably-founded opinions on issues that are not of immediate relevance to her purpose. The famous statement of Clemanceau that war is too important to be left to the generals illustrates the way in which the well-informed citizen reacts to expert advice.

ing sense,[3] to a variety of less radical challenges to the universality of human rights: e.g., human rights have been interpreted as modern and Western, rather than transhistoric and universal. A body of literature has emerged in response to these challenges.[4]

Most defenders of universalism converge in a common assumption that can be summarized thus: human rights *values* are good but, when expressed in human rights *language* and put in the mouths of *politicians*, they are then either betrayed or used to mask diverging interpretations. As a value system human rights ought to be defended and promoted, and international human rights law is and should be improving. The problem is not with human rights but with politics and the way politics is pursued through international law.

The weakness of this argument is that it assumes, in the spirit of pre-Kantian worldviews, the segregation of concept and term, mind and language, content and form. I suggest bringing the argument closer to postclassical thought and temporarily bracketing the hypocrisy argument, a.k.a. "the double standards" in human rights. What if we assume that human rights values are at the core of the thinking of leading politicians, that not all politicians are hypocritical, cynical, or uninterested in human rights values; and that at least some political actors are sincere when they articulate interests in human rights terms. For the sake of analysis, I want to focus only on those political actors who speak in rights terms in good faith. This procedure leads us to an exploration of the functioning of the human rights culture at a noological, rather than socio-psychological level. We can then try to apply philosophical lessons from more recent and more sophisticated traditions than that of the eighteenth-century Enlightenment, with its psychological and moral theories of prejudice. Just as the devotion and sincerity of religious believers does not tell us anything about the truth content or the political impact of their religion, the hypocritical human rights *Realpolitik* should not be allowed to obscure the deeper questions on the nature of the human rights discourse.

According to Habermas, discourses produce communicative power, which cannot supplant the power of public bureaucracies but does have a certain impact on the latter. This impact is limited to reinforcing or undermining

3. Human rights ideology is an ideology of domination and a part of the imperialist world outlook," says Issa G. Shivji. See Issa G. Shivji, *The Concept of Human Rights in Africa*, London: Codesria Book Series (1989) XX.

4. See, e.g., Louis Henkin, *The Age of Rights*, New York: Columbia University Press (1996). Henkin interprets universality as that of the values underlying modern human rights. See also Jack Donnelly, "Human Rights and Asian Values: In Defense of 'Western' Universalism," in Joanne R. Bauer and Daniel A. Bell (eds.), *The East Asian Challenge for Human Rights*, New York: Carnegie Council on Ethics and International Affairs (1999) 60-87.

legitimacy. The question that has preoccupied me with respect to the human rights discourse is when, where, and how the discourse strengthens or weakens the legitimacy of power actors? And which actors are affected? But a separate and equally relevant question concerns the legitimacy of discourses themselves—in our case the legitimacy of the human rights discourse. In this discussion, therefore, *the object of reflection is double-layered: we look at how the human rights discourse as such adds legitimacy to power actors and at how social and economic rights add legitimacy to the human rights discourse.*

When speaking of the political functions of the human rights discourse, we should be careful not to regard the discourse as an undifferentiated whole. While the present analysis is motivated by the wish to formulate general comments on the issue, the heterogeneity inside the human rights discourse remains. In this regard, the legal defense of human rights in courts should be singled out and perhaps even treated separately, for the following reason. In my view, law fulfills two different though complementary functions in society in regard to patterns of power. On the one hand, law is one of the forms in which power is established and reproduced. Whereas, on the other hand, *law reproduces the limits to power*. Legal protections available to the individual function as a more or less reliable guarantee that power directed at her will not be endlessly oppressive or completely arbitrary. While the legal normative regime legitimizes the dominant status of the stronger groups, it nevertheless also protects the weaker. Human rights law is par excellence in performing the second protective function, ensuring that power over the individual is regulated.

With this stipulation in mind, I feel that a radical immanent (as opposed to external) critique of the human rights discourse is in order. The universalism debate will likely be implicated in this critique. Postcommunist individuals like myself may have something to contribute, since we have experienced the demise of one powerful and lasting ideology and developed insights regarding its functioning and dynamics, both when it was strong and unchallenged and when it entered a legitimacy crisis. We see simultaneously the totality of Marxist-communist ideology and the totality of the human rights ideology. Needless to say, this privilege is at the same time a limitation, just like any bias.

3. Is Human Rights an "Ideology"?

People are motivated to action in countless ways; but in their articulations, they always tend toward the mainstream, especially at the level of social and political activism, by utilizing the language of the dominant paradigms, worldviews, cultures, discourses, or ideologies. Each epoch and each culture has its dominant patterns of expression, including its ideologies. It is useful to remember that, possibly, Marx was correct to think that the dominant ideology in a society is that of those in power, or in Marxian terms, the "dominant classes."

Let me return now to the question asked above: namely, is there some tendency or direction to the process of multiplying the political functions of human rights? Or is this process going nowhere, chaotic and unpredictable, except at the level of fragments and void of any inherent logic? It seems to me that a tendency exists. The process of political participation of human rights follows a certain path—and throughout the world of politics, the political functions of the human rights discourse may be imagined as flowing in one direction, though inside the flow there are rapids, countercurrents, whirlpools, and swamps. Since the concept of discourse would not be very helpful at this point, I would prefer to borrow one old-fashioned but somewhat more illuminating dichotomy from Karl Mannheim, that of the "total concepts" of ideology and utopia, developed in the 1920s.[5] Though the choice is one of many, and though other traditions may offer better conceptual tools, I find these two categories and the whole sociology of knowledge, built on the "critique of ideology," quite useful for my interpretation of the present-day human rights discourse.

According to Mannheim's theory, the concept of ideology reflects the first discovery which emerged out of the modern political conflict, namely, that in their thinking ruling groups can become so strongly bound to a state of affairs which secures their interests, that they are simply no longer capable of seeing certain facts that would challenge their sense of domination. The concept of utopian thinking reflects the contrary discovery of modern political struggle: certain oppressed groups are so invested intellectually in the destruction and transformation of certain social conditions that they, unwillingly, see only those elements of the situation which tend to deny its continued existence.

Utopia and ideology are two types of false consciousness, not in the sense of deception but of cognitive bias: utopia is a vision that is not yet adequate to social reality, while ideology is no longer adequate. Each of these biases is noological rather than psychological. In principle, while utopia is realizable as a transformation project, ideology cannot be "fulfilled." Ideological

5. See Karl Mannheim, *Ideology and Utopia*, A Harvest Book reprint edition, Harcourt, Inc. (1985). (The reprint is of the 1936 English translation of the 1929 German original.) The history of ideas is rich in intellectual traditions of interpreting the concept and the reality of "ideology," from Proudhon to some of the most far-reaching and comprehensive views developed in the Frankfurt School of social research. Here, however, I have chosen Mannheim's conceptual dualism as a tool for conveying a hypothesis, and not as a substantial view to which I subscribe.

concepts are forms of interpretation and justification of the status quo in the disguise of normative values setting the direction of development. Ideologies may be former utopias which have "come to power," and therefore, are no longer tools of radical social change. They have turned into tools for preserving the essential definitions of the status quo.

We can now consider the human rights discourse as a utopia and/or ideology by its very raison d'être. There are at least two critical "witnesses" which attest that the human rights discourse is suspiciously similar to phenomena of an utopian-ideological nature.

a) Liberal fundamentalism: A characteristic tendency of every ideology, as well as of every utopia, is to reify certain human relations and express them as "things" or "properties"; to posit certain values as metaphysical "entities." The sophistication of ideological constructions notwithstanding, such reification takes place also at the profane everyday level where ideology lives and labors. The political exaggeration of this tendency, as we find it in the nonreflexive everyday mind, is the absolutization or universalization of certain values. Thus, ironically, even in the deeply anti-fundamentalist (in the political sense) human rights paradigm, we can note the development of a fundamentalist (in the philosophical sense) tendency. The more human rights function to either negate or legitimize a status quo, the more one is able to register a kind of liberal fundamentalism: a hypostatization of Liberty and Rights.

b) Claims to universality, while applying universal principles selectively: A clear and broadly discussed symptom of ideology is what is popularly known as the politics of "double standards." The rhetoric of universals fails to translate to all cases consistently. Ideologies typically contain this claim to universalism, while plagued by selective blindness. But it seems that early on, already at the utopian stage, the presence of double standards reveals an ideologizing potential in a doctrine. In the case of the Western liberal-democratic "utopias," on the basis of which the human rights paradigm took shape, the same original sin is noteworthy. Tocqueville, for example, criticized democracy in America and denounced American mistreatment of Indians and black slaves. But when it came to French colonial policies in Algeria during the late 1830s and 1840s, where the French fought a war of pacification against the Muslims, he suspended his normative standards.

The central hypothesis of this paper is that the human rights discourse is undergoing a transformation in respect to its political functions both at the global and regional levels. At the global level, the tendency of change is from utopia to ideology, i.e., *from a critique to a justification or defense of the global order* with its power structures.

In the global context, the tendency is expressed in region-specific ways, defying generalization. Yet I would venture the following observations: (i) in Western liberal democracies human rights have moved from critique to legitimation of the social order, or in Mannheim's terms, from utopia to ideology; (ii) in oppressive undemocratic societies human rights function as utopia—the stronger the grip of an oppressive regime, the more subversive the utopian function; (iii) in transition societies where democracy-building is ongoing, the teleology is towards legitimation with human rights still serving a more or less significant utopian function; (iv) the societies in which profound change is underway, but in which the direction of change is unclear, must be left out of these three broad categories and considered on a case by case basis.

One stipulation is due here: the above characterization of the political function of human rights is not burdened by a moral judgement on power as such. I am not assuming that to oppose governments/powers is good and to legitimize them is bad. The value of these positions depends on the nature of the government/power in question. In fact, I am not sure that any of the existing international protest movements has a better vision of the future to offer than liberal democracy; and human rights discourse tends to legitimize power in the form of liberal democracy establishments. What matters most here is that the more human rights discourse becomes a legitimation strategy, the more it loses its initial potential as a tool of progressive social change.[6]

The diversity of social environments and the complexity of each polity qualifies the functions of human rights in each country, limiting and at times prohibiting placement in the above general types. The hypothesis proposed here is meant as a temporary strategy of seeking some orientation in the heteronomy, some logos in the chaos. The postmodernist will therefore be justified in discarding it as Archimedean, Cartesian, classical. I leave aside now the philosophical question of whether my generalizations are ultimately foundationalist, or pure empirical observations, not necessarily founded in some sort of historical grand narrative. But I would reiterate the political anchorage of my analysis: the human rights discourse is predominantly a critique of the social order in most parts of the globe. If this is the case, a critique of the legitimation function of human rights should at this stage remain limited and be placed within the global context.

The mechanism of the transformation of human rights into ideology in democratic and transition societies is similar to the mechanism of transfor-

6. I must admit that the remaining value anchor here is "progressive social change": in trying to define the latter, will I not need the ideas of dignity, freedom, rights, well-being? Human civilization may or may not be inseparable from value rationality. But at this time in history, humans are trapped in value language as long as they want to relate to existing political discourses and communities.

mation of other great "utopias" of humankind—namely, a *gradual usurpation* of the "utopian" discourse by the forces of the status quo, in our case, by the social and political elites at the global and national level. From the point of view of discourse semiotics, the process of ideologization can be presented as a gradual but irreversible pluralization of the core value expressions of the human rights discourse.[7]

In view of the foregoing, the *usurpation* of the human rights discourse by power elites is the essential definition of two interrelated tendencies: (i) "mainstreaming" of human rights: human rights considerations are increasingly present in non-rights agendas; (ii) "mainstreaming" of issues by articulating them in human rights terms: advocates of various concrete issues express their claims in terms of rights, since this increases the chance that the issue will be addressed. Both tendencies are a result from and a further strengthening of the *power of human rights.*

The concepts of ideology and utopia are somewhat obsolete today and not many scholars are comfortable with them. However, my view does not depend on these terms. As demonstrated above, I formulate essentially the same view on the political functions of human rights by employing the legitimation discourse. At the expense of losing some of the richness and profundity of the Mannheimian or Habermasian theories, we might even prefer the everyday terms, such as "justification" or "apology" of the social and political system. Whatever the terms, such a large and rich discourse as human rights, once it has begun to develop into ideology, prolongs its life via the added legitimacy of its emerging apologetic status. I offer below comments on several mechanisms of adding legitimacy, first *in abstracto* as in any ideology, then by considering the specific contributions of the social and economic dimensions of universal rights to the legitimacy of the entire human rights discourse. It is not a surprise that in its legitimation function, the human rights discourse exhibits a number of suspicious similarities with other formerly oppositional, even revolutionary ideologies, such as Christianity or Marxist communism.

7. I have developed elsewhere a theory on the semiotic pluralization of value categories in the context of a specific understanding of values as such. In my theory of value rationality, the defining characteristic of values, their very raison d'être, is their functioning as false common *loci* of opposing positions. I refer to the ideological space of communication as the "false common *locus*" in order to grasp the presence of two opposing aspects: (i) the commonality, meaning the possibility of conversation, as opposed to violent conflict; and (ii) the falsity of this very commonality, insofar as the ideological discourse itself does not resolve in practice the conflict between adversarial positions. See Dimitrina Petrova, *Utopia i tsennostna ratsionalnost* [Utopia and Value Rationality], Doctoral Dissertation, Sofia: Vissha atestatsionna komisia (1993).

4. Evolution of the Social and Economic Dimensions of Rights Inside the Human Rights Discourse

The chief venue through which social and economic issues have been entering the human rights discourse is the conceptualization of social and economic rights. Additionally, social and economic issues work their way into the core of the human rights movement through the articulation of rights for specific categories of human subjects: women, children, migrants, indigenous people, people with disabilities, people with HIV/AIDS, people living in extreme poverty, etc. A special role has been played in this process by efforts to elaborate the content of the right to development.

Outside the individualistic Anglo-American tradition of understanding rights, the history of ideas contains a second tradition in which rights are understood as much closer to and based on such values as community, solidarity, and fraternity. This second tradition was strongly present in the codification of the international human rights bill.

The UN Charter created the UN Economic and Social Council (ECOSOC)—the body in the framework of which the drafting of the Universal Declaration on Human Rights (UDHR) took place and the subsequent UN Covenants and further conventions evolved. The ECOSOC achieved, already in its first years, incorporation of the most important ILO standards on labor conditions to be developed prior to World War II. Social and economic rights were included in the UDHR with little opposition. Recent studies highlight the contribution of non-Western representatives in this process.[8]

In the Communist system, the supremacy of social and economic rights followed from the basic tenets of Marxism: economic determinism and the understanding of politics as derivative of and secondary to the economy; the primacy of social class and class struggle as the driving force of history; and the high value placed on social equality. In the name of achieving a classless society and eliminating economic inequalities altogether, Communist regimes downplayed civil and political rights and, following Marx, even discarded them as merely formal bourgeois rights which did not endow the individual with a real freedom.

Some Western human rights advocates of the 1970s and thereafter expressly refused to consider social and economic rights as real human rights, pointing out their alleged non-enforceability or limited enforceability by the

8. See, e.g., Mary Ann Glendon, *A World Made New: Eleanor Roosevelt and the Universal Declaration on Human Rights*, New York: Random House (2001).

state, subject to available resources. According to this argument, since governments cannot be held accountable for noncompliance, and since human rights are about the relationship of the individual vs. the state, social and economic rights cannot be taken seriously. Their inclusion in the canon would even undermine the real, i.e., civil and political rights.

Overall, by the late 1980s and despite the Helsinki Accords of 1975, there existed a clear Cold War divide in the interpretation of social and economic, as opposed to civil and political rights.

The main global instrument on social and economic rights is the 1966 International Covenant on Economic, Social and Cultural Rights (ICESCR), which has been ratified by 142 states as of 13 June 2002.[9] Currently there is an initiative to adopt an Optional Protocol to provide for individual complaints.

In the 1990s, especially around and after the 1993 Vienna World Conference on Human Rights, the divide remained between social, economic, and cultural rights on the one hand, and civil and political rights on the other, but began to mean something very different in political legitimation terms. Some Asian governments, such as Singapore represented by Lee Kuan Yew, argued for a suspension, or a reduced and secondary role, for civil and political rights in the name of economic development and prosperity. Others, predominantly from developing countries, grounded the supremacy of economic, social, and cultural rights in the allegedly non-Western value of community over the individual. Both arguments were purported to be formulated in resistance to Western imperialism and colonialism.

The United Nations human rights regime is currently struggling to integrate economic, social, and cultural rights with civil and political rights. The Human Rights Commission has adopted in recent years resolutions on the eradication of extreme poverty, the right to education, the right to an adequate standard of living, and others—in which the principle of indivisibility of all human rights is applied. While the United States is the biggest opponent to the recognition, on an equal footing, of social and economic rights,[10] the European Union fully supports the UN Secretary General's efforts to integrate human rights within the system of the United Nations.[11] One of the UN treaties which is strongly based on the wish to integrate economic, social, and cultural rights with civil and political rights is the Convention on the Rights of the Child (CRC). The CRC Committee has taken the approach

9. http://www1.umn.edu/humanrts/instree/b2esc.htm, visited 13 June 2002.

10. See Philip Alston, "U.S. Ratification of the Covenant on Economic, Social and Cultural Rights," 84, 2 *American Journal of International Law* (1990) 365-393.

11. European Union Annual Report on Human Rights, Brussels (2001) 88.

that rights are indivisible and interrelated, and that each right is equally important and fundamental to the dignity of the child.

The Committee of the ICESCR has been commended by experts for having taken steps in the direction of more vigorous rights protection and raising the appeal and meaningfulness of economic and social rights. Scott Leckie states that, in comparison with other UN treaty bodies, this committee has made the most significant progress in improving the reporting process, and that it has been the most open to alternative sources of information, especially from NGOs.[12]

The UN Office of the High Commissioner on Human Rights (OHCHR) has also been in the forefront of integrating economic and social rights in the last five years. There have been internal (inside the UN institutions, especially between the treaty bodies and the OHCHR) hurdles in the actual implementation of this approach, especially at the level of the Technical Cooperation Program.[13]

In my view, the principle of indivisibility of human rights is in need of further elaboration. Although this principle has been officially adopted by the United Nations, its implications remain unclear. In international human rights case law indivisibility means little. In domestic litigation in particular the defense of social and economic rights remains very different from the defense of civil rights. Social and economic rights should be very welcome in the human rights discourse as factors contributing to its empowerment. Still, one fundamental accomplishment of the human rights paradigm must be reaffirmed: the justiceability of rights, the possibility to defend in a court of law a person whose rights have been violated. Similarly rigorous legal standards must be developed and applied in the litigation of social and economic rights. There are neither logical nor juridical obstacles to the applicability of social and economic rights.

In the analysis of recent developments on social and economic rights in the human rights discourse, the policy reorientation of Amnesty International (AI) provides an important case study. According to Pierre Sane, the former secretary general of AI, *globalization* has created an unprecedented potential to eradicate poverty and fulfill the aspirations of the UDHR—freedom from fear and freedom from want. But globalization has also brought economic volatility and instability. Deregulation, privatization, and the dismantling of welfare provision have led to widening inequalities in many countries.

---

12. Scott Leckie, "The Committee on Economic, Social and Cultural Rights: Catalyst for Change in a System Needing Reform," in Philip Alston and James Crawford (eds.), *The Future of UN Human Rights Treaty Monitoring*, Cambridge: Cambridge University Press (2000) 129-130.

13. See Anne Gallagher, "Making Human Rights Treaty Obligations a Reality: Working with New Actors and Partners," in Alston and Crawford, *op. cit.*, note 12, 223-224.

In large parts of the world corruption has increased and personal, political, and social insecurity has spread. The predictable and almost inevitable consequence of this growth in poverty has been a parallel escalation in violations of all human rights. The new human rights challenges arising from globalization have stimulated AI to take on new areas of work, namely, socio-economic rights and economic actors.[14]

A few years earlier, in a 1997 policy decision, while reaffirming their determination to promote *all* human rights, AI members began work on social and economic rights. Pierre Sane wrote: "AI has acknowledged the relative neglect of economic, social and cultural rights by the international human rights movement, and has taken steps to address these rights more directly in its own work."[15] AI also began to target the corporate world in its advocacy work. AI promoted a set of human rights principles for companies which cover issues such as security arrangements, community consultation, labor rights and fair working conditions, as well as non-discrimination. AI attended the launch of the Global Sullivan Principles and the Global Compact, an initiative of the UN Secretary General aimed at injecting universal values into the working of global markets. At present, AI campaigns for the implementation of these principles as minimum standards. However, as Sane explains, it would be naïve not to recognize the potential conflict between the pursuit of profit and the protection of human rights. An example is the proposed Multilateral Agreement on Investment (MAI) which would have restricted the ability of states to regulate the conduct of multinational corporations. Additionally, it would have limited the capacity of states to enforce certain human rights, while not imposing any binding obligations on multinational corporations to protect such rights. A broad coalition of NGOs, trade unions, and political parties lobbied against the MAI and as a result it was not adopted.[16]

At present the work of AI and other human rights NGOs on social and economic rights is informed by a sense of urgency. Poverty, hunger, and homelessness are not inevitable—the world has the resources to overcome them if we can generate the political will. This utopia is within reach. The new context within which social and economic rights must be viewed is globalization. According to Sane,

> In a world where globalization is undermining many nation-states and bringing poverty to the forefront of the human rights agenda, the challenge for AI is to remain relevant. In my opinion, this means broadening our aim from

---

14. See Pierre Sane, forward to *Amnesty International Report 2001*, London: AI Publications (2001) 5.
15. *Ibid.*
16. *Ibid.*, 6.

> the protection of civil and political rights to embrace all human rights. The indivisibility of human rights is not an abstraction: the context which gives rise to human rights violations is invariably complex and cannot be divorced from issues of wealth and status, injustice and impunity... In the minds of the drafters of the UDHR, freedom from fear and freedom from want have been inseparable. And the indivisible link between socio-economic and political rights has been mirrored in the emergence of a new network of protest movements. Globalization has brought together activists on issues such as child labor, the environment, anti-capitalism, Third World debt and human rights, creating an international, grassroots movement... A global solidarity movement to address the negative consequences of globalization is in the making. AI will bring its unique contribution to this endeavor.[17]

Globalization and the struggle for social and economic rights also shifts the focus of advocacy and protest, to some extent remove the burden of accountability for human rights violations from individual governments. The nation-state can neither control global trends, nor easily accommodate the demands of different groups living within its borders. Many states have claimed that they have been forced to adopt economic policies which undermine social and economic rights.

In addition to this new orientation in policy, AI, together with numerous other groups, began working on cases that directly demonstrate the indivisibility of universal rights. Violence over land rights in Brazil is an example of such a case. Conflict in Brazil over land rights continues to generate violence as land activists are harassed, threatened, and killed by military police carrying out evictions, or policing demonstrations. Activists have also been attacked by gunmen hired by landowners, with the apparent acquiescence of police authorities.

Another human rights development in which the social and economic dimensions of rights are inseparable from political rights issues is the protest movement in China. Human rights organizations reported that in 2000 the enormous social cost of economic restructuring in China continued to provoke social unrest. The absence of effective social welfare provisions left in acute poverty many of the millions of workers who had lost their jobs in recent years. A severe drought also brought hardship and disquiet among the country's rural population. Tens of thousands of demonstrations were believed to have taken place during 2000, although most were not reported by China's tightly controlled official media.

In the Republic of Korea, the police used excessive force to repress strikes and protests by trade unionists. The impact of the 1997 economic crisis was felt over the last several years. Trade unions organized protests against harsh

17. *Ibid.*, 7.

employment conditions which are particularly severe in the service industries. Labor activists were held as political prisoners.

Let me now turn to the question of how the relationship between the *local and the universal* in human rights affects the articulation and the political functioning of social and economic rights? The important distinction from my point of view is not between universalist and localist positions and movements, but between positions in support of and positions against the established social and political order, be it at a global, regional, or local level. The way we recognize the former from the latter is increasingly less dependent on whether recourse is made to the universal character or the local specificity of social cnd economic rights.

Human rights language is increasingly ideological. It is the adopted universal language of more and more movements at all levels (international, regional and local) of those who seek to empower themselves. But pluralization of ideological meanings is also in rapid progress. Thus, the fact that a movement formulates its agenda in rights language says little about its political orientation. Contrary claims are being expressed in rights terms: the right to life of the fetus as opposed to the right of women to choose abortion is an example. Potentially, any social and political agenda can be translated into social and economic rights language. The tendency is towards a further expansion of rights claims, as social and economic rights are, globally, a means of legitimation as well as a challenge to power.

There are social movements at the international level which are trying to express their demands in terms of social and economic rights, or the right to development, from which a variety of rights are formulated: the right to benefit from all natural resources; worker rights claimed against multinational corporations; rights to a healthy life and safe environment; the right to health care for those with HIV/AIDS; the right to be free from extreme poverty; etc. These movements are actually trying to enter the dominant discourses of the democratic West. Speaking rights language is a means of self-empowerment for them.

Furthermore, there are local social movements in liberal democratic and transition societies whose agendas are compatible with and dependent upon liberal democracy as a socio-political system. These movements naturally try to speak the social and economic rights language as a way of mainstreaming themselves.

There are domestic movements in the South and the East whose agendas involve a radical change in the oppressive social and political order. Their "utopian" reference framework is set within liberal democracy, and these domestic movements speak the social and economic rights language as a way to relate to it, while opposing their regimes. The trouble, however, is that the oppressive governments themselves also claim that they promote human rights.

One thing is quite certain: we live in a world in which social and economic rights will be implemented at accelerating rates. Unfortunately, this is not a metaphysically, socially, or politically optimistic statement. All I expect is that—whatever the nature of real change in living standards, educational opportunities, access to food, employer policies, health care reform, etc.—a variety of future actions and processes will be formulated as "implementation of social and economic rights." This will be the legitimate way of accounting for success, for yet some time.

5. Mechanisms of Adding Legitimacy

If we look at social and economic rights separately from human rights in general, we will see that they lag behind in their apologetic function in the West. Social and economic rights were incorporated into the official ideology of Communist societies and have been harnessed for ideological usage more recently by Asian and African power elites. Yet, the discourse on social and economic rights (not the level of their actual implementation!) is still more utopian than ideological, not only in the Third World/global South, but also in the developed liberal democracies.

Social and economic issues today seem to add legitimacy to the human rights discourse, and thus postpone its legitimation crisis. From the area of social and economic rights, new topics, concerns, and advocacy groups are integrated in the human rights movement. Dialectically, social and economic issues simultaneously advance the semantic pluralization tendency. In what follows I present some ideas of how this works.

5.1 Adding actors

Most simply, legitimacy may be increased by increasing the number of actors interested in the ideological discourse. A very important feature in the process of ideologizing human rights, and perhaps the most visible side of the usurpation, is the growing control of governments and other elites over the human rights agendas as a whole. It is increasingly governments and their multilateral formations that define the priorities and the standards of human rights research, monitoring, reporting, and even advocacy. Citizens and their organizations seem to be—through conscious choice or not—less militant, less confrontational, and more cooperative with "democratic" governments and IGOs than a decade ago.

If we now compare social and economic to civil and political rights from the point of view of the question, who defines the agenda and sets the priorities, we can observe that—since the articulation of both new issues in rights terms and of new rights is more recent with respect to social and economic rights—the driving force seems to be the Third World/global South social movements, such as those of the shack dwellers or the homeless, or indigenous peoples struggling to regain control over natural resources. The areas of social and economic rights are still in a process of fermentation, and the canon has not yet been settled to the same extent as with civil and political rights. On the whole, the pressure to expand the social and economic boundaries of universal rights comes from the oppressed and the powerless and thus makes these aspects somewhat more utopian at the global level than civil and political rights. Legitimacy in this case is increased by the ever larger number of utopian actors—thus integrating the oppressed.

5.2 Adding meanings

The meanings of ideological concepts have something in common with cancer cells: they multiply uncontrollably. The process of semantic pluralization is checked only by the death of an ideology. (Though elements of a dead ideology can return to life and join future canons.) Argumentation and the redefinition of terms is central to any ideology. The evolution of an ideology can be seen as a progressive absorption—with the continued interpretation of reality (events, processes, and problems) from the point of view of the basic tenets as expressed in value concepts. This evolution leads inevitably to the expansion of the original meanings of the central value concepts. We often witness how opposing ideologies compete over the interpretation of the same events or processes, how each ideology strives to herd expressions towards its own ideological pen. Examples of ideological homing: "the caste system in India is racism"; "The treatment of Palestinians by the Israeli authorities is racism"; "The treatment of Roma in Europe is racism"; or "The treatment of asylum seekers in Western Europe is racism." This is the anti-racism ideology at work, expanding and at the same time pluralizing its central concept. One day, the concept will be so broad that it will lose its potential to mobilize for social change. The trumpet call will turn into a lullaby. But until then, the capacity of an ideology to incorporate new meanings prolongs its legitimacy.

In this respect, social and economic aspects contribute to a faster accumulation of new meanings of rights, therefore adding new legitimacy to the human rights discourse as a whole, keeping its utopian function alive. Yet in a dialectically contradictory way, the multiplying of meanings also leads towards a semantic terminus.[18]

18. The word "progress" for example has reached a semantic terminus—it has no agreed meaning and can be used by advocates of diametrically opposite ideas.

5.3 Adding expertise and efficient ignorance

In ideologies one observes a parallel growth of expertise and ignorance. Within the guild of the human rights professionals, the narrow specialization of experts is in progress. The number of international human rights instruments is growing progressively; hence the growing number of institutions, international and domestic, created to ensure monitoring and implementation. New bureaucracies follow each new convention. Scores of NGOs, not as digitally challenged as the UN treaty bodies, participate at all stages and levels. At the same time, the general public and the majority of those who are dressed up in the human rights legitimating uniform, especially the "human rights" functionaries in governments and GONGOs, remain pathetically ignorant about the basics of human rights philosophy, international human rights law, relevant case law, etc. But the most curious fact is that the members of the fast-growing group of human rights functionaries can in fact do their job without possessing substantial knowledge on human rights. This has been typical of the functioning of other ideologies: for a growing group of people across society competence regarding the original doctrines is increasingly irrelevant, while for the growing group of experts preoccupation with specialized subjects is obvious. For example, in the new transition "democracies" of the 1990s, numerous officials have been appointed to deal with "human rights" or aspects thereof. Many of their speeches reveal little understanding of rights. They contain the needed rights references but only in the most trivial ways. From the point of view of the human rights sages, this type of speaker does not know what she is saying—and few in the audience are listening anyway. When the speech ends with appeals no one feels inspired. This fellow is not one of our family, but only imitates us, the sages decide, and fail to notice the critical fact that the imitation is—politically—not just necessary, but also sufficient.

Under this mechanism then, social and economic dimensions of rights legitimize by contributing to both the growth of expert networks and the accompanying efficient ignorance.

5.4 Adding ceremony

Ideology can be recognized by the characteristic atmosphere created through rituals and metaphors, the mixture of church and vulgarity, which accompanies the progress of human rights performance. The fiftieth anniversary of the Universal Declaration in 1998, celebrated at numerous fora, provided abundant evidence of such ceremony. Audiences honored human rights heroes with minutes of silence. A well-known writer, speaking about human rights, said at one conference that human rights are the tables of humanism. Another dignitary said that human rights are a ship which cleaves the waves in the storm, and furthermore, that "Human rights will guarantee the flight of progress over the abyss of our time." Federico Major, the president of UNESCO, declared on 10 December 1998 that the twenty-first century will be the century of human rights. If he is right, there will be no shortage of such rhetoric.

Obviously, social and economic aspects of rights (including social and economic rights in the strict sense) are well-disposed to rhetoric and to the addition of ceremony and spectacle to the human rights discourse. Recently, many more awards as well as fellowships and other opportunities have been announced for people and organizations working on the social and economic aspects of rights.

5.5 Adding talent

The advance of ideology is also an advance of mediocrity. One notes the political weakness of the human rights community and its increased susceptibility to manipulation. The human rights networks, assemblies, and audiences seem to be increasingly uncritical in their reception of ideas and agendas by leaders of the movement. This tendency, too, is a symptom of advancing ideology. A process of personnel counterselection may also be expected, in view of the fact that as human rights ascends to power, the people attracted to it will be those who attracted to power, who are more amenable to established procedure and less likely to worry about whether they make a difference in the lives of real people. A new generation of human rights activists is being agglutinated to our generation, but it is coming along by roads very different from the ones that brought us to human rights.

In many recent cases when a certain policy has been enacted on behalf of human rights, the human rights community was not among the key players, as in the 1999 NATO bombing of Yugoslavia. It is in the midst of such crises that the voice of the human rights community matters most; yet it is during such developments that human rights activism and advocacy become epiphenomenal, spectral, nonconsequential, while the rhetoric is everywhere about it.

By bringing new thematic aspects and new energy to the human rights discourse, social and economic issue advocates are less involved in professional counterselection and more likely to bring new reserves of inspiration and talent to the human rights discourse.

5.6 Adding morality

In view of the above, we should not be surprised by the authenticity of the appeals by veterans of the human rights movement. As a moral reaction to ritualization and metaphoric disaster, those who were born to be reformers but were bound in their loyalty to an ideologizing discourse start to dream for a rediscovery of the moral value system. Such appeals to authenticity in the human rights community are already voiced by individuals who are sympathetic to the original human rights moral impulse, even if they have ascended high in governmental hierarchies.[19]

Social and economic dimensions of rights add legitimacy to the human rights discourse by providing new moral impetus, deriving from the very substance of respective preoccupations: eradication of extreme poverty, relief of hunger, child labor, women's reproductive health, etc.

5.7 Adding interaction with neighboring discourses

The interpretation of social and economic rights is certainly influenced by developments in many different areas and discourses including: conflict prevention/resolution; building of democratic institutions; development; poverty alleviation; security; humanitarian intervention; peace-building and peace activism; educational policies; transitional justice; globalization; anti-racism; the women's movements; indigenous movements; migration and refugees-related work; environmentalism; etc. In its integration of social and economic dimensions the human rights movement has begun to share advocacy campaigns with neighboring movements. This opening up of the human rights discourse to interaction with and influence from other discourses extends the viability of human rights.

6. Water Under the Bridge

The dialectics of legitimation is such that whatever is at work in adding legitimacy to a discourse simultaneously and ipso facto brings nearer the final eclipse of that discourse. There are intrinsic limits to power legitimation, such that the very same forces that build a tendency are also those that bring it to an end. Social and economic dimensions of rights, at this stage adding

19. At a conference in Vienna in October 1998, Catherine Lalumiere stated that if the European Union does not hurry to develop a human rights policy, Europe would lose its soul. Peter Leuprecht left his high post in the Council of Europe, questioning the departure from original standards which was demonstrated in the acceptance of countries like Russia and Albania into the organization. Human rights professionals in prominent positions such as Aaron Rhodes, the executive director of the International Federation of Human Rights, have been trying to reestablish the movement's claims on the moral realm in press publications, interviews, and other formats.

legitimacy to the human rights discourse, also ensure that the discourse will become so integrated as to lose its political potential to transform.

Is it possible to change the direction of the process? My answer is negative. It is inevitable that human rights will experience a legitimation crisis in the future, no matter how long one is delayed by the infusion of social and economic dimensions of universal rights. According to some, and judging by the defensive reactions of others, a legitimation crisis is already looming on the horizon. But if understood in its totality, those who believe in human rights should not view the process with dread. Every advancing ideology is ultimately self-defeating because it is primarily (and despite the secondary regulatory functions of human rights—defending the weaker and limiting power) a form of justification. When it advances to a state where it can be used to justify anything whatsoever, and therefore also obviously immoral acts, the critique and demise of the ideology are in order, at least logically if not historically. While we cannot win the battle for recapturing the original value of human rights, we can try to understand what is happening with the role human rights play in politics. With this attitude we are philosophers wondering, after Aristotle, at things as they are and mindful of Hegel's ineluctable metaphor in the introduction to the Philosophy of Law: when philosophy begins to paint with its gray colors on gray, a certain form of life has grown old. With its gray on gray, philosophy cannot change but only understand. The owl of Minerva flies at dusk.

7. Social and Economic Rights and the Human Rights Defenders

As noted above, there are many signs that "human rights defenders" in democratic and transition societies are now more closely aligned with power coalitions, and that their agendas are quite similar to governmental agendas. Or, otherwise put and without any ironic intent, they are winning the struggle and forcing governments to adopt their views. At the same time, in many countries on the dark side of the Earth, a human rights defender is a candidate for prison, if not a prisoner already. Who then are the human rights defenders? And how is the community of defenders influenced by the social and economic dimensions of universal rights?

Human rights defenders differ in several important ways; and the strong emphasis on social and economic dimensions in their field of work is *positively correlated* with several other characteristics—as described below.

In December 1998, a group of over five hundred human rights defenders gathered in Palais de Chaillot in Paris to celebrate the fiftieth anniversary of the UDHR, at the same place where it was originally adopted. The majority of defenders came from Asia, Africa, and Latin America. Each of those present was undoubtedly a genuine human rights defender, carefully selected, according to common criteria of efficient and courageous human rights work, by an inclusive and well-informed steering committee put together by four international human rights networks. As a member of that committee, I had observed that already during the selection process deep differences between the human rights defenders in the different parts of the world began to emerge, and this struck me as a phenomenon of daunting significance which requires analysis. Since then I have been studying the human rights movement from the perspective of my 1998 impressions, and what follows is a snapshot which has validity only at this stage—for it is unclear how the future will shape the human rights community.

I would suggest that, based on their country of residence, there are at least three different types of human rights defenders: those living in the established Western democracies; those in societies undergoing a "transition to democracy"; and all others. A large part of these others live on the dark side of the Earth, in non-democratic oppressive societies or dictatorships, but I put them in the same group with those who come from the economically undeveloped Third World. This is a gross oversimplification, which I will be the first to dispose of as soon as reality calls. For the time being, I propose grouping together all the countries that remain after we deduct the liberal democracies and the societies undergoing a transition to a democratic political system. I believe that all the differences listed below, between the human rights defenders in the different parts of the world, are expressions of the fact that while human rights still function as a protest and critique in oppressive societies, they are already an apology in democratic and transition societies.

The picture is complex and heavily country-specific, but certain approximate tendencies can be grasped.

7.1 Attitude toward the Great Powers

Strong anti-American sentiment is typical of a large number of Third World human rights defenders; more generally, they reveal a strong antipathy to all Great Powers. When one radical peace activist said at the fiftieth anniversary of the UDHR that the Great Powers have obtained for themselves "the democratic license to kill together with the democratic license to plunder," the audience, numerically dominated by Third World activists, applauded enthusiastically. The Third World activists see a natural link between imperialist "plundering" that violates social and economic rights and the impunity in the abuse of civil and political rights by those who can afford to ignore criticism, i.e., the Great Powers. The colonial past and the condemnation of colonialism are formative influences for these defenders. Fighting against the consequences of colonialism, they stand in defense of social and economic (as well as cultural) rights.

Western human rights defenders, on the other hand, typically view their own governments with more amity. Because many NGOs cooperate with governments in the West, Western activists do not view government as the major evil—but frequently as guarantors or sources of pressure for rights protection. A strong group of NGOs in the World Conference Against Racism in Durban (August-September 2001) was reluctant to support the claims of Third World networks for compensations to be exacted from the former colonial powers, as part of an effort to defend their dignity—understood to include the enjoyment of economic rights.

7.2 Attitude to communism and the radical Left

Though not necessarily articulated, the Third World human rights movement is impregnated with communist attitudes, including at times a communist type of combative intolerance. In contrast, the human rights defenders in the postcommunist space are on the whole anticommunist, even though many would describe themselves as socialist or center-left. Accordingly, human rights defenders from democratic and transition societies seem to be less sensitive to economic inequality and hence less responsive to issues of social and economic rights. Eastern European human rights activists are still more committed to civil liberties, as a natural reaction to communist totalitarianism, and only in the last few years have social and economic rights entered upon their agenda. For example, the European Roma Rights Center followed the same path: having focused on issues of police brutality and racist violence in its first years, it then took on issues of systemic, especially indirect, discrimination against the Roma in Europe and on this basis developed strategies for integrating social and economic rights in its monitoring, legal defense, and advocacy projects.

7.3 Position in the social stratification

Human rights defenders in established democracies and transition societies are mediators, occupying a median position between the powerful and the powerless. They do not belong fully in the world of the powerful because human rights careers are usually less financially rewarding than alternative careers open to individuals with their background and skills. Hence, they often are people who have made a status "sacrifice." But apparently they do not belong in the world of the powerless either; to date, they as a rule remain distinct from those whose rights they defend. From this median position some descend while others ascend, but once there, they usually defend the rights of others, especially of disadvantaged groups. They are rarely themselves "victims of human rights violations."

In contrast, Third World human rights defenders usually belong to groups whose rights have been abused. They are themselves victims, and they are more or less legitimate "representatives" of groups or communities struggling for their rights. In fact, many are political leaders and political activists, in the narrow sense of participating in the struggle for political power. Since most human rights professionals in democratic societies are in human rights because of their liberal democratic views and related concerns with civil and political rights, they have until recently been less ardent on social and economic rights, as compared to those who are themselves victims of violations. This may be so because the victim consciousness is more easily generalized, and the wronged person experiences a generalized suffering which includes social and economic dimensions.

7.4 Existential mode

In the richer Western democracies, the activities of human rights defenders amounts to work. In poor countries, and those under authoritarian and other oppressive regimes, human rights defenders are freedom fighters. In repressive environments, work vs. struggle also implies a difference in the personal price exacted: while human rights defenders in democratic societies are usually salaried employees, or are self-employed and raise funds for their cause, defenders in non-democratic regimes *struggle for liberation*. The latter activists are often paid nothing and indeed pay a personal price for their efforts. They are often actual or potential victims and therefore legitimately represent victims. The personal prices they pay often include exposing or subjecting themselves to killings, forced disappearances, torture, imprisonment, unfair trials, harassment of family members, threats, etc. In transition societies, human rights defenders are in differing country-specific stages between peaceful enjoyment of their jobs and self-sacrificial heroism. The personal experience of material insecurity by Third World activists is also a factor informing their stronger inclination to prioritize social and economic rights.

7.5 Attitude toward political parties

In democracies human rights defenders emphasize their political independence. They proclaim their nonpartisan approach and avoid any affiliation with political parties struggling for power. On the other extreme, in some dictatorships, human rights defenders are the leaders of the opposition. This is only logical: if a regime is generally abusive, its opponents function as human rights defenders and remain as such at least as long as they remain in opposition. (However, they tend to change when they ascend to power, or gain positions of power in oppositional armed groups on the side of non-state actors who often compete with the government in violating human rights.) Since Third World activists do not shy away from party politics, they are drawn into formulating party policies and platforms, which by definition engage with social and economic issues.

7.6 Political constituencies

In the West human rights defenders are frequently quite individualistic professionals with sophisticated motivations and moral scruples, whose constituencies—if any—are not clearly defined and may be spread across political divides. Political affiliations in democratic and transition societies are formed around agendas in which human rights are rarely the critical issues of the day. In contrast, in countries in which the political regime is authoritarian or abusive, human rights defenders are active opponents of the regime. In Iran during the 1990s, or in present-day China, political dissidents overlap with human rights defenders. The prominent activists have a political constituency of a certain size and type, varying from country to country. Since they are at least informally accountable to broad collectivities, they have to appeal to social and economic rights in order to maintain their political basis.

8. Conclusion: What Then Constitutes the Unity of the Human Rights Movement?

There is no such real political unity. A human rights community—of scholars, activists, and functionaries—united by common aims and common standards hardly exists at present. But on the other hand, there is a quasi-unity at a discursive level, if hundreds and even thousands of defenders of all backgrounds vote in favor of the same declarations and plans of action. This quasi-unity is the false common *locus* that I call "human rights ideology," a communicative space inclusive of a variety of not necessarily compatible political interests, positions, and attitudes.

Political differences among human rights defenders are expressed in ways other than simply stating that "we belong to the human rights movement." Human rights defenders are faced with an identity crisis because belonging to the "human rights community" has ceased to be a marker or indicator of political affiliation. It is more and more difficult to build alliances solely on the basis of supporting human rights.[20] In order to decide whether a group is a potential partner or an adversary, we are not satisfied to learn only that it is pro-human rights. We will want to know its concrete issues, agenda, policy choices, and will make no judgment before we figure out the local context in which the group operates.

Finally, in my view, there is a sense in which the unity and solidarity of the human rights movement is not discursive but deep and real. As maintained above, human rights advocates who care about the moral foundations of human rights will not try to salvage the totality and purity of the human rights ideology. If the human rights discourse is usurped by powers, there can be no winning back of this territory. After all, who won the battle for redefining Reason in the eighteenth century, or Progress in the nineteenth century, or the battle for the meaning of real Marxism and real socialism in our time? Such battles are neither won nor lost. Ideological discourses become eclipsed and sink into oblivion. Basic values currently expressed in the language of rights will be expressed in ways we cannot even imagine today.

Beyond all words, and apart from all discourses, and regardless of occupation, cultural identity or other status, some people simply refuse to sit still in the face of injustice. There is a kind of wordless clarity among them. Their solidarity may even survive any possible justification. Wittgenstein says: "If I have exhausted the justifications I have reached bedrock, and my spade is turned. Then I am inclined to say: 'This is simply what I do.'"

20. The European Union funding for human rights is mainly channeled through the European Initiative on Democratization and Human Rights (EIDHR), but only a very small portion of the funding goes to groups that do strictly human rights work. All grantees technically should define themselves as human rights defenders, but this would contribute little to striking alliances on issues.

Chapter 9

Eva Brems

Reconciling Universality and Diversity in International Human Rights Law

Today, the concept of universality is inherent in that of human rights. Human rights are by definition the rights of all human beings around the world. At the same time, human rights are increasingly considered to be the most fundamental norms, which should receive priority over all other norms and interests. Human rights are presented as the ultimate criteria of human behavior: of government behavior but also increasingly of the behavior of economic actors and private individuals. The question that is addressed here relates to the tension between this claim of universality and the reality of enormous diversity in the world.

1. Universality versus Cultural Relativism

Defending the universality claim of international human rights is often equated with defeating so-called cultural relativism. The position of cultural relativism, a view most often held by anthropologists and philosophers, is that moral values are necessarily relative, and as a result, it is not possible to

András Sajó (ed.), Human Rights with Modesty: The Problem of Universalism, *213-230.*

use uniform criteria for judging human behavior across a diversity of contexts, which means that universal norms are not desirable.

Originally, cultural relativism was the name of a school of anthropology that had its peak in the first half of the twentieth century. This school introduced some valid insights in reaction to the ethnocentrism and imperialism that characterized the anthropology of earlier periods. One of their main conclusions was the rejection of absolutes and the tolerance of diversity. Cultural relativists claimed that the principles used for judging behavior are valid only within a particular culture. On this basis, they rejected the idea of universal human rights in its entirety.

1.1 The AAA statement

The cultural relativists did not hesitate to say as much in a statement on behalf of the American Anthropological Association in 1947, addressed to the United Nations Commission on Human Rights, which was at that time drafting the Universal Declaration of Human Rights (UDHR):

> The problem of drawing up a Declaration of Human Rights was relatively simple in the eighteenth century, because it was not a matter of *human* rights, but of the rights of men within the framework of the sanctions laid by a single society....
>
> Today the problem is complicated by the fact that the Declaration must be of worldwide applicability. It must embrace and recognize the validity of many different ways of life. It will not be convincing to the Indonesian, the African, the Indian, the Chinese, if it lies on the same plane as like documents of an earlier period. The rights of Man in the twentieth century cannot be circumscribed by the standards of any single culture or be dictated by the aspirations of any single people. Such a document will lead to frustration, not realization of the personalities of vast numbers of human beings.[1]

The cultural relativist critique of human rights is a harsh one: it is a square rejection of the concept of universal human rights, based on the absence of empirical evidence which might confirm the existence of universal values.

Today, other schools have replaced cultural relativism in the social sciences, but the same arguments are still heard, mainly among philosophers. The rejection of absolutes and universals fits well into a postmodern framework.

---

1. American Anthropological Association, "Statement on Human Rights," 49, 4 *American Anthropologist*, (1947) 539-543, reprinted in Morton E. Winston, (ed.), *The Philosophy of Human Rights*, Belmont: Wadsworth (1989) 116-120.

1.2 The search for mother notions

In order to defeat this line of argument much effort has gone into research that attempts to contest the empirical basis of relativism. Many people have tried to show that international human rights have a basis in all the cultures of the world. The search for this basis is sometimes an anthropological one, focusing on institutions, rules, traditions, etc., that can be linked to human rights. At other times it is a philosophical search, looking for similarities between the ideas and values circulating in a particular society on the one hand, and the principles of human rights on the other. Often both aspects are intertwined.

The approach is frequently that of a search for a "mother notion" of human rights. A mother notion is a moral principle that is situated on a more general level than human rights. A typical example is the principle of human dignity. As a first step, it is argued that this mother notion can be found in all cultures. This means that it is universal in the empirical sense. Then, as a second step, it is argued that all specific human rights can be derived from this one mother notion. The idea is that since the mother notion is universal, there can be no objection against the universal application of the specific rights.

In my view, both steps in this reasoning are problematic. In the first place, it has not yet been empirically demonstrated that such a universal mother notion actually exists. Presumably, the best evidence of such a notion is a norm or value that can be found in the majority of human cultures, yet not in all of them. The question then is whether the exceptions do not undermine the universality of the norm or value. If you want to establish universality on an empirical basis is quasi-universality as good as full universality?

Second, the movement from the universal mother notion to universal human rights is also problematic. Here the problem is the operationalization of general values. Human rights strive to be more than general moral values: they must be operational. In this light, one may wonder whether the consensus that exists on the general level of the mother notion also exists on the more specific level of human rights. Even if people in all societies respect the value of human dignity, they may have extremely diverse ways of interpreting and expressing it, to the extent that in certain societies some human rights may be considered as unnecessary, incomprehensible, or undesirable.

Hence, in my opinion, the empirical approach to the issue of universality is not the right one. First, the result is inevitably unsatisfactory. The list of norms and values shared by all cultures will either include only a few of the extensive international catalogue of human rights, or it will consist of notions that are so vague and general that they resist operationalization. Second, this approach results in an unnecessarily vulnerable universality. There is a very real possibility that no empirical universal basis can be found for all human rights; which would seem to lead to the conclusion that human rights are not universal. The weakness of cultural relativism is then not its reliance upon empirical analysis, but the conclusions it draws from such analysis. Whoever wants to defeat cultural relativism through empirical research is repeating the same mistake: the mistake of jumping from "*Sein*" to "*Sollen*," from description to prescription.

Why on earth must the universality of human rights rest on an empirical basis? What prevents a good idea such as human rights from spreading outside the society in which it originated? Cultures are not static. One of the ways in which they change is through contact with other cultures—and norms and values are certainly not immune to this kind of change. In order to judge whether something is worthwhile, it is not particularly important to know where it comes from.

2. Universality as Choice

If the universality of human rights is not based upon the empirical existence of universal values, then what is it based upon? In my opinion, the universality of human rights is not something inevitable or mystical, but rather a deliberate choice that we make. I prefer to view universality as a normative and not a descriptive concept.

In 1948 the international community chose to draft a catalogue of fundamental norms for all human beings everywhere. The important question is not whether these norms could be found in all human societies, nor whether all societies were represented at the conference. It is clear that this was not the case. The significant fact is that a choice was made to give these norms universal validity.

In the half-century since 1948, international human rights have been further developed in numerous international treaties. What is remarkable is that in practice there seems to be a worldwide consensus on this choice in favor of universal validity. This consensus is expressed whenever human beings who experience oppression and injustice appeal to human rights. During the period of decolonization, the independence movements in Asia, Africa, and Latin America employed human rights discourse. Today, women's movements, labor unions, indigenous peoples, and innumerable other groups and individuals appeal to human rights each day. This type of universality in practice is not limited to the organized exercise of rights. Gross human rights violations, which are remarkably similar all around the world, create a rights-awareness in the minds of the people who are confronted with them. UN Secretary-General Annan expresses this as follows:

> You do not need to explain the meaning of human rights to an Asian mother or an African father whose son or daughter has been tortured or killed. They understand it—tragically—far better than we ever will.[2]

Human rights discourse is so successful that governments generally support it, even though by design human rights are intended to protect citizens against their government. When a regime is accused of violating human rights, the regime only rarely questions the validity of human rights as criteria for judging their behavior. They may contest facts; they may contest the right of the accusers to interfere with their domestic affairs; or they may advance "mitigating circumstances"—but the basic principle that those human rights have to be respected everywhere is accepted either implicitly or explicitly.

Is it then necessary to find a universal foundation in order to confirm the universal validity of human rights? I think not. If we want to use human rights as a fundamental and ultimate criterion for judging human behavior, it is important that they have legitimacy in all societies and for all individuals. Linking human rights to God or to human nature may strengthen this legitimacy. Yet the foundation of universality need not be universal itself. In practice, states, organizations, and individuals support the universality of human rights for a diversity of philosophical, ideological, religious, and political reasons.

3. Universality and Contextual Diversity: A Different Debate

There is another more relevant question than that concerning the foundation of the universality of human rights: what does the decision to establish universality mean concretely for human rights? In other words, what are the consequences of this choice?

The question touches on another debate besides that between universality and cultural relativism, which takes place mainly among Western academics. This other debate is also partly academic, but to an important degree it is fought in the political arena. It is not however a debate on the theoretical possibility of universal rights within the West, but rather takes place between representatives of the West and representatives of non-Western societies regarding the modalities of universal rights.

The challengers in this debate represent several non-Western societies, in particular: East Asia, sub-Saharan Africa, and the Islamic world. These non-Western representatives claim that "universal human rights"—in their

2. Kofi Annan, "Statement of UN Secretary-General Annan, delivered on Saturday, 18 October 1997, to the Communications Conference at the Aspen Institute, Colorado," United Nations Press Release SG/SM/6366 (20 October 1997).

present state of development and evolution within international law and especially as applied in international relations—cater overly to the West and do not sufficiently take into account the needs and values of other people and other societies. The reaction to this claim, by representatives of both the West and the international human rights community, is generally defensive. The critique is considered an attack on human rights, and in particular, a threat to the fundamental principle of universality. Yet it is worth having a closer look at the main arguments advanced in this discourse.

3.1 Asia and Africa

The Asian and African critical discourses on human rights are different in tone but quite similar in content.[3] Asian particularist views on human rights are often expressed in a very assertive manner, taking the shape of a real critique. The best example remains that of the United Nations World Conference on Human Rights in Vienna in 1993. At the Asian preparatory conference in Bangkok, a declaration was adopted expressing particularist views, which were then repeated during the Vienna conference by the representatives of East Asian governments. The Bangkok Declaration stated:[4]

> [The Asian states]
>
> 5. Emphasize the principles of respect for *national sovereignty and territorial integrity as well as non-interference in the internal affairs of states*, and the non-use of human rights as an instrument of political pressure...
> 7. Stress the universality, objectivity and non-selectivity of all human rights and the need to avoid the application of *double standards* in the implementation of human rights and its *politicization*, and that no violation of human rights can be justified;
> 8. Recognize that while human rights are universal in nature, *they must be considered in the context of a dynamic and evolving process of international norm-setting, bearing in mind the significance of national and religious particularities and various historical, cultural and religious backgrounds.*

The above positions were perceived as an attack on the universality principle and became one of the dominant themes of the conference, forcing the Western states to the defense of universal human rights.

---

3. For an extensive analysis of the Asian and African particularist critiques of international human rights, see Eva Brems, *Human Rights: Universality and Diversity*, Martinus Nijhoff (2001), 33-90 (Asia) and 91-181 (Africa).
4. Bangkok Declaration: final declaration of the regional meeting for Asia of the 1993 United Nations World Conference on Human Rights, 29 March-April 1993 (A/CONF.157/ASRM/8-A/CONF.157/PC/59).

The African discourse is much more moderate, and today is more frequently found among academics than among politicians. This is related to the fact that Africa has its own regional human rights protection system based on the African Charter of Human and Peoples' Rights, which resulted partly out of the desire to "Africanize" human rights and is now a central reference point in the discussion about "African human rights views."

Despite the difference in tone, it is remarkable that the particularities invoked by both Asians and Africans largely coincide. The main areas of difference with the West are apparently the same in both regions.

In the *economic sphere*, differences arise about the priority given to development. There is much discussion of the link between development and human rights and a strong focus on the human right to development. In the same context, Asians and Africans stress the importance of economic and social rights such as the right to food, to health care, and to education, as well as the principle of the indivisibility of human rights on the basis of which economic and social rights should have the same importance as civil and political rights.

In the *political sphere*, many arguments center around the question of internal and external instability, and the conditions under which a repressive style of government can be justified. Both types of instability result from the fact that many states in Asia and Africa are relatively young, meaning that their regimes and borders are not always solidly established. Another factor contributing to instability is the heterogeneous composition of the population in ethnic or religious terms.

Finally, there are the *cultural arguments*, where the central theme is the rejection of extreme individualism and the focus on communality. This leads to support for collective rights and for restrictions of individual rights in the interest of the community, in addition to support for the establishment of individual duties and responsibilities. Also, in the cultural field, there is the specific issue of the so-called harmful cultural practices. These are practices that are positive in value for some participants within the cultural context, yet are difficult for outsiders to reconcile with human rights. The most frequently cited example is the practice of female genital mutilation (*cf. infra*).

The flavor of the non-Western particularist critique of international human rights is best illustrated with some samples. The first example is an extract from a text written by Bilahari Kausikan, an official of the Ministry of Foreign Affairs of Singapore. Despite its small size, Singapore is very vocal on the issue of differing human rights standards which reflect "Asian values." In Singapore itself, some of the most problematic human rights issues concern corporal punishment (caning is a common sentence for minor offences) and freedom of expression, in particular, for political dissidents. These issues are addressed in the following extract from Kausikan:

> Singapore has had differences of opinion with several Western governments as regards capital punishment, corporal punishment and limits to freedom of expression. How are such disagreements to be resolved? International law prescribes no single international standard that can be applied to any of these issues... The days are gone when any single country can insist on its own practices as a "universal norm"...
>
> My point is not that Singapore should never adopt a more liberal standard for freedom of expression or that we should never abolish capital or corporal punishment. It is simply that these are choices that Singaporeans must make for themselves...
>
> I am not arguing that national sovereignty precludes all international discussions on human rights. International law has evolved to the point that how a country treats its citizens is no longer a matter for its exclusive determination. But international law still co-exists uneasily, and in as yet an unresolved manner, with the fundamental principle of national sovereignty. It would thus be prudent to restrict such discussions to gross and egregious violations of human rights, which clearly admit of no derogation on the grounds of national sovereignty. Attempting to expand the debate to areas where there are legitimate national differences of interpretation or implementation only exacerbates misunderstanding and prevents consensus...
>
> A focus on a more restricted but precise core of basic human rights that must be accepted irrespective of culture or development, and that are fundamental enough to restrict the room for interpretation, is a more productive approach.[5]

This rather sophisticated argument is based on the room for interpretation that is left by international human rights norms. The treaties prohibit "inhuman or degrading punishment"; though they do not prohibit caning as such. This means that there is room for debate about whether or not caning falls under the qualification "inhuman or degrading punishment." Similarly, freedom of expression is not an absolute freedom. In international human rights law (e.g. Art. 19 ICCPR), restrictions of this freedom are acceptable if they are proportionate to such goals as the protection of public order and national security, or the protection of morals, rights, or the reputations of others. Again, there is room for discussion about what this means concretely.

The next example is from sub-Saharan Africa. Claude Ake is a Nigerian professor of political science who writes about the need to "domesticate"

5. Bilahari Kausikan, "An Asian Approach to Human Rights," *American Society of International Law Proceedings* (1995) 146-152.

human rights, to recreate them in the light of African conditions in order to make them relevant for African people:

> First, we have to understand that the idea of legal rights presupposes social atomization and individualism, and a conflict model of society for which legal rights are the necessary mediation. However, in most of Africa, the extent of social atomization is very limited mainly because of the limited penetration of capitalism and commodity relations. Many people are still locked into natural economies and have a sense of belonging to an organic whole, be it a family, a clan, a lineage or an ethnic group...
> All this means that abstract legal rights attributed to individuals will not make much sense for most of our people; neither will they be relevant to their consciousness and living conditions. It is necessary to extend the idea of human rights to include collective human rights for corporate social groups such as the family, the lineage, the ethnic group. Our people still think largely in terms of collective rights and express their commitment to it constantly in their behavior... If the idea of human rights is to make any sense at all in the African context, it has to incorporate them in a concept of communal human rights.
> For reasons that need not detain us here some of the rights important in the West are of no interest and no value to most Africans. For instance, freedom of speech and freedom of the press do not mean much to a largely illiterate rural community completely absorbed in the daily rigours of the struggle for survival.
> African conditions shift the emphasis to a different kind of rights. Rights which can mean something for poor people fighting to survive and burdened by ignorance, poverty and disease, rights which can mean something for women who are cruelly used. Rights which can mean something for the youth whose future we render more improbable every day. If a bill of rights is to make any sense, it must include among others, a right to work and to a living wage, a right to shelter, to health, to education. [6]

This is a different kind of argument, one that focuses on change and shifting priorities within international human rights: collective rights instead of, or in addition to, individual rights; basic economic and social rights rather than civil and political rights.

3.2 Islam

The debate about Islamic views on human rights is a quite distinct discourse.[7] Different tendencies can be distinguished. The so-called apologetics claim

6. Claude Ake, "The African Context of Human Rights," *Africa Today* (1987) 5-12.
7. For an extensive analysis, see Brems, *op. cit.*, note 3, 183-290.

that the *Shari'ah*, Islamic law, offers complete protection for human rights. More progressive Muslims are of the opinion that this is not the case and try by way of interpretation to make Islamic law compatible with international human rights. Finally, there are secularists who believe that it is not possible to reconcile human rights and Islamic law.

In comparison with the Asian and African discourses, the Islamic human rights discourse comes closest to rejecting the universality of human rights. This is particularly the case when Islamic law is represented as an alternative human rights model, such as in the 1990 Cairo Declaration on Human Rights in Islam (Organization of Islamic Conference). These models combine Islamic rules with international human rights norms, yet typically, give priority to Islamic law over human rights. As a result, they do not provide protection in those fields where Islamic law itself violates international human rights norms, which is especially the case with regard to religious freedom, discrimination on the basis of religion, women's rights, and corporal punishment. Take for example Art. 6 of the Cairo Declaration on the equality of men and women:

> a. Woman is equal to man in human dignity and has rights to enjoy as well as duties to perform; she has her own civil entity and financial independence, and the right to retain her name and lineage.
> b. The husband is responsible for the support and welfare of the family.

While recognizing the equal dignity of men and women, this provision does not endorse the principle of equal rights regardless of sex. To the contrary, it sanctions a system in which men and women have separate roles, to which correspond separate rights and duties. Art. 10 is the provision of the Cairo Declaration protecting religious freedom:

> Islam is the religion of unspoiled nature. It is prohibited to exercise any form of compulsion on man or to exploit his poverty or ignorance in order to convert him to another religion or to atheism.

This is obviously a very limited conception of freedom of religion. Not only is it limited to one religion (Islam), but it also protects only the freedom not to be drawn away from Islam. In other words: everyone is free to be a Muslim, but not necessarily to practice another religion or to live without religion.

Other provisions of the Cairo Declaration seem to protect rights rather well (e.g., Art. 2: right to life; Art. 9: right to education; Art. 11: freedom of the person; Art. 12: freedom of movement). However, whatever guarantees are contained in the declaration are seriously undermined by the final Arts. 24 and 25:

> Article 24: All the rights and freedoms stipulated in this Declaration are subject to the Islamic *Shari'ah*.
> Article 25: The Islamic *Shari'ah* is the only source of reference for the explanation or clarification of any of the articles of this Declaration.

Art. 24 is a limitation clause and Art. 25 an interpretation clause. Both have the effect of establishing the Islamic *Shari'ah* as a higher set of norms than the human rights that are protected in the Cairo Declaration. For these articles require that human rights be interpreted in such a way as to conform to the Islamic *Shari'ah*. Where this is not possible, any conflict must be resolved by giving priority to the rule of the *Shari'ah* over human rights.

4. Toward Inclusive Universality of Human Rights

4.1 Principle

When human rights activists are confronted with a cultural relativist discourse questioning the universality of human rights, they have no other choice but to try and defeat the relativist arguments in order to justify the principle of universality. Very often, this is the Western reaction to the non-Western particularist human rights discourse. Yet this approach ignores the differences between the particularlist discourse and cultural relativism, in particular the fact that most of the particularist critique of international human rights remains situated in a framework which accepts the worldwide validity of human rights as a matter of principle. This is a crucial distinction—for contemporary particularist discourse does not threaten to undermine the universality of human rights. Hence, it is not necessary to react in such a defensive manner.

On the contrary, with respect to the universality concept that I promote here in this chapter, it is essential to take the particularist critique seriously in order to promote the universality of human rights. In this view, called "inclusive universality," the universality of human rights is interpreted as the inclusion of all human beings in the human rights protection system. Inclusion has to be more than formal. In essence, it is a democratic criterion implying equal participation in the human rights system. If human rights are valid for all people in all societies, they must then reflect in an equal manner the needs and values of all human beings. Moreover, all human beings must be able to participate equally in their drafting, as well as in their interpretation and application, and in determining the international human rights agenda.

This view is based not only on a democratic principle but also on a pragmatic one. Human rights make very little sense unless they are alive among the people. This means that they must be connected to the way people think and feel. Only the people themselves can activate and strengthen human rights; if the people do not care about them, how can governments be expected to care? When human rights are insufficiently connected to human reality in a certain society, the position of human rights in that society is undermined.

How does this relate to the non-Western particularist human rights discourses from East Asia, sub-Saharan Africa, and the Islamic world? First of all, it should be recognized that diversity arguments are often abused by authoritarian governments who pretend to be protecting the particularity of their society, but whose only real interest is to protect their shameful human rights record from international scrutiny. This should not obscure the fact that many of these arguments are bona fide. The aim of this bona fide discourse is precisely to improve the connection between international human rights and the reality of human life in non-Western contexts.

It cannot be denied that international human rights disproportionately reflect Western needs and values. The founding document of international human rights, the Universal Declaration of Human Rights (1948), is closely linked to the eighteenth-century declarations of rights in France and America, expressing European Enlightenment thought. In the fifty-five years since 1948 during which international human rights have been in a process of development, they have been subject to diverse influences which still could not undo their overwhelmingly Western character. Some of these influences such as socialism and the labor movement are also mainly of Western origin. Other influences express non-Western concerns. In particular, the right to self-determination and the right to development both originated from the postcolonial self-affirmation of the non-Western world. Still, even today there is an important imbalance of power in the international forum where the West dominates the international agenda. International human rights are no exception in this sense: both with regard to the formulation of new norms and to the interpretation, application, and policy of such rights. Non-Western people and their cultures, societies, and states have simply always had less influence on the international level. Thus, to the extent that they live in circumstances that differ from those in the West, it is to be expected that those will be insufficiently reflected in international human rights.

The non-Western particularist human rights critique is an expression of the limited influence of non-Western actors on the international stage. Hence, if the goal is that of inclusive universality, this critique should not be seen as a threat to the universality of human rights, but rather as an expression of the struggle for increased inclusiveness from which follows increased universality of human rights. Inclusive universality demands that we take this critique seriously and make an attempt to account for contextual diversity in international human rights.

4.2 Flexibility and transformation

I can imagine two ways of accounting for diversity: contextual flexibility of human rights norms and the transformation of human rights norms.

Flexibility of human rights norms means that the same rule can be interpreted or applied in different ways in different contexts. Flexibility is already accepted in the formulation of human rights standards, as evidenced by the fact that the same rights are expressed in different formulations in the European, African, and American regional conventions. We can also accept flexibility in the interpretation of universal texts. For example, if everyone has the right to the protection of family life, there may be good reason to understand the term "family" in a different way in Europe than in Africa, where it may be appropriate to include the extended family.

A very promising area for the application of flexibility is the balance between rights and their restriction grounds. Human rights in the legal sense are not absolute. They can be restricted if certain conditions are met: generally the restriction has to be proportionate to the protection of the common good. It has been accepted, for example, in the case law of the European Court of Human Rights, that this balance between a right and its restriction ground can be struck in different ways in different circumstances.[8]

Take as another example the rule "everyone has a right to freedom of expression, yet this right can be restricted in the interest of public order, the protection of morals and the protection of the rights of others" (cf. Art. 19 ICCPR). The appreciation of which restrictions are necessary in the interest of the protection of morals differs from one society to another.[9] The same movie may enjoy the protection of freedom of expression in one country, and in the name of the protection of morals, be forbidden in another; yet, both actions can be acceptable applications of the above cited rule (Art. 19 ICCPR), and this need not threaten the universality of the rule.

While flexibility leaves international human rights standards intact, *transformation* of human rights norms involves altering the norms themselves in response to claims from non-Western contexts. For example, one may consider formulating more collective human rights, or recognizing individual responsibilities next to individual rights, or upgrading economic and social rights and the right to development.[10] This can be done in a way that does not threaten the "*acquis*" of international human rights, but that rather provides an increased protection of human rights for all, including in the West.

8. See Eva Brems, "The Margin of Appreciation in Europe," in David P. Forsythe and Patrice C. McMahon (eds.), *Human Rights and Diversity: Area Studies Revisited*, Lincoln, Nebr.: University of Nebraska Press (due in 2003).
9. Cf. the argument made in Kausikan, *op. cit.*, note 5.
10. Cf. the argument made in Ake, *op. cit.*, note 6.

5. Limits of Adaptation to Diversity

It is self-evident that there should be limits to the adaptation of human rights to cultural and other contextual factors. Human rights are not a neutral mirror of society; they are intended to direct society. Human rights must necessarily change certain traditions and certain contexts—this is their revolutionary calling. Therefore when trying to realize inclusive universality, the challenge is to constantly seek a balance between this revolutionary calling and the accommodation of contextual particularities that is necessary for inclusiveness.

5.1 Double approach

Therefore a double approach is needed. In order to bridge the gap between international human rights and those non-Western societies that experience certain aspects of human rights as inadequate, work is required on two fronts. On the one hand, international human rights can be adapted, through flexibility and transformation, so that they become more receptive to contextual differences. While on the other hand, work has to be done from inside those societies, in order to make them more receptive to international human rights.

In particular when cultural differences are at stake, one should not forget that culture is not static. Cultures are dynamic and heterogeneous. If all cultural factors are accepted as given and if the human rights concept is adapted accordingly, this would result in an extremely conservative and limited stance. Very often cultural elements that are hard to reconcile with international human rights are the object of internal debate within a society. For example, in the Islamic world there are many scholars who have developed a flexible interpretation of the *Shari'ah*, which allows most conflicts with human rights to be eliminated.

What can Westerners do to support this? In these internal debates, interference by Western outsiders runs the risk of producing a counterproductive effect by creating an impression of imperialism and paternalism. Yet what we can do is insist on the freedom of internal debate and offer support to those participants in the debate who promote human rights. Moreover, next to these internal cultural discourses about human rights, there is a need for intercivilizational dialogue on human rights.[11] One of the objectives of this dialogue should be the correction of the Western bias inherent in international human rights.

11. See the work of Abdullahi Ahmed An-Na'im, *Human Rights in Cross-cultural Perspectives: A Quest for Consensus*, Philadelphia: University of Pennsylvania Press (1991).

Summing up, there are two complementary approaches to the issue of human rights and cultural diversity: the adaptation of cultural norms and practices to human rights, and the adaptation of human rights to cultural diversity. There is of course a tension between the two approaches. When do we expect cultures/societies to adapt and when do we expect international human rights standards to adapt? There is no set answer to the question. The answers will be borne from intercivilizational dialogue on human rights. As an outsider to those societies who claim legitimate cultural (or other) difference in the face of human rights, I have chosen to adopt in my research the perspective of international human rights law. This has led to a focus on the second element: how international human rights standards can adapt to become more inclusive, in the sense of being more receptive to cultural diversity.

5.2 Some criteria

Nevertheless, we can try to formulate a few criteria that demarcate the limits within which the accommodation of cultural and other contextual particularities promotes inclusive universality. First, it is important to determine who is formulating a particularist claim. Claims should be given more credit to the extent that they are shared by a more diverse group of claimants. In particular government claims are to be treated with care. As human rights are largely intended to protect against governmental abuse of power, governments have their own interests and agendas concerning human rights; hence the tendency to manipulate cultural and other contextual elements in their own interest. In such cases critical reservation is appropriate.

Next, the extent to which a particularist human rights claim can be accommodated must also depend on the type of human rights violation at issue. There can be no room for cultural flexibility with regard to gross human rights violations. Flexibility only comes into play when human rights discourse attains a certain level of sophistication. A very substantial part of human rights discourse, especially at the level of public opinion, concerns gross violations: torture, arbitrary arrest, the prohibition of a religion, the destruction of crops and houses, slavery-like labor conditions, etc. These cannot be justified in any context.

Finally, some limitations are inherent in the concept of inclusive universality. If inclusion is the goal, we have to be critical about particularist arguments that lead to the exclusion of certain categories of individuals from under the protection of human rights. This is the case for many rules that discriminate against women or against ethnic or religious minorities. Moreover, the ultimate goal is that of worldwide effective human rights protection. Therefore, particularist claims that would result in decreasing the effective protection of human rights cannot be accommodated. For example, in the "transformation" wing, a possible approach is to complement the existing catalogue of individual rights with a list of individual duties. This would promote inclusive universality to the extent that in many cultures human rights are seen as too individualist and people feel a greater affinity with a discourse of duties. In legal terms, the formulation of such duties could be an alternative to the formulation of restrictions of rights. Yet, if one were to replace rights with duties or if one were to make the enjoyment of individual rights dependent upon the performance of individual duties, effective human rights protection would be threatened. Therefore, such measures do not fit in the framework of inclusive universality.

6. Focus on Concrete Problems

Many concrete conflicts between cultural elements and mainstream international human rights occur in the field of women's rights. From a legal perspective one can imagine two types of situations.

The first situation occurs when the law of a state endorses certain "cultural" rules. For example, family law in many states is based on Islamic law. This often implies significant discriminations against women; for example, by endorsing polygamy, by establishing the authority of the husband over his wife, by limiting women's access to divorce procedures, and by providing that men inherit twice as much as women when both are in the same relation to the deceased. In the eyes of human rights activists, these laws seriously violate the fundamental principle of equal rights for men and women.

The second situation is that in which the conflict between culture and women's rights results not from law, but originates instead from practices and traditions that are not endorsed by law and may even be expressly prohibited by law. Such practices are generally known in the language of international human rights as "harmful cultural practices." Examples of cultural practices that are seen as harmful to women include widow burning in India (sati), widow inheritance, child marriage, arranged or forced marriage, polygamy, seclusion and veiling, and food taboos for women. But the focal point of feminist activism is the practice of female circumcision, often referred to as FGM: female genital mutilation. This is a practice occurring mainly in Africa, undergone by women or girls (most commonly between the ages of four and eight), often as part of an initiation ceremony, and consisting of the cutting of the clitoris and sometimes other parts of the female genitalia. In Africa, this practice occurs in more than twenty-eight countries. In some of these, including Egypt, Ethiopia, Mali and Somalia, it is estimated that more than ninety percent of women undergo the operation. This practice abhorred

Westerners when they learned of it, and continues to do so. Today, female circumcision is the object of numerous campaigns. Some human rights activists label it a form of torture, others see it as a violation of the right to health because many of these "operations" are performed under poor conditions and have serious medical consequences. Some of the campaigns conducted by Western feminists, however, have been counterproductive because they were lacking in cultural sensitivity.

How to deal with the two types of situations? The concept of "inclusive universality" suggests a few lines of thinking.

In the first place, there have to be efforts from within the cultures concerned: e.g., reinterpretation of the *Shari'ah*, cultural change that replaces serious genital mutilations with minor or even symbolic ones...all this is possible from within the affected communities. Western governments, NGOs, IGOs, etc., should probably not campaign directly, but rather support internal pro-human rights forces in the target societies. Only insiders can accurately grasp the complex situation of the women who are directly concerned.

But what should then be the response of international human rights to these cultural norms and practices? Within the societies concerned, there are women who claim human rights protection against these laws and practices: Muslim women seeking equal rights and African women rejecting FGM. But there are also women who object to the interference of human rights discourse and activism in this sphere of their lives. These women are attached to their traditions; they experience them in a positive manner; and they certainly do not feel that they are victims of human rights violations. So the situation is quite complex.

One line of thought that I would like to suggest is that of the centrality of the individual in human rights protection. In my view, despite the stress on communalism in the cultural critique and despite my willingness to meet that critique to a certain extent, the centrality of the individual is crucial. Conflicts between women's rights and cultural practices or norms can be seen as conflicts between the right of an individual (to non-discrimination, to physical integrity, to health...) and the right of a group to protection of its cultural or religious norms or practices. I am willing to recognize the existence of such a collective right, but collective rights must always be conceived in function of the individual. What is the value of a collective right to a cultural practice, if not the fact that the members of the collectivity experience the cultural practice as valuable? When this is no longer the case, that collective cultural right becomes void.

The way I see it, human rights have to maintain the centrality of the individual, especially when we are trying to make them more inclusive by taking into account cultural and other contexts. This is so because of the heterogeneity of human societies and the multiplication of particular contexts to be taken into account. Within a group of people sharing a certain particularity, for example cultural membership, people differ according to other particularities that may be equally relevant for human rights protection, for example, economic means, or gender. When the focus is on the group, the particularities shared by its members can be taken into account, but other specificities that may be equally relevant but are not shared by all group members cannot be done justice. In today's complex world, only a focus on the individual makes it possible to adequately take into consideration all relevant contextual factors.

More concretely, people dealing with claims of human rights violations should adopt the viewpoint of the subject of human rights, the "insider" perspective of the (potential) victim of human rights violations. With regard to "harmful" cultural rules or practices, this implies that the human rights protection system has to guarantee the individual the option of not participating in a traditional practice or community, his or her right to "opt out" of it.[12] When an individual feels victimized by one of her society's practices, and then makes a balanced decision to oppose the practice, the international human rights system has to offer that individual its full support.

This holds not only for the international human rights system, but also for Western states committed to human rights who judge other states on that basis. If they seriously believe that particular cultural practices violate human rights, the minimum these states should do is to accord refugee status to women fleeing such practices. Conversely, if other members of that community voluntarily participate in the same practices and obey the same rules, it should be assumed that they have found their own balance between the value of this cultural rule or practice on the one hand, and that of the individual right it may infringe upon on the other; and this is to be respected as an exercise of their individual or collective cultural or religious right. If this right is to be conceived in function of the individual, as I have suggested, then collectivities cannot impose cultural practices or norms on dissidents.

All this would mean that "harmful" cultural rules or practices could neither be prohibited nor endorsed by the law. An unqualified legal prohibition, such as exists with regard to FGM, for example, in Burkina Fasso, Egypt, Ghana and Sudan, would violate the (collective or individual) right to cultural or religious practice. While an unqualified legal endorsement, such as the endorsement of discriminatory *Shari'ah* rules in the law of some Islamic states, violates the individual rights of dissidents.

---

12. Cf. Rhoda E. Howard, *Human Rights in Commonwealth Africa*, Totowa, N.J.: Rowman & Littlefield (1986) 198-200.

Chapter 10

Ruti Teitel

Global Rule of Law: Universal and Particular

Contemporary manifestations of the protection of international human rights are overwhelmingly humanitarian in character: the convening of the Hague Tribunals for the former Yugoslavia and Rwanda, the recent ratification of the Rome Treaty establishing a Nuremberg-style International Criminal Court, as well as transnational proceedings, such as that initiated against General Augusto Pinochet, the former Chilean dictator. Contemporary responses to political violence and human rights violations equate the rule of law with international criminal justice.

This paper explores contemporary understanding of the global rule of law by analyzing developments in international humanitarian law and expanded law of war as the leading form of protection of human rights worldwide. In particular, it focuses on some of the tensions in the extension of the use of this area of law to enforce human rights norms in global politics.

Consider the aims of international criminal justice in the enforcement and advancement of human rights. This rule of law regime, while aspiring to a universal ethics, is ultimately ambivalent in this regard. This essay contends that international criminal justice advances competing normative paradigms: a "politics of universalism," and a "politics of difference." In large part, a universalistic politics drives the postwar paradigm, where both principles of jurisdiction and substantive criminal justice are guided by the standard of

András Sajó (ed.), Human Rights with Modesty: The Problem of Universalism, *231-247.*

"humanity."[1] Beyond the universalist paradigm is another dimension; in the "politics of difference" international criminal justice moves beyond its ordinary role of identifying individual wrongdoing, to emphasize the group character of an offense. Accordingly, the contemporary international human rights regime is in considerable tension as it both affirms the protection of individual rights, as well as that of collectives often threatened in contemporary political violence. These two paradigms are in some tension, apparent in the manner in which the purposes and role of international criminal justice mediate the universal and the particular. Ultimately, contemporary attempts to model a coherent conception of the global rule of law on criminal justice culminate in a minimalist process-based conception and a limited or baseline understanding of the relevant human rights, as the basis of the global rule of law. As is elaborated below, insofar as there has developed a basis for universal human rights, it is a minimalist threshold notion of securing bodily integrity.

This essay explores dimensions of the universal and the particular in international humanitarian law, towards a better understanding of the distinctive global rule of law peculiar to the contemporary moment. It suggests that the humanitarian regime has a mixed character, an amalgam of human rights law and the law of war. This hybrid regime reflects the state of present political realities, of transition from an international legal system premised on sovereign states to a more interconnected system aimed at mere threshold governance of global politics.

1. The Politics of Universalism

1.1 Contemporary debates

The contemporary debate over the newest international institution, the International Criminal Court, raises a question of jurisprudence that relates to the broader topic of human rights.

The Rome Statute has been signed by the sixtieth country and thereby entered into force—in line with its Art. 126—on July 1, 2002, establishing a permanent International Criminal Court which will adjudicate the most

1. The term "humanity" has a historical provenance, which appeals to universal, transnational norms of consensus. Its historical roots, as well as its more contemporary versions, lack a process for grounding moral consensus, but rather derive from moral values grounded in particular religious ideas. These differences lie at the basis of this conception of humanity. Beyond this basis is a more practice oriented understanding chiefly represented in the custom that has become codified in the law of war. See generally, Christophe Swinarski (ed.), *Studies and Essays on International Humanitarian Law and Red Cross Principles in Honour of Jean Pictet*, Geneva and Boston: ICRC/Martinus Nijhoff Publishers (1984).

serious violations of humanitarian law.[2] The Court will begin its work shortly thereafter by taking jurisdiction over charges of genocide, crimes against humanity, and crimes of war.[3]

The debate over the Court has raised the question of the extent to which the Court depends on universality of jurisdiction, as opposed to its underlying charter as ratified by particular states. The United States has said that it does not intend to become a party to the treaty. Whereas the Bush administration's "unsigning" of the treaty constitutes a formal renunciation of involvement in the Court, and an act of heightened positive law,[4] nevertheless, its actions belie the administration's asserted interpretation of the ICC treaty regime.

The United States opposes the ICC, contending that the Court's jurisdiction is "overreaching" and that its authority is based on "universality" with the potential of binding "non-state parties" through the exercise of jurisdiction over its nationals. Whereas the United States insisted that the ICC's authority ought to be highly restrictive, and should depend solely on acceptance of the Court's jurisdiction by the state of nationality of the accused. Wherever a conflict might arise between the principle of nationality and other possible jurisdiction principles, such as the state of nationality or the principle of jurisdiction based on territory, the United States has claimed to be able to either exercise a veto through the Security Council, or have a full exemption.[5]

The United States, while justifying its withdrawal by claiming that the ICC has unbounded "universal" jurisdiction, has expressed with its "unsigning," conversely, a highly positivistic understanding of the ICC regime as premised on state consent. The role of universality in the ICC treaty regime is complex, as it is plausible that signing on to the ICC regime, rather than *expanding* the potential of universal jurisdiction, instead, may actually *limit* such jurisdiction; since the majority of the offenses in the ICC Charter are crimes which, under general international law, arguably any nation in the world would have the authority to prosecute under the aegis of "universal" jurisdiction.[6] The univer-

---

2. Rome Statute of the International Criminal Court, UN Diplomatic Conference of Plenipotentiaries on the Establishment of an International Criminal Court, UN Doc. A/CONF.183/9 (1998) [hereinafter Rome Statute].
3. *Ibid.*
4. The Undersecretary of State for Arms Control and International Security stated in a letter to Kofi Annan, the secretary-general of the United Nations, that "the United States does not intend to become a party to the treaty" and, therefore, "the U.S. has no legal obligations arising from its signature on 31 December 2000."
5. See Ruth Wedgwood, "The United States and the International Criminal Court: The Irresolution of Rome," 64 *Law and Contemporary Problems* (2001) 193.
6. See Restatement (third) of the Foreign Relations Law of the United States, paragraph 404 (1987). Such crimes of universal concerns include "piracy, slave trade, attacks on or hijacking of aircrafts, genocide, war crimes..."

sality principle has been applied in a number of cases discussed further on, e.g., Adolf Eichmann, as well as Alien Tort Claims Acts civil actions in the United States.[7] Universal jurisdiction would ordinarily be exercised without necessary prior consent of the state of nationality of the accused, or any other state.

Ultimately, the ICC establishes a consent scheme, where its jurisdiction is arguably much more limited than existing universal jurisdiction. The ICC treaty[8] contemplates that the state of "territory or nationality" must have ratified the treaty, or, have accepted its authority, thereby imposing preconditions on its exercise of jurisdiction that would not be imposed by an exercise of universal jurisdiction.[9]

These deliberations reflect the extent to which even this newest institution and treaty system represents continued adherence to positive law and to a consent regime in international law.[10] Further, the contemporary debate over the new International Criminal Court, to some extent, reflects a historical exchange about the role of natural law in international law. Instances of "universal" jurisdiction are few and far between, and for the most part, tend to coincide with other more traditional principles of jurisdiction.

1.2 Historical roots

For at least half a century, international criminal institutions and processes have reflected aspirations toward the representation of the universal in human rights. In the postwar period, the modern international human rights movement commenced with the Universal Declaration of Human Rights which followed on the heels of the Charter of the International Military Tribunal at Nuremberg.[11] The International Military Tribunal at Nuremberg constituted a potent symbol of law's universality: the proceedings, the sub-

7. While there had been a proposal to have a much broader jurisdiction in the ICC premised on universality, such jurisdiction was opposed by most delegations. The German delegation was the primary promoter of universal jurisdiction in the ICC, arguing that the crimes were punishable by virtue of the principle of universality. Moreover, it might have conflicted with at least some international law. See Rome Statute, *op. cit.*, note 2, Art. 6, which provides inherent jurisdiction only for genocide.
8. See Rome Statute, *op. cit.*, note 2, Art. 12.
9. *Ibid.*
10. *Ibid.*
11. Universal Declaration of Human Rights, 10 Dec. 1948, G.A. Res. 217A, UN GAOR, 3d Sess., UN Doc. A/810 (1948) and the Charter of the International Military Tribunal, 8 Aug. 1945, Art. 1, 59 Stat. 1544, 1546, 82 UNTS 279, 284. Moreover, these understandings of human rights as universal share affinities with the constitutional developments that accompanied the beginning of the international human rights movement. See Louis Henkin, *The Age of Rights*, New York: Columbia University Press (1990) 16-17, observing that "universalization" is reflected in national constitutions.

stantive charges—in particular, "crimes against humanity" proscribing inhumane acts committed against civilians[12]—and the subsequent trials have long been understood to reflect universal standards of humanity.[13] To this day the Tribunal's normative legacy has laid the basis of the core concepts of universal human dignity.[14] The aspiration of the time was the advancement of "universal" values, as reflected not only in the Tribunal but also in the postwar Universal Declaration of Human Rights.[15] The modern international rights regime sought to construct human rights as universal by framing sovereign individual rights in terms of a universal human condition. This phenomenon can also be witnessed in the adjudications of human rights violations in the postwar "crimes against humanity" proceedings in a manner that encompassed natural law understandings.[16] It is also evident in the norms ratified in the many postwar instruments.

Despite the aspiration towards universalism, historically, there were also other more particular dimensions. The natural law theory animating the postwar legal responses—whether in its criminal or constitutional forms—was also tempered by the various legal and political traditions prevailing in the postwar period.

---

12. See generally, Telford Taylor, *The Anatomy of the Nuremberg Trials: A Personal Memoir*, New York: Alfred A. Knopf (1992).
13. Compare Allied Control Council Law No. 10, Punishment of Persons Guilty of War Crimes, Crimes Against Peace and Against Humanity, 20 Dec. 1945, reprinted in Benjamin B. Ferencz, *An International Criminal Court: A Step Toward World Peace* (1980) 488, with the Charter of the International Military Tribunal, *op. cit.*, note 11, Art. 6(c). Art. 6(c) of the Nuremberg Charter defines "crimes against humanity" as

    > Murder, extermination, enslavement, deportation, and other inhumane acts committed against any civilian population, before or during the war, or persecutions on political, racial or religious grounds in execution of or in connection with any crime within the jurisdiction of the Tribunal, whether or not in violation of the domestic law of the country where perpetrated.

    Art. 7 of the Rome Statute of the International Criminal Court (*op. cit.*, note 2) expands upon the definition of "crimes against humanity":

    > [T]he following acts when committed as part of a widespread or systematic attack directed against any civilian population, with knowledge of the attack: (a) Murder; (b) Extermination; (c) Enslavement; (d) Deportation or forcible transfer of population; (e) Imprisonment...; (f) Torture; (g) Rape, sexual slavery...; (h) Persecution against any identifiable group or collectivity on political, racial, national, ethnic, cultural, religious, gender...grounds...; (i) Enforced disappearance of persons; (j) The crime of apartheid; and (k) Other inhumane acts of a similar character....

14. See Ruti Teitel, "Nuremberg and Its Legacy, Fifty Years Later," in Belinda Cooper (ed.), *War Crimes: The Legacy of Nuremberg*, New York: T.V. Books Inc. (1999).
15. The Universal Declaration of Human Rights, *op. cit.*, note 11.
16. See Judith N. Shklar, *Legalism: Law, Morals, and Political Trials*, 2d ed., Cambridge, Mass.: Harvard University Press (1986).

In some regard, the very framing of the postwar human rights scheme constitutes a response to a failed predecessor, the "minority rights" regimes.[17] The war had shown that minority rights could not be left to protection by states and consent regimes, where states were themselves pursuing ethnic cleansing. The very understanding of what was deemed "universal" was informed by Allied traditions, as well as by the transitional critical response to fascism at the time. Indeed, the turn of postwar legal responses to the universal reflected the view at the time that Nazi repression was associated with a positivist legal philosophy.[18] Therefore, the response to totalitarianism was to move to the natural law concepts implicated by the universal rights ideology. This conception of universal human rights is evident in the postwar international criminal proceedings, as well as in the ascendance of American rights traditions in constitutional developments in postwar Europe.

Further, notwithstanding the above, the asserted universalist rights conception is always animated by, and contingent upon, its particular political context. While the postwar trials had pretensions to universality,[19] their wartime political context had a pervasive and ongoing force; which operated as a substantive restrictive principle, limiting the Tribunal's jurisdiction. Thus, despite the expansive Charter jurisdiction, the prosecutions in the Nuremberg proceedings were limited to inhumane acts, with a demonstrable nexus to war.[20] Despite the rubric of universality, the adjudications of human rights were limited by more conventional jurisdictional principles.

The emerging postwar international human rights movement and the wave of constitutionalism of the time shared a common theory of rights, generally conceived as traditional Anglo-American rights at law, as norms backed by sanctions.[21] Postwar justice was conceived of as a system of judicially enforced rights. What was distinctive about this conception is that, whereas traditionally the predicate to enforceable rights was a functioning nation-state, the postwar responses reflect the landmark uses of a new legal

17. For discussion of historical minority treaties that protected ethnic minorities within states, see *Minority Schools in Albania* (1935), Permanent Court of International Justice, Ser. A/B, No. 64, 17.

18. The judiciary's philosophy of law under the Reich was considerably more complicated. See, e.g., Ingo Müller, *Hitler's Justice: The Courts of the Third Reich*, trans. Deborah Lucas Schneider, Cambridge, Mass.: Harvard University Press (1991) 68-81; Ruti Teitel, "Transitional Jurisprudence: The Role of Law in Political Transformation," 106 *Yale Law Journal* (1997) 2009, 2025 and note 52.

19. For support, see United Nation Secretary-General, The Charter and Judgment of the Nuremberg Tribunal: History and Analysis, UN Doc. A/CN. 4/5 (1949). See UN General Assembly Resolution, 95 (I) at 188, UN Doc. A/64/Add. 1 (1946).

20. For a discussion of this prudential self-limiting of the scope of the postwar trials, see Taylor, *op. cit.*, note 12, 113-15.

21. See Herbert L.A. Hart, *The Concept of Law* (1961), Oxford: Clarendon Press (1997) 218.

system which sought to internationalize a traditional domestic form of rights protection by judicial processes.

The judicialized human rights conception associated with the postwar period persists to the present day. It appears only to have become more generalized. Human rights protection is said to be universally attainable through international justice processes; and this is said to be one of the rights movement's central aims. Yet, despite numerous genocidal campaigns and the commission of other atrocities in the last century, such criminal proceedings have been few and far between. There has only been sporadic application of the Genocide Convention,[22] with the adjudication of genocide limited to the Nuremberg trials and to analogous atrocities relating to the Balkan and Rwandan conflicts.[23] The international proceedings convened as a result of ethnic cleansing in Europe, the International Criminal Tribunal for the Former Yugoslavia, was the first such effort since the World War II-related trials.[24] While appealing to a shared commitment against genocide, the Genocide Convention stopped short of creating jurisdiction on the basis of universality. Neither did the Convention provide for an international institution or mechanisms to enforce the rights it recognized.

The postwar judicial rights paradigm emphasized the judicial protection of norms considered universal.[25] While the theory may be universal, its instantiations and its enforcement has always been local. However, the rights model raises profound issues regarding enforceability as well as the apparent antinome of so-called positive and negative rights, going to the heart of the meaning of international human rights. Understandings of the justiciability of rights associated with domestic law also play a significant role in delimiting rights on the international scene.[26]

---

22. See Convention on the Prevention and Punishment of the Crime of Genocide, 9 Dec. 1948, 78 UNTS 277 (entered into force 12 Jan. 1951).
23. For a discussion of the particularist limits in the definition of genocide, see Beth Van Schaack, "The Crime of Political Genocide: Repairing the Genocide Convention's Blind Spot," 106 *Yale Law Journal* (1997) 2259.
24. See Annex IV, *The Policy of Ethnic Cleansing* 17, 21-36, in Annexes to the Final Report of the Commission of Experts Established Pursuant to Security Council Resolution 780 919920, Vol. I, UN Doc. S/1994/674/Add.2 (Vol. I)/Annex IV (1994).
25. See Kenneth Randall, "Universal Jurisdiction under International Law," 66 *Texas Law Review* (1988) 785; for the "Princeton Principles," see Princeton Project on Universal Jurisdiction, The Princeton Principles on Universal Jurisdiction (2001).
26. See Maurice William Cranston, *What Are Human Rights?*, London: Bodley Head (1962) 84-85.

2. The Politics of Particularism

More contemporary adjudications of human rights violations reflect a more complicated view of rights, as these proceedings attempt to reconcile the postwar universalizing human rights norms with a view of norms that is also sensitive to context. In its rights instantiations, the application of the concept of "universality" in the postwar human rights regime is reconciled by limiting jurisdictional principles based on more particularist norms of political identity, such as nationality and ethnicity. To elaborate, whereas offenses at Nuremberg were prosecuted as "crimes against humanity" on a universalizing basis, in the subsequent national trials of the 1950s and 1960s these offenses were prosecuted in terms explicitly relating to the collective.[27] As such, many of these trials were conducted in the service of the consolidation of national politics. Thus, for example, in a fairly newly established state of Israel, Adolf Eichmann was prosecuted for commission of "crime[s] against the Jewish people." Assertion of the principle of universal jurisdiction underlying the prosecution of crimes against humanity was, in justification of the judgment of Eichmann, beyond the state of nationality or territoriality.[28]

Similarly, a more particularized notion of rights marks a number of deliberations over adjudicating the "crime against humanity" offense within national jurisdictions throughout Europe. In 1960s Germany, a debate ensued over whether and to what extent to continue the trials related to World War II. This debate revealed the tension in international criminal justice between the universal and the particular, as it juxtaposed universalizing ideas of jurisdiction against more particularist notions of justice reconciled in national statutes of limitations. Ultimately, the wartime trials were continued but with significant limits. The change in jurisdictional principles represented the transitions in sovereignty, and thus, illuminated law's relation to politics.

Another European trial for World War II-related atrocities, the prosecution of Klaus Barbie in late 1980s France for wartime deportations of civilians, raised the question of the extent to which asserted universal human rights were reconcilable with local legal cultures. Whereas in the 1960s, France had incorporated the Nuremberg Charter's definition of "crimes against human-

27. See Cr.C. (Jm.) 40/61 *Attorney General of Israel v. Eichmann*, 1961, reprinted in 56 *American Journal of International Law* (1962) 805. See discussion of the representation in the trial of Adolf Eichmann, of the contextualized account of the wartime atrocities as committed "against the Jewish people." See, e.g., Hannah Arendt, *Eichmann in Jerusalem: A Report on the Banality of Evil* (1963), New York: Penguin Books (1994) 275-76.

28. See *Attorney General of Israel v. Eichmann*, 36 *International Law Review*, 50 (1968), (Israel Supreme Court 1962). Full justification was found for applying the principle of universal jurisdiction since the international character of "crimes against humanity" dealt with in this instant case is no longer in doubt.

ity" into its criminal justice system. This attempt to incorporate the principle of universal jurisdiction[29] posed tension with other preexisting, and more limiting, domestic legal principles of prescription. The case demonstrates the extent to which prosecutions of war crimes, even years after the fact, continue to be shaped by a state's legal culture and political circumstances. National adjudications of rights norms create a space for contestation of these values. Adjudicating crimes against humanity implies displacing the domestic law principles that would ordinarily apply, some of which go to procedure, others to the substance of the relevant offenses, signaling an attempt to depoliticize and universalize. Nevertheless, what those contemporary trials show is that rights are protected and adjudicated within the distinct parameters of a political context, jurisdiction, and related principles. While the adjudication of "crimes against humanity" historically implied features of normative universalism, its treatment in the Barbie Trial in contemporary France ultimately represented another identity politics.[30] The controversy concerned the meaning of "crimes against humanity" as incorporated in French law; and whether the prosecution of "crimes against humanity" could go beyond the atrocities committed against Jews to include members of the Resistance,[31] igniting a normative debate about the subject of the "crime against humanity" and the reach of humanitarian law. Moving beyond an objective conceptualization of the protected subject to a more complex understanding of the scope of the "humanity" crime, France's High Court focused not only on the victims' status, but on the perpetrators' motives against the backdrop of state policy to include crimes against members of the Resistance, and in so doing, expanded the parameters of the "humanity" offense.[32]

Contemporary post-Cold War transitions raised again the dilemma of how to reconcile the precepts of universalism versus particularism in application of the principles of jurisdiction to prior rights violations. Where atrocities were being prosecuted, and though committed in the distant past, jurisdiction depended on recurring to timeless universal offenses of "crimes against humanity." In the postcommunist trials in Hungary, rights violations committed in the repression of the 1956 uprising were conceived as war crimes, and prosecuted despite the passage of time.[33]

29. See Code Pénal, Arts. 211-1, 212-1.

30. See Guyora Binder, "Representing Nazism: Advocacy and Identity at the Trial of Klaus Barbie," 98 *Yale Law Journal* (1989) 1321, 1281.

31. See *Fédération Nationale des Déportés et Internés Résistants et Patriotes and Others v. Barbie*, 78 *International Law Review* (1988) 139-140. (France, Court de Cassation, Criminal Chamber, 20 Dec. 1985).

32. *Ibid.*

33. See Act No. XC of 1993 on Procedures Concerning Certain Crimes Committed During the 1956 Revolution. (The Act has been declared null and void as unconstitutional by the

3. Globalizing Human Rights Protection

In the contemporary moment, the assumption of universal jurisdiction on the basis of the principle of "crimes against humanity" is increasingly made independent of the affected states, promoting, it is said, a form of global legal sovereignty. Pursuant to this new globalizing rule of law, human rights norms are protected not only by affected states, or by international institutions; indeed, contemporary instantiations of international criminal justice appear to operate independent of conventional nexus, such as territoriality or nationality.[34] Contemporary globalization of rights enforcement, albeit in sporadic adjudications, challenges both the immediate postwar emphasis on internationalist, as well as, local understandings of justice. The expansion beyond these traditional bases for jurisdiction points to new directions for normative principles for assuming jurisdiction. Rights norms are developing in an unsystematic way. Jurisdiction is often taken by states with little or no connection to the instant controversy.

Contemporary rights globalization is highlighted in the ad hoc international tribunals for the former Yugoslavia and Rwanda. In *Prosecutor v. Anto Furundzija,* the International Criminal Tribunal for the Former Yugoslavia endorsed the principle of universal jurisdiction in the case of torture:

> It would seem that one of the consequences of the *jus cogens* character bestowed by the international community upon the prohibition of torture is that every State is entitled to investigate, prosecute and punish or extradite individuals accused of torture, who are present in a territory under its jurisdiction. Indeed, it would be inconsistent on the one hand to prohibit torture to such an extent as to restrict the normally unfettered treaty-making power of sovereign States, and on the other hand bar States from prosecuting and punishing those torturers who have engaged in this odious practice abroad. This legal basis for States' universal jurisdiction over torture bears out and strengthens the legal foundation for such jurisdiction found by other courts in the inherently universal character of the crime. It has been held that international crimes being universally condemned wherever they occur, every State has the right to prosecute and punish the authors of such crimes. As stated in general terms by the Supreme Court of Israel in *Eichmann,*[35] and echoed by the USA

decision 36/1996 AB hat. (IX. 4.) of the Hungarian Constitutional Court.

34. There are traditional jurisdictional principles that criminal prosecution connect up to the implicated states. See Restatement (Third) of Foreign Relations Law of the United States § 402 (1987). The Comment to section 402 provides that a state has jurisdiction to prescribe law under general principles of: (1) territoriality; (2) nationality; (3) affects within the territory; (4) protection of the state's security; (5) passive personality. (Cmts. 1-g.)

35. *Attorney General of Israel v. Eichmann*, 36 *International Law Review*, 277 (1968), (Israel Supreme Court 1962).

> court in *Demjanjuk*,[36] "it is the universal character of the crimes in question *i.e.*, international crimes which vest in every State the authority to try and punish those who participate in their commission."[37]

Another instance is seen in a recent opinion invoking the principle of universal jurisdiction in regard to genocide. In *Bosnia and Herzegovina v. Yugoslavia*, the World Court emphasized the universal character of the crime of genocide:[38] "It follows that the rights and obligations *erga omnes*."The Court notes that the obligation each state has to prevent and to punish the crime of genocide is not territorially limited by the Convention.[39]

Universalizing jurisdiction can be seen also in occasional national cases, such as Spain's extradition request of General Pinochet for human rights violations perpetrated in Chile under military rule.[40] On 25 November 1998, the judiciary committee of the British House of Lords concluded that "international law has made it plain that certain types of conduct...are not acceptable conduct on the part of anyone." As far as application of the principle of universal jurisdiction, the Judgment in the House of Lords is complex; and reflects a similar ambivalence regarding the principle of universal jurisdiction. While it recognized that the "*jus cogens*" nature of torture justifies states in taking universal jurisdiction over torture wherever committed, nevertheless, the Court did not accept that, prior to the enactment of the Criminal Justice Act of 1988 in British courts, acts of torture could be prosecuted by virtue of the principle of universal jurisdiction.[41]

Another instance is Germany's indictment of Dusko Tadic for war crimes in the Balkans, before turning him over to The Hague. The indictments for genocide were based on a 1995 German statute predicated upon

36. *Demjanjuk v. Petrovsky*, 776 F. 2nd 571 (6th Circuit 1985).
37. *Prosecutor v. Anto Furundzija*, 38 *International Law Materials* 317, para 156 (International Criminal Tribunal For Former Yugoslavia 1999).
38. G.A. Res. 96 (I), UN GAOR, 1st Sess., Par II (Resolutions), UN Doc. A/64/Add.1 (1947); see also Reservations to the Convention on the Prevention and Punishment of the Crime of Genocide, 1951 I.C.J. 14, 23 (28 May); Case Concerning Application of the Convention on the Prevention and Punishment of the Crime of Genocide (*Bosnia and Herzegovina v. Yugoslavia* (Serbia and Montenegro)), 1993 I.C.J. 1 (8 April); Case Concerning Application of the Convention on the Prevention and Punishment of the Crime of Genocide (*Bosnia and Herzegovina v. Yugoslavia* (Serbia and Montenegro)), 1993 I.C.J. 325, 348 (13 Sept.).
39. Case Concerning Application of the Convention on the Prevention and Punishment of the Crime of Genocide (*Bosnia and Herzegovina v. Yugoslavia*), 1996 I.C.J. 595, 616 (11 July).
40. See in Re Pinochet, Opinions of the Lords of Appeal for Judgment in the Cause (15 Jan. 1999) (visited 6 Feb. 1999) http://www.parliament.the-stationer-off...pa/ld199899/ldjudgmt/jd990115/pino01.htm.
41. The extradition of Pinochet was authorized only with respect to acts of torture committed after 8 December 1988.

the principles of universality.[42] There are illustrations from civil law in the United States where jurisdiction has been taken on the basis of universality in extreme rights abuses, in cases brought under the Alien Tort Claims Act against Radovan Karadzic for damages relating to "crimes against humanity," which depends upon the concept of "universality" as comprehended by the "law of nations" in U.S. law.[43]

Human rights globalization through international humanitarian law suggests there is a change afoot in the sources, content, and form of rights norms. This is seen in the application of international human rights norms through judicial proceedings occurring outside of the traditional spaces of contestation. To some extent, these adjudications signal the universal in human rights, but they also generate complex issues as the concept of universality interacts with the legal traditions and political agreements of the relevant countries, pointing to a transformative relationship in law, politics, and justice in the international arena.

Globalization poses contradictory ramifications for international criminal justice.[44] To some degree, globalization implies closer connections between countries' criminal justice systems, as is reflected in the adoption of conventions and extradition treaties that facilitate transnational cooperation, as well as in the recent adoption of the International Criminal Court. Changes in the traditional understandings of the bounds of national sovereignty appear to lead to the expansion of criminal jurisdiction and to universal cooperation across jurisdictions.

However, globalization also implies changes that point in another direction: toward the breakdown in traditional ideas of causation, agency, and responsibility.[45] Whereas, theoretically, jurisdiction over international human rights violations may well be expanded, greater rights enforcement by this means is challenged by other contemporary developments such as mass murder and systematic repression, which by their character imply more than individual responsibility; and are often predicated upon a complicated rela-

42. See *The Prosecutor v. Dusko Tadic a/k/a "Dule,"* Case No. IT-94-1-T, Opinion and Judgment, pt. I.B., paras 6-9 (7 May 1997) (visited 11 May 1999) http://www.un.org/icty/tadic/trialc2/jugement-e/970507jt.htm. See also in Nov. 1997 Press Release GA/9345.

43. See *Kadic v. Karadzic*, 70 F. 3d 232 (2d. Civ. 1993): "We hold that certain forms of conduct [including genocide] violate the law of nations whether undertaken by those acting under the authority of a state or only as private individuals."

44. See David Held, Anthony Mcgrew, David Goldblatt and Jonathan Perraton, *Global Transformation: Politics, Economics, and Culture*, Stanford University Press (1999). See also Michael Likosky, (ed.), *Transnational Legal Processes: Globalization and Power Disparities*, London: Butterworths (2002).

45. See Samuel Scheffler, "Individual Responsibility in a Global Age," in Ellen Frankel Paul et al. (eds.), *Contemporary Political and Social Philosophy* (1995) 219, 228-29.

tion between the individual, the collective, and the regime. Accordingly, contemporary globalizing politics puts pressure on the modern judicial rights model and implies the elaboration of restrictive principles, which limit the protection of human rights through criminal justice.[46]

4. International Humanitarian Law: Mediating the Universal and the Particular

International humanitarian law is the preeminent response to the political violence and grave rights violations that have characterized the end of the twentieth century and the beginning of the next—it is thought to be the apt response to communal violence and disorder by establishing a threshold basis for the global rule of law. International criminal justice's normative potential is evident in the various legal constructs that attempt to reconcile the universal and the particular. This can be seen in the ongoing trials at The Hague that adjudicate "ethnic cleansing" in the Balkans and Rwanda,[47] in the ad hoc codifications being applied,[48] or in the statute for the proposed permanent International Criminal Court.[49]

The asserted aims of the current uses of humanitarian law are ambitious: to move from ethnic conflict and to usher in peace and the rule of law.[50] The

46. Namely, at present, we are seeing the development of immunity principles; most recently, in response to Pinochet litigation and the ICC, ranging from the diplomatic to the invocation by the United States of "peacekeeping" immunity. For a recent instance of resort to official immunity principles, see *Congo v. Belgium*, (I.C.T., 14 Feb 2002), http://www.ics-cij.org/icjwww/idecisions.htm. For discussion of U.S. appeal to peacekeeping immunity, see Serge Schmemann, "U.S. Links Peacekeeping to Immunity From New Court," *New York Times* (19 June 2002) A3.
47. See Annex IV, The Policy of Ethnic Cleansing, *op. cit.*, note 24.
48. Statute of the International Tribunal [for the Prosecution of Persons responsible for Serious Violations of International Humanitarian Law Committed in the Territory of the Former Yugoslavia], Annex to *Report of the Secretary-General Pursuant to Paragraph 2 of Security Council Resolution* 808 (1993), UN SCOR, 48th Sess., Supp. for Apr.-June 1993, at 134-38, UN Doc. S/25704 (1993) [hereinafter ICTY Statute].
    Statute of the International Tribunal for Rwanda [for the Prosecution of Persons Responsible for Genocide and other Serious Violations of International Humanitarian Law Committed in the Territory of Rwanda and Rwandan Citizens Responsible for Genocide and Other Such Violations Committed in the Territory of Neighboring States], Annex to S.C. Res. 955, UN SCOR, 49th Sess., 3453d mtg. at 15, UN Doc. S/RES/955 (1994) [hereinafter ICTR Statute].
49. See Rome Statute, *op. cit.*, note 2.
50. The Security Council's decision to establish the International Tribunal for the Former Yugoslavia (later expanded to include Rwanda) was motivated not only by an intent to punish and to prosecute, see *Final Report of the Commission of Experts Established Pursuant*

aim of prosecuting the most serious violations of international humanitarian law is to establish individual accountability to break cycles of ethnic retribution.[51] Accordingly, "crimes against humanity" are defined to encompass widespread and systematic inhumane acts "directed against any civilian population" including "persecutions on political, racial and religious ground."[52] Where intent to destroy "a national, ethnical, racial or religious group" can be shown, such persecution is also prosecutable as "genocide."[53]

At present, international humanitarian law bears a complex relationship to current transformations in global sovereignty. These norms comprehend the contemporary challenge of rights enforcement in light of changes in the public and private realms, between state and non-state actors, and in the apparent normalization of extraordinary situations of conflict.

In the contemporary moment, rights norms comprehend current political realities which address the fact of transnational persecution, with destabilizing effects beyond the state to the international community. Accordingly, at present, universalist ideas are being extended beyond the postwar consensus. "Crimes against humanity"—whether or not committed in the course of international armed conflict—are being adjudicated across national borders. This is vividly demonstrated in the international adjudication of the attempted genocide of approximately one million Tutsi and Hutu moderates in Rwanda, persecution committed entirely in that country's internal conflict.[54] In these proceedings, universalizing norms appear to have transcended traditional limits on adjudicating international offenses.[55]

International humanitarian law is also most apt to adjudicate contemporary human rights violations for other dimensions relating to present politics, for the relevance of the move to international humanitarian law is precisely

---

to Security Council Resolution 780 (1992) paras 3-4, Annex to *Letter Dated 24 May 1994 from the Secretary-General to the President of the Security Council,* UN Doc. S/1994/674 (1994) [hereinafter *Final Report*], but also as a measure to bring about peace. See *Report of the Secretary-General to Pursuant to Paragraph 2 of Security Council Resolution* 808 (1993), 48th Sess., Supp. for Apr.-June 1993, paras 10, 22, UN Doc. S/25704 (1993); S.C. Res. 808, UN SCOR, 48th Sess., 3175th mtg. at 28, UN Doc. S/RES/808 (1993). This use of judicial proceedings to bring about peace had no precedent in the postwar paradigm.

51. See Response to the Motion of the Defence on the Jurisdiction of the Tribunal at 23, (filed 7 July 1995), *The Prosecutor v. Dusko Tadic a/k/a "Dule,"* Case No. IT-94-IT.

52. See ICTY Statute, *op. cit.*, note 48, Art. 5.

53. *Ibid.*, Art. 4, para 2. See also *Final Report, op. cit.*, note 50, para 182. Conclusion is that the actions perpetrated in Opština Prijedor against non-Serbs would likely be confirmed in court as constituting genocide.

54. See ICTR Statute, *op. cit.*, note 48.

55. For a discussion on the relevance of characterization of conflict to subject matter jurisdiction, see Theodor Meron, "Classification of Armed Conflict in the Former Yugoslavia; Nicaragua's Fallout," 92 *American Journal of International Law* (1998) 2361.

that it allows the condemnation of repressive systemic policy. Through the application of principles of superior authority linking up the individual to the collective, the political leadership can be held to account for its role in repressive policy.[56] In contemporary international humanitarian law, the constructs of "genocide" and "crimes against humanity," by their very definition, are rights which incorporate highly nuanced understandings linking up the individual and the collective. Through principles that emphasize persecutory motive, trials at the ad hoc tribunals at The Hague take note of ethnicity, if only to transcend it. The new humanitarian regime has significant normative potential, as its expanded enforcement enables the transformation of traditional understandings of responsibility in the international sphere, from the national to the international, from the individual to the collective.[57] Another core change that emerges in the new regime is the application of the rules of the game—beyond states to private actors, with jurisdiction extended often through principles of universality.[58]

Whereas, in its traditional domestic role, the primary aim of criminal justice is to ascribe individual responsibility, nevertheless, in adjudicating modern human rights violations this goal is more complicated because individual proceedings may obscure the role in repression of systemic policy. Where the emphasis is on individual accountability, and where prosecuted "bottom-up," contemporary war crimes trials often end up obfuscating the relevant politics. Further, representations of "crimes against humanity" which highlight universality and adjudicate persecution as offenses against the entire international community (as at The Hague Tribunal), also risk decontextualization from the relevant politics. Finally, where the international criminal proceedings are convened in a political vacuum (as at the Hague Tribunal), largely independent of their national jurisdictions, such proceedings can obscure the significance of broader state policies and failings in the rule of law.[59]

The continued expansion of international humanitarian law to protect human rights is being reaffirmed in the contemporary consensus on establishing the new permanent International Criminal Court. The establishment of an international criminal court appears to entrench the postwar tribunal

56. See Rome Statute, *op. cit.*, note 2, Art. 25.

57. See Ruti Teitel, "Humanity's Law: Rule of Law for the New Global Politics," 35 *Cornell International Law Journal* (2002) 101.

58. See Rome Statute, *op. cit.*, note 2, Art 7. See also Minimum Humanitarian Standards: Analytical Report of the Secretary-General submitted pursuant to Commission on Human Rights Resolution 1997/21, UN Doc. E/CN.4/1998/87, para. 74 (1998).

59. See Ruti Teitel, "Bringing the Messiah through the Law," in Carla Hesse and Robert Post (eds.), *Human Rights in Political Transitions: Gettysburg to Bosnia*, New York: Zone Books (1999).

for the next millennium. Going beyond the construct at Nuremberg, the statute for the new International Criminal Court reveals the dynamic tension discussed here between the politics of the universal and the particular, which comprehends the contradictions posed by contemporary globalization.[60]

In the new global order, the traditional bases for jurisdiction have given way to more expansive, transnational principles. The breadth of offenses for which jurisdiction is "universal" suggests a similar expansion of transnational consensus, reflected in its being a regime of state consent. The Charter for the new International Criminal Court extends the reach of international humanitarian law to offenses many of which had already been recognized as human rights violations at customary law, the most heinous known as *jus cogens*.[61] This is explicit in the expansion of the definition of "crimes against humanity" in the new codifications.[62] The use of international humanitarian law to protect a more pluralist human rights law is evident in the transformation of what currently counts as "persecution." Thus, the Rome Statute includes "persecution on political, racial, national, ethnic, cultural, religious, or gender grounds" as a crime against humanity.[63] Further, the Rome Statute's codification of "crimes against humanity" encompasses the crimes of "apartheid" as well as the "disappearance" policies of military regimes in Latin America and Africa, in what is a recognition of contemporary political change.[64] This is also seen in the Rome Statute's heightened protection against sexual violence.[65]

The global human rights regime constitutes a paradoxical normative order. There appears to be increased normative consensus on the most grave rights offenses, and hence, in theory, upon principles of universal jurisdiction.

---

60. See Rome Statute, *op. cit.*, note 2.
61. For elaboration of the meaning of *jus cogens*, see Michael Akehurst, "The Hierarchy of the Sources of International Law," 47 *British Year Book of International Law* (1974-75) 273, 281-82; Vienna Convention on the Law of Treaties, Art. 53, opened for signature 23 May 1969, 1155 UNTS 331 (entered into force 27 Jan. 1980), defines *jus cogens* as peremptory norm. For a discussion of these "preemptory norms from which no derogation by treaty is permitted," see Oscar Schachter, *International Law in Theory and Practice*, Norwell, Mass.: Kluwer Academic Publishers (1991) 342-45.
62. See Rome Statute, *op. cit.*, note 2, Art. 7.
63. *Ibid.*, Art. 7, para 1 (h). This definition goes beyond the postwar consensus where even the definition of genocide excluded political leaders. See Van Schaack, *op. cit.*, note 23, 2259.
64. Enforced disappearances and apartheid are now codified as "crimes against humanity," *Ibid.*, Art. 7, paras 1 (i), 1 (j).
65. Rape is codified at several places in the statute. Crimes against humanity include "[r]ape, sexual slavery, enforced prostitution, forced pregnancy,...or any other form of sexual violence of comparable gravity." *Ibid.*, Art. 7, para 1 (g). Under the statute, rape is also a war crime, see *id.*, Art. 8, para 2 (b) (xxii), and potentially a form of genocide. *id.*, Art. 6 (b)-(d). *Op. cit.*, notes 47-49.

Under the new rights regime, these offenses have been codified and ratified as conventional law, adding democratic-based legitimacy. For the first time since the immediate postwar period, there are renewed expectations of a shared international normative consensus. Nevertheless, it is important to concede the limits of contemporary developments, which, while universal in aspiration, continue by and large to reflect continued adherence to traditional principles of state consent, nationality, and territoriality.[66]

The globalization of humanitarian law, though occasional and erratic, has some limited normative force. Wherever states adjudicate crimes against humanity, or similar universalizing offenses, these instantiations represent a limited consensus upon a narrow constraint on national sovereignty posed by persecutory politics. This rule of law, however, is thin, as it involves protection only of the most basic bodily integrity rights. Moreover, to the extent judicial sovereignty attempts to represent an autonomous rule of law norm, free of national and political predicates, it is vulnerable. Human rights remain at great risk where their protection lacks the legal and political institutions and processes of a working rule of law state. Removed from national contexts and thicker political constructs, this largely symbolic normative order can offer only glimmerings of a transcendent rule of law.

5. Conclusion

The new international human rights legalism has been heralded as a form of transformative jurisprudence with the ambitious aim of laying the foundation for world society—often in the absence of any other predicate political consensus. As discussed above, law plays a leading role in the emergent humanitarian rights regime as it supports the international legal system's present shift from its historical guardianship of the politics of nationalism, to those of globalization. The humanitarian regime's transformative potential in the contemporary moment derives from its competence to span particularist human rights values to constitute a threshold rule of law capable of guiding present global politics.

66. See Rome Statute, *op. cit.*, note 2, Art. 5.

Part III
Rule of Law: Local Experiences

Chapter 11

Martin Krygier

False Dichotomies, True Perplexities, and the Rule of Law

"In many of his writings," Philip Selznick tells us, John Dewey "hammered away at what he took to be pernicious dualisms...[that] transform analytical or functional distinctions into ontological divisions...the effect of the transformation is to frustrate inquiry and limit achievement."[1] However pernicious they may be, and notwithstanding Dewey's best efforts, such dualisms remain remarkably popular. Dichotomies that allegedly necessitate choice, perhaps tragic, proliferate: individual (or civil society) versus the state, liberty versus equality, liberalism versus communitarianism, universal versus local, are just a few examples. It is left to a few old fogies to mumble that these dichotomies might just be aspects of complex phenomena which can manage to include them both. Few find such reminders convincing, still even fewer interesting. Nevertheless, I'm with the fogies. One aim of this chapter is to suggest the inadequacy of a forced choice between universal or local in relation to the rule of law. Another is to suggest the universal complexity and local variability of the achievement it represents.

There are many ways in which the taste for dichotomies might "frustrate inquiry." I will mention two. One is by implying that the choice on offer is

1. Philip Selznick, *The Moral Commonwealth*, Berkeley: University of California Press (1992) 21.

András Sajó (ed.), Human Rights with Modesty: The Problem of Universalism, *251-277.*

exhaustive, that one is faced with *nothing but* the alternatives presented. This rules out, a priori, such wisdom as Adam Michnik displayed, when asked in 1988 whether he would prefer General Jaruzelski or General Pinochet. Michnik replied that offered such alternatives, he would choose Marlene Dietrich.[2] Many would applaud his choice.

Again, familiar dichotomies often present as incompatible—unable to share the same space—alternatives that might be amenable to combination. Out of differences that might be complementary, or tensions that might be resolved, or lived with, they postulate contradictions between which one *must* choose. That does not merely present what might be a false choice, but by the way it frames a problem it makes *choice*, between exclusive and binary alternatives, the first task of thought and action. By implication that excludes other, and perhaps more appropriate, ways of thinking and doing. Like refusing to choose.

Faced with such stark options, one does well at least to begin with a Deweyite presumption and try to finesse them. The presumption might be quickly rebutted and finessing may not be possible, for sometimes stark choices are inescapable, but we should not strive to multiply such situations. Rather, since the questions we ask delimit the answers we give, we often do better to ask how the two sides of a dichotomy, in our case universal and local, might—and do—combine and connect, and how best they might be made to combine and connect. That way we might relieve, on the one hand, the abstraction and arrogance that can go with single-minded insistence on purported universals (which have all *originated* somewhere in particular) and, on the other, the parochialism and relativism that can flow from excessive devotion to the local.

One way of combining apparent incompatibles is to distinguish levels or moments in the phenomena under discussion, some of which might have claims to universality, and others which are intrinsically, perhaps necessarily, local. Since the subjects of this book—human rights and the rule of law—are complex phenomena with many aspects, it might make sense to think of them as both universal and local, in parts and at once.

In discussion of the universality of human rights, for example, several authors have suggested that there are a number of questions at issue, which are often not distinguished among, but which demand answers at different levels of generality.[3] The rule of law, too, is a layered phenomenon. In the past

2. *Times Literary Supplement* (19-25 February 1988). Things have changed since. I do not know whether Michnik would prefer Jaruzelski to Dietrich even today, but he does appear to prefer him to Pinochet.

3. See Jack Donnelly, "Human Rights and Asian Values: A Defense of 'Western' Universalism," in Joanne R. Bauer and Daniel A. Bell (eds.), *The East Asian Challenge for Human Rights*, New York: Cambridge University Press (1999) 60-87 and Charles Taylor's

few years, I have sought to distinguish three questions that need to be asked in relation to it, some of which are appropriately answered only locally, others which have larger scope. This essay continues that program.[4] My terminology has changed a bit, since I have been learning on the job, but for the present I distinguish ends, conditions, and means. My claim is that it is important to separate questions about the point of the rule of law, about what in general it depends upon, and about what forms it should take. It is also important to treat these matters in that order: why? what? and only then how? Questions about universal and local will have different resonance depending on the specific aspect of concern within this complex of values, conditions, and institutions. It is a mistake to homogenize the considerations involved and force a melodramatic once-for-all choice in relation to the range of considerations which must go into any serious consideration of bringing human rights to earth.

Distinguishing levels will not solve all disputes, however, particularly not some of the most contentious. Some purported values are contested at every level. There are also, as I will mention, real problems about the character, conditions, and value of the rule of law, which even the sort of wimpish ecumenism I recommend does not solve or dissolve. These problems are important and in some, not rare, circumstances morally fundamental. The fifth and last part of my article will address some of them.

1. An Unqualified Human Good?

Almost thirty years ago, E.P. Thompson disconcerted many fellow radicals who had long admired him and considered him their ally, even mentor. He did so by asserting that "the notion of the regulation and reconciliation of conflicts through the rule of law—and the elaboration of rules and procedures which, on occasion, made some approximate approach towards the ideal—seems to me a cultural achievement of universal significance."[5] To cap this injury with what Marxists had to recognize as insult, he went on to explain:

> I am insisting only upon the obvious point, which some modern Marxists have overlooked, that there is a difference between arbitrary power and the

"Conditions of an Unforced Consensus on Human Rights" in the same volume, 124-46.

4. Begun in Martin Krygier, "The Rule of Law," 20 *International Encyclopedia of the Social and Behavioral Sciences*, editors-in-chief Neil J. Smelser and Paul B. Bates, Oxford: Elsevier Science (2001) 13403-408 and "Transitional Questions about the Rule of Law: Why, What, and How?" 28, 1 *East Central Europe/L'Europe du Centre-Est* (2001) 1-34.
5. Edward P. Thompson, *Whigs and Hunters: The Origin of the Black Act*, Harmondsworth: Penguin (1977) 265.

> rule of law. We ought to expose the shams and inequities which may be concealed beneath the law. But the rule of law itself, the imposing of effective inhibitions upon power and the defense of the citizen from power's all-intrusive claims, seems to me an unqualified human good.[6]

Orthodox Marxists, by contrast, knew that the rule of law was neither universal nor good. Not universal, since after the revolution there *would* be no place for it, and in some views (such as those of E. B. Pashukanis), before capitalism there *had* been no place for it. Not good either, since it was an ideological crutch of the bourgeois order. In any event, the ideology of the rule of law (and the French Revolutionary "natural" precursors of "human" rights, which some supposed it to protect) presupposed a malign and atomistic universal anthropology for which the social plasticity of our natures and the promise of communist species-sociability gave no warrant.[7] And so, as Hugh Collins unabashedly explained rather late in the day, "[t]he principal aim of Marxist jurisprudence [*sic*] is to criticize the center piece of liberal political philosophy, the ideal called the Rule of Law."[8] Late twentieth-century Marxists, somewhat bruised after sixty years of "really existing socialism," might reluctantly come to a tepid and guarded truce with capitalism-with-the-rule-of-law rather than without it, but not a "universal," "unqualified" variant. It might need to be tolerated, perhaps even valued a little, but hardly welcomed and still less applauded. And so Thompson was rebuffed, rebutted, and rebuked by people half his size.[9]

At least in the West. In the East, on the other hand, it would have been hard even then, let alone by the time European Communism collapsed, to see what the fuss was about. One can even imagine ill-mannered questions, like why it had taken Thompson so long to get to where Locke and Madison, not to mention Aristotle, had gotten somewhat earlier. Marxism was out the window, and the call was for the rule of law to be brought in—without adjectives, unmodified, as Catharine MacKinnon might say.[10] Timothy Garton

6. *Ibid.*, 266.
7. I discuss these claims at length in "Marxism and the Rule of Law: Reflections after the Collapse of Communism," *Law and Social Inquiry* (1990) 633-64. That discussion in turn caused some controversy. See the debate in the same issue at 665-730.
8. Hugh Collins, *Marxism and Law*, Oxford: Oxford University Press (1982) 1.
9. *Ibid.*; Bob Fine, *Democracy and the Rule of Law: Liberal Ideas and Marxist Critiques*, London: Pluto Press (1984); Morton J. Horwitz, "The Rule of Law: An Unqualified Human Good?" 86 *Yale Law Journal* (1977) 561; Adrian Merritt, "The Nature of Law: A Criticism of Edward P. Thompson's *Whigs and Hunters*," 7 *British Journal of Law and* Society (1980) 194. There is a later and more sympathetic discussion of Thompson's claims, and of the controversy they caused among the believers, in Daniel H. Cole, "'An Unqualified Human Good': Edward P. Thompson and the Rule of Law," 28, 2 *Journal of Law and Society* (June 2001) 177-203.
10. Catharine MacKinnon, *Feminism Unmodified: Discourses on Life and Law*, Cambridge, Mass.: Harvard University Press (1987).

Ash faithfully captures the spirit of that time, at least as expressed by many prominent activists:

> In politics they are all saying: There is no "socialist democracy," there is only democracy. And by democracy they mean multi-party, parliamentary democracy as practised in contemporary Western, Northern, and Southern Europe. They are all saying: There is no "socialist legality," there is only legality. And by that they mean the rule of law, guaranteed by the constitutionally anchored independence of the judiciary.[11]

I have to confess to a deep and long-held sympathy for Thompson's claim and those characterized by Garton Ash. Faced with the choice between arbitrary power and the rule of law, the latter gets my vote every time. This is one dichotomy which seems to me worth insisting on, and one of its alternatives is immeasurably preferable to the other. And the reasons for that are pretty simple, about as simple as Thompson suggests. Some truths really are as simple as they sound, and the comparative virtues of the rule of law have seemed to me among them.

However, not everything about the rule of law is simple, and some important things about it are neither universal nor unqualified. In recent years I have been led to think about those things in two rather different and distant contexts: that of the postcommunist European "transitions" of the last dozen years or so, and that of an earlier and no less dramatic transition in my own country, Australia, since the arrival of Europeans two centuries ago. Thinking about each has spurred me to think about the other and to recognize that not everything that can be said in either context has the same resonance elsewhere. This essay is a preliminary attempt to come to terms with this uneasy combination: some fundamental rule of law values that make sense pretty well anywhere, anytime, together with ways in which they have and might be realized, that vary greatly and whose sense is at times questionable.

2. Ends

Perhaps fortunately, Thompson was not a lawyer, and unlike the doyen of English rule-of-lawyers, A.V. Dicey,[12] and most other lawyers who write about the rule of law, he did not seek to spell out just what legal elements allegedly produced it. In an "I know it when I see it" way, he insisted upon

11. Timothy Garton Ash, "Eastern Europe: The Year of Truth," *New York Review of Books* (15 February 1990) 21.

12. Albert Ven Dicey, *Introduction to the Study of the Law of the Constitution*, London: MacMillan, (1st ed. 1885, 10th ed. 1959).

the "obvious point" that "there is a difference between arbitrary power and the rule of law," and that the latter was identified by what it was claimed to achieve rather than by any recipe or précis of ingredients. Thompson identified the rule of law by the good it did—"the imposing of effective inhibitions upon power and the defense of the citizen from power's all-intrusive claims." For Thompson, it was only if and to the extent that law and the rule of law made this sort of difference that it mattered.

Of course, analysis of the rule of law must go further than this, if only to ensure that the cause of the good attributed to it has been well identified. But I think Thompson was right at least to start where he did. For I believe it is always preferable to start with the *values* that inspire concern for the rule of law, with why it might matter, what its point might be, than with contingent descriptions of institutional particulars said to further these ends.[13] Still more, to avoid taking these contingent particular elements, as Dicey took them, to be their universal essence.

There are several reasons for preferring to start with the end, as it were, but here I will mention only one, well known in the study of organizations: the dangers of "goal displacement." An organizational pathology occurs when institutions initially introduced—or even not deliberately introduced—but taken to serve as a way of achieving goals, come to be reified as the best, and often soon after as the only way, to fulfill those goals. That assumed, it is easy to forget the goals altogether and remember only the means, or identify the two and then only talk about the means. When means thus effectively displace ends, people continue doing things or try copying what others are doing, often with great conviction but with little idea why. These means are often the stuff of institutional fashion, and when one forgets what was supposed to justify them, institutions are often stuck with them until the fashion changes. And in the case of government institutions, we are all stuck with them. It should never be forgotten that means are just instruments which are not self-justifying. Unfortunately, they are often self-perpetuating.

Such self-perpetuation can be contagious as, for example, when models presumed successful in one place are offered for export under misleading labels. The early history of the "transitional rule of law" was full of such offers, confidently given, enthusiastically received, and frequently disappointing. The export of models can lead to two different but similarly derived errors. On the one hand, the possibility that there might be other ways of attaining valued results is not explored. On the other hand, institutional emulation is taken to have done the job when models from prestigious places are copied in less prestigious ones; regardless of whether the transplanted models work in ways similar to the original or whether they have any salutary impact at all.

13. Krygier, "Transitional Questions," note 4.

My preference, then, is to start with the end, as it were, and only when that is clear move to means.

The end that matters to Thompson—restraint on arbitrary power—is not eccentric. The rule of law is commonly understood and valued by contrast with circumstances where it is lacking, and arbitrary exercise of power, above all, is the evil that it is supposed to curb. The concept and the contrast, though not always the specific verbal formulations, embody ideals that have been central to political and constitutional discourse at least since Aristotle. Means thought to achieve those ideals, needless to say, have varied over that time.

There are three common ways to reply to this encomium to the rule of law by contrast to arbitrary power. One is to opt for the other alternative, which despots (and, as Weber observed, populist demagogues) often do, but their subjects not always. Another possibility might be to adopt the Michnik strategy and insist on what today might be called a third way. Some of Thompson's critics seem attracted to this move. But, of course, one then has to consider whether such a way is open even in principle—to anyone, anywhere, anytime—and if so, whether it is open to us, here and now. I will return to this point. Third, one might deny that the rule of law is indeed an antidote to be preferred to arbitrariness, either because it is no antidote or because its own consequences are worse than the disease it is supposed to cure. Such claims require a response.

I will take these proposals in turn. Though real and aspirant power-holders are often keen on unrestrained power, there is little to be said for it, and much to be said in favor of trying to curb it. Today this is fairly well accepted, so I will be brief. The *reasons* one might want arbitrary power to be restrained are various; there are two that seem to me most general. The first aspect might be called *protective*, the second *facilitative*. A third has to do with substantive values of legality in the exercise of public power, but I think that is less general than the first two. Since at the moment my focus is on the most universalizable of rule of law values, I will leave this third aspect aside.[14]

The protective aspect has to do with fear, fear of surprise, of assault, of interference, of dispossession, of whatever dangers might flow from unbounded power, whether public or private. The sources of well-grounded fear vary—between societies, within them, and over time. Under Communism, public power was overwhelming, and could at times inspire overwhelming fear. Today an excess of state power is often the least of a postcommunist citizen's problems, and impunity of powerful private actors is what most needs to be addressed. Either way, legal attempts to constrain arbitrariness are at the core of what Judith Shklar has aptly called the "liberalism of fear," and that is a

14. *Ibid.*, 6-8 and Krygier, "The Rule of Law," note 4, 13406-408.

good cause. Fear of arbitrary power is a terrible thing; power which can be exercised without check is a good reason for such fear; ways of lessening both are to be commended.[15]

In a world which routinely includes strangers, fruitful and cooperative rather than fearful, distrustful, and solipsistic relations among citizens, and between citizens and officials, depend on it being reasonable to assume that relations among non-intimates will not, as a rule, be inclined to be predatory; that opponents will not be able to mobilize the state against you; that in relation to the state you will not be defenseless, and so on. These are not natural or inevitable assumptions, and it takes much to make them plausible. The hope is that an effective rule of law regime will contribute to citizens' confidence that such assumptions are neither foolish nor heroic.

Fear is not, however, the only reason for the rule of law, nor is government its only subject. We all are. Madison wrote that if we were angels we would not need any laws. Unfortunately, so the familiar argument goes: we are not, so we do. However, even angels and, indeed, all but the omniscient might benefit from the rule of law. We can all become confused and lose our way, not necessarily due to our or others' evil but merely to the superfluity of possibilities in an unordered world. All the more when that world is, as ours, full of large and mobile societies of strangers, where ties of kinship, locality, and familiarity can only partially bind, reassure, or inform.

The predicament of a member of such a "civilized" society, as Adam Smith already identified it in the eighteenth century, is that he "stands at all times in need of the cooperation and assistance of great multitudes, while his whole life is scarce sufficient to gain the friendship of a few persons."[16] What is needed is "a basis for legitimate expectations,"[17] without which the "cooperation and assistance of great multitudes" will necessarily be a more chancy affair. Where such a basis exists and though strangers are abundant, fellow citizens can know a good deal about each other; coordinate their actions with others; and feel some security and predictability in their dealings with them. Such a basis can, of course, never make everything predictable. The hope is that it can tie down enough so that matters, which would otherwise be up

15. Cf. Judith Shklar, "The Liberalism of Fear," in Nancy L. Rosenblum (ed.), *Liberalism and the Moral Life*, Cambridge, Mass.: Harvard University Press (1984) and "Political Theory and the Rule of Law," in Shklar, *Political Thought and Political Thinkers*, in Stanley Hoffmann (ed.), Chicago: University of Chicago Press (1998). I have tried to explore some implications of the liberalism of fear in "Ethical Positivism and the Liberalism of Fear," in Tom D. Campbell and Jeffrey Goldsworthy (eds.), *Judicial Power, Democracy and Legal Positivism*, Dartmouth: Aldershot (1999) 59-86.

16. Adam Smith, An Inquiry into the Nature and Causes of the Wealth of Nations, vol. 1, Indianapolis: Liberty fund (1981) 26.

17. John Rawls, *A Theory of Justice*, Cambridge, Mass.: Harvard University Press (1971) 238.

for grabs, serve as fixed and knowable points in the landscape; on the basis of which the strangers who routinely interact in modern societies can do so with some security and autonomy, and be enabled to cooperate, to plan, and to choose.

The key to cooperative encounters with others is commonly shared knowledge that there exist limitations on options, which in principle might be unlimited or at least too many in number to deal with, together with common knowledge of the available options. Road rules are a good example, literally and metaphorically, of such facilitative option-specifying rules. Rules which can limit and signal options, and which can be assumed to have done so, even for strangers, are important simply for us to be able to communicate and engage with others, all the more so whenever it is important to coordinate activities with them. Commonly known and acknowledged rules of the game contribute to interpersonal knowability and predictability, from which might arise mutual confidence, coordination and cooperation, without which such things will not easily develop.

Limits on sources of fear, and commonly understood and reliable rules of the game are good things to have; and it is hard to see where they would not be. They are also necessary conditions for most plausible candidates for human rights, unless it is thought there should be human rights to terror and confusion. Where in the world would it be better to be unprotected against potential dangers from, among other things, our political rulers and our fellows? Where would confused and lonely solipsism be better than the possibility of productive cooperation? The difficult questions, and the contingent limitations to the answers, have to do with how we can serve these goals.

Which leads to the second counterproposal to the choice between arbitrariness and the rule of law: a third way. It would be foolish to reject this in principle for all places and times. Variations in the nature, size, and complexity, or in the degree of differentiation, institutionalization, and—connected with these—modernity of societies are of great significance in affecting institutional possibilities; and arguments about universality can scarcely ignore such variations. There are other variations, too, but I will start with these.

There is plenty of evidence that small or nomadic or what used to be called "stateless"[18] pre-modern societies, without our sorts of institutional apparatus— legislatures, executives, judiciaries—can nevertheless contrive to protect their members from familiar dangers (unfamiliar dangers, particularly unprecedented and overwhelming ones such as alien invasions, are a dif-

18. See Meyer Fortes and E.E. Evans Pritchard, (eds.), *African Political Systems*, Oxford: Oxford University Press (1948). Cf., Martin Krygier, "Anthropological Approaches," in Eugene Kamenka and Alice Erh-Soon Tay (eds.), *Law and Social Control*, London: Edward Arnold (1980) 27-59.

ferent matter) and encourage certain sorts of necessary cooperation, without a war of all against all. We might not recognize the means by which these ends are accomplished as legal, but that is of little moment. It is an empirical matter how these ends are achieved and a normative one how well.

But there are ecological limits to this, and they are of two familiar sorts. One has to do with size, the other with modernity (which also affects size). Beyond a very small size, as Weber among others has observed, societies will develop institutionalized apparatuses of rule. This is inevitable, and in modern societies it is also in principle good. We *need* states with adequate powers to do what only they are capable.[19] This Hobbesian insight has not yet been washed away by the tides of globalization or the tremors of September 11. On the contrary, those in control of such states are able to amass great power, which it is difficult to restrain routinely without some institutionalized countervailing measures. Unrestrained, it is reasonable to fear them. Moreover, large societies generate coordination problems no longer amenable to purely informal resolution on the basis of common understandings; for common knowledge fades with complexity and distance. To be sure, rules of law are never self-sufficient unmoved movers, nor are they sufficient for whatever good we want, but in large societies they can contribute to the lessening of fear and confusion, both of which would be natural enough without rules of law. They don't do this *necessarily*, for rules of certain sorts can do as much harm as rules of other sorts do good, and much is required besides rules, but to limit fear and confusion they are arguably necessary.

Moreover, modernity militates against the endurance of small societies on the basis of their internal social control mechanisms alone. It destroys many and renders others ineffective. Among those things that wreak such destruction are modern states and law. There is abundant evidence for this, and such destruction and erosion have occurred in many parts of the world. Size is an important part of this, but only a part. Other parts include the thinning of cultural density, competition from other options, freedom of movement, infections and corruptions of every literal and metaphorical sort. So, for better or worse, there are many places where concerns to institutionalize ways to protect and facilitate, which motivate rule of law thought, are or have become indispensable, if only to restrain the power of the institutions they presuppose. In societies with large and concentrated centers of power (traditionally political power, but the point can be generalized), and large physically and culturally dispersed and mobile populations, we do better if we can

19. On this, see esp. Stephen Holmes, *Passions and Constraint*, Chicago: University of Chicago Press (1995); Cass Sunstein and Stephen Holmes, *The Cost of Rights*, New York: Norton (1999); and Linda Weiss and John Hobson, *States and Economic Development*, Cambridge: Polity Press (1995).

rely on institutions that are able to lessen the chances of power being exercised arbitrarily, capriciously, without authority or redress. We do better, too, in large societies, where we are constantly interacting with non-intimates, if we can know important things about people we may not know well in other respects. Such things include their and our rights, responsibilities, risks, and constraints. In small and pre-modern societies, as in families, we can know many of these things from personal everyday experience. In larger, more various, agglomerations such knowledge and the shared normative understandings that make it possible, are often not available. Where the rule of law *matters* in a society, however, we can know many of these things even about strangers. That makes their and our activities more predictable to one another and might make us less fearful of and more cooperative with them, and of course, them of and with us. This can lead to a productive spiral of virtuous circles,[20] where each gains by reasonable trust in others. So while, as we will see, the rule of law can be sought along a variety of routes and through a variety of means, I do not see any acceptable alternative to it.

But—and this is the third complaint—perhaps the rule of law does not do what is needed, or what its partisans promise, or does these things at too great an expense. Here three elementary points are worth recalling. First, no one suggests that the ideal achievement of the rule of law, whatever that would be, is possible. The rule of law is not something you either have or not, like a rare painting. Rather, like wealth, one has more or less of it. Whether one has enough of it is a judgment to be made along continua— multiple continua— not a choice between binary alternatives. One seeks to *reduce* arbitrariness, to *increase* the sway of the rule of law, not to eliminate the former by installing a new, and fortunately unrealizable, dystopia consisting of nothing but the latter. Second, the rule of law is obviously not *sufficient* for a good society. At most it is necessary—but this is true too of oxygen—and does not make irrelevant the rule of law. Third, it is not the only game in town. Where other values conflict with it, they need to be taken into account and compromises in pursuit of one or another might be necessary. That is not a new problem in human affairs. Perhaps, unlike oxygen, single-minded devotion to the rule of law is harmful to other good things we would want to do, like extend certain benevolent government activities. There are arguments to this effect[21] and it might be so, though I believe that both partisans of the welfare state and its critics exaggerate the inconsistencies. And to the extent that they do not, this

20. See Martin Krygier, "Virtuous Circles: Antipodean Thoughts on Power, Institutions, and Civil Society," 11, 1 *East European Politics and Societies* (1997) 36-88.

21. See, e.g., Friedrich A. von Hayek, *Law Legislation and Liberty*, 3 vols., Chicago: University of Chicago Press (1973, 1976, 1979) and Geoffrey de Q. Qalker, *The Rule of Law: Foundation of Constitutional Democracy*, Melbourne: Melbourne University Press (1988).

simply makes the rule of law another of those things we value that live in tension with other things of value. Since little is pure in social life—not even oxygen—it remains to be shown that active government (which I support) and the rule of law (which I also support) cannot be achieved together. At least the tensions between the two are likely to be highly variable. As Philip Selznick has insisted, what in weak legal orders might be mere and dangerous opportunism that threatens a fragile order of constraint, might in stronger ones be a "responsive" leavening of the rigidities of legal orders well able to take care of themselves.[22]

In any event, there are good reasons to believe that, both in principle and in historical experience, constitutionally restrained government is, in important and valuable ways, more usefully strong than governments whose power is unrestrained, and that to be effective such a government has much to do.[23] And not only are restrained governments stronger than arbitrary ones, so are the societies which depend upon them.

Therefore, I conclude, some of the central values informing the pursuit of the rule of law are generally good, if I were less modest I might say universally so, as is their pursuit. But what of the means? Here it is worth distinguishing between broad conditions such means need to satisfy: qualities they must possess, on the one hand, and the particular sorts of institutions that might be thought to possess them, on the other. The former can be stated with some degree of generality, but not fully; the latter even less so.

3. Conditions

This is not to deride the ideal of the rule of law, for that ideal is not a recipe for detailed institutional design. It is rather a value, or interconnected cluster of values, that might inform the determination of such design, and which might be—and have been—pursued and institutionalized in a variety of ways. So specifying the values the rule of law is to secure is not yet to describe how these values are to be achieved. And perhaps such specification can never be achieved with any combination of generality and precision. In different societies, with different histories, traditions, circumstances and problems, law has contributed to securing these (and other) values in different ways, and argu-

22. See, e.g., Philippe Nonet and Philip Selznick, *Law and Society in Transition: Toward Responsive Law,* 2d ed., New Brunswick, N.J.: Transaction Publishers (2001) 116, and Selznick, *op. cit.*, note 1, 336.

23. See Krygier, *op. cit.*, note 20, and "The Quality of Civility: Post-Anti-Communist Thoughts on Civil Society and the Rule of Law," in András Sajó (ed.), *Out of and Into Authoritarian Law*, The Hague: Kluwer Law International (2003).

ably could not have secured them all in the same way. And there are many ways to fail, too. Nevertheless, there are some general conditions which need substantially to be fulfilled by whatever normative and institutional setups available within a society. These are variably fulfilled in different societies and times, and thus the ends of the rule of law are variably attained. In principle, these conditions are highly general goods, for they are jointly necessary for the achievement of the values specified above. In practice, however, they have only rarely existed in abundance. Elsewhere I have explored four such conditions,[24] which I will briefly summarize here.

First, *scope* of restraint on and channeling of power is crucial. To the extent that powerful players are above or beyond the reach of the law, the rule of law will not apply to them.

Second, people will not be able to use the law as a guide for their own actions, or for their expectations of others, unless they can know and understand it or it can readily be made known and understood to them. So the law must be of a *character* such that it can be known. It will rarely be universally known anywhere, but where it is unknowable so is the rule of law.

A third condition of the rule of law takes us beyond the rules to the ways they are administered. The law must be administered in a manner in which its terms are taken seriously and thus allow citizens to do the same, e.g., interpreted in non-arbitrary ways that can be known and understood publicly, and enforced in accordance with such interpretations.

Finally, to be of social and political, rather than merely legal, consequence the law must actually, and be widely expected and assumed to, *matter*, or *count*, as a constituent and as a frame in the exercise of social power, both by those who exercise it (which, where citizens make *use* of the law, should comprise more than just officials) and by those who are affected by its exercise. What is involved when the law counts is a complex sociological question on which the law bears. But it is not in itself an internal legal question, or even a question solely about legal institutions, for it depends as much on characteristics of the society as of the law, and on their interactions. And, although the literature of the rule of law has almost nothing useful to say about it, the rule of law depends upon it.

Recall Thompson. What was key for him, as it has been for dissidents under countless despotisms, was "the imposing of *effective* inhibitions upon power and the defense of the citizen from power's all-intrusive clams." This is a social result, to which law is supposed to be able to contribute, and needless to say, it depends on many things beside the qualities of the formal law. Yet, far too often lawyers and philosophers when discussing the rule of law

24. Krygier, "Transitional Questions," note 4, 9-17.

move from some legalistic conception of the first three of the above conditions to the assumption that where they exist so does the rule of law. Which it might, if the law were the single unmoved mover of the social world. But since no one seriously believes that, this move is as odd as it is common.

Take for example, knowledge of the law. Lawyers have developed lists of the particular characteristics necessary for law to be known. Often indeed these are taken together to add up to what the rule of law means. The law, they say, must at least exist, of course, but it must also be public, comprehensible, relatively clear, precise, stable, non-contradictory, unambiguous, prospective, and so on.[25] These lists are well known, and regardless of their length their rationale is the same: the law must be of a character that people can align their actions and expectations with it. Since this is the desired end, it is easy for lawyers to stipulate what, from the legal *sender's* viewpoint, contributes to legal knowability.

But whether the law is known or knowable cannot just be read off merely from legal forms. For success in the communication of law surely depends on how the law is *received*, not on how it is expressed or even delivered. And that depends on many various factors that intervene between law and life. But what in a particular society are the sources and impediments to orienting one's actions by law are essentially empirical, socio-legal questions to which we have few certain answers. And since we do not it is odd that lawyers and philosophers are so confident that we do.

One a priori hypothesis, which is extremely common among lawyers, is that whatever contributes to making legal rules less vague, ambiguous, open-ended and, thus, renders them more precise, tightly-specified, and univocal contributes to making law more certain, and therefore reliable. It seems to stand to reason, after all, that if a rule is sharper, more precise, less open to interpretation, then it is easier to understand and follow. This assumption underlay both Max Weber's and Evgenii Pashukanis's sociology of law and capitalism, and it remains popular, particularly among legal positivists. Thus Joseph Raz gives as one "fairly obvious" reason for preferring rules to principles in the direct regulation of behavior that "[p]rinciples, because they prescribe highly unspecific acts, tend to be more vague and less certain than rules" and "since the law should strive to balance certainty and reliability against flexibility, it is on the whole wise legal policy to use rules as much as possible for regulating human behavior because they are more certain than principles and lend themselves more easily to uniform and predictable application."[26] On that assumption,

25. E.g. Lon Fuller, *The Morality of Law*, 2d ed., New Haven: Yale University Press (1969) chapter 2; Joseph Raz, "The Rule of Law and its Virtue," in *The Authority of Law: Essays on Law and Morality*, Oxford: Clarendon Press (1979).

26. Joseph Raz, "Legal Principles and the Limits of Law," 81 *Yale Law Journal* (1972) 823, 841.

numerous advocates of the rule of law insist that it should be a "law of rules,"[27] where rules are understood to act as "exclusionary reasons"[28] rather than more open-ended principles, since the former are more certain and predictable than the latter.[29] Even those, like Ronald Dworkin, who are fond of principles are not so on the grounds that they are as predictable as rules, indeed they concede that they are not. Dworkin commends them for offering other virtues of justice which a strict regime of rules might thwart.

It is a major and unresolved issue of socio-legal investigation whether precision of rules yields certainty of law. Not only is it unresolved, it is very difficult to resolve, since it is an empirical question for which it is hard to gather evidence. Such evidence as we have suggests, at least to John Braithwaite, that while rules might be more certain than principles in relation to "simple, stable patterns of action that do not involve high economic stakes"—like driving a car—"with complex actions in changing environments where large economic interests are at stake" principles are more likely to enable legal certainty than rules. Indeed, Braithwaite argues, "[w]hen flux is great it can be obvious that radically abandoning the precision of rules can increase certainty."[30] The argument is complex and the evidence, as Braithwaite readily concedes, incomplete and hard to obtain, but his arguments are powerful and the evidence on which he draws, though limited, is strong. A complex order of fixed and rigid rules, for example, is typically more open to "creative compliance," "legal entrepreneurship" and "contrived complexity" particularly at "the big end of town." This is both because certain precise rules, and regimes where such rules predominate, lend themselves to such exploitation more readily than certain principles, and too, because "there is uncertainty that is structurally predictable by features of power in society rather than by features

27. Cf., Antonin Scalia, "The Rule of Law as a Law of Rules," 56 *University of Chicago Law Review* (1989) 1175. This is the central theme of Tom Campbell's, *The Legal Theory of Ethical Positivism*. Dartmouth: Aldershot (1996). Campbell's "ethical positivism" is "an aspirational model of law according to which it is a presumptive condition of the legitimacy of governments that they function through the medium of specific rules capable of being identified and applied by citizens and officials without recourse to contentious personal or group political presuppositions, beliefs and commitments."

28. Joseph Raz, *Practical Reasons and Norms*, London: Hutchinson (1975) 15-84. See Campbell, *op. cit.*, note 27, 5: "a system of law ought to be a system of rules. Further, the rules in question must be 'real' rules, that is rules which have, in Raz's term, 'exclusionary force.'"

29. See Tom D. Campbell, Antonin Scalia and Geoffrey de Q. Walker, The Rule of Law: Foundation of Constitutional Democracy, Melbourne: Melbourne University Press (1988); P. S. Atiyah, From Principles to Pragmatism: Changes in the Function of the Judicial Process and the Law, Inaugural Lecture delivered at Oxford University (17 February 1978), later published by the Clarendon Press.

30. John Braithwaite, "Rules and Principles: A Theory of Legal Certainty," 27 *Australian Journal of Legal Philosophy* (2002) 54.

of the law."[31] One might speculate that some of the tendencies Braithwaite identifies might even be stronger in less ruly countries than the Western, comparatively law-abiding polities (Australia, United Kingdom, United States) on which this and allied research primarily draws.

Whether or not Braithwaite's particular hypotheses are confirmed by further work, the point remains that we will not be able to confirm or deny them without such work. Yet the literature of the rule of law is largely innocent of these sorts of inquiry. Lawyers often stop at the place where social investigation should start, at the legal vehicle of transmission, or later, at a somewhat skewed sample of law-affected behavior. They do not regularly investigate those places where legal transmissions are most typically and crucially received and acted upon—in the myriad of law-affected everyday interactions of individuals and groups with which lawyers or officials do not come in contact, but where law in a rule of law society does its most important work. Moreover, sources of and impediments to legal knowledge differ between societies. Even were lawyers interested and equipped to look more widely, they would still typically have only local knowledge. And since philosophers of law rarely go beyond the writings of lawyers for their data, they have even less to work with: vicarious local knowledge. This would need to be supplemented by comparison and reflection, and with additional knowledge of sorts which needs to go beyond where lawyers usually feel comfortable looking or philosophers thinking. I do not expect lawyers or philosophers to do something alien to their natures, viz. empirical social research, but it would be gratifying if, once in a while, they acknowledged the significance of such investigations for so much that they say is in ignorance of them.

This is just one example of a more general point, that the successful attainment of the rule of law is a *social* outcome, not merely a legal one. What matters, here as everywhere with the rule of law, is how the law affects subjects. But since the distance between law in books and action is often great, and the gap full of many other things, and in different places full of different things, it is a matter of comparative social investigation and theorization what might best, in particular circumstances, in particular societies, further that goal. A docket of the *rechtstaatlich* features of legal instruments, even buttressed by citations to Fuller, Hayek, or Raz, will not do the trick.

The only time the *rule* of law can occur, when law might then be said to rule, is when the law counts significantly, is distinct and in competition with other sources of influence, in the different realms of thoughts and behavior, the normative economy, and significant sectors of a society. But we do not know what makes law count.[32] Knowability of legal provisions is obvi-

31. *Ibid.*, 58-59.

32. For some intelligent, still controversial and unsettled, speculations in a particular con-

ously only a part of the story. Jurists say little about this large issue, beyond bromides about "legal effectiveness" or, more occasionally, the importance of legal culture or a culture of lawfulness. However, as seekers of the rule of law from societies without it are discovering in many parts of the world, what these generalities depend upon, and, even more, how to produce them, are mysteries. Furthermore, what works in one place does not necessarily work elsewhere in the same way, or at all—mysteries abound.

What does it mean for law to count in a society in such a way that we feel confident saying that the rule of law exists there? All the questions asked here have a sociological dimension, this one above all. It asks about the social *reach* and *weight* of law, and the answers, whatever they are, will have to attend to questions of sociology and politics, as much as of law. These answers must vary between societies, whether or not the formal rules do. This is not because the law has no significance, but because what in law does have significance, how it does, and the fact that so many other things do as well, that little about the nature and extent of the significance of law can be read off from the law itself.

The notion of legal effectiveness merely hints at the complexity of the conditions of the rule of law, far greater complexity than is needed merely (!) to ensure the effectiveness of a legal order. That is no simple matter either, of course, but one can imagine that, for a while at least, effectiveness might come "out of the barrel of a gun." But not the rule of law.

Both effectiveness and the rule of law begin with obedience in any legal order. For the rule of law to exist, obedience must be manifest to a considerable degree both on the part of ordinary citizens and the powerful. But for the rule of law to thrive, beyond mere obedience, *use and manner of use* matter as well.

If the laws are there but governments bypass them, it is not the law that rules. Therefore exercise of governmental power must be predominantly channeled through laws that people can know. But governments, as we have seen, are not the only addressees of the rule of law. For the rule of law to count in the life of its subjects a less frequently remarked upon condition must be present—one as important as mere *submission* to law, or even adequate *access* to and *supply* of laws and legal institutions— that is constraint by *demand* for and (often unreflective) use of legal services and resources.[33] Such

text, see Kathryn Hendley, Stephen Holmes, Anders Åslund and András Sajó, "Debate: Demand for Law," 8:4 *East European Constitutional Review* (1999) 88-108. Cf. also "Citizen and Law after Communism," 7:1 *East European Constitutional Review* (Winter 1998) 70-88 and Ilian G. Cashu and Mitchell A. Orenstein, "The Pensioners' Court Campaign: Making Law Matter in Russia" with reply by Kathryn Hendley, "'Demand' for Law—A Mixed Picture," 10:4 *East European Constitutional Review* (Fall 2001).

33. See Hendley et al., *ibid.*

demand and use extend beyond, and frequently will not involve, direct enlistment of legal officials or institutions. They are manifest in the extent to which legal institutions, concepts, options, and resources serve to frame, inform, and support the choices of citizens.

More socially significant than citizens' (generally rare) direct invocations of official channels, is the extent to which they are able and willing to use and to rely upon legal resources such as cues, standards, models, "bargaining chips," "regulatory endowments," authorizations, and immunities in relations with each other and with the state as realistic (even if necessarily imperfect) indicators of what they and others can and are likely to do. For it is a socio-legal truism, which still escapes many lawyers, that the importance of legal institutions is poorly indicated by the numbers who make direct use of them. The primary impact of such institutions, as Marc Galanter has emphasized,[34] is not as magnets for social disputes, a very small proportion of which ever reach appropriate legal institutions, but as beacons sending signals about law, rights, costs, delays, advantages, disadvantages, and other possibilities, into the community. Of course it helps if the beacons are bright rather than dim, but that is not all that is needed. It is the job of legal officials to make the signals they send clear and encouraging (or, in the case of criminal law discouraging), and of enforcement agencies to make them salient. But even when these signals are bright and visible, they are not the only ones that are sent out or received in a society.[35] They can be blotted out by more immediate, urgent, extra-legal, often anti-legal messages sent from many quarters. Or by discouraging messages, such as that whatever the courts say, it won't be implemented (often alleged in Russia), or that the courts are less powerful than local patrons (ditto and elsewhere), or that whatever one obtains from the courts won't compensate for the costs, difficulties, delays and even dangers involved in obtaining it. And other systems, not always cooperative with the law, come into play. Finally, even after the legal messages have been sent, and not diverted, occluded or misdirected, there are still the receivers, who are nowhere a single entity or homogeneous group but plural, different, self-and-other-directed,

---

34. See Marc Galanter, "Justice in Many Rooms: Courts, Private Ordering, and Indigenous Law," 19 *Journal of Legal Pluralism* (1981) 1-47. As Galanter observes, "[t]he mainstream of legal scholarship has tended to look out from within the official legal order, abetting the pretensions of the official law to stand in a relationship of hierarchic control to other normative orderings in society. Social research on law has been characterized by a repeated rediscovery of the other hemisphere of the legal world. This has entailed recurrent rediscovery that law in modern society is plural rather than monolithic, that it is private as well as public in character and that the national (public, official) legal system is often a secondary rather than a primary locus of regulation" (p. 20).

35. For a classic statement of these points, see Sally Falk Moore, "Law and Social Change: The Semi-Autonomous Social Field as an Appropriate Subject of Study," in *Law as Process*, London: Routledge and Kegan Paul (1978) 54-81.

members of numerous, often distinct, sometimes and in some respects overlapping, "semi-autonomous" groups which affect them, often deeply. Law "means" different things to different "communities of interpreters," especially since for most of them interpretation of law is not their major interest.

The extent to which citizens are able and willing to use and to rely upon legal institutions to protect and advance their interests varies, again, within and between societies and over time. In many times and places citizens are willing to use the law but excluded from access to it. In others, including contemporary Russia, it appears that despite having access they are unwilling to make much use of laws. In yet others such as the United States, many citizens, perhaps too many, are both willing and able. We know a bit about how to affect the supply of law, but we know a good deal less than we might about how to affect demand for it.

Law never means everything in people's lives, and it rarely means nothing either. But to speak sensibly of the rule of law as a significant element in the life of a society, the law's norms must be socially *normative.* If people know nothing of the law, or knowing something think nothing of it, or think of it but do not take it seriously, or even, taking it seriously do not know what to do about it, then their lives will not be enriched by the rule of law (though as it applies to governments they might still be partly protected by it). As to how such normativity might be generated, we have few universal prescriptions worth offering.

4. Means

We have, then, few recipes for producing the legal normativity in a society on which the rule of law depends. Its ingredients vary, some do not travel well, some turn out on arrival to depend upon others which went unnoticed at home, let alone packed; resources and equipment in some places are more welcoming than in others. This is not even to mention *tastes,* which everyone knows are beyond discussion. And if this is all true of the prerequisite conditions needed to establish the rule of law, it is much more so of the particular institutions and practices that might satisfy such conditions. Here the variety is enormous. This is true both in a positive sense: there are many ways in which comparable achievements can be arranged;[36] and negatively: the same institutional arrangements work differently,[37] and some do not work at all.

36. See Philip Selznick, "Legal Cultures and the Rule of Law," in Martin Krygier and Adam Czarnota (eds.), *The Rule of Law after Communism,* Darthmoth/Ashgate: Aldershot (1999) 21-38.

37. See, e.g., András Sajó's observation, based on experience in postcommunist Europe, par-

This has been vivid in the experience of countries that have embarked upon hoped for "transitions" to the rule of law. Like Thompson, dissidents knew what they wanted from the rule of law—above all a curb on arbitrary power. They knew less how to achieve it, though they fancied that it existed in "normal countries" of the West. That led to initial optimism that it could be directly imported by constructing institutions modeled on those of the West. That optimism has proved excessive, though it is not altogether and everywhere misplaced.

On the one hand, ideals of the rule of law have been better served in some nations and by some institutions than others. Institutional possibilities are not infinite; institutions have consequences; different institutions have different consequences; learning can and does occur, and you have to start somewhere. So it would be absurd to ignore what Dewey called the "funded experience" of generations, among them truisms that have proved valuable again and again. One of these is that only power can tame power.

Some arrangements work well in many contexts; others less so or only in some contexts. One is often warranted in starting with presumptions in favor of institutional models which have worked elsewhere. On the other hand, one should be wary of too swiftly converting presumptions into prescriptions, particularly prescriptions that are highly specific, let alone that hold out particular institutions as universal models to be emulated. When that occurs without answers to deeper questions about conditions and possibilities of institutional transplantation, about how to mesh with (and yet transform) local institutions, expectations, social interests and history, frustration will threaten even—perhaps especially—the best laid plans and transitional societies will be the unhappy beneficiaries of uncontextualized, and commonly unsuccessful, offerings and borrowings.

Here it is important to keep the point(s) of the rule of law in mind. Rather than conclude from institutional variety that new contexts are "*sui generis*"[38] (as all contexts are in part but not completely), pursuit of the rule of law requires reflection in particular contexts on how some generally valuable goods might be achieved. That is an urgent problem in some contexts, and one which might seem to be unprecedented in many. However, while in particular details the context might indeed be unique, the *sort* of problem is not often likely to be. Rather, as Lon Fuller has observed, law is "purposive activ-

---

ticularly Hungary: "Where the cabinet is endowed with its own anti-corruption police, that police will investigate those whom the majority in the cabinet dislike. The rule of law will be stabbed in the back by a partisan and arbitrary knife, although the use of that knife was originally authorized to protect the rule of law." ("Corruption, Clientelism, and the Future of the Constitutional State in Eastern Europe," 7:2 *East European Constitutional Review* (Spring 1998) 46.

38. Cf. Ruti Teitel, *Transitional Justice*, New York: Oxford University Press (2000) *passim*.

ity attended by certain difficulties that it must surmount if it is to succeed in attaining its ends."[39] The difficulties will vary, and so, too, will the best ways to meet them. Wherever the location, the rule of law should be approached with a combination of its *point(s)* in mind, including an acquaintance with various attempts to ground and institutionalize such ends, *together with* a great deal of reflected-upon local knowledge. What needs to be avoided is the Scylla of abstract universalism which has no understanding of the significance, and variable significances, of particular contexts and the Charybdis of a "po-mo" relativism, for which context is all. The former often generates "off-the-shelf blueprint"[40] approaches to the rule of law; the latter, sometimes in justified but unfortunately symmetrical reaction against excessive faith in blueprints, threatens to sever the moorings of the rule of law in the human condition and more general human purposes. That is why I have been recommending that "in this, as in many other contexts, we should resist pressure to *choose* between universal and particular. Rather we should ask how best they might be combined, to relieve both the abstraction that commonly goes with the former and the solipsistic idiosyncrasy that can flow from excessive devotion to the latter."[41] In principle, I still believe that should be attempted.

5. Antipodean Antinomies

Even this compromise is too neat. Doubts and perplexities remain. I have been moved to them by the Australian experience, so let me close with it.[42] In relation to the rule of law it is at the same time exemplary and fraught, and thus another example, though this time not a uniformly happy one, of dichotomies that resist easy choice.

In January 1788, Governor Arthur Philip landed in Sydney with 9 officials, 212 marines, 759 convicts and all the laws of England that were "applicable to their own situation and condition of any infant colony."[43] The aim was to establish a penal colony for convicts who could no longer be transported to America.

39. Fuller, *op. cit.*, note 25, 117.

40. Wade Jacoby, "Priest and Penitent: The European Union as a Force in the Domestic Politics of Eastern Europe," 8:2 *East European Constitutional Review* (Winter/Spring 1999) 62.

41. Krygier, "Transitional Questions," note 4, 3.

42. Here I draw on my "The Grammar of Colonial Legality: Subjects, Objects and the Rule of Law," in Geoffrey Brennan and Francis G. Castles (eds.), *Australia Reshaped: Essays on 200 Years of Institutional Transformation*, Cambridge: Cambridge University Press (2002) 220-60.

43. Blackstone, *Commentaries on the Laws of England*, 18th ed., Book 1, 111.

Thus began what by most criteria and for most inhabitants has been a remarkably successful and long-lived transition to democracy and the rule of law.

The experiment was paradoxical, or two-faced, from the start, however, and it is worth emphasizing both faces, since one or the other is often ignored and rarely are they confronted with each other. The first is that, along with the convicts, the settlers brought not just law but the rule of law. Indeed, it sometimes appears that they brought more of the rule of law than of the law itself. For there were all sorts of legal peculiarities in the colony. After all, the first white settlers did not go there for a holiday, nor did they get one when they arrived. Early New South Wales was all very strange, and it was not a pleasant or easy place to be. Apart from the harshness of everyday life there was "one fact that everyone in the colony knew, both convict and free: convicts were sent there as a punishment."[44] In accordance with that fundamental fact and purpose, the nascent penal colony had no representative political institutions, no jury trials, and almost no lawyers (except for some convicts), but did enjoy a dominant military presence and governors whose formal powers were great and whose practical autonomy, in this wilderness at the end of the world, was even greater. It almost did not have courts. That was not intended until as late as November 1786, when Lord Sydney, the British home secretary, "seems to have decided that too much was being left to chance."[45] Fifty years later, however, while the majority of its population was still convict or ex-convict, it was a free society with considerable legal protection against arbitrary power and a representative legislature. There is no evidence that the British government planned it that way; nor was the result inevitable. Nevertheless, the transformation occurred, and most Australians are its beneficiaries. Why this happened is a matter of more than local or antiquarian interest.

There are, needless to say, many reasons for these changes. But one of the central reasons that New South Wales became a free society, as David Neal has argued, has to do with law, in a very special sense. His argument is that it was not just convicts who were transported, but particular ideas and ideals about law. What transformed Australia from penal colony to free society was what the convicts carried from Britain in their heads, "as part of their cultural baggage." Central to the cultural baggage was belief in the rule of law,

44. David Neal, *The Rule of Law in a Penal Colony,* Cambridge: Cambridge University Press (1991) 45-46. Neal's book is the major source of my argument here. See also Alan Atkinson, *The Europeans in Australia: A History,* vol. 1: *The Beginning,* Melbourne: Oxford University Press (1997); John Braithwaite, "Crime in a Convict Republic," 64 *The Modern Law Review* (January 2001) 11-50; John Hirst, *Convict Society and its Enemies,* Sydney: Allen and Unwin (1983) and John Hirst, "The Australian Experience: The Convict Colony," in Norval Morris and David J. Rothman (eds.), *The Oxford History of the Prison,* New York: Oxford University Press (1995).

45. Atkinson, *ibid.*, 89.

belief that the law should and could matter, that it should be respected by their rulers and that it should and could form the basis of challenge to these rulers. "A cluster of ideas known as the rule of law provided the major institutions, arguments, vocabulary and symbols with which the convicts forged the transformation."[46] Convicts fought battles for status and recognition in terms of their entitlements under the law, believed in the rule of law, insisted that the authorities should respect it, and demanded rights that they believed flowed from it. A great deal flowed from these beliefs. Following the terminology already introduced, the *scope* of the law reached both high and low, to the governor and to the convicts; convicts knew and insisted upon that; they were rather liberally granted legal rights; and they made use of them, often to good effect. When they won, it was because their opponents' hands were tied. They too, after all, had the same baggage in their heads. And even where they did not, the courts did, insisting on their independence under British law, and the subordination of the apparently autocratic governors to that same law.

A striking feature underpinning this story, for all its brutality, corruption, and harshness, is that convicts were conceived not only as "British subjects," as they were in law, but "subjects" in a much more robust sense of the word. There were things that could not be done to them, facilities that must be afforded to them, demands that they could make, which were listened to. They could use the law, not merely suffer it. They would undoubtedly have preferred not to be convicts, and they were often treated extremely harshly, but they could not complain that they were systematically treated in ways that denied their humanity or personhood.

All the more striking, then, is what happened at the hands of the same people, thinking the same thoughts, wielding the same law, to the indigenous inhabitants of Australia. For white settlers were never on their own here. Though their jurisprudence denied it, and treated Australia as *terra nullius*, in fact there were scores (maybe hundreds) of thousands of people and several hundred Aboriginal societies here when whites arrived. Yet the same processes that installed English law and the rule of law in a penal colony led to the wholesale dispossession of those people and decimation of their societies.

The plight of Australia's indigenes was so overdetermined that it is difficult to estimate the role of law in it, but it has surely been considerable. That of itself does not necessarily implicate the rule of law. We know that many legal systems are not rule of law systems, and that law itself is compatible with great iniquity. We know too of what Ernst Fraenkel called a "Dual State," dual for it includes both a "normative" and a "prerogative" component.[47] Nazi Germany

46. Neal, *ibid.*, 62.

47. Ernst Fraenkel, *The Dual State*, trans. E.A. Shils et al., New York: Oxford University Press (1941) xiii.

was his example, apartheid South Africa might be another, arguably some moments in Australian colonial (and other colonial) history also had a dual character. And so an easy way to exculpate the rule of law from this terrible story is to deny that it was tried: the Aborigines were simply denied it. And for at least the first half of the nineteenth century that was true. For much of that time, whatever the motives of governors, their means were inadequate to prevent what was going on at the frontiers, and what was going on was at times terrible. As Hobbes understood, protection from arbitrariness requires a government with a monopoly over the imposition of force, and in the early years of settlement in New South Wales there was no such government much beyond the limits of Sydney. Thus, on the relentlessly expanding frontier, restrictions on the use of force by settlers (and natives) were not enforced, and given the nature of white settlement, could not have been. Settlers were often isolated, frightened,[48] and, in the nature of things, on the make. And what they were intent on making, pastoral success, involved taking Aborigines' land, their water holes, killing their game as pests, and killing them, too, for a variety of reasons. This is precisely the sort of situation Hobbes envisaged, that stems from a truth often enough manifested and noted: *homo homini lupus*. Often nothing more highfalutin is necessary to explain it. In the nineteenth century, not always but often, it was as basic and shabby as that. Sometimes it was better, and not infrequently it was worse, helped along as it was by the weakness of restraints on the frontier, the superior power of the settlers, the fact that real interests were at stake, and beliefs that Aborigines were barbarian, not quite human, anyway nothing like us, and, by the late nineteenth century, doomed to die out.

By the middle of the century, however, the newly emerged colonies of Australia had won self-government and a measure of control. Sometimes, and particularly in Queensland, that was used for murderous purposes against Aborigines. More commonly, Aborigines came to be defined (on the basis of variable and often inconsistent classifications based on race) and dealt with under comprehensive special-purpose legislation that appointed "Protectors" with discretionary and unappealable powers over the minutest details of the lives of "aboriginal natives." Legally the latter had virtually nothing to protect them against the comprehensive powers of such men. That was true whether one interprets the purposes of such legislation as being for the sake of whites or of the Aborigines themselves. It was a thoroughgoing denial of the rule of law, sometimes imposed with the very best will in the world.

While this sad history suggests the rule of law was not applied to Aborigines, none of it necessarily makes the normative appeal or reach of the

48. The significance of fear in the frontier setting is emphasized by Henry Reynolds in *Frontier*, Sydney: Allen and Unwin (1996) 9-31, 44-50.

rule of law any less general. One could always say: if only the rule of law *had* been applied. And in many respects it would have been better if the government had been willing, and when willing, able to insist on the rule of law in encounters between whites and Aborigines, as plaintive Imperial directives kept demanding. At least there would have been restraint on power, some protection from fear, if the most powerful actors had been required to stay within legal bounds. But what of facilitation of cooperative encounters? By the 1830s, the official interpretation was settled and clear: Aborigines were British subjects, in principle protected by and able to make use of British law. However, if it is hard to see how Aborigines were or could have been protected by law in the circumstances I have sketched, it is even less clear how they could make use of it.

In the first stages of contact, this was not primarily or even significantly a result of the character of the formal law. With a few exceptions, law had yet to be devised specifically for Aborigines. The "law in the books" was generally that which applied to convicts. But contact brought out, in the most dramatic and extreme forms, the depth of those truisms of sociology of law that stress the distance between "law in books" and "law in action," or between official law and what Ehrlich and Petrażycki, respectively, call "living" or "intuitive" law. These distances exist in every society, however familiar and obedient to positive law. But some societies are not at all familiar with it, and among those who are, not all are obedient. In this connection, I would repeat the following observation, born of reflection on Eastern Europe, which is even more dramatically applicable of the Aboriginal experience:

> for the rule of law to *count*, rather than simply to be announced or decreed, people must *care* about what the law says—the rules themselves must be taken seriously, and the institutions must come to matter. They must enter into the psychological economy of everyday life—to bear both on calculations of likely official responses *and* on those many circumstances in which one's actions are very unlikely to come to any officials' attention at all. They must mesh with, rather than contradict or be irrelevant to the "intuitive law" of which Leon Petrażycki wrote, in terms of which people think about and organize their everyday lives. None of this can be simply decreed.[49]

Whatever the formal law was like, Aborigines did not and for a long time could not know it, or understand it. If Poles under Russian or Prussian or Austro-Hungarian rule throughout the nineteenth century, or under Communism in the twentieth, taking the law to be alien and imposed, were

49. "Institutional Optimism, Cultural Pessimism, and the Rule of Law," in Martin Krygier and Adam Czarnota (eds.), *The Rule of Law after Communism*, Dartmouth, England: Ashgate, (1999) 89-90.

reluctant to enlist the legal system and did not have much practice doing so, then early nineteenth-century Aborigines, assailed with the finest fruits of the common law tradition, were astronomically less well placed. And how could it have been otherwise? As Paul Hasluck, onetime historian and later minister for Aboriginal affairs, comments:

> These new British subjects did not know British law and they did not believe it was a good law, and even if they had known and believed, their situation and condition meant that the law was not accessible to them and that they were not amenable to it. They knew nothing of the process of sworn complaint, warrant, arrest, committal for trial, challenging the jury, pleading, legal defense, recovery of costs, suit for damages, summons for assault, evidence on oath, and so on. Those living in the bush did not know that it was wrong to resist arrest or hinder a policeman in the execution of his duty and they also frequently refused to stop when called upon to do so.[50]

The notion in such circumstances of Aborigines *using* the law makes little sense. That is dramatically true of criminal law, where the process was in the hands of whites, and it was even more true of civil law. For, as Hasluck reminds us, "in any civil relation...the move for redressing injury or maintaining a right rests with the wronged person."[51] It takes a great deal to imagine crowds of avid Aboriginal litigants in the early years of settlement. Still less can we imagine the Aborigines abiding by the far more important service that the rule of law is supposed to provide, in informing and supporting the relations of citizens who never go to court but act on understandings of the law in countless routine individual acts, accidents, and forms of cooperation in daily life. None of this "tacit knowledge" was or could quickly be available to the Aborigines upon which the penal colony had been inflicted. In the long meantime, at so many levels in so many ways, British law contradicted exactly that "living," "intuitive" law that legal sociology has shown to be fundamental to people's ordinary lives, and to the structures, roles, culture, and expectations that underpin them.

The rule of law, then, presupposes much to be effective and much to be good. In early contact with Aboriginal society, these presuppositions did not exist even where the will to adhere to it did. And as we have seen that often did not exist either. Most unsettling for my argument is that it is hard to see how a will more concerned to bring the rule of law could have done much to alter the tragedy that became the Aboriginal story in my country, and it is not clear that the entry of European law into Aboriginal societies could be

50. Paul Hasluck, *Black Australians* (1942), Melbourne: Melbourne University Press (1970), 123.

51. *Ibid.*, 147-48.

said by anyone to be an "unqualified human good." Indeed, in the context I have described, and even more in the light of the relative impotence of the imposed law for much of the century, the rule of law more likely served as what some of Thompson's critics have taken it more generally to be. It justified, mythologized, and may well have blinded the perpetrators to the horror of relationships of domination and exploitation out of which, systematically and unavoidably, there could be only one set of winners.

Today several of the milestones in the struggle of Aborigines for recognition and improvement of their condition have issued from the law and the depth of the rule of law in Australia. That is no small matter, but fearful damage has already been done, much of it according to law, and most of it, of course, law cannot undo. Perhaps all that can be said is that if invaders have to come, it is better when they bring the rule of law with them. But it is not always obviously that much better.

So my reflections on the rule of law end on a somber note. It still seems to me a "cultural achievement of universal significance," if only because the sources of threat and confusion throughout the world are so pervasive that a life without the rule of law, virtually anywhere today, is likely to be worse than a life with it. And in most cases, very much worse. But what "it" will turn out to be in any particular case is best known, perhaps only known, after the event, and, as the Aboriginal experience with one of the great purveyors of that achievement suggests, as human goods go it is at times somewhat qualified.

Chapter 12

Frank K. Upham*

The Illusory Promise of the Rule of Law

In this chapter I argue that the seemingly universal advocacy of the rule of law as an instrument for economic development is premised on a mistaken understanding of both law and its relationship to economic development. Rule of law advocates too often treat formal legal institutions as the only means by which developing societies may resolve disputes and regulate markets efficiently without the corruption and political intervention that have crippled economic growth in many parts of the developing world. In doing so, they fail to recognize that a successful legal system plays a deeply political role in its society and is dependent on particular political conditions to be effective. They assume that formal legal institutions are necessary elements for economic growth without realizing that there is little empirical evidence showing that such institutions and doctrines have contributed to economic growth in any way that can be generalized and applied to developing countries today.

Mainstream legal reformers observe the fact that developed countries invariably have some form of the rule of law and inductively conclude that the rule of law must have contributed to development. It is more likely that

* I would like to thank Owen Lefkon and Arun Thiruvengadam for their excellent research support and critical insight in the preparation of this chapter.

András Sajó (ed.), Human Rights with Modesty: The Problem of Universalism, *279-313.*

an effective formal legal system is a desirable result of economic and political development, rather than its cause. Nonetheless, the rule of law retains a strong allure for those interested in development, both the aspiring countries and well-intentioned development "practitioners." It is difficult to find anyone, whether in government, foundations, corporations, or universities, who does not favor encouraging the rule of law in virtually every country and society.

The rule of law appeals to two powerful strains in contemporary intellectual and political thought. First, it speaks to the desire for universal truths in a global world. It simplifies complex realities by transforming social and political behavior into legal categories, and it promises to make mutually comprehensible the processes and practices of societies as different as those of Nigeria and Nebraska.[1] Second, the rule of law appeals to our mistrust of politics and political action. It promises order without bureaucracy; governance without government; social choice without politics. Just as the invisible hand of the market produces wealth without intentional human agency, the black box of legal reasoning resolves social and economic disputes without moral judgment or political bias. In an age when politics and social engineering are reviled as wasteful and corrupt, the rule of law presents itself as the perfect complement for a free-market based view of development, offering to fix whatever problems the market fails to fix on its own.

At times, it seems that any issue, no matter how far removed from what we normally think of as the province of law, can be addressed profitably via legal reforms. Within months after September 11, 2001, and weeks after America's entrance into Kabul, American observers were calling on the Bush administration to focus on the rule of law. The *Baltimore Sun* editorialized in April 2002 that "Establishing the rule of law... must be the first priority in Afghanistan. Enduring stability and security can only be achieved under a widely accepted and viable legal and regulatory framework." Michael Ignatieff agreed, arguing in the *New York Times* that "helping the Afghans to rewrite the criminal and civil code and train a new generation of lawyers, prosecutors, and criminal investigators" was a necessary first step in Afghan reconstruction and a prerequisite to economic recovery. Raj Bhala, a law professor at George Washington University, argued that "There has to be a 'rule of law' culture in place" for reconstruction to succeed, and estimated that an effective legal system could be operational within three years.

The idea that training judges or rewriting laws could significantly help reverse the legacies of twenty-five years of civil war, religious zealotry, and political disintegration in the same amount of time that it takes an American law student to become a lawyer is perhaps the most bizarre example of exag-

1. For a discussion of how mapping played an analogous role in the formation of early states, *see* James Scott, *Seeing Like a State*, New Haven, Conn.: Yale University Press (1998).

gerated hopes for the rule of law, but it is only one of many. Senator Joseph Biden, former chair of the Senate Foreign Relations Committee, has identified the failure of the Chinese to develop the rule of law as "the one thing" that could disrupt U.S.-Chinese relations, while the U.S. government, the Ford Foundation, and others have launched an expensive campaign to engender the rule of law in China. Similarly, a major part of America's effort to help sub-Saharan Africa has been the African Growth Opportunities Act of 2001 ("AGOA"), which conditions trade liberalization for African exports on a showing that individual countries are establishing the rule of law. While examples are ubiquitous, the message remains the same: appropriate legal institutions have become a core component of any strategy to overcome the poverty, ethnic strife, corruption, economic decline, and political oppression that have plagued parts of the developing world for decades.

Such a heavy reliance on legal reform to accomplish political and economic goals is not harmless or risk free. While it is easiest to attack the expense of hiring legal consultants, flying them to exotic locales, and housing them in the proverbial five star hotels, this is not where the real danger lies. Although this cost is not *de minimus*, neither is it huge in the overall scheme of foreign assistance, and many programs incrementally improve professional competence. Even failed programs may build intellectual and personal bridges that remain beneficial after the fact. Of more concern is the likelihood that Western mischaracterization of the appropriate roles of law will be accepted by developing countries, thus leading to misallocation of domestic effort and attention, and perhaps most important, eventually to deep disillusionment with the potential of law. When the revision of the criminal code does not prevent warlords from creating havoc in Afghanistan and the training of Chinese judges by American law professors does not prevent the detention of political dissidents—or, perversely, enables judges to provide plausible legal reasons for their detention—political leaders on all sides may turn away from law completely and miss the modest role that law can play in political and economic development.

This chapter proceeds as follows. In part 1, I distill from the myriad uses of the term "rule of law" two versions that are most relevant and explain why neither is very useful to those interested in economic development. I explain that legal reformers have chosen a narrowly technical and highly formalistic definition of law that denies its political nature and raises false hopes of achieving political goals without the messiness of politics. In part 2, I review the role of law in economic and social development, in the United States and Japan. I argue that law has not played the role expected of it in these cases. I do not deny that law and legal institutions have been important in these countries. Rather, I argue that neither country can provide empirical justification for the types of legal models now being advocated as necessary for economic development in contemporary developing countries. Part 2 ends with the assertion that rule of law advocacy as presently practiced raises false hopes for developing countries and diverts the attention of the development community away from more productive approaches both to the creation of effective legal systems and to development itself. In part 3 I attempt to explain why the rule of law retains such a strong hold over the imaginations of contemporary policymakers despite its poor record in practice.

1. The Many Faces of the "Rule of Law"

The rhetoric of rule of law in the contemporary world is so vast and varied that it is difficult to summarize. For our purposes, it will suffice to establish two rough categories. What I call the normative version is the broad appeal to the rule of law as a political value and as an end in itself. This type of rule of law discourse is about the structure of democracy and the distribution of power within a society. It talks in terms of justice and is most frequently used in settings where specifics would spoil the mood if not destroy the political consensus to which the speaker aspires. Senator Biden's statement regarding China's legal failings is a prominent example. If we assume that part of his concern was the detention of Americans, it is likely that his concerns would be effectively dispelled if China simply stopped detaining Americans for politically sensitive offenses like espionage even when they had legally unimpeachable grounds for doing so. It is unlikely that American senators' admiration for legality would lead them to encourage the legally appropriate arrest and detention of American citizens spying for Taiwan or the United States. Conversely, even if China demonstrated that its detention of *falun gong* adherents was scrupulously consistent with properly promulgated statutes limiting activities of religious institutions and that all arrests had followed China's Code of Criminal Procedure, it would be unlikely to silence the call for rule of law. These examples show not that rule of law diplomacy is hypocritical or inconsistent, but that the rule of law in this normative sense is an expression of broad political values with virtually nothing useful to say about the institutional structure or operation of a legal system beyond the demand that it produce results congenial to the speaker's biases.

The second category of rule of law discourse I call the technical version. It is more narrowly focused on the details of legal institutions and provides more or less clear guidelines for legal reform projects. The rule of law in this technical sense is not an end in itself but is rather a prerequisite to economic growth. It requires, on the substantive side, clear property rights, efficiently enforced contracts, a market friendly framework of economic laws, guarantees of judicial independence, and active judicial restraint on political meddling in economic matters. On the institutional side, it calls for building courtrooms, training judges, instituting computer-based case management systems, etc. It talks in detail about the content of laws and regulations and about the appropriate structures and procedures for litigation, case management, legal reasoning, and dispute resolution. It is most often used by economists and bureaucrats, as well as the lawyers and law professors whom they hire.

At the extremes, these two types of rule of law discourse are quite distinct—statements like Biden's are political, not legal, and the introduction of computerized case management is technical, not political. Problems arise, however, when the two are confused, when we mistake political oratory for legal advice or when efficient judicial machinery is manipulated for political purposes. I discuss each category in turn.

1.1 The rule of law as political virtue

In his final convocation speech as dean of New York University School of Law, John Sexton, now president of NYU, defined the rule of law as "government by reason, not arbitrary power." Undoubtedly many other law school deans mentioned the rule of law in their graduation speeches, likely with no more elaboration of what it entails. E.P. Thompson in characterizing the rule of law as "an unqualified human good" was somewhat more specific, describing it as "the regulation and reconciliation of conflicts through...the elaboration of rules and procedures." He, too, found the core of the rule of law in its opposition to arbitrary power: "the imposing of effective inhibitions upon power and the defence of the citizen from power's all-intrusive claims."[2] Most likely the editors of the *Baltimore Sun* had something of this sort in mind when they opined that the rule of law was the path to "enduring stability and security" in Afghanistan.

Few would disagree. I doubt that even the biggest bugaboos of Western civilization—Saddam Hussein or Robert Mugabe, for example—would defend "arbitrary power" or admit to practicing it. They might even claim to use "rules and procedures." Presumably there are legal processes for recognizing marriages in Baghdad and for issuing drivers licenses in Harare, and they are likely followed most of the time. If the governments of Cuba or Vietnam made the same claim, their case would be even stronger—indeed, many would argue that communist regimes had too many "rules and procedures," but few of us would grant them the status of rule of law regimes.

The reason is simple but often missed: rule of law rhetoric like the above—when it has any meaning at all—refers to the distinct power of legal institu-

2. Edward P. Thompson, *Whigs and Hunters: The Origin of the Black Act*, New York: Pantheon Books (1975).

tions relative to other centers of political power. It is about the capacity of courts to check the power of a dictator, a ruling party, or concentrated private wealth. Although this rhetoric portrays the judicial role as legal and hence as "rules and procedures," it is not. It is political. It is not their faithfulness to clear rules, for example, that allow American courts successfully to integrate schools, name presidents, or dismantle (or not dismantle) Microsoft; it is their political legitimacy. It is not legal technique that leads courts to one decision or another when there is a lot at stake; it is political affiliation and preference. As Thompson so memorably demonstrated, elaborate processes and arcane jargon can be important, even indispensable to maintaining legitimacy, but it does not follow that they are sufficient or necessary to acquire it. Legitimacy is itself a political phenomenon and thus is acquired by politically acceptable actions, whether they are judicial opinions boldly proclaiming limits on executive or legislative power, reticent statements of judicial incapacity to decide political questions, or simply interminable delay. Outside of the legal academy, it rarely matters whether those actions are "legally" correct. What matters is whether they are popular over the long run with those who wield political power. This fact should not be reason for despair; all the public choice limitations and qualifications notwithstanding, in any regime where this type of rule of law system will have a chance of developing, the politically powerful will include the electorate, otherwise known as "the people."

In successful rule of law regimes, political power is diffused, with courts holding what power the other state institutions have lost. It is the opportunities for leverage that this fragmentation of power gives to the relatively weak that makes rule of law rhetoric so universally popular. In this broad sense the rule of law is for most people "an unqualified human good," as Thompson put it, that is just as valuable for developing countries as it is for developed ones. Indeed, the stable diffusion of power among state institutions may be an important measure of development. Even observers sympathetic to black Zimbabweans' desire for land would likely agree that all that country's citizens would have a better future had the Supreme Court been successful in preventing the brutality of recent land occupations there. Its failure was not a legal failure, however, but a political one. It did not occur because the judiciary discovered legal reasons that white farmers' land titles were invalid or because judges were not well trained or competent. In fact, the Zimbabwean judiciary was relatively respected for its technical expertise and competence. Conversely, had the court's initial attempts to oppose Mugabe been successful, it would not have been because of the white farmers' superior legal claim but because the court was able to back it up with its own political legitimacy. In this sense, the Zimbabwean events illustrate that rule of law rhetoric of this sort has little to do with law. Legal doctrine and expertise by themselves rarely trump political power; they must be part of a powerful political institution before these legal niceties matter.

Most legal assistance taken under the rule of law rubric ignores these political realities, probably for good reasons. How, after all, could a few million dollars and a series of workshops by foreign experts build a politically legitimate and powerful institution in a developing country? Given the colonial history of much of the developing world, just the mention of political goals in foreign assistance might well doom it to failure. Even if that were not true, it is highly unlikely that foreign experts could devise a workable scheme to transfer political power from existing institutions to ones newly created or rehabilitated in the Western image. Nor is it likely that existing political entities would allow the attempt. It was not the English common law inherited by the young United States that made *Marbury v. Madison*[3] possible, but the domestic context and the political skill of John Marshall. Otherwise most Anglophone African nations, which also inherited the common law, would have already developed the rule of law. "Nation building" of this type must be done domestically either directly by the politically powerful or with their acquiescence. They don't have to be happy about it. It is enough for them to see it as their only means to staying in power or for guaranteeing their wealth or status should they lose power.

Rule of law in this sense is almost always the result of domestic political compromise. This does not mean that foreign intervention or pressure in the form of Biden's threats or the AGOA's inducements cannot alter the political balance in a way that might lead to devolution of power to the courts. But practitioners of this rule of law diplomacy should be aware that they are playing a deeply political game and have little chance of controlling the result.

1.2 The rule of law as technical fix

Given this disconnect between rule of law rhetoric and political result, it is not surprising, therefore, that legal assistance programs focus on strengthening technical capacities and justify their existence and expense not in terms of political makeovers but in terms of economic growth. The various types of programs are mostly premised on a highly formalist conception of the legal process and commonly focus on legislative drafting or strengthening judicial capacity. While the former tend to enlist law professors who are experts in the area to be reformed, judicial reform programs are more varied. Some train judges and other court personnel by either bringing in Western lecturers or by sending the trainees to American law schools or other developed world legal institutions. Other programs provide equipment and focus on admin-

3. 5 U.S. 137 (1803).

istrative efficiency, for example, by computerizing the management of cases. The judicial programs share the goal of creating a judiciary that is honest, competent, and efficient; most also try to nurture political independence and neutrality, not primarily for normative political reasons but because independent courts are presumed to settle economic disputes effectively and be more willing to prevent political intrusion into the market. In sharp contrast to the normative version, this version of the rule of law ignores the judiciary's need for political power and concentrates instead on building its technical capacity. This "technical fix" vision sounds both desirable and possible, but before endorsing these programs, let's look at the elements of the rule of law to see if they are indeed as uncontroversial and attainable as they appear.

Issues in legislative drafting assistance. Legislative drafting would seem to have little potential for mischief. One might imagine that the worst that could happen is that the new statutes would be ignored, a situation resulting in little net harm beyond the direct costs of the drafting process. Unfortunately, the potential risks are greater than this scenario suggests. Legal rules provide opportunities to reallocate power and are thus rarely ignored by political actors. Laws are most obviously susceptible to manipulation at the drafting stage, but the risks hardly stop upon promulgation. Legal rules never unambiguously answer every issue, and complex areas like economic or environmental regulation are not an exception. Even artfully drafted statutes provide opportunities for further manipulation—in fact, much of American legal education focuses on such rule manipulation.

These problems multiply when foreign legal models are imported; they may become insuperable when not only the model but also the incentive comes from outside the domestic political environment. Laws are usually drafted to achieve specific goals and are premised on certain preexisting conditions. In the prototypical situation where democratically elected politicians draft the laws, one can assume that they are at least aware, if not responsive to, conditions in the country or among their constituents. The interests of their constituents may be overwhelmed by the wiles and incentives of lobbyists, their personal greed or ambition, or the necessities of political bargaining, but politicians are rarely ignorant of the social preconditions and political/pragmatic goals of the legislation they draft.

Foreign experts operate very differently. Although personal greed and ambition play a role here too—the U.S. government has sued the Harvard Institute for International Development and a Harvard professor for corruption in a contract to supply developmental advice to Russia[4]—foreign reformers at least hold the potential of being neutral in domestic political

4. Bruce Rubenstein, "Harvard Accused of Ignoring Russian Aid Scam: Academics Rigged Russian Market," *Corporate Legal Times* (Jan. 2001) 60, available on LexisNexis; "New

battles. Indeed, it is often this apparent neutrality that gives outsiders currency in the domestic political environment. Unfortunately, the allure of this theoretical possibility must be balanced against foreigners' inherent disadvantages. By definition, foreign legal experts are relatively ignorant of local conditions. Unless the local language happens to be a colonial one, they usually cannot speak or read it. Moreover, they are sometimes totally clueless about the particularities of the problems that they are meant to address. This is not a criticism of development practitioners; it is built into the system. Being both "foreign" and "expert," they are holders of specialized knowledge gained by experience and learning in a technical field rather than in a particular society or economy. On occasion, an expert may have developed local knowledge from years of field experience, but it would pervert the purpose of external legal assistance to select advisors primarily on the basis of their time in-country or ability to speak indigenous languages. The fundamental goal of rule of law assistance is to bring to developing countries the legal expertise of the West, which means that in most instances the carriers of the expertise are dependent on whomever they work with in-country and whoever can tutor them before they leave or between trips.

Who then should fill this "native informant" role? A reliance on local politicians and/or business people with firsthand knowledge and experience with the encountered problems would at least address the problem of ignorance. The problem of course is that local politicians or economic figures will have stakes in the outcome of legal reform, and thus have strong incentives to steer the process according to their own interests. While this inclination can be balanced by others' similar ambitions in the process of ordinary domestic legislation, it is virtually impossible for foreign experts to find a balance, to know whom to trust for a neutral perspective (no one, most likely), or how to discount individuals' biases. Another possibility is turning to local experts, technicians with backgrounds very much like those of the foreign experts themselves. Unfortunately, to the degree that technical proficiency tempers local political biases, it threatens to reintroduce the local knowledge problem. The local economists, law professors, or elite junior bureaucrats often have been educated in the developed world, thus sharing the assumptions and perspectives of the foreigners, and lacking the firsthand experience with the issues, politics, and personalities relevant to legal drafting in the local context. Although at least marginally more able to discern local elites' motivations and biases, they are also correspondingly more likely to share them.

False Claims Suit Targets Harvard," 14, 7 *Government Contract Litigations Reporter* (26 Oct. 2000) 6, available on LexisNexis.

None of these obstacles means that foreign reformers cannot contribute substantially and successfully to developing country legislation. There are myriad instances of experts playing precisely this role with sensitivity and sophistication. My point is simply that an effective program of external legal assistance is difficult, time-consuming, and relatively expensive, none of which any candid rule of law practitioner would deny. What may be less obvious, at least to casual observers, is that the most important element may not be getting it technically right according to the imported Western model, but structuring the domestic team to mimic the political process of legislation to the greatest degree possible. Unfortunately, the contemporary bias against all things political and the consequent tendency to portray legal assistance as the faithful servant to an apolitical and neutral market militate against openly embracing the political reality of legislation. Without political acceptability, however, any legislation is doomed.

Issues in judicial reform assistance. Let's assume for the moment that the problems enumerated above have been solved and that a team of international and local experts has cooperated with domestic political forces to draft an appropriate statute for local conditions. There remains the question whether the judiciary can and will interpret and enforce the statute in a manner that will carry out its drafters' intentions. Here again we encounter in rule of law advocacy what appear to be truisms about effective judiciaries only to discover that things are not so simple as they initially seem.

The most prominent example is the quest for a politically neutral and independent judiciary. The rhetoric of the World Bank, perhaps the most sophisticated practitioner of rule of law assistance, illustrates the ideal. In a memorandum addressing the Bank's desire to improve the economic performance of borrowing nations, then General Counsel Ibrahim F. I. Shihata argued that good "governance" should be a core criterion for lending to developing countries, and further, that governance was dependent on the rule of law, which he defined at one point as a "system based on abstract *rules* which are actually applied and on functioning *institutions* which ensure the appropriate application of such rules" (emphases in original). Such a system, Shihata claimed, provides a legal foundation for social stability and economic growth and should be a prerequisite for the effective use of World Bank assistance and, by implication, all legal reform efforts:

> Reform cannot be effective in the absence of a system which translates them into workable rules and makes sure they are complied with. Such a system assumes that: a) there is a set of rules which are known in advance, b) such rules are actually in force, c) mechanisms exist to ensure the proper application of the rules and to allow for departure from them as needed according to established procedures, d) conflicts in the application of the rules can

be resolved through binding decisions of an independent judicial or arbitral body and e) there are known procedures for amending the rules when they no longer serve their purpose.[5]

Shihata went on to state that in the absence of such a system the fates of both individuals and enterprises will be left "to the whims of the ruling individual or clique" and that only such a system of predictable rules and due process can provide the "general social discipline" that makes economic reform possible.

Such sentiments are intoxicating. The attraction of the ideal of uniform rules impartially applied is apparent to any parent with more than one child and is undiminished when it comes to the allocation of resources within an economy. Initial normative appeal should not, however, preclude analysis. Nor does it mean that the ideal is either possible or desirable in all circumstances. Shihata's formalistic model is arguably neither, and many legal reform practitioners have indicated deep skepticism on both counts. Professional doubt has not, however, led to second thoughts among policymakers.

The sources of the strong appeal and tenacity of rule of law rhetoric will be addressed in part 3, but before we reach that point, let's look briefly at the way legal institutions have worked in two developed countries: the United States and Japan. We find that neither country has even tried to create a formalistic and apolitical judiciary, and for very good reasons.

2. Law in Action and Inaction

2.1 The United States

A Politicized Judiciary. The American judiciary is a good place to begin. The political nature of the federal judiciary is a major issue in every national election, and most state judges are elected on partisan platforms. As a result, political affiliation is perhaps the single most important attribute for a lawyer aspiring to a judicial position in the United States. Moreover, the appointment of judges is a constant political issue in Washington; in the last decade it has

5. Ibrahim F. I. Shihata, "The World Bank and 'Governance' Issues in Its Borrowing Members," in Franziska Tschofen and Antonio R. Parra (eds.), *The World Bank in a Changing World*, Dordrecht: Martinus Nijhoff (1991) 85. For similar ideas, see Edgardo Boeninger, "Governance and Development: Issues and Constraints," Pierre Landell-Mills and Ismaïl Serageldin, "Governance and the External Factor," Denis-Constant Martin, "The Cultural Dimensions of Governance," in *Proceedings of the World Bank Annual Conference on Development Economics, 1993*, Washington, D.C.: World Bank (1994). See also Clive S. Gray, "Reform of the Legal, Regulatory, and Judicial Environment: What Importance for Development Strategy?", Development Discussion Paper No. 403, Cambridge, Mass.: Harvard Institute for International Development, Harvard University (Sept. 1991).

most dramatically taken the form of whether the Senate Judiciary Committee will have hearings on nominees of a president whose party is the minority in the Senate. The former Democratic chairman of the committee is the same Senator Biden who urged China to build the rule of law and who supported the AGOA and its requirement that African nations create the rule of law. It is highly unlikely that Mr. Biden has in mind African or Chinese rulers handpicking judges on the basis of whether they will serve partisan interests, despite the fact that this would be closer to his own American reality than the conventional interpretation of such remarks. A few examples will illustrate.

The case of Rose Bird, in which the Chief Justice of the California Supreme Court was removed from office by California voters for her stubborn opposition to the death penalty, is one of the best known instances of a judge being punished for fidelity to her vision of the law. More typical, however, is the recent transformation of the Texas judiciary at the hands of competing commercial interests.[6] In the early 1980s, wealthy trial lawyers succeeded in transforming the historically pro-business Texas Supreme Court into an "all-Democratic, lawsuit-friendly court that began upholding enormous jury verdicts against corporate and medical defendants." In response, corporations and doctors struck back and reversed the court's politics, again through partisan elections, so that by the mid-1990s the winning record of defendants before the court had risen from 40 to 83 per cent. By 2000, with a governor running for president as a "compassionate conservative" using his interim appointment powers to portray a picture of moderation, the pendulum had swung back once again toward the center.

Parties to such controversies often claim that their position is faithful to the correct interpretation of the law and that their opponents' position is not legally correct but, on the contrary, is a politically motivated distortion of the law. What is striking about these arguments—and vital to understanding the psychological hold of the rule of law ideology—is the deep conviction of participants on both sides that their side alone is being faithful to the letter of the law and that the other side, most charitably put, is mistaken. Unfortunately, the sincere belief in these claims does not make them true.

But it is not the number of judges who lose their jobs that is important. The vast majority of elected judges are reelected, often without significant opposition. That phenomenon does not mean that judicial elections are apolitical any more than the ease of reelection for incumbents in the U.S. House of Representatives or state legislatures means that these positions are apolitical.

6. Jim Yardley, "Bush's Choices for Court Seen as Moderates," *New York Times* (9 July 2000) A6. Also representative are William Glaberson, "Fierce Campaigns Signal a New Era for State Courts," *New York Times* (5 June 2000) A1; and Kevin Sack, "Judge Trades on Renown in Race," *New York Times* (5 June 2000) A22.

What is important is the numbers who have remained in their positions either because the political position that got them elected has remained the dominant position or because they have bowed to political expediency when their views lost electoral support. This number would give us a more accurate view of the extent of direct political influence on United States judges. Unfortunately, this number is uncountable, but it may be the vast majority of state judges.

Moving from the state to the federal judiciary, the picture becomes more complex, but fundamentally similar. Federal judges are appointed, not elected. They serve for life, subject only to impeachment for egregious misbehavior; the story of the politically conservative judge becoming a liberal on the bench (or the reverse) is a warhorse of American platitudes about the rule of law. Such inspiring stories of life tenure giving judges the security to grow in their jobs or to adhere to principle or their consciences should not blind us to reality. The appointment process is overwhelmingly political, and federal judges rarely experience substantial conversions. It would be difficult to imagine it otherwise, since they are appointed largely in their fifties after decades of professional and political activity. Of course, the ultimate proof of the infrequency of judicial bench conversions is the role of judicial appointments in federal politics, both during presidential elections and in the relationship between the president, who nominates federal judges, and the Senate, which must confirm them. If judicial behavior was unpredictable, judicial appointments would not loom so large in political campaigns.

Less well known than the open political behavior of those appointing judges are the political activities of sitting American judges. Judge Richard Posner of the Court of Appeals for the Seventh Circuit, for example, published a book arguing for the prosecution of President Clinton for perjury in the Monica Lewinsky affair while that very issue was being considered by the Office of Independent Counsel. While controversial, this action was not generally criticized as crossing the bounds of judicial propriety. Indeed, after the remarkable case of *Bush v. Gore* that decided the 2000 presidential election, several Supreme Court justices took to the road to justify and explain the court's action.

Less flamboyant, but more common, is the commitment of sitting judges to the implementation of a particular political philosophy in the legal system and through the courts. While usually done quietly and perhaps subconsciously, one aspect of this approach to judging—the cultivation of young lawyers who share your philosophy—is well illustrated by the following published dialogue between Judge Alex Kozinski of the Court of Appeals for the Ninth Circuit and his clerk, Fred Bernstein:[7]

7. Alex Kozinski and Fred Bernstein, "Clerkship Politics," 2, 1 *The Green Bag* (Autumn 1998) 57-64. Although it might be said that the publication of this dialogue is evidence of the rarity of its subject, i.e., of the open desire of judges to support young lawyers with simi-

Kozinski: The reality is that law schools are pumping out liberals. Not every law school, obviously, but the overwhelming number of students at the top-notch schools tend to be liberal. I can't afford to cross liberals off my list, the way Judge Reinhardt crosses conservatives off his.

Bernstein: Does he?

Kozinski: Judge Reinhardt says, "I'm not interested in hiring conservatives. I'm not even interested in hiring people who are moderately liberal. I'm only interested in hiring committed liberals, who are going to spend their careers promoting liberal causes. I don't train corporate lawyers." That's a paraphrase, but it's accurate.

Bernstein: How do you feel about that?

Kozinski: He justly sees himself as providing a unique opportunity to advance the careers of young lawyers. And I feel the same way. I think I owe an extra measure of consideration to conservative and libertarian law students. First of all, I feel an obligation to train conservative and libertarian lawyers. There are a lot of liberal judges out there, not as many conservatives and libertarians. Second, there are a lot of cases, and having a clerk who basically agrees with me makes for an easier year. In my heart of hearts, I know it's a good thing to have dissent in chambers, but sometimes I'd just as soon have an easier year.[8]

Nowhere in the dialogue is there any sense that either participant fears that the use of a judicial position to "advance the careers of young lawyers" with certain political opinions would be considered illegitimate. Indeed, at one point Judge Kozinski remarks that although doing so may sometimes be hard, "following the law is good practice."[9] So, one must presume that Kozinski considers the politicization of legal decisions either desirable or unavoidable whenever the cases demand or allow judicial interpretation. In either case, he would be keeping company with the vast majority of American social scientists, if not law professors, who long ago rejected the possibility, if not desirability, of the rule of law ideology advocated by Shihata and the World Bank. The belief that one's political beliefs affect one's interpretation of the law, and hence judicial decisions, is not limited, therefore, to politicians running for office and those voting for them; the judges themselves recognize it as well.

---

lar political sympathies, *The Green Bag* is not an academic journal and the subject is not treated as controversial. It is treated as entertaining and of interest to potential clerks, especially liberal ones facing the prospect of serving conservative judges.

8. *Ibid.*, 58, emphasis added.

9. *Ibid.*, 61.

The result is apparent in judges' behavior on the bench. Despite unending proclamations of fidelity to precedent, political neutrality, judicial restraint, and other legal virtues, American judges overwhelmingly follow their political preferences when the opportunity presents itself.[10] As mentioned above, the most powerful evidence of this fact is the amount of attention given to judicial appointments in presidential campaigns and Senate confirmation hearings, but more direct examination of judicial behavior bears out this common sense observation. A 1993 study by social scientists Segal and Spaeth on the implementation of judicial restraint by Supreme Court justices between 1953 and 1989 can serve as an example.[11] The authors studied the voting patterns of justices on the Warren, Burger, and Rehnquist courts in cases involving labor rights, civil liberties, federalism, and economic regulation. They then compared them with the justices' professed fidelity to judicial restraint. The result was that justices, whether liberal or conservative, were only restrained when it suited their preexisting political preferences. Otherwise, they found a reason to overcome their devotion to restraint. In a testament to the power of the rule of law myth, one of the worst "offenders" was Justice Felix Frankfurter, an icon of judicial restraint in the eyes of generations of law professors and students.[12]

Structured irrationality. It is not just the politicization of the judiciary that contradicts the formalist model. Four fundamental aspects of the structure of the American legal system demonstrate that the World Bank version of the rule of law has almost no grounding in the legal system on which most observers believe it to be based. First, federalism guarantees, indeed celebrates, national inconsistencies in legal rules and results. Each state enjoys its own legislative and judicial sovereignty, limited only by the supremacy clause of the federal Constitution. As a result, many laws governing commercial or financial activity are state laws and vary significantly among the fifty-one jurisdictions. Model codes like the Uniform Commercial Code substantially reduce the disparities in many areas, but do not eliminate them. Nor do they touch the procedural and institutional differences that make "forum shop-

10. Richard L. Revesz, "Environmental Regulation, Ideology and the D.C. Circuit" 83 *Vanderbilt Law Review* (1997) 1717- 1772.

11. Jeffrey A. Segal and Harold J. Spaeth, *The Supreme Court and the Attitudinal Mode*, Cambridge: Cambridge University Press (1993). See also Jonathan D. Casper, "The Supreme Court and National Policy Making," 70 *American Political Science Review* (1976) 50-63; and Robert Dahl, "Decision-Making in a Democracy: The Supreme Court as National Policy-Maker," 6 *Journal of Public Law* (1957) 279-295.

12. Segal and Spaeth, *ibid.*, 316-319. Segal and Spaeth discovered a number of other interesting surprises. For example, despite the rhetoric of state sovereignty and federalism, justices were less deferential to state government decisions than to those of the federal government. *Ibid.*, 311.

ping" an integral part of much commercial and products liability litigation. It is not, for example, a coincidence that the vast majority of large American corporations are incorporated under the laws of Delaware. Delaware has triumphed in the interstate competition to attract corporate headquarters because it created a legal regime that most corporations have found sufficiently different and more attractive than those found in their states of origin to justify the cost and inconvenience of incorporating in a state distant from their places of business. Far from being condemned by scholars or politicians, this interstate competition is valued as creating a series of jurisdictional laboratories, on the one hand, and deterring states from stifling economic activity by creating legal regimes less favorable to corporations on the other.

The second structural aspect of the United States legal system that deviates substantially from the idealized technical view of rule of law is the jury system. As with federalism, there are myriad rationales for a jury system, but fidelity to the rule of law is not one. Whether one defines the rule of law as the rational application of rules to facts or, more abstractly, as the converse of "rule by men," juries simply do not fit. It is true that juries are theoretically limited to deciding questions of fact and are generally prohibited from relying on their own interpretation of legal rules. However, even if the distinction between law and fact were clear—and dozens of scholarly careers have been made disputing that point—many juries do not even understand the law that they are to apply. This misunderstanding has nothing to do with intelligence or good-will. It is an intentional part of the system. Lawyers spend three years of postgraduate education learning the techniques necessary to analyze, interpret, and apply legal rules in a professionally acceptable manner. Judges usually have spent decades honing these skills. To expect a jury to understand legal rules with the same depth just because they are patiently explained by a judge borders on the fantastic. A jury may well have a good intuitive understanding of the judge's instructions, and hence a good common sense handle on the rules, but it is imperative to note than a common sense understanding of the law is a far cry from what the rule of law ideal requires. Common sense, community norms, customary practices, and other systems of informal norms cannot provide a sound basis for the rule of law, however defined. Indeed, the supposedly "common sense" decision-making of the village elder or neighborhood boss is precisely the image against which the rule of law is most frequently contrasted. To argue for a common sense application of the law is to argue against the rule of law in its technical sense.

The third structural aspect of the American legal system that leads to deviations from Shihata's rule of law ideal is its system of civil procedure and, specifically, its adversarial basis. Here, two aspects deviate from fidelity to rules: the lawyers' obligations to their clients and the passive role of the judges. Ethical rules require lawyers to represent their clients zealously, to keep virtually all information received from clients confidential, including information of illegal acts, to work to discredit the opposing party's evidence regardless of its truth, and, perhaps summing up the result of all the other duties, to give their primary loyalty to their client, not to truth or law.

As with federalism and juries, there are powerful arguments for requiring attorneys to give their primary loyalty to their clients. Many of these, however, relate to political theory, rather than a conception of the rule of law as an accurate mechanism for uniformly applying rules to facts. It is true that many attorneys and law professors defend adversarial procedures by arguing that zealous advocacy by two equally talented partisans is the best path to truth. Even if one accepts this position in theory, the social reality is that opposing sides are rarely represented by equally talented lawyers with equal resources. All too often one side has vastly more talent and money than the other, so much so that the weaker party is not likely even to bring the matter to litigation, much less win if it did.

One might expect that, where presented with such an unequal playing field, the judge would have an obligation to step in to correct the imbalance. This, however, is not the case; the common law judge's role is more akin to a referee than to a guarantor of rule-based justice. She is not ethically required to redress inequalities of resources, talent, or dedication that threaten to lead to inaccuracy or injustice. Nor must she structure the trial so that truth wills out, or prevent an advocate from misleading the jury with a deceptive cross-examination that remains within the bounds of legitimate zealousness. Her role is to create a space where the opposing lawyers can compete. Admittedly, lawyers compete within boundaries provided by rules, but their primary obligations are to their clients, not to the law. Then, at the end of this unevenly matched competition, the judge turns the result over to a group of citizens whose legal education is usually limited to television shows.[13]

A final anomaly of the U.S. legal system as an exemplar of the rule of law ideal is the government's extreme reluctance to make the law accessible to people with little or no means.[14] Perhaps the most fundamental norm of

---

13. The reader should not take from this comment any bias against television dramas. As indicated in the text, the television version of law may have a great deal more to do with common concepts of the rule of law than does the professional version.

14. I am referring here to civil cases only. Legal representation is provided to criminal defendants, although with varying degrees of success. Civil cases are of more direct interest to the present topic, since it is largely civil law that shapes the economy and on which economic actors rely to provide the framework for their activities. For a comparison of United States provision of civil legal services with those of European countries, see: 5 the *Maryland Journal of Contemporary Legal Issues*, 2 (1994) Symposium Issue. Statistics in this chapter are drawn from Earl Johnson, Jr., "Toward Equal Justice: Where the United States Stands Two Decades Later" at page 199 of the same issue.

rule of law ideology is the uniform application of the law, without which the universality of norms means little. Society will not enjoy the benefits of the rule of law if the rules are not enforced evenhandedly or where one side to a dispute cannot bring the matter to the attention of the law due to a lack of resources. Despite the simplicity of this concept, American governments have never devoted even a fraction of the resources necessary to ensure that poor people have significant access to the courts. The United States, for example, spent approximately one-ninth as much per capita on civil legal services for lower income persons as England.[15] The implication is that the uniform application of law is not an important enough goal on which to spend significant resources, a policy judgment that seems unlikely if Americans were as convinced as the World Bank or the State Department that the rule of law is indispensable to economic growth or stability.

Such a great deviation from the rule of law is neither a failure of execution, nor the inevitable falling short of an ideal. On the contrary, it results from the conscious choice to subordinate fidelity to rules to other institutional goals or political values. First, as for the substance of legal rules, the interstate competition and the freedom to experiment afforded by federalism are preferred to universality. Second, as for the judiciary, democratic control via the election or political appointment of judges with broad social experience virtually guarantees a politically active judiciary. Third, in the realm of process and procedure, the drama of the lawyer as gunslinger and the democratic symbolism of the jury are chosen despite the knowledge that they will substantially impair, if not destroy, uniformity and consistency even within a single jurisdiction. And finally, the provision of adequate or even minimal access to justice for the majority of individuals is simply not a powerful political issue.

A legitimately politicized institution. The foregoing is intended to convince the reader that the American legal system is a thoroughly and intentionally politicized institution. It is emphatically not intended to portray the legal system as illegitimate, ineffective, or undeserving of political or intellectual support. It is important in this context to remember several aspects about politics. First, politics and politicization are not equivalent to corruption. Second, politics is the life blood of all regimes, especially democratic ones. Unfortunately, observers within the rule of law movement tend to equate politics with corruption. In the black-and-white world of rule of law advocacy, law and judging are clean, procedurally transparent, and stable; politics is dirty, procedurally opaque, and chaotic. Consequently, the sins of corrupt

15. The comparisons with some of the other north Atlantic societies were better, but the United States was still outspent by a factor of 2.5:1 by France and Germany, the next lowest two countries on the list of per capita expense. Johnson, Jr., *op. cit.*, note 14, 212. On the other hand, Japan through the 1990s spent even less than the United States.

judges in developing countries and elsewhere are conceived of as the result of political interference, and an "independent judiciary" is defined as one free of any political influence without any consideration of whether such a judiciary is possible or advisable. Instead of trying to depoliticize the judiciary, international financial institutions and other purveyors of the rule of law ideology should focus on the judiciary's legitimacy and effectiveness, not its political purity.

The question then becomes not whether courts play a political role but how that role is structured and managed. In the United States it is handled very well. Politics in the American judiciary has not led to the "telephone justice" of Russia, where the judge changes her mind at the order of a politician, or the "local protectionism" of the People's Republic of China, where the courts favor local enterprises because the local governments control their budgets. American justice is a deeply institutionalized form of politics that operates over relatively long timespans, either the terms of elected state judges or the political cycles of presidentially appointed federal ones. More fundamentally, it operates within a very narrow political spectrum. The difference between Democrats and Republicans is tiny compared to the differences among political interests in most developing countries. Moreover, judges are likely to be moderates within their parties. In most American jurisdictions, it is also true that parties rotate in power so that the judiciary is not totally dominated by one party or one political view. While this mix of political preferences on the bench makes the political dimension of decisions more apparent in controversial cases like *Bush v. Gore*, it probably has the long-term effect of moderating political swings within the law.

Important consequences follow from political stability. Because judges' political preferences are concentrated at the middle of the political spectrum, their socialization to their roles as judges, although superficial compared to civil law countries like Japan, is more successful in overcoming personal preferences than it would be if political differences among them or within society were more dramatic. Equally important, most cases will not pose issues that appear political to most judges. As opposed to persons at more extreme ends of the political spectrum, judges accept the legitimacy of both positions in the vast majority of cases brought before them. The result is stable doctrine that appears like the rule of law but owes more to the political stability of the United States than to the political independence of the American judiciary.

The difference between American judges, on the one hand, and Russian or Chinese judges, on the other, is thus more complicated than might first appear. If the "telephone justice" of Russia is motivated by a financial interest in one of the litigants' success, the issue is one of corruption and distinct from questions of the independence of the judiciary, politics, or the rule of law. A corrupt judge who affirms the decision of a corrupt bureaucrat is more like a criminal than he is like an honest judge. If, however, the judge decides for one litigant over the other because she is convinced that that decision is better for society and will strengthen her political allies, then the comparison with American judges becomes more a matter of degree and institutional style than one of principle. Similarly, if Chinese judges decide for a local litigant in order to retain their budget allocation or get desirable housing, this is corruption; as such, it is the equivalent of a bureaucrat denying a license because the licensee would compete with local industry. If, on the other hand, the conference of judges within the particular court discuss the case and decide that one result is more consistent with the guidelines set out by the National Peoples Congress as interpreted by the Chinese Communist Party, then we again have an institutionalized politics that is structurally comparable to American courts and particularly to appellate courts where negotiated collegial decisions are the norm and where political preferences are arguably clearer than at the trial level.

The foregoing discussion may seem both shocking and wildly implausible. How could the Russian or Chinese judiciaries be compared to the American? I agree that the American legal system is incomparably better, but the reason is not that the American judiciary is independent of politics and the Chinese and Russians are enmeshed in it. American courts are better because they are largely honest and because American politics is better. Chinese and Russian judges are much more likely to be corrupt, to be part of corrupt institutions, and to be so poorly paid and trained that resisting corruption simply does not make practical sense. The politicization of the American judiciary is not generally considered a problem because the political processes by which judges are chosen and removed are thoroughly democratic. The National Peoples Congress and the Chinese Communist Party are decidedly not democratic. Nor are they generally considered to be free of corruption. The distinction, therefore, is not the apolitical character of judges, but the democratic quality of the politics within which they operate. While this distinction may make little difference to a politically naïve and unconnected litigant—as most foreign enterprises or financial institutions are likely to be—it makes a great deal of difference to those wishing to help China or Russia build an effective judiciary.

Hard cases: law, politics, and economic growth. At this point, it may be useful to return briefly to an implicit aspect of rule of law discourse: the conviction that politics is bad for economic growth and a formalistic rule of law good. The argument is that the vigorous and unyielding enforcement of legal rights, especially property rights, is indispensable to growth because it creates predictability in the legal process, and that politics is antithetical to it precisely because politics destroys that predictability. Although virtually a mantra in development circles, the reality is a great deal more complex. Economic growth disrupts societies, and economic growth driven by technological change—which would certainly be the case for most growth in contemporary developing countries—invariably requires deep changes in economic, social, and physical structures. Recognizing this, the role of the legal system becomes far more complicated than that of simply protecting rights; it becomes the mediation and justification of fundamental and often wrenching change that often produces, at least in the short run, as many losers as winners.

A digression to a nineteenth-century Pennsylvanian fishpond will illustrate both the problem and one plausible judicial role. Mrs. Sanderson had a riparian lot that she used commercially for both fish and ice. After she had bought and improved the lot, a coal company opened a mine upstream, eventually polluting the fishpond rendering it useless. Pennsylvania's prior case law considered the "natural flow" of water a property right, that is, the law gave Mrs. Sanderson the right to an injunction against the further polluting of the stream. The Pennsylvania Supreme Court, in a marathon of judicial waffling requiring three separate judgments, eventually decided that the law could not possibly mean what it said and rejected her suit without even granting her damages. No matter how clear the right, the court could not or would not bring coal mining to a halt in favor of fishponds.

Mrs. Sanderson's fate is typical of what happened to agrarian interests across America in the nineteenth century as courts had to choose between new and old industries. In the face of technological change, the courts could either enforce established property rights as exemplified by Mrs. Sanderson's right to the natural flow of a stream, or they could destroy those rights in favor of what must have appeared to be the greater good of mining and industry. The rhetoric and prescriptions of today's rule of law advocates would argue for an injunction against the coal mine. This would mean that the mine would have to buy out the injunctive rights of every downstream owner, a task that would have been economically efficient in terms of market theory but almost certainly impossible to achieve in practice. On the other hand, to rule against Sanderson, as the Pennsylvania Supreme Court did, would mean not only a radical departure from the formalist ideal of a law of rules, but also the deliberate embrace of instability and opacity in law, instability because the decision reversed settled doctrine, opacity because an intellectually dishonest judicial opinion is far from the transparency considered necessary for growth. Given the consequences, one wonders whether the rule of law advocates, from Ibrahim Shihata to the senators who voted for the African Growth and Opportunities Act, would really prefer stability and predictability.

Of course, one could argue that the nineteenth century was an exceptional time, that technology does not change substantially at frequent intervals, and that what really matters is a highly competent, independent judiciary for the majority of times. Even if, the argument might go, it is occasionally necessary to change the law judicially as in *Sanderson*, such decisions should be recognized as exceptional, and all efforts should be made to ensure that the great majority of disputes will be decided according to established rules. It follows that, if necessary, resources should be diverted from other productive activities to building that rule of law. Unfortunately, this argument has two difficulties for developing countries. First, how are judges, especially the politically insulated judges of the rule of law model, to recognize those few exceptional cases? Second, the exception is likely to be the rule for the short term in developing countries, that is, judges are likely to encounter this type of case frequently because their economies are likely to face technological changes of precisely the *Sanderson* sort. It was, after all, economic growth that precipitated the *Sanderson* dilemma. To insist on developing countries installing a legal system that would have decided for Mrs. Sanderson on the ground of fidelity to law may be attractive in some abstract rule of law fashion, but it would be the height of folly if it prevented the very growth that today's rule of law advocates see as the eventual goal of development.

Paradoxically if developing countries do not grow, or if growth were somehow to take place without any significant technological or structural changes, the rule of law looks much more attractive. Judges can follow the dictates of the doctrine without any worry that they will be thwarting beneficial developments. But even here where we postulate social and economic stability, the rule of law, when examined closely, loses much of its luster, at least when one remembers that a formal rule of law-type legal system does not come cheaply. This is because in stable times, when the political interests and economic structures remain more or less unchanging, it may not be necessary to create an elaborate system of professional jurists. Decisions can be made by bureaucrats or police, village or ward political committees, private commercial associations, formal or informal mediators, and an unlimited variety of other lay persons and organizations. One need not have three to four years of formal legal education, maybe an LL.M. from Oxford or NYU, a year of articles or apprenticeship with a law firm, and a staff of court officers to apply stable rules to disputes occurring within stable societies. It is exactly when norms, political interests, or markets change that specially trained and socialized judges with a professional jargon and backed up by elaborate institutions are needed. But they are needed, I argue, not to enforce the law in the "rule of law, not men" sense, but because they have the practical wisdom to recognize the need to change the rules and the political legitimacy to get away with doing so.

2.2 Japan

One would think that postwar Japan would be an obvious model for the rule of law movement. It was the first non-Western economy to develop; it did so relatively quickly; and it did so under a democratic regime. To my knowledge, however, legal reformers seldom consult the Japanese experience. A possible reason is lack of knowledge about Japan, but a more likely explanation is the institutional structure of the movement, particularly its fragmentation into national factions. The U.S. State Department is not likely to let a contract to disseminate the Japanese model. Perhaps most important, however, is the general sense, often encouraged by the Japanese themselves, that Japan is culturally unique and that its experience is thus of little practical use to others. Closely related is the belief that consulting Japan's legal experience would be worthless because Japanese life is hardly affected by law, because law is disfavored as a means of dispute resolution, and because the Japanese economy is ruled by powerful bureaucrats unhindered by legal restrictions.

It is true that law has played a less visible role in Japan than in the United States, but it has not been for the assumed cultural reasons. Much of this conventional wisdom is either exaggerated or simplistic,[16] and I will try briefly to correct some of these misunderstandings in the next section. My purpose in this chapter, however, is not to argue that Japan should be a model for legal development. Japan's small, politically insulated, and elite judiciary would seem of more relevance to most developing countries than that of the United States, but to advocate that Japan should become a model for contemporary developing countries would be beyond the scope of this article. My primary point here is that the Japanese experience stands, as does the American, in sharp contrast to the assumptions of the rule of law ideology.

I attempt to make two main points. First, the Japanese developed an economic and political system that kept the formal legal system out of the economic policymaking process to a much greater extent than in the United States. Japan chose to isolate the judiciary from major issues despite having a judiciary much closer to the rule of law ideal than the deeply involved judiciary of the United States. Second, for the settlement of individual disputes as opposed to the development of policy, Japan developed a broad system of informal mechanisms to keep most disputes out of the courts altogether. It is the success of this system of informal alternatives, rather than cultural antipathy to law, that has kept the legal system in the background and given

16. It is also outdated, more representative of the first three decades of the postwar period than of the last two, but since we are concerned primarily with Japan's period of high growth, the outdated nature of these assertions is largely irrelevant to us.

empirical weight to the rhetoric that Japanese culture does not support legal action.[17]

The incredible shrinking legal system. In the Middle Ages, when the English were still throwing litigants in rivers to see if they would float, Japan had developed a legal system to adjudicate competing land claims that valued procedural regularity, the right to confront hostile witnesses, and objective third party adjudication based on evidence instead of magic or divine ritual.[18] Even during the Tokugawa Period—seen largely as the heyday of neo-Confucian authoritarianism and the flat prohibition of the legal profession—formal legal institutions were overloaded with lawsuits, legal advice was a significant industry, and legal justice was accessible for even the most downtrodden. Although commercial matters and debt collection cases dominated, the courts were also used for disputes concerning property rights and personal status.

Law continued to play a significant role in the seventy years from the Meiji Restoration up to World War II, and not solely as a superficial ornament borrowed from the West. Legal rules, and litigation to enforce them, became an important tool both to defend privilege and to challenge it.[19] As landlords exploited their rights under the Civil Code, demanding rent legally—although perhaps not morally—due, tenants sued landlords for overreaching. Husbands exercised their rights to quick and simple divorce, while wives countered with suits for damages suffered because of their husbands' adultery. Contracting parties sued each other for default and neighbors sued each other for irritating and harassing land use practices. Lawyers were numerous, litigation was common, and the results were not always to

---

17. I will not describe the judiciary that Japan has created, and is now considering substantially expanding, for those few disputes that persist or which fall outside the informal mechanisms. The Japanese judiciary is more like a highly structured and closely monitored bureaucracy than like the American judiciary and therefore has created a much more predictable and stable set of doctrines and decisions. In many ways, it may be more readily reproduced in the developing world than its American counterpart, but it has not been central to the Japanese story and a full explication of its creation and structure is beyond the scope of this chapter.

18. The reference is to the *shiki* system of land rights adjudication developed during the Kamakura Period. See Jeffrey Mass, *The Development of Kamakura Rule, 1180–1250,* Stanford: Stanford University Press (1979). For discussions of the role of law and legal institutions in later periods of Japanese history, see Frank K. Upham, "Weak Legal Consciousness as Invented Tradition," in Stephen Vlastos (ed.), *Mirror of Modernity: Invented Traditions of Modern Japan,* Berkeley: University of California Press (1998) 48-64; and Herman Ooms, *Tokugawa Village Practice: Class, Status, Power, Law,* Berkeley: University of California Press (1996).

19. Sources include J. Mark Ramseyer, *Odd Markets in Japanese History: Law and Economic Growth,* Cambridge: Cambridge University Press (1996); and John O. Haley, "The Politics of Informal Justice: The Japanese Experience, 1922–1942," in Richard Abel (ed.), *The Politics of Informal Justice,* New York: Academic Press (1982) 125-147.

the liking of the political elite. Litigation against the government was less common, although even here courts occasionally provided relief.

The leading politicians within the Imperial Diet reacted to this blossoming of legal activity with horror. By the 1920s, they were passing progressively harsher statutes to restrict litigation and protect the "beautiful customs" of Japan's imaginary past from the corrupting influences of law, individualism, and modernity. But this was to little avail. While the onset of militarism in the 1930s brought litigation rates and, not incidentally, the number of lawyers down drastically, it was not until the advent of postwar democracy that the government's efforts to restrict the role and size of formal legal institutions became an unquestioned aspect of Japanese culture and society. This was largely due to a governmental limitation on the number of lawyers. For most of the second half of the twentieth century, the government simply set the maximum annual production of legal professionals, including judges and procurators, at five hundred. The policy succeeded: a country that had had over 7,000 lawyers in 1932 had less than 7,000 thirty years later.[20] The number of attorneys per million people dropped by over one-third, from 107.1 to 71.3. While the absolute number of attorneys rose slowly after the 1960s, it remains tiny today, especially when viewed in relation to either population or economic activity. Litigation rates are harder to characterize, but by one count they dropped by over 75 percent in the century between 1883 and 1990.[21] The absolute number of cases, as opposed to per capita rates, varied during that period, ebbing and flowing in rough but clear positive correlation with economic recessions. The number of judges and procurators remained virtually constant from the immediate postwar period through the 1990s.

What is remarkable about this shrinking of the legal sector is that it occurred at a time of rapid economic expansion, population growth, and social dislocation. That is well illustrated by the share of the national budget spent on the court system: it went from an already low 0.91% in 1955 to an infinitesimally small 0.36% in 1999.[22] Also striking is the fact that from

20. The precise figure was 7,136. Dan Fenno Henderson, "The Role of Lawyers in Japan," in Harald Baum (ed.), *Japan: Economic Success and Legal System*, Berlin: Walter de Gruyter (1997) 40.

21. I cite these statistics for dramatic purposes only. Comparing lawsuits is an excellent illustration of the adage, "lies, damn lies, and statistics," especially when the comparison crosses eras or jurisdictional borders. The most recent attempt to evaluate Japanese litigiousness that I know of is Christian Wollschläger, "Historical Trends of Civil Litigation," in Harald Baum (ed.), *Japan: Economic Success and Legal System*, Berlin: Walter de Gruyter (1997). The figures for the 75% drop come from Figure 1 at page 94 of Wollschläger. The specific figures are virtually meaningless but they express both the direction and degree of litigation rates.

22. Curtis Milhaupt and Mark West, "Law's Dominion and the Market for Legal Elites in Japan," 34 *Law and Policy in International Business* (forthcoming Winter 2003).

1950 to 1970, the percentage of Japanese living in cities practically doubled, presumably increasing the need for the social ordering of formal law.[23] Put simply but accurately, during the very same period that the economy boomed and society underwent substantial changes, the number of legal professionals per capita declined, the litigation rate fell, and the size of the formal legal system relative to the population and economy shrank substantially. It is difficult to exaggerate the importance of the juxtaposition of these phenomena to the topic of this chapter. If formal legal institutions were necessary for either social order or economic growth, or even just weakly associated with it, one would expect the de-emphasis of formal law to have hindered growth. Instead, the shrinkage of legal institutions is positively correlated with growth, although of course no causal connection—that the deliberate shrinkage of formal legal institutions created growth—can be proved.[24]

The regulatory environment. According to neoclassical economists, optimal economic growth in a capitalist setting requires certain social preconditions. Investors must expect to capture a reasonable return on their investment. Part of that expectation is that the government will not take property or allow others to do so without good reason and compensation. A second part is that investors will have adequate knowledge of the markets to allocate their resources to pursue the greatest gain and that those markets will be stable and relatively free of unpredictable public intervention or private manipulation. Government's role is to create open and stable markets, correct market failures via clear and predictable regulation, and otherwise stay on the sidelines. For most observers of successful economies—and certainly for those within the rule of law movement—the easiest and most common way to achieve these characteristics is by creating a set of incentives that align private behavior with public benefit. The mechanism for establishing these incentives is most commonly law and the formal legal institutions that apply and enforce legal rules.

For Japan, however, a legally established and maintained system of private incentives is not the dominant explanation for the rapid economic growth over the last fifty years. Although there are forceful exceptions, the conventional explanation is that the Japanese economy developed under the strong guidance of a dedicated and talented cadre of powerful central governmental bureaucrats who created what has become known as the developmental

23. Japan Access, "The High Growth Era," *Mainichi Interactive*, available at http://jin.or.jp/access/economy/grow.html.

24. It is also impossible to prove that Japan would not have grown even faster had it put more resources into formal legal institutions and relied more heavily on them to regulate its economy and society. To state this hypothetical claim, however, is to demonstrate its implausibility.

state.[25] According to this view, bureaucrats decided where Japan's resources should be invested and who should receive them, and then did their best to make sure their choices were successful. The market played a crucial but passive role; it was there to ratify bureaucratic choices and to reward the winners, but it did not allocate investment resources as required by the economists. On the contrary, the market was intentionally bypassed and distorted both to provide emerging sectors the necessary resources and to provide a soft landing to the losers. For the proponents of the developmental state model of Japan, the law played virtually no role.

The centrality and independence of the bureaucrats stressed in this explanation is strongly debated, with some critics stressing the role of politicians and others that of the private sector.[26] The crucial point is that bureaucrats acted within an environment where judicial attack on bureaucratic action was rare. This should not be surprising. Restrictive threshold doctrines prevented lawsuits by anyone but the most directly affected parties, so that competitors, consumers, or advocates of indirectly affected interests like the environment were effectively shut out of the courts. Insiders, on the other hand, had little reason to complain. Their interests had invariably been considered, and any use of the courts threatened not only their cooperative relationships with competitors and bureaucrats but also the overall regulatory structure that was working so well to all of their benefits. It is important to note that bureaucrats did not arbitrarily deprive individuals or corporations of property or profits. That would have been as foreign and destructive to the system as constant resort to litigation by disgruntled insiders. My point is not that the bureaucrats dominated private interests or directed the economy; it is simply that economic policy was discussed, formed, and implemented largely through informal mechanisms that were consciously shielded from the interference of the formal legal system.

---

25. Chalmers Johnson, *MITI and the Japanese Miracle*, Stanford, Calif.: Stanford University Press (1982) is the classic. Ironically Johnson and his followers are known as revisionists, but within Japanese studies, both of the academic and popular varieties, it is those who argue that economic orthodoxy works as well with Japan as with anywhere else that are the outsiders. A prominent example of this heterodoxy is J. Mark Ramseyer and Frances McCall Rosenbluth, *Japan's Political Marketplace*, Cambridge: Harvard University Press (1993).

26. A major focus of this debate is the role of the bureaucrats and whether they deserve credit for Japan's success or whether they acted at the behest and under the control of Japanese politicians. Although potentially crucial for a general model of development and the question of the relative roles of democracy and expertise, this issue is not central to our immediate purposes. In fact, I have argued elsewhere that these two viewpoints underestimate the role of private parties in the formation and implementation of economic policy. Frank K. Upham, "Privatized Regulation: Japanese Regulatory Style in Comparative and International Perspective," 20 *Fordham International Law Journal* (1997) 396-511.

An example of how these arrangements worked in practice will illustrate. The Large Scale Retail Stores Law (LSRSL) was passed in 1973 to protect small and medium retailers from high volume discount stores. The law required operators of prospective large stores to submit their plans to the Ministry of International Trade and Industry (MITI) and required MITI to determine, according to specified timelines and procedures, whether the store's opening would substantially injure existing merchants. If MITI decided that there was danger of injury, it could suggest changes in the plans. The store was under no obligation to make changes; MITI's suggestion had no binding legal effect. If the store failed to implement the suggestion, however, MITI could reissue it as a formal order. Only if the store continued to defy its wishes, did MITI have legal power to curtail the store's operations. Despite these procedural quirks, the statutory language contemplated a process similar to permit processes in the United States. Large retailers would make their expansion plans based on market forces, and then apply to open a new store whenever those calculations indicated that it would be successful. MITI would then evaluate the new store's impact on neighborhood merchants according to the statutory criteria and make its decision. If dissatisfied therewith, the interested party (either the large retailer or a local merchant) could ignore the suggestion and, if MITI followed up with a binding order, sue.

In practice the statute operated in an entirely different manner. MITI made it known that it would only accept store notifications that were accompanied by a written statement that local merchants did not oppose the opening. The large retailers formed a cartel to allocate annually the number of new stores and floor space for each of its members, and when a retailer was ready to put one of its allocated stores in a particular location, its representatives would bargain with local merchants for their permission to open. After permission was obtained and the statement filed with the store's plans, things usually went smoothly and the store opened as stated in the filed plans.

For the private sector participants, the LSRSL was a great success. The retail market was severely restricted; the profits of large stores skyrocketed; and small retailers were given some respite from more efficient competitors. MITI was also happy because it did not have to make any regulatory decisions, thus insulating it from political criticism and saving it administrative time and expense. Despite the total distortion of the statute's formal intent and language, virtually no one sued. Why would they? The only losers were potential entrants to the market and consumers. Neither of them had any specific knowledge of what was going on, nor would they have had standing to sue even if they had. This system was stable and predictable, investors and market participants knew the rules, and it was not until the law became a trade issue with the United States that change occurred.

The dominant reason for the stability of such arrangements, both in the retail sector under the LSRSL and elsewhere, was that it was not in the long run interest of most firms to fight the system. Cartels were usually organized by and for the industry with the relevant government ministry policing the industry's agreement. Since the ultimate losers of these arrangements were usually Japanese consumers or potential foreign entrants, there was no immediate reason for firms to resist; resisting would have meant not merely fighting the bureaucracy but also fighting the other firms in the industry, the trade association, and the relevant Liberal Democratic Party politicians. It often would have resulted in bad publicity as well, since they would be portrayed as greedy renegades, destroying the economic order that had brought prosperity to postwar Japan. Although this economic system undoubtedly harmed individual companies from time to time, they were not without recourse. If they had significant political power, they could go to the politicians or battle within the policymaking framework and, even if they lost, could be assured that their interests would not be forever ignored. They could also cheat, which individual firms certainly did, sometimes openly, sometimes covertly.

When these arrangements were working well, the formal legal system was irrelevant. Even when things went wrong—when technology or market structures changed or when a renegade entrepreneur tried to break the cartel—law's role hardly amounted to what the World Bank would argue was necessary. Because the government's own actions were often legally indefensible, the threat of litigation was an option for aggrieved or greedy firms. It was not easy, however. Litigation could proceed only if the firm satisfied a series of doctrinal hurdles governing who can sue the government for an official decision. First, the government action had to constitute an official act that immediately and directly infringed on one's legal rights, known technically as an administrative disposition. This meant that all informal activities of administrative agencies including administrative guidance like the LSRSL "suggestions" were immune from suit. The second doctrinal requirement was standing, which focused on who could sue to challenge government acts that constituted an administrative disposition, such as denials of requests for permits, licenses, etc. Standing was limited to the direct applicant, which meant that the interests of competitors, consumers, and the general public were beyond judicial scrutiny. Thus, both consumers and local merchants were effectively denied legal protection.

Even upon satisfying the requirements of standing and administrative disposition, winning was difficult. In the first place, the firm had to convince the agency to accept the notification. It was common bureaucratic practice simply to refuse to accept troublesome applications unless the applicant agreed to amend its application to fit agency policy.[27] As long as the application had not been denied, the firm could sue only to force the agency to accept the application. Only after it had won on that level could it resubmit and get official action, presumably a denial. Then, and only then, could the firm sue on the merits of that denial and, given the breadth of discretion granted to agencies under administrative statutes and the agency's opportunity to craft its decision to withstand judicial review, victory was hardly assured. Considering this tortuous path and the benefits that the regulatory structure conferred on the industry, it is not surprising that such suits were rare and more often driven by ideological rather than commercial motives.

More curious was the absence of lawsuits brought by consumers, Japanese firms excluded from the deals cut by industry and the bureaucracy, or foreign firms, who were underrepresented in policy formation and were the real losers in industrial and financial policy. The reasons were simple and had little to do with the oft-mentioned Japanese preferences for consensus or submissiveness to authority. First, these policies were on the whole at least implicitly approved by Liberal Democratic Party politicians and frequently taken at their explicit direction. Although informal approval could not transform an illegal cartel into a legal one, it did give the activity institutional and political legitimacy. Second, the formation and enforcement of informal cartels were never so transparent as to be part of the public record and were often totally opaque. Knowing exactly what was going on was difficult, gathering evidence even more so. Third, civil plaintiffs had little chance of success in court. Although Japanese competition law explicitly authorizes a private cause of action for its violation, the courts required such onerous proof of causation and damages that no consumer ever won a case under it during this period.

These various factors—the long-term self-interest of the insiders, the invisibility of the mechanisms used, the political legitimacy of the cross subsidies implicit in the cartels, and the doctrinal difficulties of challenging either the process or its results—combined to create a system that heavily discouraged opposition through the formal legal system. It did not mean of course that the legal system ceased operation or became irrelevant. A series of tort cases brought in the 1960s and 1970s by victims of industrial pollution started a process that resulted in the eventual reform of Japan's environmental law and policy. Shortly thereafter the construction industry used the courts to break a system of informal restrictions placed by opposition mayors

27. It was illegal for an agency to refuse to accept an application that was on its face complete, but judicial relief was arduous and uncertain. The practice continued at least into the '90s, so much so that the Diet had to restate the law in the Administrative Procedure Act of 1993. *Ibid.*, 470. See also Kenneth Duck, "Now That the Fog Has Lifted: The Impact of Japan's Administrative Procedure Law on the Regulation of Industry and Market Governance," 19 *Fordham International Law Journal* (1996) 1686-1763.

on development in affluent suburbs. For relatively weak insiders, like the Fair Trade Commission or a renegade firm inside a cartelized industry, the formal legal system provided a tool that could be used to increase one's bargaining power. Although one might not win the litigation, the mere threat of exposing the informal deals struck by the insiders was embarrassing enough to provide important leverage. But when the system was stable and operating within the norms of fairness of its participants, there was simply little reason for anyone to resort to law.

This portrait of the role of the legal system in Japanese society falls well short of that portrayed by the rule of law advocates. To paraphrase Shihata, such a system requires that rules governing the state's intervention in the market are known in advance, properly interpreted, and vigorously enforced; that exceptions to a rule's application occur only according to established procedures; and that conflicts in the application or interpretation of the rules are formally adjudicated by an independent judicial body. In other words, transparency, uniform application, and arms length conflict resolution—all three comprise Shihata's rule of law system. It is hard to argue that the regulation of the Japanese economy for the first three to four decades of the post-war period had any of these characteristics. Yet it would be equally difficult to argue that the Japanese system was not successful, either in terms of economic growth, the preservation of civil order, or the guaranteeing of a high degree of social justice.

Although this chapter is not the place to discuss in depth the factors that made this possible, a few are worth mentioning. First, the actors involved in economic policy formation and implementation were stable institutions staffed by dedicated and competent businessmen and bureaucrats. Whether it was the corporations, the trade associations that represented them, or the ministries that had responsibility for their regulation, their staffs were well educated and trained and generally remained with the same institution for most of their career. Second, there were pervasive and institutionalized means of communication between public and private institutions. The most famous is the *amakudari* system whereby bureaucrats retired to the private sector, but *amakudari* has been generally limited to sectors and firms heavily dependent on government regulation. More important was the informal interaction sometimes on an almost daily basis between regulated and regulator, if not via individual firms, then via trade associations and similar institutions. Third, Japanese bureaucrats were widely perceived as competent and honest. Fourth, Japan was a democracy. The politicians and the voters behind them always had a veto power if either a policy failed disastrously or important interests were ignored. Fifth, the courts did, in fact, intervene at crucial times and provided an outside limit to the flexibility and arrogance of the insiders. Their power came, however, not from formal allegiance to rules and procedures, but through the public exposure of violations of accepted political, social, and moral norms. Finally, as we see in the next section, these regulatory institutions existed within a society where most conflict was handled by informal mechanisms consciously created to channel it away from the courts and other public institutions that might bring it into the public sphere.

Dispute resolution. In this section, I outline how Japan has managed conflict that fell outside of the regulatory context described above. The focus is on the myriad informal mechanisms generally lumped under the rubric of alternative dispute resolution. Japan is rightfully renowned for such devices, but it will suffice here to look briefly at two instances: one in the politically charged arena of environmental disputes and the other in the routine sphere of automobile accidents. These examples will convey some sense of how Japan has dealt with the inevitable social dislocation caused by economic growth without resorting to a rule of law system.

Prior to the current decade-long recession, perhaps the greatest social crisis faced by Japan in the postwar period was the environmental degradation of the 1950s and 1960s. The Japanese government was unable to respond decisively to pollution, despite clear evidence that unrestrained industrialization was destroying Japan's social fabric. The postwar pro-development consensus made protest unpopular and pollution victims had few allies in the Diet or the powerful ministries. Although opposition parties controlled many local governments, they were unable to take effective action. In the end, it was a litigation campaign that broke the political logjam and forced the central government to respond. The result was an effective and comprehensive regulation of industrial pollution that was stricter than that of the United States and most of Europe, but it is how Japan chose to deal with subsequent environmental disputes that is of interest here. Despite the demonstrated success of tort litigation in exposing and redressing pollution, the Japanese government explicitly rejected using the legal system for future conflict. Instead it established bureaucratically managed compensation and mediation schemes to channel disputes out of the courts.

This environmental dispute system was a direct response to a political crisis, but it is representative of similar informal systems that cover virtually every field of social interaction conceivable in Japan's modern polity. From divorce or adoption to human rights or employment, there is a government-created conflict resolution scheme ready to address the concerns of potential litigants. They range from conciliation programs attached to family courts to human rights committees under local government supervision. Many observers of Japan attribute these devices to a cultural preference for harmony and consensus over the divisiveness of litigation. Others see a political conspiracy to use an imagined culture and tradition to keep political issues out of the courts where they may escape elite control.[28] Undoubtedly, both views have some currency—there are historical antecedents for mediation in the Tokugawa Period and the political advantage of bureaucratically administered mediation is clear—but what is of interest here is the success of these devices in managing social conflict without direct resort to the formal legal system.

Traffic accidents provide an excellent example of how this has been achieved.[29] As Tanase Takao, a leading Japanese sociologist of law, put it:

> [W]hile in the United States, except in minor injuries, people routinely bring their claims to lawyers, in Japan nearly all the injured parties handle compensation disputes themselves without the aid of lawyers. Only when they encounter extraordinary difficulty and feel that, as a very last resort, they will have to use the court, do the Japanese ask the help of lawyers.

According to Tanase, less than one per cent of total accidents end up in court and no more than two per cent involve private attorneys at any stage. Those who believe that harmonious dispute resolution is the natural result of Japanese culture may be surprised to learn that such was not always the case. Traffic litigation was common in the 1960s and peaked in 1971. Thereafter the government, the police, insurance companies, bar associations, and the courts took measures that reduced the number of absolute cases by two-thirds in a decade. There was nothing spontaneous or uniquely Japanese about the process. On the contrary, it was carefully structured to provide adequate compensation to accident victims without the expense of the formal legal process. Nor was it developed without attention to legal rules; a key aspect of the process is the provision of free legal consultation by police, insurance companies, and lawyers. The emphasis in these consultations is on the ability of the parties to handle the vast majority of accident claims without litigation or professional involvement. The judiciary played a role by carefully and consistently simplifying liability rules and compensation formulae, a task well suited to the Japanese judiciary which more closely resembles a tightly controlled and regimented bureaucracy than its American counterpart.

As is implied by the involvement of the bar and the judiciary in the automobile accident scheme, legal institutions can play important supporting and enabling roles in Japan's informal dispute resolution mechanisms. Family

28. For examples and analysis of "invented tradition" in Japan, see Stephen Vlastos, (ed.), *Mirror of Modernity: Invented Traditions of Modern Japan*, Berkeley: University of California Press (1998).

29. The system for automobile accidents is beautifully described by Japanese legal sociologist Takao Tanase in "The Management of Disputes: Automobile Accident Compensation in Japan," 24, 3 *Law and Society Review* (1990) 651-691. His article puts the automobile accident scheme in the context of general conflict control and is an excellent source for understanding the Japanese approach to litigation and social conflict.

court conciliation is another such example, although in this instance the legal role has often been the processing of complaints rather than ensuring fidelity to legal rights. In other areas, especially those under the jurisdiction or policy sphere of particular ministries, processes are conducted with considerably less involvement of legal rules, institutions, or personnel.

The common denominator for all dispute procedures, however, is a concerted and largely successful effort to avoid the cost and formality of litigation. To this extent, the use of informal mechanisms such as the ones I've described arising in Japan, and similar ones in every developed country, may be a more attractive route for developing countries to pursue than attempting to create a full-blown formalistic legal system. Again, it is necessary to stress that these systems have not arisen spontaneously from the depths of Japanese culture, but on the contrary, were specifically designed by the government to discourage litigation. They are not, in other words, uniquely Japanese; nor do they depend on a culturally submissive population, ready to compromise their interests in the name of harmony. They may depend, however, on a degree of internal social cohesion that many developing countries will lack. Even more important, they clearly require an effective bureaucracy, another state institution that is in short supply in much of the developing world. Even so, informality may still be preferable to the formality of a rule of law judiciary, which is at least equally dependent on social conditions and vastly more expensive.

3. Explaining the Appeal of the Rule of Law

Despite these difficulties, rule of law rhetoric remains a staple of diplomacy. Legal assistance programs continue to garner relatively scarce foreign aid funds through use of such rhetoric. The reason for both the failure to develop a workable definition of rule of law and its enduring appeal is law's unrecognized political nature. While political institutions are not intrinsically indefinable, their nature must be recognized to be defined, and the single most important reason for the universal appeal of rule of law rhetoric is the refusal of rule of law practitioners and advocates to recognize, much less analyze, law's political side. Instead, law is envisioned as technical knowledge and hence as readily transferable from one context to another as are best practices in chip design or inventory control.

Portraying law as technical is important for several reasons. First, it means that the "exporting" country is not advocating any particular political norms or institutions and hence not infringing on the "importing" country's sovereignty. Being able to deny any political goal is important for the legitimacy of developed world diplomacy. Perhaps of even greater importance, however, is that the apolitical nature of rule of law assistance makes it more palatable to the recipient country since it removes any obvious taint of colonialism or geopolitical maneuvering from the offered assistance. This matters both for the legitimacy of the leaders of the recipient country, and for the legitimacy of the assistance program itself. Moreover, in some instances this explicit denial of political goals is legally required for international aid agencies such as the World Bank to even participate in an assistance program.

A second explanation of the appeal of "law as technique" is its resonance with the *Zeitgeist* of the late twentieth century, which strongly prefers non-state solutions to the "social engineering" of overtly political solutions. Although legal history has not provided us with a phrase equivalent to Smith's "invisible hand," the law, like the market, is seen as operating without human agency and hence without the vices of bureaucracies and politicians, two of our time's least favorite institutions. Just as a market needs only clear property rights and freedom of exchange, the rule of law needs only the correct rules and institutions. It can then be left alone to operate free of the messiness and inefficiency of government.

Finally, the rule of law is appealing because it is an elegant concept that can explain away much of the complexity of human life while also solving many of its moral problems. Again, in the same way as market fundamentalists need only a few assumptions to create wealth, all a rule of law advocate needs to provide the answers to many difficult questions is a few key conditions. Rarely are these conditions considered consciously—they are simply assumed to exist—and they are even less frequently acknowledged as necessary to the practical success of the theoretical promises of the rule of law. Unfortunately, these conditions almost never exist in developing countries. If they did, the countries would already be developed. More striking, these conditions often do not exist even in the rule of law advocates' own home countries and may, like the assumptions of a perfect market, be impossible to achieve.

Part IV
Many Faces of Religion: Case Studies on Iran

Chapter 13

Shlomo Avineri

The Paradox of Religion and the Universality of Human Rights

The issue of how religion as such, and various religious traditions in particular, relate to the possibility of universalizing human rights or lending them legitimacy can be dealt with on two levels: the theological and the historical. I will try to combine both—being well aware that there are obvious methodological and factual pitfalls in such an attempt. What I will try to avoid are some of the more conventional approaches which have recently become extremely popular among participants in inter-religious dialogues, when mere theological texts are quoted as proof as to whether a religious tradition is, or is not, compatible with human norms. In such instances, what is not addressed by the discussants is the question, which is far more relevant to an historical or social science approach, about the real historical praxis prevalent in those societies which adhere to the religion in question. It thus happens that many of these inter-religious dialogues tend to degenerate into a series of sermons by true believers preaching to one another, reminiscent of medieval disputations, real or imaginary, about the relative truth of each disputant's respective religion or revelatory tradition.

Any discussion of human rights cannot avoid admitting that on a most fundamental level the respect for universal human rights and human dignity has to be seen as deriving from the biblical tradition, common to the three Abrahamic faiths. It is true that none of these three religions view human

András Sajó (ed.), Human Rights with Modesty: The Problem of Universalism, *317-326.*

rights as an intrinsic constitutive aspect of its credo. Yet it is in the belief that human beings were created in God's image that we can discern the metaphysical origins of the train of thought that in its secularized version eventually led to the development of the idea of human rights and their universality. That the Judaic tradition insisted on this idea is, of course, also the normative foundation of many of the explicit moral precepts of Judaism, which were then integrated, though with different accents, into Christianity and Islam. It is an historical fact that the ideas of human rights, not least their universality, were developed within these traditions. To state this may sound to many as Eurocentric hubris, or another expression of Western hegemonism or intellectual imperialism: it is, however, true. It is the secularization of the idea that human beings were created in God's image that led to the development of the ideas of human rights and their universal application.

In this context it should be mentioned that while many elements of the modern democratic political culture derive from the Greco-Roman republican classical tradition, the idea of human rights, and certainly their universality, were not bequeathed to the modern democratic and liberal discourse from this source. While modern concepts of citizenship, elections, and political consent have their origins in the traditions of the Greek *polis* and the Roman republic, this is not the case regarding the question of rights. This should be stressed because it is often overlooked that neither the Greek nor the Roman tradition had a concept of rights in the sense of a sphere of individual entitlements *vis-à-vis* political power. *Libertas* did not mean freedom from the state, but freedom to participate in the deliberations and decisions of the *polis* or *civitas.* The trial of Socrates epitomizes this lack of rights against the state in democratic Athens: for all of what we may think today of the trial, it was, in procedure as well as in substance, a legitimate trial given the laws of Athens; and Socrates was, of course, the first one to admit this when in the *Critias* he refuses to flee and accepts the legitimacy of the laws that led to his trial and death sentence. The Greek and Roman traditions had no mechanisms of rights against the state.

Even the later broadening of citizenship rights under the influence of Stoic ideas and the legal development of *ius gentium* and eventually *ius naturale* meant only that all citizens had the same standing in law, not that they had the same rights against the state; certainly the granting, under Caracalla, of Roman citizenship rights to all free inhabitants of the Empire did not mean that all had rights *vis-à-vis* the state: it meant that the historically-developed differentiated rights among citizens of different status (*cives, socii,* etc.) were abolished, not that they had not acquired any rights against the state. In the late Roman Empire whatever remained of republican political rights had totally disappeared, and in the third century C.E. to say '*civis Romanus sum*' certainly had very little meaning in the terms in which we understand political rights today, as a weapon defending the individual citizen against arbitrariness of state power.

Similarly, neither had the classical tradition any notion of the universality of the human race. The conventional Greek distinction between Hellenes and barbarians makes this clear, and is central to the whole Greek political culture. Philosophically it was even underpinned and given added legitimacy by the Aristotelian distinction between free and unfree human beings, anchoring this distinction in nature, and not in the vagaries of war or serendipity of human biography.

I want to stress the biblical tradition in the case of universal human rights not for reasons of making a religious argument, but for the sake of historical accuracy. Modern historiography, as well as modern theoretical republicanism, is so steeped in the Enlightenment tradition and the idealization of Greco-Roman republicanism that both sometimes find it difficult to admit that something as central as the concept of rights against the state, and the universality of these rights, does not stem from classical republicanism but from the Judeo-Christian tradition. That this idealization of the classical tradition was common to both Jacobins like Robespierre and liberal conservatives like Mommsen may explain its prevalence: it does not detract from the fact that it overlooked the issues of rights (ironically, both Robespierre and Mommsen, for opposite reasons, might not have been bothered too much by it). This historical renaissance of classical republicanism in political theory, which modern political thought owes to such disparate thinkers as Machiavelli and Harrington, was equally silent on issues of citizens' rights *vis-à-vis* the state: and the sometimes extreme laicism of many thinkers of the Enlightenment made it even difficult for them to admit that much of their most prized ideas have roots and origins in theological traditions which they viewed merely as *l'infame.*

Yet on the other hand, there is no doubt that the religious traditions we refer to here are Janus-like, and that it was the introduction of monotheism which contributed to persecution and lack of tolerance towards those holding different views: non-monotheistic religions (once called pagan or polytheistic) are free from these intolerant tendencies. It is the very ontological certainty in the metaphysical truth immanent in their revelatory origin, which makes monotheistic religions intolerant in their historical impact: it was these faiths which introduced religious persecution into the world and gave it the highest possible legitimacy—the word of God. In the case of Catholic Christianity, the eventual need to navigate between the Sermon of the Mount and the Inquisition has been a constant dilemma which cannot be easily solved by praying for the souls of the damned burned at the stake *ad magnam Dei gloriam.* Certainly Vatican II and similar—and earlier—Protestant developments have made the issue of religious persecution anathema to the churches today: but it was an arduous and difficult path. And after all, both Christianity as well as Islam owe their worldwide presence to the sword as much as to the word. Muhammad and Charlemagne stand out as prototypes of the bloody way in which the Gospel and the Qur'an were spread among the infidels.

In this respect Judaism is strangely different: Judaism's particularism tended to make it exclusive and tribal—for which it has been criticized by a long list of polemicists—from the Alexandrian Apion, through the Church Fathers, to the eighteenth-century Enlightenment and radical Protestants in the Ludwig Feuerbach and Bruno Bauer tradition. It is an argument sometimes still made by contemporary writers, who find Judaism wanting when compared to the universalism of Christianity and Islam. Yet it was precisely the universalism of Christianity and Islam which contributed to intolerance, forced conversions, expulsions, and the "*Ausgrenzung*" of the "Other" as an infidel to be overcome, subjugated, or (at best) persuaded. And when persuasion failed, an auto-da-fe could at least save the apostate's eternal soul from eternal damnation. In the particularism of Judaism, on the other hand, lies a kernel for pluralism, tolerance, and multiculturalism: usually these traits are attributed to modern Jewish thinkers as a natural position taken by members of a minority religion. This, of course, is true: yet there are also deeper theoretical and theological reasons here, embedded in a non-proselytizing creed. Exclusivism and an elevated view of one's being divinely chosen can, paradoxically, lead to a "live and let live" attitude.

On another theoretical level, the Judaic tradition knows also elements of universalism which draw on the basic common humanity of all beings created in God's image. In the biblical narrative the particularistic covenant between God and His people, the Covenant of Sinai, is supplemented, and even preceded, by a universal covenant, the Noahite Covenant, where all people are supposed after the Deluge to have taken upon themselves seven basic precepts which are common to all humanity—and it is the tensions between the Sinaitic and Noahite Covenants which inform even contradicting versions of the Jewish messianic vision, which tends to oscillate, in its different modes, between the ethno-centric and the universal.

On another level this internal tension is exemplified by the Talmudic exegesis on the reason for the creation of humanity in the form of one person (or two—Adam and Eve). The reason that human beings are all supposed to be descendants of one ancestor is explained in the Talmud by the following counter-example: had human beings been descended from different ancestors, one person could say to another that his own ancestors were superior to the other's; since all have the same one ancestor in common, no one can say to the other: "My ancestor is of a more elevated standing than yours." Similarly, the descent of all humanity from one ancestor also legitimizes the importance of every individual human life, since every individual stands for the original one human creature who equaled the totality of the human species. Yet (as if to exemplify the internal tension between particularism and universality) there are two versions of this dictum: one says, "Anyone who saves the life of one human being is deemed to have saved all of humanity"; the other version, however, runs: "Anyone who saves the life of one Israelite is deemed to have saved all of humanity."

But beyond this metaphysical foundation of human rights in the tradition that all human beings were created in God's image, there is another ingredient hailing from a specific Christian tradition, which has contributed, conceptually and institutionally, to the anchoring of human rights in the modern polity: it is the tension between state and church and the institutional apartness (I am careful not to say: separation) of the two.

The Christian tradition of the "two swords," the sacred and the secular, running from Gelasius to Aquinas and coming to a head in the High Middle Ages in the Wars of the Investiture, created a legitimate institutional corrective to the claims to absolute power on the part of the secular ruler. Again, this is something that does not originate in the Greco-Roman tradition, though one could argue that the Roman republican tension between consular and tribunician power, between the senate and the popular assemblies, as well as the duality of consular power, created a balance of power in the forms of practical checks and balances.

But the Christian theory of the two swords introduced a totally different notion into the nature of political power and gave a normative dimension to its limitation. By institutionalizing the Hebraic prophetic tradition of speaking truth to power, the medieval Papacy endowed itself with the ultimate power of resisting and, if necessary, dethroning imperial and royal rulers in the name of the moral religious imperatives of the message of the Christian faith. In this Catholic Christianity went one significant step further than Judaism. The Hebrew prophets—Nathan, Elijah—could castigate the powers-that-be by accusing King David of murdering the husband of the desired Bat Sheba or killing Navot of Jezreel because King Ahab coveted his vineyard. But they did not have the power to dethrone him (though Samuel, in a way, did it to Saul). The Church, by institutionalizing—through the act of papal coronation, deriving from the Samuelite coronation—the right of taking away divine grace from the anointed emperor or king and transferring it to another person, forged a powerful weapon for limiting secular power. Post-Renaissance absolutism did overcome much of this, as did the Protestant development of national churches. Yet the idea of a legitimate institutionalized ability to speak truth to power, limit it and—if necessary—depose it, has its roots in this Western Christian tradition, which became secularized by transferring what was once the prophetic power vested in the holder of the Keys of St. Peter to parliaments, the electorate, and an independent court system. It is difficult to imagine the development of a parliamentary tradition and modern republicanism without this historical background—and it is a fact, that outside the European Christian and post-Christian orbit, similar developments did not occur independently.

Even within Christianity, the cesaro-papist Byzantine traditions of Eastern Orthodoxy lacked this duality and internal tension: consequently, Orthodox societies lacked the institutionalized structures which could then be transformed into the secular mechanisms of controlling and limiting power. In a way this can be seen until this very day in those countries of Central and Eastern Europe with an Orthodox tradition, where the church has remained ultimately subservient to the state. With the rise of modern nationalism in these regions, and the emergence of autocephalous national churches, the combination of state power and a national church in areas of ethno-religious conflict had obvious and extremely pernicious effects on issues of human rights. When an ideological nationalist or ethnic message is combined with a religious legitimacy, it is a powerful bulwark which trumps human rights and a universal concept of citizenship. The different role of the Catholic Church in Communist Poland as compared to that of the Russian Orthodox Church in the Soviet Union cannot be totally divorced from these different historical theological and institutional differences.

A development similar to the role of national churches in Central and Eastern Europe (and, one should add, in Ireland) can be seen in the Middle East, where the Arab-Israeli conflict, originally a secular conflict between two national movements, has recently become radicalized with the overlaying of deeply religious connotations on both sides.

Within the Islamic orbit, one should again be able to differentiate. Recent, mainly post-September 11 conventional wisdom that Islam as a religion is incompatible with democracy and human rights development is as irrelevant as views, quite prevalent in the nineteenth and even twentieth century, that had maintained that Catholicism is *per se* incompatible with democracy or human rights. Again, it is not a question of theology but of the wider political and social context within which a religious faith operates, and Catholicism today plays a completely different role regarding issues of democracy and human rights from the one it played in the nineteenth century.

It is not the theology of Islam which hinders democratization or the spread of human rights; but the fact that Islam lacks the distinction—crucial to the Christian tradition—between the sacred and the profane, which appears to be a hindrance to the development of internal mechanisms for the defense of human rights. That there are no two swords in Islam, and the Caliph is also the Commander of the Faithful (*Amir al-Mu'amiyin*), is no doubt at the root of some of the difficulties Islamic societies have in creating and safeguarding a public space for human rights which is distinct from, but defended by, the state. Consequently, Islamic societies did not develop institutional mechanisms of a countervailing power: the absence of an institutionalized church in Islam also weakened the affective power of whatever resistance could be made against the powers-that-be in the name of religious precepts. Contrary to some conventional liberal wisdom, the existence of an institutionalized church can—under conditions which we have tried to explain—contribute towards the development of human rights in specific historical contexts. What is sometimes lost in the current, sometimes hysterical and not very well-informed debate about Islam, is that (just like Judaism) Islam is a religion, not a church, and hence (paradoxically) lacks the institutional structures which can withstand political power or oppose it in the name of an alternative—and even higher—legitimacy.

Of course there exist texts in the Islamic traditions which imply criticism of tyrants: yet Islamic societies, lacking the dualism of state and church, do not have at their disposal institutionalized legitimate structures which could mobilize this criticism and turn it into a real political force. The lack of an institutionalized church also makes it easier for secular powers to control religious institutions, which appear as atomized and relatively weak individual mosques, madrassas, or *waqfs vis-à-vis* a powerful and centralized state machinery with its administrative structures and secret police. Egypt is a good (or bad) example of this imbalance, in which a secular state controls—not always successfully but basically rather harshly—religious life and institutions in a most authoritarian fashion, which would certainly be unthinkable today in any Western post-Christian society.

Insofar as liberal concepts of human rights have been developed in Islamic societies, they have been imported from the outside—i.e., from the West. Especially in the Arab Muslim world, this was one of the byproducts of European imperial expansion, and it was for this reason that the ideas of constitutionalism, liberalism, and democracy have sometimes been viewed with suspicion in Arab countries; being companions of colonialism could very easily brand them as hypocritical and lacking legitimacy. Being imported from the West in the wake of imperial conquest and sometimes subsequent missionary activity, these ideas lacked internal legitimacy—very different from the way in which they grew in the West out of the dichotomies and contradictions of its own traditions. What has complicated matters even more has been the fact that the attempt to adopt Western ideas was not limited to constitutionalism or liberalism: in various Arab countries, and in various periods, Western ideas like secular nationalism, fascism, and communism were also tried—and as writers like Fouad Ajami describe so convincingly, have all failed dismally and even further weakened these societies *vis-à-vis* the West (and Israel, which is being seen as an outgrowth of Western civilization). In the ensuing crisis of identity and values, a return to Islam became for many Muslim Arabs the only "authentic" alternative to Western ideas, now identified with materialism, imperialism, secularism, and gender equality. It is here that Edward Said's criticism of Orientalism intersects with Islamic fundamentalism in viewing Western ideas of universalism as a mere foil for imperial domination and hegemonism. In some cases, former communists have now become Islamic fundamentalists. Many Muslims feel under siege, and this gives an extremely violent interpretation to the concept of *jihad* (originally "striving"), which then can legitimate suicide murders on the scale of September 11.

Yet while this applies more or less generally to the Arab Muslim world, it does not apply in the same manner to non-Arab Muslim countries: Turkey is an obvious example. For all its flaws regarding human rights and minority protection, Turkey is a democratic country—albeit a deeply flawed one; no Arab country can even qualify as such. Yet this was achieved only through the Kemalist revolution—a radical and violent departure from Islam as a public force, combining elements of extreme French Revolutionary laicism with authoritarian etatism. That even after eighty years this structure of a secular Muslim society is beset by Islamist fundamentalists who are trying to undo the Kemalist heritage suggests how deep some of these issues run.

But the more interesting example is Iran, and it is here that the ambivalent heritage of a religious tradition becomes apparent once more. The experience of the Islamic Republic of Iran paradoxically suggests that an Islamic context can also produce different results—again, not because of theology, but because of the specific historical circumstances in which developments work themselves out. Next to an Arab Muslim world which shows very few traits of development towards a liberal society or attempts at democratization, it is Iran which suggests that even a fundamentalist Islamic republic can move in another direction. I am not in a position to explain the reasons for this difference: it may be the Persian historical background, so very different from the Arab triumphalist tradition; it may also be the Shi'a context, which after all is a minority culture, free from the universalistic urges of mainly Arab Sunni hegemonism. Be this as it may, the differences between the twenty-two countries of the Arab League and Iran are staggering and suggest, once again, that religion as such is not a hindrance towards the emergence of a culture leading to universal human rights.

For the developments in the last decade in Iran are indeed far-reaching: what started as a bloody, repressive, and violent revolution against the West and those conceived as its agents (the Shah, up to a point Israel), is now developing into a much more complex system. Looking for possible parallels in European history, the development of Calvinist Protestantism from Calvin's austere and oppressive Geneva, through the English Puritan

Revolution towards British parliamentarism may perhaps suggest—surprising as it certainly is at first sight—an interesting and helpful parallel. In both cases, what started as a biblio-centric authoritarian attempt to resurrect a mythical pristine religious community turned into a vehicle of enormous change—and openness.

Like the Puritans, lacking a church and a hierarchy, the Iranian Revolution vests ultimate power in the Community of Believers: hence elections. These elections are obviously run within a circumscribed Islamic discourse (one should recall that in elections in Great Britain, until the 1820s, only members of the established Church of England and the Church of Scotland were qualified to vote and be elected—excluding not only Jews and Papists, but also Protestant dissenters). Yet despite this obviously significant restriction, elections in Iran, both presidential and parliamentary, are a truly contested process, not a charade (as in Egypt or Syria). Despite the unequal treatment of women according to *Shari'ah*, women have suffrage in Iran—and it appears that it was the women's vote that gave Khattami his majority in both elections against the more hard-line establishment candidate. More women serve in the Iranian *Majlis* than in any Arab parliament—and one of the deputy speakers of Parliament is a woman. Despite the chador, women appear to exercise significant political power—also in matters of social legislation and even on issues like birth control. Birth control is officially encouraged by the regime under the slogan that "Good Muslim families are educated families"—thus legitimizing smaller families. This shows again how plastic and malleable religious traditions can be. After all, nothing empowers women more than the ability to control the size of their families—and this is happening, of all places, in Iran.

Debates in the *Majlis* are real debates—again, within a circumscribed Islamic discourse: but they are not sham debates. Parliamentary coalitions are formed, alliances are forged and laws are passed, after much debate, by majority voting, not by presidential decrees or by acclamation. Anyone reading the debates in the Iranian *Majlis*, in which complex issues of religion and state are more or less openly debated, cannot but be reminded of the Cromwellian debates in the Long Parliament.

Recognized minorities (Christians, Jews, Zoroastrians—not of course Baha'is) have guaranteed allocated seats in Parliament—according to the Islamic precepts of defending the "People of the Book": this may be merely symbolic, and the fact that the one Jewish member of Parliament must be as anti-Israeli as are the current policies goes without saying. Nonetheless, minorities are represented (in secular Egypt the Copts are not recognized as a minority, since "there are no minorities in Egypt").

Even the current tug of war between the President, the *Majlis*, and the self-appointed theocratic Council of Guardians suggests more than one authoritarian focus of power and the possibility of a political public discourse totally lacking in countries like Egypt. While at the moment Hattami has as yet not proved himself to be able to wrest power from the more conservative Council of Guardians, the political discourse—again, very clearly within an Islamic political culture—points to developments which are still open-ended, precisely because the Iranian Constitution legitimizes a plurality of political institutions. This does not mean that Iran will in the immediate future became a full-fledged constitutional democracy—far from it. But political reality in Iran is totally different from the authoritarianism one finds in Arab Muslim societies—be they traditional fundamentalist monarchies like Saudi Arabia or secular republican mild autocracies like Egypt, let alone straightforward tyrannies like Syria or Iraq.

All this again shows that there is no simple answer to the question posed in the title of this essay. It also suggests that religion—the same religion—can give rise to different solutions and institutional arrangements as well as value legitimation. Both Iran and Saudi Arabia are Islamic fundamentalist states, but on every issue that has an impact on human rights they differ: in Saudi Arabia women are not allowed to drive, in Iran they sit in Parliament; in Saudi Arabia amputation is still a legitimate punishment, in Iran dissidents are brought before a (more or less) open trial; Saudi Arabia is an authoritarian monarchy with no elections and no representative institutions, Iran holds elections in which women have suffrage and may even have determined the outcome of the presidential race. One does not have to believe that Iran is on the road to a Western-style democracy (certainly I do not think this is the case) to realize that religion, in this case two fundamentalist versions of Islam, can lead to totally different results.

One of the legacies of the Enlightenment has been a healthy suspicion of the oppressive potentialities of religious authority. But this has sometimes led to simplistic accounts of the role of religion in the historical development of modern polities. Yet the paradox of modernity, and of the universal concept of human rights immanent to it, resides in the fact that our concept of secular universal humanism, anchored in a system of citizens' rights against the state, derives, by complex theoretical and institutionalized routes, from developments proceeding from religious traditions. It was only their *Aufhebung*, which made the universal concept of human rights possible: but *Aufhebung* is premised on a previous reality which is then being *aufgehoben*.

Chapter 14

Shiva Balaghi

Constitutionalism and Islamic Law in Nineteenth-Century Iran: Mirza Malkum Khan and Qanun*

Where are we?

– In the prison of injustice.

What must be done?

– We must break down the walls of this prison.

With what power?

– With the power of humanity.

What is the basis of the power of humanity?

– The power of humanity rests on the basis of those truths that the Prophets have placed in the repository of universal knowledge.

Where is that repository of knowledge?

– In the noble *Shari'a* of Islam.

---

* I would like to thank the participants of the 10th Annual Conference on the Individual vs.

András Sajó (ed.), Human Rights with Modesty: The Problem of Universalism, *327-348.*

This colloquy was published by Mirza Malkum Khan, one of the main proponents of constitutionalism in nineteenth-century Iran, in his newspaper *Qanun* (Law).[1] Malkum was amongst the first Iranians to articulate a notion of parliamentary government; his views were "central to the emerging revolutionary fervor" that resulted in the Constitutional Revolution (1905-11).[2]

Throughout the nineteenth century, Iran had come to occupy the geopolitical nexus of the imperialist contest for power. As Russia advanced further into Central Asia and Britain resolved to maintain control over its Indian and Arab territories, colonial attention became increasingly focused on Iran. Wars, border skirmishes, and damaging political treaties that extracted land and tariffs were a part of the history of Qajar Iran, but by the mid- to late-nineteenth century colonial control over Iran had become more indirect and discreet. Economic concessions and development schemes—for mineral extraction, railroad construction, banking, river navigation—figured largely in the competition for power over Iranian territory. At the same time, the cultural terrain became a significant space for constructing and resisting colonial influence. In the Iranian context, the nationalist struggle took shape against the backdrop of internal absolutism and colonial aggression; this struggle ultimately manifested itself as a constitutionalist movement.

As one of the main ideologues who helped shape notions of constitutionalism in the critical years leading up to the Constitutional Revolution, Malkum sought to reconcile notions of citizenship and representative government with Islamic precepts. He argued that Islam and constitutionalism were complimentary and compatible, and he was not alone in this belief. A significant source of support for constitutionalism came from the ranks of the *ulama*. As early as 1902, some leading clerics sent a telegraph to the Shah calling for the establishment of a chamber of representatives.[3] One of the leading clerics of the time, Sayyid Muhammad Tabataba'i, wrote in his diary about his advocacy of constitutionalism: "Right from my arrival in Tehran [in 1894] I had planned to establish constitutionalism (*mashrutah*) and a national consultative assembly in Iran. From pulpits I used to talk about these two.

the State held at the Central European University in Budapest for their helpful comments on an earlier version of this paper. This paper owes much to the intellectual companionship of Geoff Eley and Haggai Ram whose readings of multiple drafts of this paper have proved invaluable.

1. *Qanun*, no. 21, p. 1. Translations are my own, unless otherwise noted.
2. Abbas Amanat, "Constitutional Revolution," in Ehsan Yarshater (ed.), *Encyclopeadia Iranica*, vol. 6, London: Routledge (1982-) 163-176.
3. Abdul-Hadi Hairi, "Why Did the Ulama Participate in the Persian Constitutional Revolution of 1905–1909?" 17, 1-4 *Die Welt des Islams* (1976-7) 128.

Nasir al-Din Shah often complained about me and sent me messages saying that Iran was not yet prepared for constitutionalism."[4]

A dispute over sugar prices sparked the first public protests of the revolution. In 1905, the governor of Tehran ordered that some sugar merchants be bastinadoed for refusing to lower their prices. A group of merchants, tradesmen, and mullahs took sanctuary (*bast*) in a Tehran mosque. Government officials dispersed the group who then took refuge in the shrine south of Tehran. The group grew to some 2,000 people who remained in the shrine for twenty-five days. By January 1906, the Muzaffar al-Din Shah agreed to their main demands which comprised the formation of an *'adalatkhanah* (a house of justice) and the dismissal of the governor of Tehran. This *'adalatkhanah* was to be the parliament which some Iranians had been calling for, but the process by which the parliament would be established and would function was still unclear at this juncture.

Despite his assurances, the Shah did not follow up on his promise to establish the *'adalatkhanah*, leading to growing discontent and unrest. Finally, there was a confrontation involving a group of clerics and their students in which a young *sayyid* was killed. This violent encounter led to another *bast*. This time, nearly 15,000 protestors including mullahs, merchants, and tradesmen gathered in the British legation.[5] "The behavior of this vast crowd is

4. *Ibid.*, 130. Scholars writing on the constitutional period such as Hairi, Algar, Admaiyat, and Kasravi have shown that other leading clerics, such as Behbehani, Na'ini, Tehrani, Khurasani, and Mazandarani also supported the constitutionalist movement. Some clerics clearly opposed the movement. There is little consensus amongst scholars on a general historical explanation of Shiite ulama's position on constitutionalism as a concept. Scholars have suggested that ulama supported the constitutional movement because of their alliance with merchants, their sense of patriotism, their dislike for the corrupt Qajar kings, and/or their desire to ally themselves with a populist movement. Hamid Enayat outlined aspects of Shiite thought that were commensurate with constitutionalism. By the nineteenth century, he argued the development of *usul-i fiqh* or the theory of jurisprudence had developed in ways that accommodated constitutionalism. The centrality of doctrines relating to the competence of reason and the importance of consensus lent themselves to the acceptance of the role of man in lawmaking and the significance of majority opinion. These principles were reconcilable with democracy. Furthermore, Shiite ulama accepted the necessity of monarchy while recognizing the need for a *hay'at-i musaddidah* (adjusting body) that would oversee their governance. This view of the state was also compatible with notions of parliamentary government. See *ibid.*, 127-154; Hamid Enayat, *Modern Islamic Political Thought*, Austin: University of Texas Press (1982) 164-181; Faridun-i Adamiyat, *Idi'uluzhi-i Nahzat-i Mashrutiyat-i Iran*, Tehran: Payam (1976); Hamid Algar, "Religious Forces in Twentieth-Century Iran," in *The Cambridge History of Iran*, vol. 7, Cambridge: Cambridge University Press (1991) 734-5 and Ahmad Kasravi, *Tarikh-i Mashrutah-i Iran*, 16th printing, Tehran: Amir Kabir (1991).
5. For more on the importance of the *bast* for creating a revolutionary community and spreading ideas of constitutionalism, see Janet Afary, *The Iranian Constitutional Revolution, 1906–1911*, New York: Columbia University Press (1996) and see Edward G. Browne, *The Persian Revolution of 1905–1909* (1910), reprint, London: Frank Cass (1966).

described by eye-witnesses as admirable: they grouped themselves by guilds, each guild having its own tent, cooking arrangements and police," reported Edward G. Browne. "The friendliest feeling was manifested towards the English, and such of the staff of the Legation as mingled with the refugees were eagerly consulted as to the nature and formation of a Parliament, the method of election of deputies, and the like."[6] The protestors demanded that a constitution be drafted and a parliament established. The Shah finally relented and in August 1906, he issued a decree calling for the formation of a national assembly in Iran. The first *Majlis* (Parliament) convened in October 1906 and set about the task of writing a constitution. An ailing Muzaffar al-Din Shah decreed the document they produced into law in December 1906, a few days before he passed away. In October 1907, the new king Muhammad 'Ali Shah signed the Supplementary Fundamental Law. Together, the two documents formed the core of the Iranian Constitution for some seventy years.[7] The Constitution called for freedom of speech and the press, and it called for a committee of *mujtahids* who would ensure that legislation passed by the *Majlis* would be in accordance with Islam.[8]

The establishment of the *Majlis* and the issuance of the Constitution, however, did not mean the end of the Constitutional Revolution. Indeed, the course of the Revolution would remain rocky for some years to come. Internal differences amongst the revolutionaries about the nature of constitutionalism, continued reluctance by the Qajar shahs to relinquish power to the national assembly, and colonial interests in maintaining control over key aspects of governance severely hampered Iran's first experience of democratization. In August 1907, the Russians and the British signed an agreement in which Iran was divided into "spheres of influence." The convention fomented colonial influence over Iran and helped to further undermine constitutional rule.[9] The Shah, with the backing of the Cossack Brigade, carried out a violent coup in 1908, closing down the *Majlis*. Some of the leading intellectuals and activists who supported constitutionalism were imprisoned, executed, or exiled. This phase of the revolutionary years came to be known as the Lesser

6. Edward G. Browne, *A Brief Narrative of Recent Events in Persia*, London: Luzac (1909) 15.

7. For a comparative analysis of Iran's first Constitution, see Nader Sohrabi, "Historicizing Revolutions: Constitutional Revolutions in the Ottoman Empire, Iran, and Russia, 1905–1908," 100, 6 *American Journal of Sociology* (May 1995).

8. This committee was never actually formed. Throughout the twentieth century, various individuals and parties called for the formation of this committee.

9. See Nikki Keddie, *Qajar Iran and the Rise of Reza Khan, 1796–1925*, Costa Mesa, Calif.: Mazda Press (1999) 59. For a discussion of Iranian responses to the treaty, see Shiva Balaghi, "Print Culture in Late Qajar Iran: the Cartoons of *Kashkul*," 34 *Iranian Studies*, 4 (2001) 165.

Tyranny. The constitutionalists continued to struggle and eventually regained power in 1909. They forced the abdication of Muhammad 'Ali Shah, and reopened the *Majlis*.[10] While some clerics had supported the constitutional cause, others opposed it. The most famous of these was Shaikh Fazl-Allah Nuri, who called instead for *mashru'a*, a form of constitutional government that was based more rigidly on the *Shari'ah*. Concerned that the constitutionalist movement was calling for an increasingly secular form of government, Nuri eventually sided with the Shah. Following the 1909 constitutionalists countercoup against Muhammad 'Ali Shah, Nuri was brought to trial and executed.[11]

One of the primary goals of the second *Majlis* was to create an independent financial system for Iran. To that end, Morgan Shuster, an American advisor was hired to consult the new Parliament on strategies for reforming the country's finances.[12] Russian officials were displeased at growing American influence in Iran and at the possibility that their own profitable tariff agreements and concessions might be reversed. They complained that this arrangement was in violation of the Anglo-Russian Convention of 1907, which did not allow Iran to hire foreign advisors without the consent of both England and Russia. By the fall of 1911, matters had come to a head and Russia, with the support of England, gave the *Majlis* an ultimatum that would essentially nullify Iran's independence. The *Majlis* refused. Russian troops then entered northern Iran, brutally killing some of the leading constitutionalists; other intellectuals and activists fled Iran. Russian troops stormed the *Majlis*. Under threat of foreign occupation, the *Majlis* was dissolved.[13]

1. The Loyal Oppositionist as Newspaper Publisher

"The newspaper is the fountain-head for reforming the world... Without the newspaper, there is no right or bounty which is protected from the

10. A weak Ahmad Mirza took over the kingship and ruled until the 1921 coup that eventually overthrew the Qajar dynasty.
11. Algar, *op. cit.*, note 4, 734-5.
12. For more on the Shuster mission to Iran, see Robert A. McDaniel, *The Shuster Mission and the Persian Constitutional Revolution*, Minneapolis: Bibliotheca Islamica (1974).
13. For a more complete history of the Persian Revolution, see Browne, *op. cit.*, note 5; Mangol Bayat, *Iran's First Revolution: Shiism and the Constitutional Revolution of 1905–1909*, New York: Oxford University Press (1991); Nikki Keddie and Mehrdad Amanat, "Iran Under the Late Qajars, 1848–1922," in *Cambridge History of Iran*, vol. 7, note 4 and Keddie, *op. cit.*, note 9.

wickedness of fools," wrote Malkum.[14] The Cambridge Orientalist Edward G. Browne, who was actively engaged in supporting and documenting the history of the Constitutional Revolution, believed that Persian newspapers published prior to the revolution played a critical role in bringing it about. Browne argued, "in examining the causes and means which produced the prodromata of this Revolution it will be established that these publications were an important agent, and hold a conspicuous place amongst numerous other influences."[15] And Malkum's newspaper, *Qanun*, was clearly one of the most significant Persian newspapers published in its time. Fereydoun Adamiyat, one of the leading historians of modern Iran, wrote of Malkum, "We regard him as the most prominent...social critic of nineteenth-century Persia."[16] Shaul Bakhash wrote, "Of the publications that appeared in Nasir a-Din's lifetime, *Qanun* was the most important and influential."[17] Browne had this to say about Malkum's newspapers:

> By reason of the incomparable style and expression of Mirza Malkom Khan in Persian, this became the best newspaper in the Persian language, and, by reason of its effect, has an important historical position in the Persian awakening. In short, the writings of Mirza Malkom Khan have, generally speaking, a great twofold historical importance in the political and literary revolution of the latest Persian renaissance. Politically they were one of the chief supporters of the promoters of the Revolution and the renovation of Persia, and the founders of the movement of the *Risorgimento*; while from the literary point of view they were the sole originator of a peculiar style at once easy and agreeable.[18]

In some respects, *Qanun* closely resembled those newspapers that Jürgen Habermas observed normally appear in times of revolution, when politicians or intellectuals form their own newspapers and journals which become a forum for debating the pressing social and political matters of the time.[19]

14. *Qanun*, no. 4, p. 1. Unless otherwise noted, all translations from French and Persian which appear in this paper are my own.
15. Edward G. Browne, *The Press and Poetry of Modern Persia* (1914), Los Angeles: Kalimat Press (1983) 19.
16. Adamiyat as quoted in Hafez Farman Farmayan, "The Forces of Modernization in Nineteenth-Century Iran," in William Polk and Richard Chambers (eds.), *Beginnings of Modernization in the Middle East*, Chicago: University of Chicago Press (1968) 137.
17. Shaul Bakhash, Iran: Monarchy, Bureaucracy, and Reform Under the Qajars, 1858–1896, London: Ithaca Press (1978) 396.
18. Browne, *op. cit.*, note 15, 18-19.
19. Jürgen Habermas, *The Structural Transformation of the Public Sphere: An Inquiry into a Category of Bourgeois Society*, (Thomas Burger transl.), Cambridge: MIT Press (1993) 181-186. See Geoff Eley's valuable commentary on Habermas: "Nations, Publics, and Political Cultures: Placing Habermas in the Nineteenth Century," in Craig Calhoun, *Habermas and the Public Sphere*, Cambridge: MIT Press (1992).

Mirza Malkum Khan was the son of an Armenian from Isfahan.[20] At the young age of ten, he was sent to France to study. Returning to Iran in 1852, he took a position as a translator at the Dar al-Tarjumah (Translation Bureau) and joined the faculty of the Dar al-Fanun (the Polytechnic) where he taught "the new sciences." He allegedly converted from Christianity to Islam at this time, though this remains a matter of some controversy.[21] Soon after his return to Iran, Malkum founded a masonic group called the *faramushkhanah* (lit., the house of forgetting). Malkum once met the Orientalist Wilfred Blunt who said of him, "he was the most remarkable man I had ever met." During this meeting, Malkum told Blunt that his *faramushkhanah* boasted some 30,000 members, to whom he taught the "religion of humanity."[22] Many leading members of the nobility joined his secret society; some even believe that Nasir al-Din Shah was a member at one point. If so, the Shah soon lost his taste for the *faramushkhanah* and banned it.[23] Indeed, Malkum quickly became an annoyance to the government he served and was exiled from Iran in 1862 and given a series of diplomatic posts in Istanbul and Cairo. While serving as a diplomat in Istanbul, Malkum developed an important friendship with the Mushir al-Dawlah, the influential ambassador to Turkey. Apparently, it was also at this time that he made the acquaintance of Jamal al-Din al-Afghani, the famous pan-Islamist who hopscotched between Europe and the Middle East in the late nineteenth century, leaving an indelible mark on Egyptian and Iranian thinking on Islam and modernity.[24] When Mushir al-Dawlah was appointed prime minister in 1872, Malkum took a position as his assistant. Malkum then became the Persian ambassador to London, an important diplomatic post he held for some sixteen years.

In 1889, Malkum was granted a lottery concession by Nasir al-Din Shah who was visiting England. Upon returning to Iran, the Shah began to have second thoughts and rescinded the concession. In his memoirs, the Amin al-

20. A controversial character, Malkum has had his fair share of detractors. Here, I am not attempting to judge his character but to ascertain the significance of his thoughts as presented in his newspaper. Huma Natiq has written that questions about Malkum's desire for financial gain, his continued efforts to be granted titles by the Shah, and other controversies do not call into question his status as a reformer of the Qajar era. See Huma Natiq, "Ma va Mirza Malkum Khan-ha-yi Ma," in *Az Mast ke bar Mast*, Tehran: Agah, (1975-6) 136-200.
21. Farmayan, *op. cit.*, note 16, 173 and Bayat, *op. cit.*, note 13, 55-56.
22. As quoted in Browne, *op. cit*, note 5, 38.
23. Naser al-Din's successor, Muzaffar al-Din Shah, was said to have received copies of *Qanun*. *Ibid.*, 416.
24. Al-Afghani and Malkum Khan maintained a friendship and intellectual collaboration through the years. Edward G. Browne wrote of meeting Al-Afghani at the Holland Park home of Malkum Khan in the fall of 1891, at the same time that Malkum Khan was publishing *Qanun*. *Ibid.*, 45.

Dawlah wrote that the Shah came to the realization that the lottery, a form of gambling, was against the edicts of Islamic law and that this precipitated the Shah's decision to revoke the concession. Malkum, who had already sold interests in the concession for a profit of some 50,000 pounds sterling, refused to abide by the Shah's decision.[25] Needless to say, the primarily British investors in the lottery concession were little pleased at this turn of events. Many complained to the Shah and to British colonial officials in Iran, to no avail.[26] Malkum's rivalry with the influential minister Amin al-Sultan peaked during this crisis. Possibly under his advice, the Shah recalled Malkum, who refused to leave his post and return to Iran. The British minister in Tehran, Sir Henry Drummond Wolff, wrote of the diplomatic impasse to Lord Curzon, "I do not know whether you were here when Malcom Khan was recalled. He had induced the Shah when in England...to give a concession for...a lottery and roulette tables in Persian and when the Shah wanted to withdraw it he sent a telegram abusing the Amin-es-Sultan. I fancy there must be a great row going on about it in London, but the telegraph is down."[27]

Despite the Shah's desire for him to return to Tehran, Malkum stayed on in London. Once again, he refashioned himself, this time as a "loyal opposition." It was in the aftermath of this diplomatic fallout, in the years 1890-1, that Malkum began publishing *Qanun*.[28] Though Malkum had been in the service of the Qajar state for most of his adult life—as a translator for the Translation Bureau, a professor at the Polytechnic, a diplomat in Cairo and Istanbul, an assistant to a prime minister, and as the Persian representative in London—he saw himself as a credible oppositionist and turned to publishing a newspaper as his primary tool for articulating and disseminating his oppositionist views.[29] Some of Iran's historians consider his role as the editor of *Qanun* to be his most significant contribution.[30]

---

25. *Khatirat-i Siyasi-yi Amin al-Dawlah*, in Hafez Farman Farmayan (ed.), Tehran: Amir Kabir Press (1970) 138-9.
26. One British resident of Iran wrote, "The Lottery people are, I think, behaving very stupidly. They telegraph the Shah instead of persecuting Malcolm. What can the poor Shah do? He has no power whatever over Malcom now." Ironside to Curzon, Tehran (12 January 1891) MSS.EUR.F112/614, pt.1, Curzon Personal Papers, Oriental and India Office Collection, the British Museum, London. [Heretofore OIOC.]
27. Drummond Wolff to Curzon, Tehran (21 December 1889) MSS.EUR.F112/614, pt. 3, Curzon Personal Papers, OIOC.
28. *Qanun* was printed on a press with moveable type in London at an address on Lombard Street. Its pages were divided into two columns. Altogether, forty-two undated issues were published over the span of three and a half years.
29. He went on to serve as the Persian ambassador to Rome under Muzaffar al-Din Shah.
30. See Isma`il Ra'in, *Mirza Malkum Khan* (Tehran, 1350/1971-2) 11; Huma Natiq, introduction to the reprints of *Qanun*, Tehran: Amir Kabir (1976) 1; Bakhash, *op. cit.*, note 17, 382.

Qanun was seen as an influential paper not just by virtue of its political content, but also for the style of its writing. Its literary style and vocabulary left a mark on Persian writing. The words nation, nationality, and national (*millat, milliyat, milli)* were ubiquitous in the pages of *Qanun*.[31] He popularized the terms law (*qanun*), reform (*tanzimat*), and principles of administration (*usul-i idarah*).[32]

Malkum once said that *Qanun* was a culmination of forty years of effort, his thinking and planning on how to bring progress to the Iranian nation. What motivated him to produce a newspaper as his vehicle for reform, his instrument as the loyal opposition? In the first issue of *Qanun*, Malkum clearly stated his reasons for choosing to edit a newspaper:

> A small group of Iran's people, for a variety of reasons, have dragged themselves out of their familiar country and have become dispersed in foreign countries... Amongst these dispersed immigrants, those intelligent individuals who compare the progress of foreign countries with Iran have been wondering how to help the helpless ones who remain in Iran. After much thought and inquiry, they were agreed upon the idea that for the purpose of the rescue and progress of the people of Iran, no better instrument could be imagined than a free newspaper.[33]

The larger mission of his newspaper consisted of four main goals: to publish the truth, to solidify unity, to search for the law, and to assist the oppressed.[34] With the publication of *Qanun*, Malkum hoped to offer a means through which various thinkers could come together to employ their knowledge through "the power of the pen...in the service of the nation."[35] When *Qanun* was originally published, it contained a price list in its header. Soon, however, the impracticality of selling the newspaper became clear and rather than listing a monetary price, the header of the newspaper asked for other forms of payment from its readers. In the fourth issue the price of subscription was "one bit of knowledge." The thirty-seventh issue's price was listed as "patriotism" (*millat-parasti*). In exchange for payment, readers of the tenth issue were told that "understanding will suffice."

For Malkum, the publication of a free newspaper was a sign of progress as well as a vehicle with which to rescue Iran. Malkum probably had some

---

31. Bakhash, *ibid.*, 320.
32. Browne, *op. cit.*, note 15, 18; Amanat, *op. cit.*, note 2, 163.
33. *Qanun*, no. 1, p. 1. A complete English translation of the 14th issue of Qanun appears in Hamid Algar, *Mirza Malkum Khan: A Study in the History of Iranian Modernism*, Berkeley: The University of California Press (1969), Appendix C, 300-308.
34. *Ibid.*
35. *Qanun*, no. 2, p. 1.

less than benevolent reasons for publishing *Qanun* as well. It became an instrument with which to discredit his personal enemy, the Prime Minister Amin al-Sultan, who had been influential in persuading the Shah to revoke Malkum's lottery concession. Although Malkum's rivalry with Amin al-Sultan and his inevitable anger at having been stripped of his rank as ambassador to London may have fuelled his outspoken criticism of the state of affairs in Iran, *Qanun* must not be seen as a mere instrument in the intrapersonal disputes of the Qajar royal court. And if the ideas he expressed in the newspaper reflect the influence of other thinkers, they are nonetheless clearly in line with views he had long expressed.

There is a remarkable consistency in many of his central arguments when compared to discussions he had with British audiences, whether in his private diplomatic correspondence, public lectures, or articles published in England. Indeed, a study of Malkum's diplomatic correspondence shows that his concern over Iran's troubles long preceded the publication of *Qanun*. For example, in 1874, he wrote an eight-page memorandum to the British Foreign Office, sounding an alarm over the condition of Persia. The memorandum is marked "confidential: desired seen only as his personal opinion." In it, Malkum wrote, "Persia finds herself in the midst of two great dangers, one interior, the other exterior. The exterior danger, the whole world knows, is the natural and almost inevitable expansion of the Russian Empire across Asia. The internal danger is the general situation of Persia; her inability to establish a regular administration on her frontiers."[36] Malkum pleaded for British intervention, which he felt was necessary in order to assure Persian independence. He concluded, "Persia abandoned to herself can do absolutely nothing; alone, she is irrevocably lost."[37]

2. Islamism and Constitutionalism in Malkum's Thought

No longer an official diplomat, Malkum turned his attention to influencing public opinion—in England and in Iran. One of his central goals was to reconcile his call for reform in Iran with the tenets of Islam. On 6 June 1891, he published a letter in the British press under the heading "A Crisis in Persia." In the letter he said that his life's work had been to strive for "Persian regeneration." He informed the British public of the establishment of his newspaper and said, "The body of the doctrine which I seek to explain gradually

36. Memorandum from Malcom (received 8 April 1874) FO 60/166, Foreign Office, London, original in French.

37. *Ibid.*

through the instrumentality of a popular journal, diffused throughout Persia, whilst it embraces the essential conditions of modern civilization, is strictly founded upon the great principles of Islam, and largely answers to the wants and aspirations of the Persian people."[38] Malkum went on to describe what he would publish in his newspaper:

> Not a word which is not perfectly in agreement with the best science and the purest morality; not a premature idea; no pretensions to an advanced Western liberalism—nothing but the elementary principles universally recognized as just, inoffensive, and indispensable. All this I have wrapped up in formulas calculated to strike the imagination and penetrate the heart of the people. As to my immediate object, my ambition goes no further than asking humbly of our Government to give us a Law.[39]

In addition to publishing letters in the British press, Malkum gave lectures to various groups in order to affect British public opinion. One such address was given at the Queen's House in Chelsea which was the residence of the Reverend H. R. Hawels. In this lecture, Malkum asked, "Why is it that European people have made such wonderful progress, while the Asiatic races, who were the first promoters of civilisation, have lagged so far behind?"[40] For Malkum neither race nor religion were a handicap for the Asians, he remarked clearly, "The Mahomedan religion is not opposed to civilisation."[41] Malkum admonished Europeans for not sufficiently understanding Islam. He explained:

> Islamism is not known in Europe. You read the Khoran [*sic*], and you think you know Islamism. That is a great mistake. The Khoran is, as you know, a sort of revised Bible, and there is nothing in it which is directly opposed to Christian principles, but it is not the whole of Islamism. Islam is not a religion; it is a vast system which embraces the whole of society—the man from his birth to his death. There is nothing that is beyond its scope... The whole science of Asia, everything which is good or useful, has been attributed to Islam. Islam is the accumulated wisdom of the East. It is an ocean where you can find everything which is good to be known, and it offers all kinds of facilities not in the Khoran alone, but in the traditions, for the progress of the people.[42]

Malkum emphasized the importance of security and law for achieving progress: "Without security of life and property, no progress—without jus-

38. Malkum Khan, "A Crisis in Persia" (6 June 1891) newspaper clipping found in the Curzon's Personal Papers, MSS.EUR.F111/68, OIOC.

39. *Ibid.*

40. Malkum Khan, "Persian Civilization," as printed in *Contemporary Review* (1891) 238-244.

41. *Ibid.*, 238.

42. *Ibid.*, 239.

tice, no freedom—without freedom, no national prosperity, no individual contentment and peace. Europeans have somehow fought for and won in varying degrees justice, freedom, and representative government."[43] He further advised his audience that it would be preferable if Europeans interested in the Eastern Question would "present European civilization independent of Christian dogma."[44] Here, his views reflect the influence of his friend al-Afghani as he articulated an idea that has remained influential in Iranian political thought. "As to the principles which are found in Europe, which constitute the root of your civilization, we must get hold of them somehow, no doubt," Malkum argued, "but instead of taking them from London or Paris, instead of saying this comes from such an ambassador, or is adviced by such a Government (which will never be accepted), it would be very easy to say that it comes from *Islam*, and that this can be proved. We have had some experiences in this direction. We found that ideas which were by no means accepted when coming from your agents in Europe, were accepted at once with the greatest delight when it was proved that they were latent in Islam."[45] Malkum's central argument as he spoke before a British audience was to demonstrate the importance of finding ways to disentangle liberalism from its basis in Christian dogma. Malkum perceived both the possibility and the necessity of reframing key components of liberalism (justice, freedom, citizenship, rights) within an Islamic paradigm.

In his newspaper, Malkum repeated the ideas about the need for justice in Iran which he had shared with British audiences. "There is no security of life. No freedom of speech or action. All of Iran is a prison of misery...and if there is hope for salvation, from where will the sun or life arise?" For Malkum, the answer was the establishment of a legal system based on the *Shari'ah* of Islam.[46] "What does security of life and property mean?" He answered this question in an issue of *Qanun*: "It means that from now, you cannot be imprisoned without a trial and evidence of your guilt. Your home and property cannot be arbitrarily confiscated. Your wages cannot be garnished at will. Your rights as a subject... cannot be sold away. Under no circumstances will

43. *Ibid.*, 239.

44. *Ibid.*, 244.

45. *Ibid.*, 243, emphasis his. The notion of carefully presenting liberal ideas within the context of Islam in order to avert opposition from Iranians was also shared by Jamal al-Din Al-Afghani. In a letter to Tabataba'i, a *mujtahid* who supported the establishment of the Parliament, Al-Afghani encouraged him to hide his real intentions, i.e., support for constitutionalism, for tactical reasons. Subsequently, *mujtahids* such as Tabataba'i and Behbehani called for the establishment of representative government even as they claimed not to be endorsing a Western style constitutionalism. Hairi, *op. cit.*, note 3, 127-154.

46. *Qanun*, no. 9, p. 1-2.

they any longer [be able to] cut off your ear or your nose; they will not tear out your eyes."[47]

The key to the protection of these rights for Iranians was the establishment of a codified legal system. "Law is the language and power of justice," he argued.[48] All nations had a system of law by which they were governed, Malkum reported, except for Iran, Afghanistan, and Baluchistan. What must be done so that Iran, too, could have the benefits of a legal system? Universal progress had reached a stage, Malkum wrote, that the community of nations would no longer tolerate a lawless state in any corner of the world. There are two means by which Iranians can achieve their goal. Either "we can kiss the boots of foreign soldiers so they will bring law to our country or we can have enough wisdom to establish a legal system on our own in Iran."[49]

Clearly, Malkum's chief concern was to put in place an abiding code of law in Iran. "Iran is filled with God-given blessings. The thing which negates all these blessings is the absence of law. No one in Iran is the proprietor of anything, because there is no law."[50] Malkum went on to describe the anarchy that has resulted from this absence of law, "We appoint governors without law. We dismiss generals without law. We sell the rights of governance without law. We imprison the slaves of God without law. We grant concessions without law. We tear open stomachs without law."[51] Malkum asserted, "All of the progress and calm of other nations is because of the establishment of law."[52] Laws of other nations allow their citizens to know their rights and duties clearly. Such is the case in India, in Tiflis, in Egypt, in Istanbul and "even among the Turkmen."[53] In the earlier issues of the newspaper, Malkum was reticent to directly criticize the Shah. At times, he clearly stated that the flaws of the country were not due to Nasir al-Din Shah. In his discussion of the corrupt bureaucracy and the consequences of its lawlessness, he claimed that the problems were not a result of a lack of justice (*'adalat*) on the part of the Shah. However, the Shah's *'adl* was ineffectual without a system of law and an orderly bureaucratic system. He concluded, "All of the desolation and all of the tyranny have been because of lawlessness."[54]

What did Malkum have to say to those Iranians who claimed that Iran already had a system of law in the form of the Islamic law, the *Shari'ah*? Had

47. *Qanun*, no. 5, p. 1.
48. *Qanun*, no. 3, p. 1.
49. *Qanun*, no. 7, p. 1.
50. *Qanun*, no. 1, p. 1.
51. *Ibid.*
52. *Qanun*, no. 1, p. 3
53. *Qanun*, no. 1, p. 1.
54. *Qanun*, no. 3, p. 1

not the Qur'an and the *hadith* provided every Muslim with a system of law which was abiding to all men for all time? Was Malkum advocating a secular system of law over an Islamic one? Indeed, Malkum addressed this matter directly in the very first issue of *Qanun*. For several thousand years, he wrote, prophets and scholars had been collecting laws, "And the complete basis of laws we see before us in the *shari'a* of Islam as clearly as the sun. The problem is not in selecting the laws. The main issue is that good laws whether of the heavens or of the intellect, from whichever they are chosen, and in whatever language they are printed, and however much we fill our libraries with these laws, it is unlikely that they will be enacted by themselves."[55] So for Malkum, Iran's problem was not that it lacked a system of law. Indeed this passage conveys a seeming indifference as to whether the laws were divinely inspired or written by men; the focus of Malkum's discussion was on finding a system for enacting and enforcing the law. Sensitive to the possibility that his ideas might be perceived as advocating a European mode of law for Iran, he wrote, "We do not say that we want the law of Paris or the law of Russia or the law of India. The basis of good laws are universal and the best basis of laws are those which the *shari'a* of God have taught us, but from the lack of enactment of these laws, we have witnessed much damage and now we are so in need of and thirsty for law that we'll be satisfied with any law even if it is the law of the Turkmen because even the worst laws are better than lawlessness."[56]

This was a notion that Malkum repeated throughout the pages of *Qanun*. In a much later issue, he wrote, "We do not think it is necessary to refer to the laws of foreign nations. We find the *shari'a* of Islam completely sufficient for [bringing about] the calm and progress of this nation."[57] Though Malkum spoke approvingly of Islamic law throughout *Qanun*, he was clear that even Islam as witnessed in Iran at the time had been corrupted. As though responding to a question about the kind of Islam he would endorse, he wrote, "Which Islam? The Islam of learning, not the Islam of ignorance; the Islam of love, not the Islam of persecution; the Islam of progress, not the Islam of decline; the Islam of unity, not the Islam of division; the Islam of development, not the Islam of ruin; the Islam of reason (*'aql*), not the Islam of imitation (*naql*); the Islam of man, not the Islam of things."[58]

Even as Malkum criticized the state of affairs in Iran, he attempted to do so without alienating the Shah and the clergy. Alongside his bitter criticisms, he published words of conciliation. Indeed, Malkum attempted to devise a

55. *Qanun*, no. 1, p. 2.

56. *Qanun*, no. 1, p. 4.

57. *Qanun*, no. 17, pp. 1-2.

58. *Qanun*, no. 27, as translated by Bakhash, *op. cit.*, note 17, 343.

system that brought together various factions of Iranian society. He felt it was essential to forge a union amongst the people of Iran, to bring together the secular and religious scholars of the law, "The Mujtahids and scholars and the lords of the pen and owners of the words must bespeak the virtues of law and the necessity of unity night and day into the ears of the people of Iran from the schools, the pulpits, the streets, and bazaars."[59] Throughout *Qanun*, we see references to various classes of Iranian society. Developing "a union" (*ittifaq*) amongst these classes and groups was clearly one of Malkum's objectives, "All classes of people: the mullah and merchant, the general and soldier, the prince and peasant in search of law must be of one opinion, one tongue, and cooperate."[60]

What did Malkum mean by unity? He noted that in Iran the meaning of communal unity was still unclear. "Most think that when we say unity, it means that in all of our actions and in all of our thoughts, we must be unified. Such unity has never existed in this world and one cannot have such expectations from human nature."[61] What Malkum meant by unity was for the people to come together out of a common sense of knowledge—and to search for a universal law on the basis of that shared knowledge. Iran's awakening was to come through knowledge. "If there is a means to awaken us, it is that whip of the people of discourse (*ahl-i kalam*)."[62]

But Malkum also sought to bring about certain reforms in Iran—and the key to Iran's prosperity was to implement reforms that were based on knowledge. "The prosperity of Iran is linked to the prosperity of the world, and the prosperity of the world is, as we know, subject to the spread of knowledge."[63] In one of the issues of *Qanun*, he wrote that a reader had written him asking, "How can the old ways of our nation be changed?" To which Malkum responded, "The same way that forty other nations of forty other lands have changed."[64] And for Malkum, the answer to reform and progress was always to work to acquire knowledge and then to unite to spread that knowledge through the nation using a system of law. "Today, in the face of the power of neighboring states, neither Arabic words nor the bones of ancestors is of any use," he once said, "Today, what we need is knowledge."[65] Even the Shah needed to have a better understanding of "the meaning and power of knowl-

59. *Qanun*, no. 1, p.3.

60. *Ibid.*

61. *Qanun*, no. 3, p. 1.

62. *Qanun*, no. 14, as translated by Algar, *op. cit.*, note 4, 304.

63. *Qanun*, no. 17, p. 2.

64. *Qanun*, no. 29.

65. As quoted in Bakhash, *op. cit.*, note 17, 14-15.

edge" in order to better govern the country.[66] At one point, he beckoned the reader, "Arise, o champion of the wounded heart, for the days of darkness are at an end and the sun of knowledge has illuminated the world from East to West."[67]

Ultimately, what Malkum wanted for Iran was summarized in the three words constituting the motto of the newspaper: unity, justice, and progress. Clearly, uniting the people of the nation, putting knowledge at the service of that nation, and instituting a code of law were chief among the ideas that *Qanun* reiterated in issue after issue. What concrete means did Malkum propose to bring about these desired goals? In one issue, Malkum set forth four demands. First, he wanted Iranians to have security of property and life. Second, he wanted to create a framework whereby the reigns of government were in the hands of the learned men of the nation. Third, he wanted the taxes that the people paid to be used for the betterment of the country and to protect the rights of the nation, rather than be squandered by corrupt religious and government organizations. And finally, Malkum wanted Iran to have a parliament.[68] The liberation of the people of Iran, according to Malkum, depended on the creation of a national parliament whose members would bring order to the affairs of the nation in accordance with the *Shari'ah*. This national parliament would determine the limits of power, the rights of subjects, and the terms of justice according to the tenets of Islam.[69]

Throughout the issues of *Qanun*, Malkum talked about establishing a parliament. In the third issue, he wrote that codifying a system of law in Iran must be carried out by a national parliament (*Majlis-i shura-yi milli*). According to Malkum, in order for this parliament to be effective it must be granted complete autonomy and authority. Its membership should be no less than seventy officials. The supervision of the ministries and government bureaus must fall to this parliament. Further, the parliament must be allowed to decide the tax rate on an annual basis and to designate tax rates for certain groups; the parliament should also be responsible for tax collection. In order to protect its members, Malkum held that no member of parliament could be penalized for decisions taken, unless she made a clear and significant error. In such a case, it should be left to the parliament itself to determine whether the mistake made warranted recourse. The members of parliament should feel secure in their positions. And who did Malkum think belonged in this parliament? "The great *mujtahids*, the renowned intellectuals, deserving mul-

66. *Qanun*, no. 41, p. 4.

67. *Qanun*, no. 14, as translated by Algar, *op. cit.*, note 4, p. 308.

68. *Qanun*, no. 22, p.1.

69. *Qanun*, no. 9, pp 2-3.

lahs, the nobility of each province, and even the knowledgeable youth should be members of this parliament."[70]

3. Constitutionalism as Contraband: Distributing and Reading a Banned Newspaper in Qajar Iran

The question of the distribution and readership of Malkum's newspaper is important, if we are to gauge the degree of influence it may have had on Iranian thinkers and activists in the critical years leading up to the Constitutional Revolution. One cannot simply read printed texts in and of themselves in order to assess the larger historical impact of the printing revolution. Indeed the context in which these texts were produced and read is a crucial piece of the puzzle. Still, it is quite difficult as a historian to get a sense of the distribution and readership of nineteenth-century Iranian newspapers. Determining the extent of censorship is a good starting point. Given the nature of the Iranian government at the time, what exactly do we mean when we discuss censorship? How did it function? We know that censorship did indeed exist; Malkum even speculated that upon seeing *Qanun*, the Amin al-Sultan would try to get it banned.

In his memoirs, the Amin al-Dawlah, a friend of Malkum's, wrote that when issues of *Qanun* began to appear in Iran, the Shah apparently saw some of the issues and became very angry. He declared the printing and distribution of Malkum's paper to be strictly forbidden in Iran. The minister of publication, the I'timad al-Saltanah, had explained the European concept of "sansur" to the Shah.[71] The Persian government seems to have adapted this form of restriction. However, there were always authors and readers willing to actively bypass the censors. The ban on Malkum's newspaper, according to Amin al-Dawlah, simply encouraged Malkum even further and made his newspaper even more famous; people were even more eager to read this forbidden paper. Amin al-Dawlah, who as minister of post was responsible for censorship, confiscated copies of *Qanun* that were posted to Iran. Nevertheless, he claimed that copies of the newspaper continued to enter Iran from the Ottoman Empire, from the Caucasus, and from Iraq; they

70. *Qanun*, no. 3, pp. 2-3.

71. Peter Avery, "Printing, the Press and Literature in Modern Iran," in Peter Avery, Gavin Hambly and Charles Melville (eds.), *Cambridge History of Iran*, vol. 7. Cambridge: Cambridge University Press (1991) 828.

were carried in by travelers and merchants. Soon, the articles of the newspaper were read and discussed in social gatherings.[72]

Some Iranians who were suspected of helping to distribute the newspaper were punished. According to Browne, "those unfortunate Persians who were known to have received it or to be in possession of it were arrested, and in several cases severely punished."[73] Amongst these was Mirza Muhammad Baqir, who had been Browne's teacher. Browne wrote that he suffered a long and hard imprisonment. By January 1891, the arrests of readers of *Qanun* and those suspected of being affiliated with the newspaper had increased. Several mullahs were expelled. High government officials, including the Ambassador to Istanbul, lost their posts. Midlevel officials, such as the Consul General in the embassy at Baghdad, were charged with distributing the newspaper. Mirza Nasrullah Khan, a secretary to the Austrian Embassy, was arrested. He had a printing press in his house on which he reprinted copies of *Qanun* for distribution throughout Iran. Sayyid Hussein, who worked for the court translating newspapers, especially those from India, was also arrested.[74] Mirza Reza Kirmani was amongst those arrested for reading *Qanun*; in 1896, this same man assassinated Nasir al-Din Shah. These arrests demonstrate that the ban against the newspaper was seriously imposed, but that despite the dangers many were willing to read the paper at great personal risk. The readership seems to have come from various classes including the clergy, mid- to high-level Iranian bureaucrats, and merchants.[75]

It is clear then that despite the prohibition against reading *Qanun*, it had a following in Iran who read, reprinted, and distributed the newspaper. To get a better sense of the distribution of the paper and readers' reactions to it, I now turn to comments from subscribers in Mirza Malkum Khan's personal papers. One reader named Abdul-Hussein wrote that the people are complaining that one issue a month of *Qanun* was not enough and encouraged Malkum to publish the newspaper more frequently.[76] Another letter contains comments from readers living in Istanbul, Tehran, Kirman, Nizir, Zanjan, and Sirjan.[77] So *Qanun* seems to have been read in the provinces as well as Tehran. Another series of unsigned letters from a reader in Iran update Malkum on the arrival of various shipments of the newspaper. In one of these letters, we read that those issues of *Qanun* that were sent through the French post had

72. Khatirat-i Siyasi-yi Amin al-Dawlah, op. cit., note 25, 139-140.

73. Browne, *op. cit.*, note 5, 35.

74. Natiq, *op. cit.*, note 20, 10-12.

75. Bakhash, *op. cit.*, note 17, 315-7.

76. Supplement Persan, folios 99-100, Bibliothèque Nationale, Paris (1996).

77. Supplement Persan, folios 101-102, Bibliothèque Nationale, Paris (1996).

arrived.[78] In another, he mentions that the shipment of *Qanun* that was sent through the British post had been received.[79] It would appear that the French and the British cooperated in bringing the banned oppositional newspaper into Iran. The diplomatic post was not subject to the Shah's censors.

Mirza Aqa Kirmani, the editor of *Akhtar*, an influential Persian newspaper printed in Istanbul, wrote to Malkum regularly. *Akhtar* had printed articles discussing the need for instituting a code of law long before *Qanun* was published. But Natiq believes that *Qanun*, with its more simple and direct style, was read by more Iranians than *Akhtar*.[80] There seems to have been a relationship between the two newspaper publishers Kirmani and Malkum. Kirmani wrote admiringly of *Qanun*, "Each of its arguments was a spring of life-giving water; a new life came into my body...I was dead; I came to life. I was tears; I became laughter by reading its pages... After all the hopelessness and grief that I have felt for the condition of Iran, I have once again become hopeful."[81]

Another reader from Istanbul wrote to Malkum, "*Qanun* stirred a new joy in my heart and connected the roots of my soul to a divine [mystical] song...I see myself as a new person... A slave on the road of patriotic martyrdom and for the advancement of Humanity, I stand with...firm resolution." He talked of the various connections that he had in Istanbul with other Iranians, noting that soon large numbers of Iranian pilgrims would be coming through Istanbul. He asked that Malkum send him at least twenty copies of each issue of *Qanun* to be distributed to these pilgrims. He also wrote the addresses of various Iranians, mainly merchants, living in Bombay, Baghdad, Basra, Egypt, Trebizond, Erzerum, Istanbul, and Tiflis who had requested copies of *Qanun*.[82] Merchants living in Iran and in merchant communities outside of Iran clearly played a key role in the distribution of the newspaper and were among its loyal readers. They sometimes smuggled copies of the newspaper into Iran, hidden in shipments of cloth and sugar. But the correspondence also made a direct reference to working to advance Humanity, suggesting that the reader was also promoting membership in Malkum's secret society. There seems to have been a connection between Malkum's *faramushkhanah* and the distribution of his newspaper.

The letters from other readers also indicate the deep impact that the newspaper had on them. Though some of the comments could be seen as

78. Supplement Persan, folios 110-111, Bibliothèque Nationale, Paris (1996).
79. Supplement Persan, folios 66-67, Bibliothèque Nationale, Paris (1996).
80. Natiq, *op. cit.*, note 20, 3.
81. Kirmani to Malkum, Istanbul, 1308/1890, Supplement Persan, folio 63 Bibliothèque Nationale, Paris (1996).
82. Supplement Persan, folios 94-95, Bibliothèque Nationale, Paris (1996).

typical Persian polite exaggeration, one cannot dismiss these responses altogether. One reader wrote, "If Sa'adi came to life [and read *Qanun*], he would say nothing in praise of himself."[83] *Qanun* came to fore at a time of great turmoil in Iran—during its publication the Tobacco Revolt was underway. In response to the colonial pressures from Britain and Russia and the intransigence of the Qajar dynasty, Malkum's newspaper offered a democratic and nationalist solution. To those readers who were also active in the nationalist movement, such as Kirmani, the newspaper offered some hope. For some of its readers at least, it may have also offered spiritual solace.

Lahuti, who later became one of the leading nationalist poets of the Constitutional movement, described his discovery of *Qanun*:

> The first issue of *Qanun* seduced me [as I read it]. When I came to myself, I saw my father standing above me. He was staring at me. It became clear that I had been drowned in the reading of *Qanun* for hours—to the point where I did not notice my father's entrance. Sweating in fear, I pleaded for my father's forgiveness for having taken *Qanun* and read it without his permission. My father said: Dear Son! It is I who have sinned for not having informed you of the existence of this newspaper until now.[84]

Lahuti's father explained that he was a member of Malkum's secret society and that this was how he had come to own and read copies of *Qanun*. His father added, "*Qanun* was very secretive and dangerous. In any house where it is found, that house and its inhabitants will be destroyed. My wings were opened from hearing my father's words and tiredness and hopelessness left me. I told myself this is that fire which I seek."[85]

4. Conclusion

That *Qanun* was a significant influence on Iran is undeniable. It openly discussed ideas of constitutionalism in a way that fused Islamic ideology with notions of representative government. It held the Shah accountable to a body of representative officials. The law of the land could no longer be left to the will of the Shah alone. Understanding this, Malkum wrote that the ultimate authority lay with the people of Iran. Fifteen years after *Qanun* was published, the people of Iran began a revolution with the explicit purpose of establishing a constitutional government. *Qanun* helped to set the stage for that revolution. It did so by creating a shared discourse amongst various seg-

83. Supplement Persan, folios 61-62, Bibliothèque Nationale, Paris (1996).
84. As quoted in the Persan in Isma`il Ra'in, *op. cit.*, note 30, 119.
85. *Ibid.*

ments of Iranian society—a discourse with which the Iranian people could critique the state and which allowed them to imagine an entirely different relationship with the state. After *Qanun*, words like *reform* and *law* became integrated into the Persian vocabulary of governance. The act of reading and distributing an oppositional newspaper which had been banned by the Shah was itself a revolutionary act. From the comments of readers, one gets the impression that the act of importing the illegal newspaper, distributing it to other readers, reading it together in social gatherings, and passing along cherished copies was in itself a means of creating a community.

Though Malkum himself reentered the good graces of the Qajar shahs and eventually assumed the position of Iranian minister to Rome (where he passed away before the completion of the Constitutional Revolution), *Qanun* remained an important ideological impetus for constitutionalism in Iran. It was copied and redistributed during the critical revolutionary years.[86] In recognition of the importance of the newspaper in the constitutionalist struggle, Malkum's wife reported that some members of the *Majlis* "had the first numbers of the paper printed in gold letters and sent them to him as an expression of what they thought of his words."[87]

Malkum was one of the leading lay intellectuals who helped frame constitutionalism in Iran, and his newspaper, *Qanun*, was his primary vehicle for conveying his ideas. As such, it is important to note how commentaries on Islam were central in his writings. This may suggest that a bifurcated perspective of the Iranian Constitutional Revolution that divides Islamism and constitutionalism into two discreet and opposed spheres of thinking is ahistorical. Some scholars see Malkum as the archetypal secular modernizer who called for the "total Westernization of Iran."[88] If his writings in *Qanun* are any indication, we must consider the notion that he viewed Islam as central to the construction of constitutionalism in Iran and perceived the tenets of Islam as being compatible with representative government that supports the rights of the citizens of the state.

In the critical years leading up the Constitutional Revolution, Malkum's views helped Iranians imagine ways to create a form of representative government within an Islamic framework that protected the rights of Iranians as citizens. The Qajar shahs were reluctant to respond to growing demands that they share power and establish a legal framework for governance; the struggle

86. I have reviewed issues of the newspaper that were reprinted under the auspices of Hashim Aqa Rabizadeh. These issues are marked "It is a copy" in the header and were sold in bookshops in Tehran and Tabriz.

87. Princess Malkom Khan to Edward G. Browne, Paris, (7 November 1908), Box 12, bundle 2, folio 71, Browne Personal Papers, Cambridge University Library, Cambridge, UK.

88. Hamid Enayat supports the notion that this is the classic interpretation of Malkum. See Enayat, *op. cit.*, note 4, 166.

between the shahs and the revolutionaries lasted for six years. In the intervening years, Iran faced a tremendous blow to its sovereignty with the Anglo-Russian Convention of 1907 that divided her territory into colonial spheres of influence. The struggle to establish a government based on sovereignty by the people of Iran culminated in the spectacle of the Russian bombardment of the house of Parliament, an act that had the backing of the British. As Russian troops moved south through Tabriz, Rasht, and Tehran, they left behind a trail of ruin. Libraries and bookstores were destroyed; many newspapers were closed down; some intellectuals were hung; other constitutionalist thinkers fled to lives of exile in Istanbul and London. In a 1913 lecture, Edward G. Browne, the Orientalist who had devoted himself to the success of the Constitutional Revolution, observed, "The meaning and essence of the Persian Revolution [was] to keep Persia independent, and to make every Persian, even the humblest peasant, a *man* with rights and duties of a citizen."[89] Iran's first experiment with representative government, however, did not meet with a happy ending. Its legacy would cast a long shadow over the history of twentieth-century Iran.

89. Edward G. Browne, "The Persian Press and Persian Journalism," A lecture delivered to the Persia Society, London (May 1913) p. 22, emphasis his.

Chapter 15

Ann Elizabeth Mayer

Shifting Grounds for Challenging the Authority of International Human Rights Law: Religion as a Malleable and Politicized Pretext for Governmental Noncompliance with Human Rights

This chapter reviews some shifting patterns in how governments represent religion as a factor determining their responses to human rights. It proposes that religion per se is not an obstacle to human rights, that it merely offers a repertory of ideas and precepts that are selectively and opportunistically used by governments in reaction to mutations in domestic politics and broad global trends, which actually determine governmental responses to human rights.

When discussing Islam and human rights, my own special interest, it is vital to emphasize that governmental stances represent only one aspect of Muslims' responses to international human rights law, which have varied from hostility to enthusiastic support. Attempting to offer any pat general characterization of where Islam stands on human rights is an exercise in futility. Debates about the compatibility of Islam and human rights are raging in Middle Eastern Muslim countries and also in Muslim communities elsewhere, perhaps nowhere as furiously as in Iran, where these debates have been at the center of political life since the 1979 Islamic Revolution.

András Sajó (ed.), Human Rights with Modesty: The Problem of Universalism, *349-374.*

The main focus here will be on Iran's shifting official stances on human rights universality, but comparisons with China will also be made. One might expect that the way an Islamic theocracy approaches questions of human rights universality would be unlikely to have much in common with the approaches of an atheistic communist regime. However, comparisons reveal enough similarities to unsettle any preconceptions about Islam creating unique obstacles to human rights.

Iran and China share many common experiences. Both participated in the meetings that gave rise to the UN, and representatives of both were involved in the actual composition of the Universal Declaration of Human Rights (UDHR) in 1948. Both have undergone revolutionary transformations since their original votes in favor of the UDHR. Both adopted in the wake of their revolutions ideologies that called for radical change and led to wrenching upheavals in their societies that tended to isolate them from the mainstream of international developments. Having been close allies of the United States when the UN was founded, both adopted policies of intense hostility to the United States after their revolutions. As their original revolutionary fervor waned, both moderated their more extreme positions and sought closer integration in the international system. After a long campaign for membership, China has succeeded in becoming a member of the WTO, and Iran has indicated that she, too, would like to join, only to be blocked by the determined efforts of the United States to keep it isolated as a pariah state. The need to integrate in the international system has prompted leaders in both countries to call for reforms that would advance the rule of law after turbulent periods when the rule of law had been honored more in the breach than in the observance.

Iran and China both have deplorable human rights records, which have included harsh repression of dissent and the implementation of arbitrary and politicized forms of criminal justice. Both share an acute sensitivity to criticisms of these records. Both work overtime to find ways to shield their poor performance from criticism and to rationalize their noncompliance with international human rights law. Both seek pretexts to excuse their failure to implement human rights that will seem credible to other members of the international community.

Iran and China both played active roles in the Asian group that met in Bangkok shortly before the 1993 Vienna World Conference on Human Rights to hammer out an "Asian" position on human rights, a position that was never applauded by the more democratic nations in the region such as Japan and the Philippines. China was vice-chair of the meeting and Iran's chief delegate headed the committee drafting the Bangkok Declaration.[1]

1. See the discussion in Ann Kent, *China, the United Nations, and Human Rights: The Limits of Compliance*, Philadelphia: University of Pennsylvania Press (1999) 165.

This document has been strongly condemned by human rights advocates for providing states with pretexts for noncompliance with human rights. Among other things, it legitimized cultural relativist approaches to human rights via its statement that human rights "must be considered in the context of a dynamic and evolving process of international norm-setting, bearing in mind the significance of national and regional particularities and various historical, cultural and religious backgrounds." At the 1993 Vienna Conference, Iran found itself together with China in the group of countries seen to be creating obstacles in the way of human rights universality.[2]

The United States has loomed large as a force affecting Iranian and Chinese stances on human rights. Common elements in Iranian and Chinese policies may, at least in part, amount to reactions to the ever more powerful role that the United States plays globally in the domain of human rights. The United States has aggressively—although unevenly and inconsistently—promoted human rights since the presidency of Jimmy Carter, a version of human rights that emphasizes civil and political rights and that largely ignores economic and social rights. Deploying its vast influence, influence that has been magnified by the collapse of the USSR, it penalizes selected countries for not adhering to this version of human rights.

Both Iran and China have had to struggle with the consequences of the U.S. policy of selectively pummeling other countries for their human rights deficiencies; at times both Iran and China have been singled out for special opprobrium by the United States by reason of their human rights violations. (Of course, there can be alterations and gradations in the level of the consequences that flow from U.S. disapproval; now ready for constructive engagement with China, the United States has remained the arch-foe of Iran, which has recently been denounced by President Bush as a member of his "axis of evil.") Observing U.S. double standards, countries like Iran and China may feel that they are being taught lessons in duplicity rather than being instructed in principles of universality.

The preoccupation with the United States that is shared by Iran and China is reflected in a BBC report on 18 April 2002, on an editorial in English published in Tehran on the occasion of the visit to Iran by President Jiang Zemin of China, a visit reciprocating for President Khatami's 2000 trip to China. The editorial comments show Iran's awareness that Iran and China have interests in common that transcend their ideological differences. According to the *Iran News* editorial:

> Iranian diplomacy has always viewed the East with special interest. Given this orientation, cooperation with China, which, like Iran, possesses a great

2. *Ibid.*, 176-77, 179, 181.

> civilization, is in Asia, and has a revolutionary history based on an ideological foundation, is of great significance. Two countries with similar viewpoints on various regional and international topics, Iran and China have a common enemy—the United States. Since they have both come under criticism with regard to observing human rights, these are grounds for the two countries to come yet closer together. Aside from the significance of this trip within the framework of bilateral cooperation, it takes place in an era of "dialogue among civilizations" while world events have led to war. In this midst as the only remaining superpower in a unipolar world, the United States implements its own policies while not acting in a just manner with respect to Israel's crimes against the Palestinian people. China has reached a stage in the economic, political and military fields such that many analysts believe that by the year 2025 the Yellow Dragon will be the world's Number 1 economic power...

Tehran-Beijing relations are followed with sensitivity by the United States. Despite the fact that the United States attempts to characterize it as "idealistic," the strategic cooperation between Iran, India, and China is one of its worries. Iran and China may not be ideologically close, but politically they are. They both believe in a moderate and just world.[3]

Some may challenge the Chinese analogy that I am proposing because they take pronouncements by Middle Eastern governments about Islam and human rights at face value, leading them to exaggerate the impact of Islam. True—the dominant strains in statements made by Middle Eastern governments since the 1990s, if accepted uncritically, would lead to the conclusion that Islam sets them apart. Among other things, many Muslim countries have expressly appealed to Islam in the reservations that they have entered to the Women's Convention, speaking as if their duty to uphold Islamic law precluded accepting various principles guaranteeing women equality in rights.[4] A number of Middle Eastern governments have determinedly campaigned for acceptance of the proposition that Islam bars acceptance of international human rights law, pressing this idea in international forums and using it as a means to discredit external critiques of their human rights records.[5] Of course, governments are not alone in taking such stances; their stances have

---

3. See "Iran: Daily welcomes Jiang's Visit, Urges China to Play Greater Global Role," BBC Worldwide Monitoring (18 April 2002), available in LEXIS, World Library, ALLWLD file.
4. For a critical appraisal, see Ann Elizabeth Mayer, "Religious Reservations to the Convention on the Elimination of All Forms of Discrimination Against Women: What Do They Really Mean?" in Courtney Howland (ed.), *Religious Fundamentalisms and the Human Rights of Women*, New York: St. Martin's Press (1999) 105-127.
5. See generally Ann Elizabeth Mayer, "Universal versus Islamic Human Rights: A Clash of Cultures or a Clash with a Construct?", 15 *Michigan Journal of International Law* (Winter 1994) 307-404.

been buttressed by the work of conservative Muslims opposed to expanding rights and freedoms.[6]

In addition to individual countries appealing to Islam to rationalize their refusal to uphold the human rights accorded under international law, the idea that Islam must be deferred to on rights questions has also been put forward by the Organization of Islamic Conference (OIC), to which all Muslim countries belong, including those outside the Middle East. The OIC has promulgated its own separate version of human rights, the Cairo Declaration on Human Rights in Islam. Because its provisions seriously dilute and even obliterate the protections afforded under international law, the declaration is tantamount to a claim that Islam stands in the way of human rights.[7] Of course, given the generally poor and frequently abysmal human rights performance of Iran and Saudi Arabia, prominent sponsors of the declaration, it would have been astonishing if it had treated Islam as supporting international human rights law.

Significantly, although quite deliberately employing Islam to dilute and deny rights, the OIC realizes that bluntly characterizing Islam as an obstacle in the way of accepting human rights is inadvisable. It therefore attempts a common tactic—an awkward straddle of two opposing positions: support for human rights and simultaneous insistence on Islamic particularism. Thus, for example, according to a report of a March 2002 symposium held at the United Nations' European headquarters, Abdelouahed Belkeziz, OIC secretary-general, maintained that Islam was distinguishable from other religions because it advocated a "new, larger concept of human rights with more global and generalized dimensions."[8] That is, Belkeziz spoke as if the OIC supported the proposition that Islam embraced expanded human rights. In this case, as in others, we see that Islamic groups that are determined to use Islam as a bulwark against human rights are not necessarily candid in characterizing their objectives.

As already noted, there is much contention surrounding issues of Islam and human rights. Observing the recently proliferating debates about where Islam stands on human rights and the absence of such intense and far-reaching debates in the 1940s and 1950s, one might hypothesize that new trends in Islam had developed since the formulation of the UDHR and that Islam, once relatively friendly to human rights, had become transformed into a religion hostile to human rights. However, such speculation would be unfounded.

---

6. See generally Ann Elizabeth Mayer, *Islam and Human Rights: Tradition and Politics*, 3d ed., Boulder, Colo.: Westview (1999).
7. For a dissection of the treatment of rights in the Cairo Declaration, see *ibid.*, 80, 86-87, 89, 96, 120-121, 146-147, 172, 204, 206-208.
8. See, e.g., "Human Rights 'Central' to Islam," OIC tells symposium, Agence France Presse (14 March 2002), available in LEXIS, World Library, ALLWLD file.

Islam remains, as it was previously, a complex religious tradition encompassing an enormous diversity of theological and jurisprudential strains, some of which are and others of which are not favorable to the reception of human rights. Muslim societies have witnessed certain reactionary trends in Islamic thought coming to the fore over the last decades—as happened in the case of the benighted and cruel Taliban, for example—and such trends have encouraged the formulation of Islamic rationales for trampling on human rights. However, these have been matched by countervailing trends that are strongly supportive of ideals like democracy and human rights. Among other things, over the last decades, a vigorous Islamic feminism has brought new insights that provide a critical perspective on the older patriarchal jurisprudence, which traditionally placed many restrictions on women's rights. Thus, factors other than Islam per se must explain the sudden blooming of particularist rhetoric purporting to set Muslim countries apart from the international consensus on human rights.

The record demonstrates that in the period immediately leading up to the 1948 UDHR, Muslim countries, at least in their public statements, did not invoke Islamic particularism and were generally supportive of the emerging consensus on rights. Fereydoun Hoveyda, the young Iranian law graduate who advised the Iranian delegate to the Third Committee that prepared the UDHR, also served as Rene Cassin's assistant in drafting the declaration. He recalls his awareness of the distant thunder of religious opposition, having the sense that "in Muslim countries, religious leaders disapproved of the Declaration."[9] However, he notes that in Third Committee discussions, "the Muslim Delegates (except for the Saudis) kept silent or expressed approval." In private, Hoveyda reports, delegates and journalists from the Third World did criticize the project—but not necessarily on religious grounds. Those on the Left saw in it a colonialist instrument of Western domination and those on the Right saw it as destructive of local traditions that bound people together. However, they preferred not to speak out lest they offend the United States.[10] That is, Third World reactions to U.S. power seem to have encouraged the emergence of a consensus—in reality a somewhat artificial, strained consensus—on the universality of human rights. Now decades later—as will be discussed—reactions to U.S. power, which had become even more overwhelming fifty years after the UDHR than it had been in 1948, may be a factor in the breakdown of consensus on these same rights.

According to Hoveyda's account, some participants who could not see how the UDHR could be implemented in practice made the assumption that

9. Fereydoun Hoveyda, "The Universal Declaration and Fifty Years of Human Rights," 8 *Transnational Law and Contemporary Problems* (1998) 430.

10. *Ibid.*

no one was going to take the exalted ideals in the UDHR seriously or actually demand that nations make the tremendous adjustments that would be needed to comply with them. For example, Hoveyda reports that:

> after having studied the draft Declaration, I had reported to my head of delegation that it would be very difficult for the Iranian government to implement most of the articles. He told me that the Declaration was not a binding agreement, only a recommendation; and then he added: "As the Americans insisted on its adoption at the present session and we need Washington's assistance and protection, you should stand aloof of the discussions and follow for voting the lead of the U.S. delegate."[11]

Hoveyda also reports that he overheard an Iranian journalist observing the scene and telling his colleagues: "Americans are really naive. Western governments will never implement this Declaration. As for our countries, better to forget the whole thing."[12] One notes here that Hoveyda is describing a sense by Iranian participants and observers that there were practical roadblocks in the way of implementing the UDHR. This is very different from saying that there was something inherently objectionable in any of the UDHR principles or that they were Western and therefore in conflict with Islamic values.

One needs to bear in mind that U.S. support for the UDHR did not mean that the document reflected a peculiar U.S. vision of human rights. The UDHR was actually the product of collaborative efforts by many countries around the world, including some Muslim countries. Susan Waltz has established that small states and non-Western states played a crucial role in formulating principles of the UDHR in contrast to major Western countries, which were relatively minor players.[13] In another study, Waltz has examined Muslim countries' participation in setting up the modern human rights system, determining that they expressed generally favorable attitudes and made important substantive contributions to the UDHR.[14] Her research did not uncover Muslim countries making complaints that identified the Islamic tradition as a barrier to accepting the proposed human rights principles.

In the preparatory work on the UDHR, representatives of Muslim countries only occasionally tried to block provisions, according to Waltz. One instance, which has been mentioned in many studies, was the opposition

11. *Ibid.*, 432.
12. *Ibid.*, 433.
13. See Susan Waltz, "Universalizing Human Rights: The Role of Small States in the Construction of the Universal Declaration of Human Rights," 23 *Human Rights Quarterly* (2001) 44-72.
14. This essay should be forthcoming shortly in the *International Journal of Middle East Studies.*

voiced by Jamil Baroody, the representative of Saudi Arabia, to the proposed freedom to change religion that was to be guaranteed in Article 18 of the UDHR. However, could Baroody be accurately said to be speaking on behalf of Islam? This seems dubious. For one thing, he did not expressly invoke Islam as an obstacle. Furthermore, whether Baroody, a Syrian Christian, was speaking on his own behalf or whether he was following explicit instructions from religious authorities in Saudi Arabia or the Saudi government does not seem to have been traced.

As Waltz notes, Saudi Arabia was not alone in voicing misgivings about guaranteeing the freedom to change religion; Afghanistan, Egypt, Iraq, Pakistan, and Syria indicated some qualms as well. Since Islamic law as traditionally understood bars Muslims from converting to other faiths, one might have expected that the record would show Muslim countries protesting that their religion precluded accepting the Article 18 principle, but none seem to have done so. As Waltz shows, delegates from Muslim countries focused on issues other than clashes with Islamic tenets, such as their objections to Christian missionaries' efforts to convert Muslims, speaking as if blocking further missionary endeavors were their objective. (One must remember that Christian missionaries had exploited European hegemony over Muslim lands to proselytize.) Johannes Morsink in his research has uncovered that the objections to Article 18 made by Baroody included ones completely unrelated to Islam, such as his assessments that the language about the freedom to change religion was superfluous and that it was inconsistent to provide for the right to change religion as part of the freedom of religion when there were no corresponding provisions guaranteeing the right to change positions in the provisions on freedom of thought and conscience.[15] Some other delegations supported Baroody's objections, and not all of these were from Muslim countries.[16] Significantly, no Muslim countries actually voted against Article 18 when this particular article was finally put to a vote, suggesting that whatever objections they did have were not deemed vital.

Waltz discusses how some objections were also voiced by Egypt, Iraq, Saudi Arabia, and Syria to the text of what became Article 16 of the UDHR on marriage and the family. Among other things, this article provides that spouses are to have equal rights in marriage, that it should be entered into only with the free and full consent of both spouses, and that men and women have the right to marry and found a family "without any limitation due to race, nationality or religion." The family laws in force in the Muslim countries that raised objections to this article reflected traditional formulations

15. Johannes Morsink, *The Universal Declaration of Human Rights: Origins, Drafting, and Intent*, Philadelphia: University of Pennsylvania Press (1999) 25, 26.

16. *Ibid.*, 25.

of Islamic law that discriminated against women in various ways—such as barring Muslim women from marrying non-Muslim men, whereas Muslim men could marry Christians and Jews. As Waltz notes, the Egyptian delegate argued that religious restrictions on who could marry whom should be acceptable. Baroody made a vague complaint about the article's authors having presumed that standards recognized by Western civilization were superior to those in force elsewhere.[17] However, far from insisting on any irremediable conflict between the UDHR and Eastern cultures, Baroody put forward the much more ambivalent proposition that although the declaration was "frequently at variance with the patterns of culture of Eastern states, that did not mean, however, that the declaration went counter to the latter, even if it did not conform to them."[18] No Muslim countries voted against Article 16 when it was eventually put to a vote, nor did any say that they objected to the idea of women's equality in marital matters because it was precluded by Islam. That is, again, while taking stances that could certainly be interpreted as ultimately resting on convictions that the UDHR was incompatible with Islamic law, delegates from Muslim countries seem to have steered away from explicitly stating that they considered Islamic law to be in conflict with the UDHR.

When the UDHR as a whole was submitted to the General Assembly, no Muslim countries cast votes against it, and Saudi Arabia was alone among Muslim countries in abstaining. (Most abstainers were non-Muslim countries.) The support of Muslim countries was not all that surprising, since they generally seem to have associated human rights with good causes. After all, with so many fellow Muslims being under European rule, they naturally sympathized with demands for self-determination and for dismantling racism and colonialism, goals that could be advanced by the application of human rights principles. The representatives of Muslim countries were skeptical about the UDHR in part due to their suspicions that Western powers would resist compliance with principles that would require them to accept the equality of all human beings and threaten their vested interests in maintaining their domination of subjugated races and colonized peoples.

The problems that were apprehended in 1948 are not those of today's world because colonialism and racially discriminatory laws have in large measure been overcome, even if their shadows still darken the contemporary scene. Ironically, Third World countries that had once decried obstacles like colonialism and racism now figure among the ranks of those creating obstacles by asserting the incompatibility of human rights with non-Western cultures and religions. Of course, these "obstacles" do not all have the same character. Racism and colonialism were seen as evils to be overcome, whereas

17. *Ibid.*, 24.
18. *Ibid.*, 25.

calls for accommodating non-Western cultures invoke countervailing values that seem deserving of respect.

Debates regarding the universality of human rights have grown more vigorous as the stakes have risen. All around the world, people who thought they were being realistic in scoffing at the extravagant idealism of those pressing for the UDHR have been ambushed by its mounting practical impact. Over the last two decades calls for democratization and accountability have been swelling: domestic and international human rights NGOs have mobilized to condemn human rights violations; feminists have organized globally to fight for equal opportunities for women; and other signs of the revolutionary potential of human rights have been manifest. Today governments and ruling elites that are wedded to a status quo in which human rights violations are embedded have every reason to perceive human rights as a threat and to try to erect defenses. In coping with the growing authority of international human rights law in public life and global culture, contemporary Muslim countries find themselves in a predicament like that of China and other countries that have found that nonconformity with human rights entails costs that few could ever have foreseen back in 1948.

In the same way that human rights have far greater political impact today than they did back in 1948, so does Islam. Although, as noted, Islam has not been transformed into a new religion since 1948, the nature of its influence has undergone a dramatic transformation with the growing power of political Islam. Until the 1970s, nationalism and socialism provided the major ideologies of the modern Middle East. Both were essentially secular. Since the 1970s the Islamic resurgence has swept across the Middle East, augmenting pressures for Islamization. In this environment, it is not surprising that many Muslim countries emphasize their commitment to upholding Islamic law, treating it as if it could override international human rights law.

Why has Islamic law more recently been perceived and presented as a major stumbling block in the way of accepting universal human rights? One reason is that Islamic thought has become much more intensely preoccupied with human rights questions than it used to be, which has led to Islamic thought becoming much more dramatically polarized on such questions than it was some decades ago. At the same time, globalization and the shrinkage of the world have magnified the external pressures calling for compliance with human rights, in turn provoking more intense reactions. In context, it is not surprising that many such reactions appeal to Islamic tradition.

With this background, one can review Iran's recent history to see how political shifts determine whether Islam is invoked as an obstacle to human rights. That most Iranians are Muslims is hardly the determinative factor. Contrary to what its ruling theocrats would have the world believe, Iran's identity cannot be subsumed under any simple rubric. Like Egypt and

Turkey, Iran has wrestled for over a century with where it fits in the world and how its present relates to its long and complicated past. Iran's distinctive cultural heritage reflects a variety of elements, including Iran's ancient civilization and elements added by the Arab conquest. Today Iran's national identity is also tied to religion, since it is the only country in the world where Twelver Shi`ism has been enshrined as the national religion for many centuries, honored as such not only by its current theocracy but also by the Pahlavi monarchy before its overthrow.

Shah Mohammed Reza Pahlavi's repressive regime extensively violated human rights, but it did not try to defend its performance by reference to Islam. Instead, it took the time-honored route of hypocrisy. In the international arena, Iran posed as a backer of the international human rights system by mechanisms such as hosting the important 1968 International Conference on Human Rights at Tehran. No hint was made in the conference proclamation that the universality of human rights was problematic. On the contrary, the second principle in the Teheran Proclamation claimed that the UDHR "states a common understanding of the peoples of the world concerning the inalienable and inviolable rights of all members of the human family and constitutes an obligation for the members of the international community."

Under the Shah, Iran's Islamic traditions were downplayed while the monarchy sought to enhance its legitimacy by associating itself with the great Persian dynasties of antiquity like the Achaemenians. Official depictions glorified Iranian civilization as it had existed under the mighty empires *before* the Arab conquest and *before* Iranians adopted Islam. The Shah's regime emphasized Iran's Aryan origins, which linked Iran to Europe rather than to the neighboring Semitic and Turkic peoples. The Shah himself wore the title "the light of the Aryans."

Eager to see a newly affluent Iran take its place among the great powers of the West, the Iranian government was motivated to portray Iran's culture as being congenial to human rights. In an English language propaganda film produced by the government at the time of the Shah's 1971 celebration of 2500 years of Persian monarchy at the imposing ruins of the Achaemenian capital at Persepolis, the Shah and Shahbanu were portrayed as the equals of the numerous European royals and Western political leaders whom they were lavishly hosting. The final shot in the film showed an Achaemenian clay cylinder known as the Cyrus cylinder that, according to the narrator Orson Welles, set forth the world's first statement of human rights.[19] This ancient

19. After the Persian army entered Babylon in 539 BC, Cyrus the Great (580-529) issued a proclamation on a clay barrel that has since been called the Cyrus cylinder. After it was discovered in 1879 in Babylon, it was moved to the British Museum. Although it is popularly understood to be the first declaration of human rights, it did not set forth principles

cylinder was borrowed from the British Museum specially for the 1971 celebrations, and those attending were given souvenir replicas of the cylinder.[20] That is, in terms of human rights, which are considered one of the crowning achievements of modern Western civilization, the Shah's regime sought to convey the message that pre-Islamic Iran had gotten there first, being the original homeland of human rights ideas.

For reasons too complicated to be detailed here, the strong leftist opposition to the Shah was unable to launch or to control the long-promised revolution, which was instead spearheaded by Islamic clerics. With the 1979 Islamic Revolution, the overthrow of the monarchy, and the clerical seizure of the reins of power, the government's position on Islam shifted dramatically. Iran's ancient pre-Islamic culture was denigrated and Iranian culture became officially equated with Twelver Shi`ism, with clerics being portrayed as the guardians of this culture. Theoretically, the whole raison d'être of the new regime was to ensure the rigorous application of Islamic law by a form of Islamic government in which clerics would hold ultimate and unchallengeable power.

The theocratic regime soon became preoccupied with dismantling Iran's existing legal institutions, suppressing dissent, persecuting opponents and minorities, implementing various retrograde policies in the criminal justice sphere, imposing a reactionary version of Islamic morality, and seeking to relegate women to housebound maternal roles. The kind of arbitrary and cruel justice so typical of eras immediately following violent revolutionary upheavals became pervasive. The despotic mentality of their clerical rulers quickly alienated Iranians, prompting the clergy to clamp down even harder on the restive populace. Meanwhile, millions of the best educated and most accomplished Iranians fled to exile in the West.

Of course, Iran's seizure of the U.S. Embassy in Tehran, the protracted holding of U.S. diplomats as hostages, the confiscation of U.S.-owned properties, and a shift to a harshly anti-American line led to Iran becoming profoundly estranged from the United States. The United States was excoriated

---

denominated as rights or claim that any rights inhere in the human person, so that everyone could claim them as rights. It seems more accurate to describe it as a statement of policy by an unusually magnanimous and humane conqueror. Among other things, Cyrus announced that he did not allow his army to terrorize the conquered population and that he abolished forced labor, improved people's ruined housing, restored their religious sanctuaries, and ordered all the captive peoples held as slaves in Babylon to be freed and returned to their homelands. For one translation of the cylinder, see Vohuman.org, The First Declaration of Human Rights. http://www.vohuman.org/Articles/The%20First%20Declaration%20of%20Human%20Rights.htm

20. See Cyrus Kadivar, "We Are Awake: 2,500-year Celebrations Revisited," The Iranian (25 January 2002). http://www.iranian.com/CyrusKadivar/2002/January/2500
The Cyrus cylinder was also featured as the center of the emblem designed to commemorate the celebrations and as the center of a special coin minted for the occasion.

for propping up the despotic Shah and became routinely demonized as the Great Satan. In return, the United States sought to make Iran pay a heavy price.

Having been relatively indulgent of the Shah and his human rights violations, the United States became a stern taskmaster, severely castigating the Islamic Republic for its rights violations. The United States imposed many tough sanctions on the Islamic Republic, seeking to strangle its economy. Once U.S. officialdom associated Iran with fostering Islamic terrorism, the United States clamped down even harder, seeking to isolate Iran as a pariah state. Naturally, in this climate, any U.S. charges that Iran was violating human rights tended to provoke acrimonious defiance. The U.S. denunciations of the human rights violations by the new theocratic regime, after decades of U.S. acquiescence in the Shah's human rights abuses, meant that U.S. policy—and attacks on the human rights performance of the Islamic Republic, more specifically—became associated with hypocrisy and double standards. This stark inconsistency in applying human rights standards did nothing to enhance the credibility of human rights; on the contrary, human rights were seen by regime insiders as weapons that were being used in a highly selective and cynical fashion against the Islamic Republic by the greatest foe of the new Islamic order.

Quite naturally, Iran's theocratic regime both in its domestic and international statements had recourse to Islam as the ostensible justification for its manifest noncompliance with international norms. In international forums, Iran became one of the most vigorous advocates of the notion of cultural particularism as grounds for rejecting the universality of human rights. The paraphrased record of a statement in 1984 by Iran's UN representative, Said Raja'i Khorasani, expressing an extreme position that has not often been put forward in public forums, portrays him as characterizing the regime's position as follows:

> The new political order was...in full accordance and harmony with the deepest moral and religious convictions of the people and therefore most representative of the traditional, cultural, and religious beliefs of Iranian society. It recognized no authority...apart from Islamic law....[C]onventions, declarations and resolutions or decisions of international organizations, which were contrary to Islam, had no validity in the Islamic Republic of Iran....The Universal Declaration of Human Rights, which represented secular understanding of the Judaeo-Christian tradition, could not be implemented by Muslims and did not accord with the system of values recognized by the Islamic Republic of Iran; his country would therefore not hesitate to violate its prescriptions.[21]

21. See the statement and an analysis in Mayer, *op. cit.*, note 6, 8.

Several claims are being made in this statement. Iran's Islamic system is equated with popular beliefs and democratic choice. According to this portrayal, human rights that are not compatible with Iran's political order would also be incompatible with Iranians' religious beliefs. The UDHR is identified with alien traditions, Judaism and Christianity, which are presumed to be at odds with Islam. But, even worse, the UDHR is said to embody a *secular* understanding of these non-Islamic traditions, which makes the UDHR unacceptable to a country like Iran with its explicitly religious ideology. In any event, the statement amounted to an assertion that Iran, precisely because both its people and government were bound by the same Islamic values, would not recognize the authority of international human rights law and would not have qualms about violating it. Obviously, in this portrayal, Islam wound up being treated as an insurmountable obstacle in the way of accepting the universality of human rights. This was not the only such portrayal. One found related themes in the regime's defenses of its Islamic punishments, in which the use of floggings, amputations of limbs, and stonings was ascribed to Islamic requirements, these being treated as superior to international law.[22] Obviously, the mentality behind such postrevolutionary portrayals of the culturally alien character of the UDHR had nothing in common with the way Iran's representatives had originally viewed the UDHR.

The grossly inadequate human rights protections in the 1979 Iranian Constitution had already signaled that Islam would be the pretext for restricting rights, if not nullifying them altogether.[23] In the constitutional human rights provisions direct collisions were set up between human rights and Islamic qualifications that were superimposed on them. (Thus, for example, Article 20 guarantees men and women human rights "according to Islamic standards.") Not surprisingly, the constitution had no provision guaranteeing freedom of religion, freedom of conscience, or protection against discrimination based on religion. This was in dramatic contrast to the language of the Teheran Proclamation that had issued only eleven years previously, which had affirmed in one part of the fifth principle that, in order to realize the aim of each individual achieving the maximum of freedom and dignity, "the laws of every country should grant each individual, irrespective of race, language, religion or political belief, freedom of expression, of information, of conscience and of religion." This important human rights principle, which had been politically acceptable in 1968, was ruled out under the intolerant ideology embraced by Iran's theocracy.

22. See Reza Afshari, *Human Rights in Iran: The Abuse of Cultural Relativism*, Philadelphia: University of Pennsylvania Press (2001) 158-59.

23. See the discussion in Mayer, *op. cit.*, note 6, 68-76.

But, did Islam in and of itself compel this outcome? It seems simplistic to claim so. The UDHR had remained a constant since 1948, and neither Twelver Shi`ism or Iranian culture had undergone a sea change since 1968. To explain the dramatic about-face, one had to look to a fluid political constellation, including the political ascendancy of clerics with retrograde mentalities and without anything resembling the Shah's eagerness to impress the West with ostensibly enlightened rights policies.

Iran's theocratic hardliners belatedly recognized the imprudence of blatantly exposing their disdain for human rights. From candid expressions of scorn for human rights, they moved to a policy of denial and dissembling. As the years passed, the Islamic Republic generally resorted to hypocrisy and deception to try to cover up the scope and seriousness of its rights violations.[24] For example, as I have discussed elsewhere, in response to UN criticisms of the rigid state-imposed Islamic dress requirements for all women, Iran resorted to egregious misrepresentations of its domestic policy. Rather than acknowledging that its Islamic dress rules were enforced by aggressive policing and severe criminal penalties for nonconforming women, Iran insisted that all Iranians supported these dress rules and that there had been no confrontations with women who deviated from these dress rules.[25]

As Reza Afshari observes, with more experience dealing with the UN system and upon learning more about human rights, Iranian officials might come to appreciate them. Raja'i Khorasani's own initially hostile attitudes evolved over the years as he became more familiar with the meaning of human rights law. In 1994 he was mainly responsible for establishing the new human rights committee set up by the Iranian Parliament. He presented himself to international visitors as a human rights advocate who was struggling against colleagues who viewed human rights as a political tool used by the West. He confided to one visitor that "in the early days after the revolution the government purposefully characterized human rights criticism as part of the international conspiracy against it," bemoaning that "it has become extremely difficult to make people understand that human rights is not just propaganda."[26] This suggests that some of the initial post-revolutionary hostility expressed *vis-à-vis* international human rights law may have been attributable to ignorance and prejudice.

The appeals by hardline clerics to Islam to legitimize their extensive infringements of human rights simply alienated Iranians from the official Islamic ideology and fueled pressures for secularization. The hardline cler-

---

24. See, e.g., Afshari, *op. cit.*, note 22, 269, 273.

25. Ann Elizabeth Mayer, "Islamic Rights or Human Rights: An Iranian Dilemma," 29, 3-4 *Iranian Studies* (Summer/Fall 1996) 284-88.

26. Afshari, *op.cit.*, note 22, 278.

ics had their comeuppance when they made the mistake in 1997 of allowing Mohammed Khatami, a liberal reformer who was also a cleric descended from the Prophet, to run as a candidate for the presidency. Khatami was meant to serve as only pro forma opponent for their favored candidate, Ali Akbar Nateq Nuri, a stalwart advocate of upholding the supremacy of Islamic requirements at the expense of human rights, but Khatami won in a landslide. By their votes, Iranians demonstrated their hunger for the rights and freedoms that they had once hoped that the Islamic Revolution would bring them, only to be bitterly disappointed.

Campaigning as a liberal reformer, Khatami offered Iranians a program of expanded human rights and freedoms. Central to his appeal were his promises to establish constitutionalism and the rule of law, an appeal that resonated among the populace after years in which the principles of constitutionalism and the rule of law had been trampled on. Showing why conclusions that Islam is necessarily an obstacle to human rights are ill-founded, Khatami conceived of Islam and human rights as being congenial and essentially offered Iranians a vision of a Muslim society where the universality of human rights would be embraced. Khatami again won an overwhelming popular mandate the second time he ran for office in 2001. Via these elections, Iranians clearly demonstrated the inaccuracy of Raja'i Khorasani's earlier contention that the regime's official Islamic human rights policy reflected popular values.[27]

Since his 1997 victory, Khatami has not been able to convert his electoral support into the power that would be needed to carry out his reform program. The hardliners have fought him every step of the way and have managed to retain their stranglehold on vital institutions. Liberalization has proceeded in fits and starts in several arenas, only to suffer severe setbacks as the nervous hardliners lashed out. The hardliners have engineered a series of egregious human rights violations, hoping that these will keep Iran estranged from the West and demoralize the reformers. According to the hardliners' calculations, their chances of maintaining their grip on the reins of power are enhanced by maximizing tensions between Iran and the United States via flagrant human rights abuses. An example of their schemes to affront U.S. opinion was the July 2002 conviction of the Iranian-American entertainer and dance instructor Mohammad Khordadian, who had lived in exile in the West for twenty-two years and had only returned to Iran to see his ailing father. Tapes of his Los Angeles dance courses had circulated illegally in Iran. Hardliners arranged to have him prosecuted and convicted during his visit on charges that he had attempted to corrupt Iranian youth. His punishments

27. See the analysis in Ann Elizabeth Mayer, "The Universality of Human Rights: Lessons from the Islamic Republic of Iran," 67 *Social Research* (Summer 2000) 519-536.

included being prohibited from ever teaching dance again and being barred from leaving Iran for ten years.

In contrast, the liberal reformers, who would like to see a rapprochement with the West, view improvements in Iran's human rights performance as a means to foster better relations with countries like the United States. One sees in international forums that Khatami's representatives no longer press the idea that Iran is entitled to violate human rights in the interests of following Islam. On the contrary, just as they have done on the domestic scene, in international forums Khatami and his allies have tended to press the notion that Islam and human rights can be harmonized. However, they may nonetheless make claims that human rights need to take cultural diversity into account. Thus, for example, Foreign Minister Kharrazi told the UN General Assembly on 22 September 1997, that human rights had to be redefined by taking into account his country's spirituality and religious roots. According to him, human rights needed to be liberated "from the restrictive bonds and monopolistic claims of a particular culture and ideology" and redefined "through genuine respect for the plurality of beliefs, religions, traditions, value systems and modes of thinking" of different peoples.[28] In context, this invocation of a relatively mild form of multiculturalism did not necessarily mean that Islam was being conceived of as an obstacle to human rights.

Speaking at a forum in New York in November 2001, President Khatami implicitly denigrated the use of religion to justify aggression and terrorism, telling a panel of religious leaders that they must wrest the language of belief away from those "who concoct weapons out of religions." Calling for religious communities to play a vital role in the "Dialogue Among Civilizations," of which he has been a leading proponent, Khatami agreed with the other panelists that religions must be fully engaged in political efforts to resolve the Middle East crisis and the current terrorist threat. He asserted that discussions of human rights must also take into account their groundings in religious belief. According to the published report, Khatami spoke as follows:

> Purely materialistic concerns cannot suffice in laying the foundation for human rights. The discourse of human rights is apparently a secular discourse, with no essential connection with the religious outlook. However, for those familiar with the deeper layers of religious reason and understanding, it is clear that a concept of human rights is both ontologically and historically rooted in religious thoughts.
>
> ...We should free human rights from the bounds of diplomatic negotiations and regard it as a discourse for defending human life, dignity, and culture. Doing so, we ought to realize its deep religious aspect. Christian, Jewish,

28. Afshari, *op. cit.*, note 22, 285.

> Muslim, as well as thinkers from other divine traditions can collaborate on this important issue.[29]

That is, as Raja'i Khorasani had done earlier, Khatami portrayed the secular character of human rights as a defect, but unlike the latter, Khatami saw values in human rights that should be supported by elaborating their religious roots. In his view, the fact that they were secular was not a reason to say that Islam required rejecting them. Back in 1984 Raja'i Khorasani had identified human rights with the Judeo-Christian tradition—as if this tie sufficed to make them unacceptable. In contrast, Khatami proposed that members of the three Abrahamic faiths could collaborate to reach a consensus on the religious foundations of human rights. In this vision, religion was not an obstacle to human rights but a factor that should be utilized to enhance human rights.

Iran has long squirmed under the heightened scrutiny of the UN Human Rights Commission. In forums like the UN, Khatami's representatives, rather than trying to justify Iran's sorry human rights record, may acknowledge that there are problems but request that the government be given credit for seeking to address them. During the annual meeting of the commission in 2001, Iran's ambassador Ali Khorram proclaimed: "I strongly believe and loudly announce that keeping the situation of human rights in Iran on the agenda of the commission and tabling another draft resolution would give once more another wrong signal to the Iranian government."[30] In a situation where the commission's most recent report had acknowledged an overall improvement in the human rights situation in Iran while concluding that the country still had a long way to go, Khorram insisted that the progress already made warranted Iran's removal from the agenda. He practically pleaded with the commission, saying: "There are many achievements in my country and therefore, after eighteen years, Iran's situation must be excluded from the agenda of the Commission on Human Rights."[31] This was a far cry from the defiant truculence that Raja'i Khorasani had shown in the mid-1980s.

Khatami's representatives have tended to adopt conventional Third World positions on human rights issues in which Islamic particularism no longer plays much of a role. For example, in a report on 2001 debates on human rights in the UN Third Committee, Mahmoud Khani Jooyabad, the repre-

---

29. Iranian President Khatami to Religious Leaders at Episcopal Cathedral of St. John the Divine: Take Back Language of Belief From "Decadent" Terrorists; Interfaith Conversation, Education Crucial to "Dialogue Among Civilizations," Agree Participants in 12 November Symposium in New York, PR Newswire (14 November 2001) available in LEXIS, World Library, ALLWLD file.

30. "Iran Asks UN to Acknowledge Its Improved Rights Record," Agence France Presse (2 April 2001), available in LEXIS, World Library, ALLWLD file.

31. *Ibid.*

sentative of Iran, exhibited the mindset typical of Iran's current governmental spokesmen, speaking as if the full realization of human rights around the globe were a desirable goal. According to the paraphrase, he asserted that "the new process of globalization, which had increased poverty, underdevelopment and marginalization for the poorest countries in the world, should be redirected so its benefits could be enjoyed by the entire human family. Only through broad and sustained efforts by the international community to create a shared future based upon common humanity could globalization be made fully inclusive and equitable."[32] The complaint that the contemporary globalization process was not sufficiently inclusive and equitable was not surprising coming from Iran at a time when it was trying hard to join the WTO, only to be excluded due to U.S. lobbying and when threats of U.S. sanctions were hampering its efforts to attract foreign direct investment.

Jooyabad began with a reference to the Vienna Declaration and Program of Action, the document that had issued from the 1993 Vienna World Conference on Human Rights, commenting that it had "recognized that the international community should devise ways and means to remove the current obstacles and meet challenges to ensure the full realization of all human rights, and to prevent the continuation of human rights violations throughout the world."[33] That is, Iran's representative, instead of raising objections to the universality of human rights as the country's representatives had formerly done, spoke as if his government favored the removal of "the current obstacles" that were preventing the full realization of human rights. The published summary describes some of his other remarks as follows: "The promotion and protection of human rights had faced multiple obstacles throughout the history of the world. Some of those problems always existed, but there were some new challenges to human rights as well...."

Jooyabad said the process of globalization constituted a powerful and dynamic force, which offered great opportunities. Globalization contributed considerably to bringing people together to materialize the notion of a human family. It was a must for the international community to harness that trend for the benefit, development and prosperity of all countries, without exclusion. Unfortunately, the benefits of globalization were very lopsidedly shared. Developing countries faced special difficulties in responding to that central challenge. The negative effects of globalization should be prevented and mitigated. Those effects could aggravate poverty, underdevelopment, marginalization, social exclusion, cultural homogenization, and economic

32. "Globalization process should be redirected to benefit entire human family, Iran tells Third Committee, as human rights discussion continues—Part 1 of 2," M2 Presswire (16 November 2001), available in LEXIS, World Library, ALLWLD file.

33. *Ibid.*

disparities between states. Today's indications of globalization were well-known. The powerful movement towards efficiency continually increased the number of people marginalized by it, not only in the Third World, but also in developed countries. Present efforts at production rationalization pushed the poor into the margins of economy and society.[34]

One notes that this speech, which focused on globalization, was not made in a forum on globalization; it was Iran's contribution to the discussion of human rights in the Third Committee. That is, by its focus, Jooyabad's speech suggested that globalization was the phenomenon that warranted attention on the part of those who were concerned with achieving the goals of human rights. Only the faintest echo of Iran's formerly vigorous arguments for cultural particularism persisted in these paragraphs, in the form of his portrayal of "cultural homogenization" as one of the negative consequences of globalization. However, significantly, this is not in a context where a demand is being made to exempt Iran from obligations under international human rights law.

That is, since it voted in 1948 for the UDHR, Iranian policy on human rights has been reoriented more than once. Iran's government has acted the part of a staunch supporter of the universality of human rights, an ardent proponent of cultural particularism, and a believer in using religious resources to enhance human rights, as well as an advocate of generic Third World positions on the problems of globalization in which religion is not highlighted. To focus on Islam or Iranian culture as if these prompted Iran's stances on human rights and to overlook the centrality of political factors can only lead to misperceptions.

When in 1998 Fereydoun Hoveyda, who had by then become an eminent man of letters, surveyed the altered human rights landscape, he was struck by the changes that had occurred since the era when he had worked on drafting the UDHR. Obliged to live in exile in the aftermath of the Islamic Revolution, he had no love for Iran's theocracy. Having reviewed developments since 1948 and realizing that he was the lone survivor of those who had been centrally involved in producing the UDHR, Hoveyda expressed his dismay at the use of culture to rationalize rejecting human rights, reacting negatively to a subsequent Islamic declaration of human rights that, like the Cairo Declaration, had used Islamic criteria to nullify rights.[35] He commented:

> And on top of all this is the idea of multiculturalism that is spreading rapidly here and elsewhere, an idea that could harm the very concept of the Universal Declaration of Human Rights. A few years back, within the framework of UNESCO, Muslim states elaborated an Islamic Declaration of Human

34. *Ibid.*

35. I have critically assessed this so-called Universal Islamic Declaration of Human Rights. See Mayer, *op. cit.*, note 6, 52-54, 76-78, 89-94, 96, 106-113, 127, 139-141, 160-62, 177, 185, 190.

> Rights. Different ethnic communities in advanced societies like the United States claim the privilege of safeguarding their "traditions" even when some of them contradict parts of the Universal Declaration. Such a fragmentation would certainly nullify the Universal Declaration. Indeed what was new and important in the Declaration in 1948 was justly the concept of universality. Abandoning it in the name of "cultural differences" would constitute a set-back. There are no Islamic, Buddhist, Hindu, Zoroastrian, Christian, Judaic, etc. rights. There are human rights, pertaining to human beings wherever they live and whatever their creeds. The Universal Declaration was conceived as a bulwark against what happened in the thirties and forties in several European countries and that prompted World War II.[36]

The final line in Hoveyda's observations, in which he situates the UDHR in relation to its peculiar historical context, ties in with the general thesis of this essay; that it is not religion and culture that independently create obstacles in the way of international human rights law, but rather, factors associated with particular historical trends and circumstances as well as an interplay between domestic politics and global developments.

In a penetrating analysis, the Norwegian philosopher Tore Lindholm has argued that the UDHR has to be seen as a reaction to the immediately preceding historical events of the Second World War "as well as challenges, threats, and prospects harbored by the world situation." According to Lindholm, the justification for the UDHR "is neither theological nor metaphysical but rather an exercise in 'situated' geopolitical moral rationality...." Among other things, it involves "an interpretation of historically evolving global societal circumstances..."[37]

When one looks at how approaches to human rights have evolved since the inauguration of the international system of human rights in the immediate aftermath of World War II, the prescience of Lindholm's assessment is borne out. The common experience of World War II was one that brought nations together in a mutual determination to make a better world according to a shared vision of human rights that would advance freedom, justice, and peace. In contrast, strains brought on by the current globalization process—which includes the United States unilaterally wielding its vast hegemonic power without due concern for the interests of others or for its potentially harmful impact on the world—may be creating circumstances that will polarize nations rather than strengthen the global consensus on human rights.

36. Hoveyda, *op. cit.*, note 9, 435.

37. Tore Lindholm, "Prospects for Research on the Cultural Legitimacy of Human Rights: The Cases of Liberalism and Marxism," in Abdullahi An-Na`im (ed.), *Human Rights in Cross-Cultural Perspectives: A Quest for Consensus*, Philadelphia: University of Pennsylvania Press (1992) 397.

But what of China? How do its changing stances on the universality of human rights shed light on Iran's? As already noted, both China and Iran were present at the creation of the modern human rights system. Just as Iran had a representative directly involved in the work on the UDHR, so China had a representative, one who had even more impact on the document. As those who have studied the preparation of the UDHR have established, the Chinese diplomat Peng-Chun Chang was one of the most influential of all the participants in the drafting.[38] Like Fereydoun Hoveyda, he was a well-educated and deeply cultured man with an interest in the arts and letters. An expert in Confucianism, Chang found elements in Confucianism that, in his view, provided foundations for human rights principles.[39] He did not envisage that the UDHR would entail East-West clashes over competing value systems. As Mary Ann Glendon records, he understood the fallacy of stereotyping the East or the West as monoliths, each with its own uniform culture. His view was that: "Culturally, there are many "Easts" and many "Wests"; and they are by no means all necessarily irreconcilable."[40] He had been able to test his ideas about culture during a diplomatic career and travels that he used to learn about other cultures while promoting the appreciation of Chinese culture. Significantly, during his posting in Turkey, he had lectured in Baghdad on the reciprocal influences and common ground between Chinese and Arab cultures and on the relationship between Confucianism and Islam.[41] After pondering differences and similarities of cultures and religions, Chang became an advocate of the position that cultures should be left to work out their own separate elaborations of the foundations of human rights.[42] As someone who participated in developing the UDHR and who was exposed to debates about the foundations of human rights, Chang did not find cultural and religious differences an obstacle to human rights, believing that it was possible to reach an overlapping consensus on human rights starting from different cultural and religious premises. In this he took a stance closely resembling the one that President Khatami took in 2001.

Being an anti-communist, Chang naturally opposed the advance of Maoist forces. After the Communist victory in 1948, the People's Republic of China was governed by a party whose members adhered to an atheistic European ideology, for decades imposing its tenets with a steely fanaticism

38. See, e.g., Waltz, *op. cit.*, note 13, 59-60; Mary Ann Glendon, "Foundations of Human Rights: The Unfinished Business," 44 *The American Journal of Jurisprudence* (1999) 4.

39. Mary Ann Glendon, *A World Made New: Eleanor Roosevelt and the Universal Declaration of Human Rights*, New York: Random House (2001) 185.

40. Glendon, *op. cit.*, note 38, 6.

41. Glendon, *op. cit.*, note 39, 133.

42. *Ibid.*, 134.

until their ideological zeal faded and a more pragmatic mindset began to prevail in the 1980s. When one reviews China's stances, one sees that under the sway of leaders ostensibly committed to communist principles, its positions regarding religion and culture and its stances on the relationship of religion and culture to human rights have been subject to shifts and adjustments that smack of political calculations.[43]

With the Communists in power, China became the nemesis of the United States, which staunchly backed the Nationalists, who had been forced to remove to Taiwan. The two countries seemed embarked on a course that would potentially culminate in war. However, in the 1980s as China's leaders moved away from hardline Maoist tenets, the animosity between the countries abated somewhat. As China displayed its readiness to play by the rules of the international game and as it shifted in practice to a quasi-capitalist system, the United States showed itself ready to reach practical accommodations with a country whose market offered lucrative opportunities for U.S. business. Nonetheless, Chinese resentments of U.S. hegemony and U.S. suspicions of China's ambitions to establish itself as the new superpower made for a tense relationship.

Based on the much longer account offered by Ann Kent, one can briefly summarize some relevant developments in China's human rights policies after the Communist takeover. Originally kept out of the UN due to U.S. pressure, from the 1950s to the 1970s the P.R.C. critiqued Western violations of human rights in the Third World, appealing to the need to respect fundamental human rights. In 1955 the P.R.C. endorsed the communiqué issued from the important Third World conclave in Bandung, which called for respect for fundamental human rights.[44] Despite being excluded from the UN, in its 1954 constitution, the P.R.C. incorporated most of the rights in the UDHR, including many civil and political rights.[45] At the same time, patterns going back to China's ancient civilization persisted, such as deeming citizens' duties to the state to take precedence over their rights.[46] One scholar proposes that even after Mao seized power, subterranean Confucian influences persisted and that rights policy under Communist rule continued to bear "the heavy imprint of traditional Confucianism, China's state ideology for some two thousand years."[47] Just as the human rights policy of Iran's cleri-

43. For a general account, see William Theodore de Bary, *Asian Values and Human Rights*, Cambridge, Mass.: Harvard University Press (1998).

44. Kent, *op. cit.*, note 1, 29.

45. *Ibid.*

46. *Ibid.*, 30.

47. Robert Weatherley, *The Discourse of Human Rights in China: Historical and Ideological Perspectives*, New York: St. Martin's Press (1999) 102, 105, 107.

cal leaders reflected a variety of strains—some secular and some religious, so China's Communist leaders deployed a human rights policy in which traditional cultural and political-cum-ideological elements were mixed.

For a while, China under Mao was essentially a lawless society: during the Cultural Revolution, launched in 1966, the judiciary was dismantled and a particularly arbitrary and politicized form of justice was applied. The P.R.C. did not assume the UN seat that Taiwan had clung to until 1971, after the worst excesses of the Cultural Revolution were over.

In the early period of its UN membership, the P.R.C. did not formally oppose the international protection of human rights.[48] As of 1979, the P.R.C. began to play a more active role in UN human rights bodies, including the Human Rights Commission. Interestingly, although it supported UN investigations of the human rights situations in certain countries, the P.R.C. did not support such investigations in the Islamic Republic of Iran.[49] In the period 1979-89 Chinese scholars were generally unanimous about the need to support human rights in the international arena. In 1982 the climate permitted the publication of an article that argued that the Third World had a duty to support human rights and that socialism and human rights were one.[50] The 1982 Constitution afforded Chinese more rights than any of the previous P.R.C. constitutions.[51]

After tracing China's relationship with the UN human rights system, Kent calls the period 1988-89 the high point, a period when China was especially active in UN human rights activities.[52] The P.R.C. seemed to be moving towards accepting human rights universality.[53] However, a sharp deterioration in relations with the United States halted this trend. The brutal 1989 crackdown on the democracy movement prompted extensive U.S. sanctions and condemnations and ended China's honeymoon with the UN human rights system. China was also being made uneasy by the collapse of the USSR and the more fluid international situation.[54] China had to confront the United States standing by itself, and struggles about human rights became a way that the power play between the two countries was expressed.[55]

At this juncture, China was in need of a way to build a coalition to back its rejection of attacks on its human rights performance. It was in this context

48. Kent, *op. cit.*, note 1, 38.

49. *Ibid.*, 43.

50. *Ibid.*, 34.

51. Weatherly, *op. cit.*, note 47, 107.

52. Kent, *op. cit.*, note 1, 45.

53. *Ibid.*, 47.

54. *Ibid.*, 50.

55. *Ibid.*, 51.

that appeals to Asian culture were made, appeals that were incongruous on the part of a country that under Communist rule had followed policies inimical to and destructive of Asian culture and religious traditions. Notwithstanding this record, China did not hesitate to join in the chorus of Asian countries claiming in the 1990s that their dedication to Asian values stood in the way of their accepting international human rights.[56] The ancient sage Confucius had been one of the figures harshly vilified as a reactionary under Mao. In a remarkable about-face, by the late 1980s China's Communist leadership was trying to promote Confucianism, seeing in Confucianism resources that could compensate for the ideological vacuum caused by the collapse of the credibility of the official communist ideology while at the same time offering principles supportive of authoritarian rule.

The recourse to Confucianism by China's atheist Communist rulers seems incongruous, but Confucianism is only one of several tools that the P.R.C. resorts to in efforts to cover its human rights deficiencies. After analyzing China's stances Michael Sullivan has concluded that in its responses to human rights issues, the P.R.C. has been highly opportunistic.[57] According to Sullivan, Chinese political leaders can construct discourses for or against human rights depending on their political needs and goals, at various times supporting their positions on human rights via recourse to popular culture, Confucianism, Marxism, scientific thought, developmentalism, and nationalism.[58] He proposes that China's Communist rulers may be looking for ways to justify their policies on rights in ways that universalize and systematize China's development experiences.[59] This is reminiscent of Iran, where official stances on human rights have shifted with the political winds and where the government has sought to rework its stances on human rights in order to relate to more general concerns.

In examining how "culture" became a popular rallying cry for the Third World countries in the 1990s, Karen Engle points out that this coincides with their having to confront the globalization of capitalism and neoliberal economics. In these circumstances, she proposes that "culture" can become a proxy of many different ideas. For countries resisting the universality of human rights, it can mean things like sovereignty and rejection of condition-

56. A useful assessment of the Asian values debate is offered in Karen Engle, "Culture and Human Rights: The Asian Values Debate in Context," 32 *New York Journal of International Law and Politics* (2000), 291-333.
57. Michael Sullivan, "Developmentalism and China's Human Rights Policy," in Peter Van Ness (ed.), *Debating Human Rights: Critical Essays from the United States and Asia*, New York: Routledge (1999) 120-143.
58. *Ibid.*, 125-26.
59. *Ibid.*, 124.

alities, particular local knowledge, communal over individual values, the right to development, decreasing the wealth gap between the North and the South, emphasis on economic and social rights, and opposition to "Western" human rights and double standards.[60] That is, governmental appeals to culture and Asian values may have different and more multivalent implications than one would assume if one took the rubrics at face value, accepting them without paying due attention to their historical context. Engle's analysis reminds us of the need to appraise critically portrayals of religion and culture as obstacles to human rights.

The full history of the May 2001 removal of the United States from the UN Human Rights Commission has not yet been written, but it seems reasonable to assume that general resentment of U.S. unilateralism and the uses and misuses of U.S. power in the human rights domain may have prompted the decision to vote the United States off, particularly since countries like Libya and Sudan that figured among the arch-foes of the United States were voted on.

China and Iran both benefited from the exclusion of the United States. In the reconstituted commission, China was able to avoid having to deal with a resolution that the United States had repeatedly sponsored in the past that criticized China for its mistreatment of Tibetans, some Muslim groups, and other religious minorities. Furthermore, for the first time in two decades, the commission voted to take Iran off its worst-offenders list.[61] In one's imagination, one can picture the representatives of the world's last great communist power and the world's only Islamic theocracy shaking hands in the corridors of the Geneva headquarters of the UN and musing on how the global system dominated by the United States had made them allies on human rights issues. One can also resort to one's imagination to conjure up possible exchanges that Peng-Chun Chang and Fereydoun Hoveyda might have had about the UDHR back in 1948. Without being able to guess exactly what Chang and Hoveyda would have said to each other, one can safely project that this earlier conversation would have been a very different one.

60. Engle, *op. cit.*, note 56, 299.

61. See Elizabeth Olson, "UN Fears 'Bloc' Voters Are Abetting Rights Abuses," *New York Times* (28 April 2002).

Index

MIX
Papier aus verantwortungsvollen Quellen
Paper from responsible sources
FSC® C105338

If you have any concerns about our products,
you can contact us on
ProductSafety@springernature.com

In case Publisher is established outside the EU,
the EU authorized representative is:
Springer Nature Customer Service Center GmbH
Europaplatz 3, 69115 Heidelberg, Germany

Printed by Libri Plureos GmbH
in Hamburg, Germany